THE VICTORIAN WORKING CLASS

THE VICTORIAN WORKING CLASS

Selections from Letters to the
Morning Chronicle

Edited and with introductions by

P. E. RAZZELL
Bedford College, University of London

and

R. W. WAINWRIGHT
Extra Mural Department, University of London

FRANK CASS: LONDON

First published in 1973 in Great Britain by
FRANK CASS AND COMPANY LIMITED
67 Great Russell Street, London WC1B 3BT, England
and in United States of America by
FRANK CASS AND COMPANY LIMITED
c/o International Scholarly Book Services Inc.
P.O. Box 4347, Portland, Oregon 97208

This selection and introductions Copyright © 1973
P. E. Razzell and R. W. Wainwright

Letters first published
in the *Morning Chronicle* 1849–1851
New edition   1973

ISBN 0 7146 2957 X

Library of Congress Catalog Card No. 72–90155

Printed in Great Britain by
The Garden City Press Limited,
Letchworth, Hertfordshire SG6 1JS

Contents

List of Illustrations

A note on the illustrations: the letters from the *Morning Chronicle* were not illustrated, but the following illustrations have been included to illuminate the text. All are reproduced by courtesy of the Trustees of the British Museum, except the Demonstration of Trade Unionists which is reproduced by courtesy of the Mansell Collection.

Preface

The *Morning Chronicle* account of *Labour and the Poor* is a unique descriptive social survey of the whole country at one point in time. Although it was ostensibly confined to a study of the "industrial poor", it broadened at times to become an account of the social structure of whole communities. In addition to a general coverage of regions and large towns, the survey described in detail particular types of occupational community illustrating what was both typical and exceptional. We have attempted to preserve this combination of the general and the particular in the belief that the survey provides a classic introduction to the social structure of England during the Industrial Revolution. The detailed accounts of the social life of particular occupational communities include information on their economic organisation and associated leisure, family, trade union, religious and political activity. We feel that this type of comprehensive information is invaluable to the sociological historian and have therefore selected all occupational communities for which such information is available: the silk-weavers of Middleton, the pitmen of Durham and Northumberland, the tin and copper miners of Cornwall, the stone quarriers of Swanage and the shoemakers of Northampton. Cities such as Manchester, Birmingham, Liverpool and London were too large to be described in such comprehensive detail, but here we have included occupational groups for which the fullest sociological information is given. We have also selected information which is of interest in its own right, independent of any direct structural context: retrospective accounts of economic change, the leisure activities of the great city populations and the small village communities; vivid descriptions of criminal and delinquent sub-cultures; personal biographies which reveal the social experiences of ordinary people. We have included a few of the detailed descriptions of the economic organisation of occupations and trades where they are central to the main focus of the text, but a great deal of this material has been excluded, as it has already been well handled in *The Unknown Mayhew* by E. P. Thompson and Eileen Yeo and in the forthcoming Cass publication of J. Ginswick's edition of the whole of the provincial series of *Labour and the Poor*. Similarly the vivid descriptions of housing, sanitary conditions, dietary standards and the standard of living occupy a peripheral place in this text, as a great variety of this kind of material has been made available in collections of nineteenth-century documentary sources published int he last few years. The relatively "open" nature of the edited survey will, we hope, allow the reader to come to his own historical and sociological conclusions.

The more positive editorial principles which guided the selection of the material can best be seen through reading our introductions. Wainwright has been concerned to place the survey within the context of the contemporary response to industrialisation and to demonstrate its relevance to certain kinds of historical analysis; he concentrates mainly on social change, particularly the effects of economic transformation. Razzell has attempted to show the relevance of the survey to a sociological understanding of the period, particularly with reference to the structure of different types of working-class community, as well as the way sociological ideas may be evaluated and developed in relation to historical evidence. He focuses on the static variations of social life which are viewed as being significantly determined by the geographically based economic structure of community life. In these introductions we have not attempted to discuss anything like the full range of information in the survey. Our main preoccupation is with the edited text itself, which is intended as a contribution to the historical sociology of the nineteenth century.

January, 1973

Introduction

by R. W. Wainwright

We publish this the first of a series of communications in which it is proposed to give a full and detailed description of the moral intellectual, material, and physical condition of the industrial poor throughout England. . . .

The metropolis and the provinces, the town and country, the manufacturing, the maritime, mining and agricultural population will be equally included in our plans; . . . .[1]

This announcement by the *Morning Chronicle* on October 18, 1849, introduced a survey to be carried out "on the spot", which continued for eighteen months. It is unique in the history of British social enquiry in that it provides a detailed account of working class life on a national scale. The only other attempt at such an enterprise is *The Condition of the Working Class in England*, in which the range of subject is more limited and the approach less detailed.

The *Morning Chronicle* had been a successful Whig/Liberal newspaper. During the 1840s its circulation and prestige declined somewhat, due mainly to its flirtation with Palmerstonian politics and the appearance in 1846 of the cheaper priced and more efficiently organised *Daily News*, which drew from the *Chronicle* a large section of its readership and by the offer of higher salaries, some of its staff.[2] In order to compete with its new rival, the Chronicle reduced its price, but failed in so doing to increase circulation appreciably. Faced with imminent insolvency and a diminished reputation, the paper was sold in February 1848 by its owner Sir John Easthope and given a fresh start under a new proprietorship, which included the Duke of Newcastle, Anthony Beresford-Hope and Sidney Herbert; described by Fox-Bourne as "a wealthy group of Peelites, who were willing to spend money in pushing the interests of their party . . .".[3] John Douglas-Cook, a reporter with the *Times* moved to the *Chronicle* to become its new editor. Little more than a year later, he and the managers of the paper were persuaded by Henry Mayhew, then one of its leader writers, of the need for a comprehensive survey of *Labour and the Poor*.

The proposed survey commenced a year after the dispersal of the Chartist demonstration and was set in the immediate context of concern over the cholera epidemic of 1848/49, which received a great deal of attention in the columns of virtually every newspaper in the country. The tension involved in relief from one and anxiety over the other of these events provoked a perturbed public interest in the poor. Two reports from Mayhew on Jacob's Island in Bermondsey immediately preceded the enquiry. In terms which an upper and middle class readership would find little to be joyful about, he reflects here on the grotesque lessons to be learned from cholera.

The history of the late epidemic, which now seems to have almost spent its total fling upon us, has taught us that the masses of filth and corruption round the metropolis area are, as it were, the nauseous nests of plague and pestilence. Indeed, so well known are the localities of fever and disease, that London would almost admit of being mapped out pathologically, and divided into its districts and deadly cantons. We might lay our fingers on the ordnance map and say, here is the typhoid parish and there the ward of cholera; for truly as the West End rejoices in the title of Belgravia, so might the southern shores of the Thames be christened Pestilentia.[4]

The *Morning Chronicle* enterprise and the wide public interest in the lives and whereabouts of the poor were symptoms of a complex response to industrialisation, which was manifested in parliamentary investigations, the surveys of local statistical societies and the social reporting of journalists and novelists; all committed in their various ways to defining, analysing and reflecting problems which were crucial to the "Condition of England". The ways in which social problems were being identified revealed both a change in the nature of the problems themselves and a fundamental change in the consciousness of their existence. Many old and obsolete remedies were increasingly perceived to be inadequate and doubt was cast on the relevance and efficacy of some of the new—like the 1834 Poor Law. The newspaper and the novel presented for most of the upper and middle classes the only point of contact which they had with the working class. The interest shown in the novels of Dickens, Disraeli, Kingsley and Mrs. Gaskell revealed a quite significant shift in literary bearings and public sympathy, involving a closer relationship between fiction and working class life.[5] The sub-title of *Mary Barton*: *A tale of Manchester Life* was considered a guarantee of its commercial success, though Mrs. Gaskell was unknown before the book appeared.[6] Much of the success of the rival *Daily News* was attributed to the style and content of its social reporting. Dickens, the initial editor, emphasised its tone of concern when he introduced the first copy:

> Very much is to be done, and must be done, towards the bodily comfort, moral elevation and general contentment of the English people.[7]

Considerations such as these gave to Mayhew's proposal the double purpose of supplying to a receptive reading public a wider range of empirical information about the working class than had ever appeared in one place and of restoring the *Chronicle* to its former eminence.

From the start the survey was designed to cover three general types of area —the Manufacturing Districts, the Rural Districts and the Metropolitan Districts. Angus Bethune Reach was the first correspondent for the manufacturing areas, which comprised the factory, mining and large town populations. He covered the northern industrial areas. Charles Mackay collected the information for Liverpool and Birmingham. He was called to the project when Reach was dispatched to report on the agricultural areas of Southern France and Denmark. The rural areas, which covered agricultural labour, the fishing and tin mining communities and, in addition, the rural and small town industries, were started by Alexander Mackay. Like Angus Reach he was assigned to another project, though not by the *Chronicle*. A group of Manchester manufacturers sponsored him to report on the difficulties of cotton cultivation in India. He was replaced by Charles Shirley Brooks. London, the subject of a single study, was undertaken by Mayhew who received a good deal of collaborative help from his brother "Gus".[8]

None of the correspondents possessed the formal credentials of a modern social investigator; a fact which accounts both for the peculiar strengths and weaknesses of the survey. They were selected for the job on the basis of their skills in descriptive reporting. Reach and Shirley Brooks had both been parliamentary reporters with the *Chronicle*. They combined these posts with the activities of literary Jacks of all Trades. Their work was of varying seriousness, ranging from satire, caricature and farce to literary criticism and lightweight novels.[9] Both found their way to *Punch*, where Mayhew had been before them as founding editor. Charles Mackay had been a reporter with the *Chronicle* between 1835-44. He left to accept more relaxed responsibilities as editor of the *Glasgow Argus*. He felt that this would leave him more time for his fairly catholic interests as a poet, critic and essayist and allow him to preserve more than a nodding acquaintance with London literary circles.[10] Alexander Mackay, like Reach and Shirley Brooks, was on the regular staff of the paper. Outside this post he was known particularly for his descriptive work on travel.[11] The observation made by Sutherland Edwards or Shirley Brooks: that he was the epitome of the talented Victorian amateur, really applied to them all, though Mayhew eludes such a generalised placing. Having escaped a legal career for which he had no relish, he came to the popular London journalism of the early 1830s, before it became altogether respectable and robust Georgian popular tastes were neutralised by a Victorian reform of manners. Following his involvement in a number of lightweight literary ventures: farces, satires, novels: often in association with his brothers, he founded *Punch*, or was certainly a moving spirit in its creation.[12] Of all the correspondents who contributed to the survey, Mayhew had the most direct acquaintance with his subject. His incomparable openness to the experience of the poor and the sense of relationship which he had with them, compelled him, as it were, to see them from the inside. As E. P. Thompson has indicated, this capacity was complementary to the interests which originally led him to "low life" journalism.[13] One of his contemporaries, Henry Vizetelly, commends him to us as "a singular combination of the humourist and the sociologist"[14] His work as the London correspondent led him finally to the four volume *London Labour and the London Poor* published in 1861/62. The best sections of this monumental study and the letters written for the Morning Chronicle more than justify the claims made for him as a great pioneering sociologist.[15]

For the first four months in the life of the survey two letters a week appeared from each of the correspondents. This was the period when public interest was at its most intense, after which there was a noticeable cooling off. The initial impact though, was enormous. Newspapers up and down the country commented on, or quoted from the most recent reports, while the correspondence columns of the *Chronicle* presented a stream of letters which had been sent in accompanied by donations for people who were described in the survey. Many letters appeared, which confirmed, modified, or contested the evidence produced, often on the basis of personal experience. For this short time there was about the whole enterprise a sense of national involvement, but it was orientated too much by charity and hysteria to be either relevant or enduring.

In order to cater for the early widespread interest, the *Chronicle* published *gratis* a series of supplements containing back numbers. Thirteen of these appeared in all, the last one on February 1st, 1850. The survey carried on until April 26, 1851, when it ended prematurely with a letter from the rural correspondent. The adjunct European section of the enquiry, to which Reach and Shirley Brooks were assigned, continued for a short while longer with descriptions of agricultural labour in France, Denmark, Southern Russia, Asia Minor and Egypt.[16] *Labour and the Poor* did not increase the circulation of the *Chronicle* by as much as its owners had hoped for and it says much for their integrity that the survey continued long after it ceased to have any great commercial possibilities.[17]

II

The editorial introduction to *Labour and the Poor* claimed that it would "equal, perhaps surpass, the official investigations for impartiality, authenticity and comprehensiveness".[18] This plan to present working class life as wholly and impersonally as possible was an integral feature of the reconciliatory nature of the survey, which, in the introductory letters of the correspondents, was placed in the context of a social malaise brought about by the disruptive force of industrialisation. In terms which were fairly common among his contemporaries, Angus Reach expressed his fears about what he considered to be the most dominant social relationship of his day:

> I fear the spirit which animates society has in it too much of cold formality, of class and of systematic want for struggling labour.
> Capital and labour look upon each other with suspicious eyes. The owner of the former characterises the owner of the latter as one of the "dangerous classes"—only perhaps to be characterised in turn as one of the "tyrannous classes".[19]

The existence of class conflict had long been noted as a symptom of industrial capitalism and urbanisation. The distance in sympathy between classes was confirmed by their increasing geographical separation. The "growing gulf" between rich and poor was recognised as a feature of Manchester life before Disraeli characterised them as the "Two Nations". The force which Cobbett had felt to be breaking "the chain of connection",[20] disturbed Carlyle with its threatening potential to "separate and isolate" society "into two contradictory masses" and he found "their mutual relation, pregnant with the elements of discord and hostility . . . far from consoling".[21] Chadwick's *Report on the Sanitary Condition of the Labouring Population of Great Britain* of 1842 brought a disturbing empirical dimension to the importance of class and geography to survival. Writers of otherwise irreconcilable persuasions were agreed on this view of society, as can be seen, for instance, in a comparison of Engels' *Condition of the Working Class in England* and Whately Cooke-Taylor's *Tour of the Manufacturing Districts*, the enquiry for which he was sponsored by the Anti-Corn Law League.

The changes in the shape and complexity of society had radically altered the consciousness of a human relationship to it. As an example of new energies which were essentially alienating, the rural correspondent, Alexander Mackay gives us the railway. While it extended geographic mobility, the numerically increased range of social contact which it made available could not be experienced, or recognised in the context of a whole way of life. In this way society is perceived as becoming less knowable through personal experience and vicarious sources of contact like *Labour and the Poor* were invested with a crucially informing role.

> He (the traveller) has little or no chance of learning the different modes of life of the people. Men travel over where they formerly travelled through the country.... The consequence is that though the gain to trade may be invaluable, the stock of general knowledge derived from a varied and personal observation is diminished. It therefore results that a generation of Englishmen now springing up will know less of the rural life of England than their forefathers unless the information which they cannot so readily gather for themselves is supplied to them.[22]

From this he proceeds to issue an urgent warning, which with a middle class accent cries out to the public to "read all about it". A crisis might be expected from the fact that "the upper and middle classes", the exclusive beneficiaries from industrial wealth, have been elevated "to a point where they more or less lose sight altogether of the lower orders". The call for a paternalistic remedy is inseparable from the fear of independent working class action in his entreaty: "a cry is coming up to us from the lower orders", which if left unheeded will unleash forces that may "come upon us with yet more startling echoes". The spectre haunting Europe no doubt.

Mayhew's tone was one more of robust irony fitting for the original editor of *Punch*:

> Our princes and nobles are no longer the patrons of prize fights, but instead the presidents of benevolent institutions. Instead of the bear-gardens and the cockpits that formerly flourished in every quarter of the town, our capital bristles and glitters with its thousand palaces for the indigent and suffering poor. If we are distinguished among nations for our exceeding wealth, assuredly we are equally illustrious for abundant charity. Almost every want or ill that can distress human nature has some palatial institution for the mitigation of it. We have rich societies for every conceivable form of benevolence:[23]

Reach and Mayhew gave brief indications of how they were to design their enquiries. Reach's intention to fulfil his commitment to comprehensiveness was expressed thus:

> I shall paint the man such as the occupation which he follows, the system in which he has been brought up, the district and the social condition of which he forms an item have made him. I shall accompany the labourer to the mill, to the mine, the forge. I shall describe his toil and the circumstances under which it is performed. I shall describe the economy of the lodging room, the cellar, the cottage.[24]

This is distinguishable from Mayhew's intention to structure his material more consciously towards a study that would reveal the economic and social causes of poverty—a basis in fact, for an emergent sociology of poverty.

> I shall consider the whole of the metropolitan poor under three separate phases, according as they will work, they can't work and they won't work.
> While treating of the poorly paid, I shall endeavour to lay before the reader

a catalogue of such occupations in London as yield a bare subsistence to the parties engaged in them. At the same time I propose, when possible, giving the weekly amount of income deriving from each, together with the cause—if discoverable—of the inadequate return. After this it is my intention to visit the dwellings of the unrelieved poor—to ascertain, by positive inspection, the condition of their homes—to learn by close communion with them, not only on how little they subsist, but how large a rate of profit they have to pay for the little upon which they do subsist—to ascertain what weekly rent they are charged for their waterless, floorless, and almost roofless tenements: and to calculate the interest which the petty capitalist reaps from their necessities.[25]

The major distinctions in approach became more obviously evident as the survey developed. The manufacturing and rural correspondents covered more ground than Mayhew and in this sense their work has about it a wider scope than his, but as itinerant reporters they were not in a position (with the exception of the smaller communities like Middleton, Swanage, the fishing and pit villages of Cornwall and Northumberland) to achieve the same depth and detail. They tended to take each area more or less as they found it and attempted, where possible, to present its typical and untypical features in the social context of a whole community. They achieved this by a combination of perceptive narrative description and the use of key witnesses, usually a long time resident in the community and who had a long standing experience of its occupations, institutions and practices. This is one of the chief reasons why the survey is such an incomparable witness to social change in the nineteenth century. Mayhew's enquiry was directed more towards detailed studies, trades, occupations and urban sub-cultures than to the kinds of community which were available to his colleagues. As his varied interest in the subject deepened, he burst out beyond the scope of the directing scheme which he had put forward in his introductory letter. Making considerable use of witnesses, he was able to show the changes which occurred in particular trades over time. His work here is quite unequalled. In the course of *London Labour* he evolved his own empirical critique of capitalism, in which casual labour and poverty could be seen to exist in a structural relationship.

Perhaps one of the simplest ways of indicating the distinctions in approach is to compare the ways in which witnesses were presented, since they are such an important part of the survey. The correspondents had a serious responsibility, as Mayhew saw it, to use the most appropriate means in giving, as a real presence, the authentic experience of the poor. Thus it was as an integral part of his whole conception of the survey, rather than the trivialising desire of an entertainer to add a bit of local colour, that he let the cockney speak with his own voice. The provincial correspondents were more content to convert the local dialects which they confronted into a standardised narrative idiom and from this they often presented a painfully contrived type of speech. The following example of a pitman giving an account of work restriction may be a little unfair to Reach, whose overall account is outstanding, but it illustrates very well how absurdly inappropriate this could sound.

"We know that there are more men in the trade than are requisite to raise the amount of coals required for the average vend, but by restricting each individual's work, we compel the masters to employ all, or nearly all of us, and thus to bring into operation, what under the competing system, would be surplus labour."[26]

There are places where the odd moralism intrudes on the evidence, though this practice cannot always be distinguished from the constraints within which the Victorian journalist had to work. The rural correspondent for instance, blunders about, in one of his best reports, making appropriate moral noises, as he confronts the tradition of pre-marital conception in Cornwall, which was sanctioned within the community and involved alike, agricultural labourers and the methodist miners and fishermen:

This practice of cohabitation before marriage is almost universal. It is not only a characteristic of low rural life; it is also so with the miners and the fishermen. Even in the fishing village of Mousehole, the people of which are in general so orderly, it is the case. And this, too, notwithstanding the extent to which temperence has prevailed amongst them. Total abstinence has not affected much in this respect for society. The miners and pitmen too, are much more under the influence of constant religious teachings than is the rural labourer; and yet they are no better than he is, so far as the practice alluded to is concerned.[27]

Disgust and sentimentality were polarised elements of upper and middle class prejudice about the poor. The South Wales correspondent echoed conventional sentiments when he reported that the squalor in which the Irish lived resulted "not from necessity, but from natural habits".[28] On the other hand the urge to romanticise the "folk" and make an emasculated quaintness of reality is indulged by the manufacturing correspondent in Middleton, where with an air of slightly patronising chumminess he gives us some local colour in the form of "the patriarch" and "his dame". She in addition to having "seen seventy winters" wore "the ordinary headress of Middleton matrons".[29]

These examples reflect the inevitable involvement of the correspondents in the very cultural process which made the survey an apparent necessity in the first place. We have at our disposal nevertheless, a marvellous range of information, which is of incomparable value to the historian and the sociologist and indeed to anybody who is seriously interested in the nineteenth century. The later surveys of Booth and Rowntree were more rigorous in method, concerned as they were with quantifying and categorising different classes of poverty.[30] *Labour and the Poor* had different interests and was projected beyond the limits of a poverty survey, as its initial terms of reference indicate. It is the wide range and penetration of its descriptions, which constitute its unique strength. In its entirety the survey stands as a monumental testament to the energies and capabilities of the early Victorian journalist.

III

I offer a brief comment on the quality of the evidence as a basis for understanding the wider social changes which resulted from industrialisation, though my discussion is restricted to only a few of the more recurring themes in the survey.

One such theme emerged from the attention given to the prevalence of small scale production, the importance of which has frequently been neglected. Too many economic historians, when demonstrating the significance of mechanisation and steam power to the process of industrialisation, have tended to understate the equally significant involvement of a mass of outworkers, "garret masters", middlemen and a vast assortment of sweated trades.[31] All the correspondents emphasise that the number of people who were thus employed increased enormously in the first half of the century. A crucial determinant of this expansion was undoubtedly the doubling during the same period, of the population, a large part of which was converted into a pool of "surplus labour". However surplus labour was both cause and effect of an increasingly competitive economic system. As such, it affected both the town and the countryside and, in addition, the relationship between the two. Its cheapness, determined largely by its abundant availability, committed it to the early ventures in the mass production of consumer goods, without involving employers in the high fixed costs of mechanisation. Thus a series of trades became crammed with a mass of small concerns, some controlled by a single wholesaler or merchant, which competed one with another in an uncontrolled progression of price cutting. This development reduced wages, a major cost item in such a system, to starvation level for many people, as a result of the effort to squeeze out surplus value. It was to this perpetual chain of exploitation that Mayhew applied his well known equation: "Underpay makes overwork" and "Overwork makes underpay". Low capital requirements, the inability to get work in the "honourable" sections of a trade and low wages for underhands in the "dishonourable" trades combined to encourage men to establish a bastardised independence as "garret masters". Some of the general features of this system, which represented a distinct form of capitalist organisation with many variations throughout the country, were explained to Mayhew by a carpenter in the "slop" cabinet trade:

> "Many works for themselves because nobody won't employ them, their work is so bad. Many weavers has took to our business of late. Thats quite common now—their own's so bad; and some that used to hawk hearthstones about is turned Pembroke table-makers. The slaughterers don't care what kind of work it is, so long as its cheap. A table's a table, they say, and thats all we want. . . . The slaughterers have cut down their prices so low that there ain't no work to be had in the better houses, so men must go on making up work for the 'butchers' (slaughterers) or starve. Those masters as really would assist the men couldn't do it because they're dead beat out of the field by the slaughter houses."[32]

Having set up for himself, the garret master was often forced to employ women and children as cheap labour. The evidence from London, Birmingham, Liverpool and Northampton demonstrates how this was an essential feature of the system and the extent to which it deviated from the honourable trades. When other men were employed they in turn would use cheap labour, often pauper apprentices, in order to squeeze out enough to stay in business, like the "chamber-masters" in the London boot and shoe trade, with the result "that our trade", said a Stepney bootmaker, "is completely overpopulated, for these boys, as soon as they get out of their time, or upon their own hands, again employ more boys, adopting the system to which they have been brought up".[33] This resembles the situation in a number of Birmingham "light trades", (described by Mackay in letters IV, VI, XII and XIV) where boys were employed by garret masters, workshop foremen and anyone "who requires assistance". At the age of sixteen, or thereabouts a youth was discarded, having had no formal apprenticeship or training, to be replaced by younger and cheaper labour. Charles Mackay reported that such youths were "only trained to one particular branch of a manufacture ... by which they learn nothing likely to be of service to them in their future life".[34] They were thus disqualified from entering the skilled trades and better workshops, becoming part of a large residual stratum of semi-skilled labour, forced either to accept the low wages and gruelling discipline of a garret master, or to become one. As such they were entirely dependent on middlemen or "factors" for the supply of materials and the distribution of their products. Not surprisingly they were compelled, in the context of this dependence, to sell in the cheapest market and buy in the dearest. They were thus motivated to employ cheap boy labour and repeat the whole process. The survey shows clearly how, as a feature of industrial development, it was this type of economic organisation, rather than the mechanised factory, which determined the process of proletarianisation for large sections of the population. While the garret master might technically have been an employer, he had little or no influence over production, distribution, or income; the levels of which were established by market mechanisms beyond his control.

The relation between the London and Northampton boot and shoe trades provides a good example of how a traditional urban trade might be affected by the establishment of a semi-rural one. In Northampton, the development of the industry during the first half of the century depended on the influx of cheap rural labour, which could quite easily be adapted to the undemanding and sub-divided skills of the ready-made trade. The garret master types of employer there, acted as outworkers to larger establishments. The increase in the numbers of London chamber masters was to some extent a direct outcome of the expansion of the Northampton trade, where cheaper labour and cheaper products encouraged merchants to buy there, thus bringing down the London prices and increasing competition.[35]

As we see from the accounts of the rural correspondents, the agricultural population suffered from the imposition of chronic insecurity, which made it an obvious source of cheap labour, enabling middlemen and wholesale organisations to increase output and reduce prices. In the metropolitan letter IX, one of the London stay stitchers, whose maximum wage had fallen from seventeen shillings and five pence to three shillings and sixpence a week, explained that the reduction was due to the fact that her employers "sent work into the country to get it done the cheapest way they could and have always been lowering the wages of the poor people". In the same letter a wholesale stay-maker corroborated this statement, saying that he could do this "owing to the number of people out of employ in those parts". Children were required as assistants to their mothers in this kind of outwork and were thus provided with an appropriate training for entering into the urban sweat shops. A Liverpool "slop" wholesaler, who employed Irish needlewomen for the "quality" and cheapness of their labour, explained this important function to Mackay:

"I have often been in the villages of Derry and Donegal where this work is done. The needlewomen seem comfortable. They employ all their children in the business as soon as their little hands are able to thread a needle. The men do not work at the business but boys of twelve and thirteen often do. The children do the hems and simpler kind of work and the women finish it off. Many boys, who afterwards became tailors, learn the first rudiments of the business at shirtmaking. When they grow up, they come over to England in search of employment as tailors, and generally have to resign themselves to work for the sweaters. They are not fit for better work. There are great numbers of Irish tailors of this class in Liverpool."[36]

It was a situation such as this which assisted in the dismemberment of the "honourable" trade in Liverpool reported by the old tailor in letter VII (Liverpool).

Rural migrants provided the basis of a progressive supply of labour to the sweated trades. Often possessing a range of skills like the country painter who told Mayhew: "...I can work as a glazier and plumber; country painters often can—I mean those apprenticed in the country...": they were unable to get into the honourable trades when these were adequately protected and were thus compelled to accept the harsh routines of the "strapping" shops and speculative builders. A foreman with one of the latter confirmed this with Mayhew:

"The speculators find plenty of cheap labour among the country lads. A hand fresh up from the country can't get employment at the best shops, unless he's got some friends, and so, after walking all London, he is generally down to look for for a job among the speculators at low wages."[37]

It was in the trades which were most susceptible to the competition and debasement of the sweater, that the skilled worker suffered, in addition to a reduction of income, a significant decline in status, determined largely by his being deprived of an acknowledged independence which had meaning within his own understood and established traditions. This experience was the outcome of a wider process whereby quasi-customary traditions capitulated before the pervasive and transforming market forces of industrialisation.[38]

The letters from the rural correspondent give an effective account of the complexity of the agricultural community. In many of his reports, we are shown how the basis of a progressive rural emigration in the nineteenth century depended for its impetus on the expelling force of a disintegrating rural community, which gave to the town and the city (often arrived at by the circuitous routes of surrounding villages) the aspect of positive centres of attraction. The rural areas were the source of growing population, but not, we are told, the scene of a corresponding growth in social resources. It was this imbalance which had a major hand in the creation of "surplus labour". The supply of housing, wages and land lay with the farmers and landlords who were largely hostile to the labourer. A particular object of this hostility was the day labourer, who gained little from staying in the countryside at a time when diminishing opportunities seemed paradoxically to be an integral feature of the expansion in agrarian productivity. In fact a complete cross section of people engaged in a host of rural occupations were caught up alike in the progressive collapse of the village economy. In this respect some of Mayhew's letters are a valuable complement to the rural series.[39]

The inadequate supply of housing forms one of the recurring themes of the rural reports. While the population was increasing cottages were often being demolished, or simply left to collapse. One of the letters from the Midlands gives a representative account of this:

> There are also many landlords who will not allow any increase in the number of cottages upon their estates, and others who destroy what few really do exist, and others who, more slowly, but no less effectually, accomplish the object of clearing their estates of labourers and paupers, by allowing all their cottages to sink into decay, without making the least exertion to prevent their ruin, and when, through age and neglect, the wretched hovels fall down, no new ones are erected in their stead.[40]

This practice was intensified by the 1834 Poor Law, with its system of chargeability and settlement, which encouraged landlords to clear their estates of surplus labour before a settlement, following five years' residence, could be claimed. As a consequence the "open" and "closed" villages were established, from which resulted the gang system and the situation whereby the labourer who had been "cleared" might have to walk up to ten or more miles a day to work on an estate where he had once been resident.[41] The Poor Law Guardians were often the landlords and farmers who had a vested interest in clearing their estates.[42]

Unless the labourer was hired by the year, like the shepherds and carters, his life was given to constant insecurity. His wages were minimal, his employment uncertain and unable to form a union he was dischargeable at any time. His relationship with the farmer is defined by a Buckinghamshire labourer:

> "You see, sir, its a matter of pounds shillings and pence throughout, not of rewarding them that faithfully serves them. . . . If a man complains they call him saucy and discharge him at once. The employers all understand each other and won't employ him again until he has learned better manners, or is punished enough for his impudence."[43]

The rural reports are full of references to the fact that the farmer's relationship to the labourer was an instrumental one. The bleakness of the labourer's involvement in industrialisation underlined the probability that he had more to gain as an urban proletarian, than as a landless rural one; though as Mayhew revealed it, the town also held out the promise of uncertainty, but life there had the implicit sanction of the momentous and often brutal force of historical change. The rural and the metropolitan letters are in many respects complementary to each other in their discussion of the poor and the principal economic and social bearings which determined their existence.

One of the great strengths of the survey is the way in which it presents its information in the context of a very wide cross section of economic organisation, ranging from large factories to the stone quarries of Swanage, where a primitive barter system still existed. We are shown particularly, the extent to which the early Victorian economy was underpinned by a complex system of sub-contractual relationships. This system had the essential function, in industrialisation, of giving continuity to production. In Birmingham, for instance, the sub-contractual relations of the small workshop were taken into the factory, which was often started by the factor who supplied raw materials and leased floor space, power, heating and light to the small master.[44] A similar situation is described in Oldham, where "there are a great number of small capitalists renting floors or small portions of factories".[45] Many of the early factories were started in this way. In the absence of a distinct managerial class, the sub-contractor combined both work and managerial roles. Being paid piece rates by the factor or factory owner, he had to ensure a certain level of production to make a living. As the factory developed, he evolved, on the one hand, into the foreman and on the other, into the reliable, respectable and salaried manager; a fact which partly helps to explain why such large numbers of managers were recruited from the "ranks".

Sub-contracting systems were not limited to small and early factories, but existed over a wide area of economic organisation, as the reports on Staffordshire, South Wales and Cornwall indicate. The abuses of truck were often the inevitable results. In the Staffordshire and South Wales collieries we see the butties and gaffers "tommying" men whose jobs depended upon a passive compliance with this form of exploitation.[46] The letters from Mayhew and Mackay reveal the endemic nature of truck around the docks of London and Liverpool, where publicans, grocers and lodging house keepers competed for contracts in order to convert an insecure labour force into customers or lodgers.[47] The tommy shop was also used as a capital reclamation and investment mechanism for the business which it accompanied. A partner in a small iron works informed the 1843 Midlands Mining Commission:

> I believe that there are many works that could not go on at all without tommy shops or truck shops. This is not only on account of the reduction in wages which the profits of the shop, in fact cause to the employer, but also on account of the capital which it is the means of supplying. The goods are purchased wholesale by the proprietor at six months credit and the men's wages have to be paid every week or fortnight.[48]

The manufacturing correspondent showed, however, that truck was not the exclusive practice of the butties and the smaller establishments. In Staffordshire he found that "the very worst 'Tommy Shops' are kept not by the ignorant butties, but by the great ironmasters—vast capitalists who employ labour by the hundred".[49]

The routinisation of work—timed, regulated and formally separated from leisure, constituted one of the most potent instruments of social change involved by industrialisation. Its capacity as a redirecting force in the community was sanctioned by quasi religious values which were not confined to church chapel and Sunday school; but found expression in teetotalism and institutions like the Lord's Day Observance Society and the R.S.P.C.A., both noted by Marx for their potential to stabilise industrial capitalism as a result of their aims to civilise the workng class.[50]

Angus Reach gives a superb example of the power of work discipline in its capacity as a compelling agent of cultural transition; dissipating traditional energies in Ashton where hunting once centred among the community sports in which the handloom weavers had been enthusiastic participants:

The mill system has, however, utterly extirpated every vestige of the ancient sporting spirit. The regulation of hours and discipline preserved seem, by rendering any such escapades out of the question, to have obliterated anything like a desire for or any idea of them.[51]

Factories had been established in Ashton for some time and the view is one of a community pretty well transformed. In Saddleworth, however, the appearance of the factory was comparatively recent. The description of this traditional woollen textile community demonstrates how pre-industrial social forms could survive, in the short term, the imposition of new and alien modes of work. It is significant that in this village hunting, sanctioned and participated in by the employers, remained an activity of the whole community:

> Even the discipline of the mills is as yet in many instances insufficient to check this inherent passion for the chase. My informant himself a millowner, told me that he had recently arranged a hunt to try the mettle of some dogs from another part of Yorkshire against the native breed. He tried to keep the matter as quiet as he could; but somehow it leaked out, and the result was, that several slubbers, spinners and weavers formed the field. The masters, however, are often too keen sportsmen themselves to grudge their hands an occasional holiday of the sort.[52]

In Birmingham where the range and type of economic organisation was highly varied, old and declining traditions persisted in a contrasted co-existence with the new. The imposition of timed work routines and the adaptation to their demands was quite widely established by 1850, but the commitment to old and hallowed institutions like "Saint Monday" still enjoyed a vestigial existence, particularly among the older workers and garret masters. In fact, the opportunity of establishing an independent work routine counted as an inducement to set up as a garret master.[53] The Birmingham working class, though increasingly separated from inherited rustic traditions, were nevertheless more closely connected with them than were the Manchester populations. This is well illustrated in the vivid descriptions of the old rough sports presented by Mackay. One of his witnesses recalled that some of these sports were carried on in secret after they had been made illegal and that they had until quite recently received the patronage of the gentry and aristocracy:

> "Noblemen and gentlemen fought for a 'main' with their cocks, and the amount of it varied according to the amount of cocks brought forward. It was frequently forty or fifty guineas and on a grand occasion as much as a hundred guineas were staked upon the result of a fight."[54]

The "gipsy parties", (forerunners of "the firm's annual outing") also described by Mackay, were representative of some of the organised leisure activities which replaced these more boistous and robust pursuits. The employer and the values which he embodied, became increasingly the identifying foci in the creation of new cultural orientations which were more appropriate to modern work procedures. This would appear to be borne out by the way in which the *"REGULATIONS TO BE OBSERVED ON THE OCCASION OF MESSRS. HINCKES, WELLS, AND CO'S PLEASURE TRIP, JULY 13, 1850"* were adhered to:

> These regulations were drawn up by a committee of the employed and the employers, and were so strictly and cheerfully adhered to, that neither in going

nor returning, nor during the stay of the party on the hills, did there occur a single instance of his disobedience to orders, of misbehaviour of any kind, or of drunkenness—[55]

New modes of work thus suggested a variety of related disciplines which provided a normative context for the rejection of older, non-rational traditions. An interesting aspect of this is illustrated by the journeyman brass worker who told Mackay:

"If one of the workmen absents himself from work for drunkenness, he returns to the manufactory amidst the ridicule and hootings of his comrades. The number of teetotallers in our establishment is considerable."[56]

The "platers" were once known as a "rough set", but, following their transformation into "electro-platers", they were distinguished "not only for their regularity and sobriety, but for their provident economy". They provide a good example of how the actual presence of the employer was an essential complement to new types of work in the formation of new cultural goals and aspirations among his employees:

They have no union of the trade, but they have founded a sick and burial club, and have it in contemplation, in conjunction, with their employer, to establish a school for their children and for the boys engaged in the manufacture, and a library and reading room for themselves.[57]

January, 1972   R. W. WAINWRIGHT

NOTES

1. *Morning Chronicle*, October 18, 1849.
2. Chas. Mackay, *Forty Years Recollections* (1877), (ii), pp. 148–57.
3. Fox-Bourne, *English Newspapers* (1887), (ii), pp. 140–63.
4. *Morning Chronicle*, September 24, 1849.
5. The fullest discussion of the social bearings of the novel in this period remain: L. Cazamion, *Le Roman en Angleterre 1830–1850* (1904); K. Tillotson, *Novels of the 1840s* (1962 ed.).
6. K. Tillotson, op. cit., p. 23.
7. Quoted Fox-Bourne, op. cit., (ii), p. 141.
8. For information on the authorship of the *Labour and the Poor* series and the careers of the correspondents see:
   Chas. Mackay, *Forty Years Recollections*, (i), pp. 148–57; (ii), pp. 148–64.
   Edmund Yates, *Recollections and Experiences* (1885), (i), pp. 190–1, 217, 240, 266, 270, 282–3, 304; (ii), pp. 83, 143–9.
   Sutherland Edwards, *Personal Recollections* (1900), pp. 59–61.
   G. Hodder, *Memories of my Time* (1870), pp. 58–66.
   H. Vizetelly, *Glances back through Seventy Years* (1893), (i), pp. 406, 408.
   M. H. Spielman, *The History of Punch* (1895), pp. 268–71, 356–8.
   Inverness Courier, January 24, 27, 31, February 3, 1905, *Two Famous Correspondents: The Reaches, Father and Son*.
   Angela Hookham, *The Literary Career of Henry Mayhew 1812–1887*, (Birmingham Univ. M.A. Thesis 1962).
   M. H. Bradley, *Selections from London Labour and the London Poor* (1965).
   E. P. Thompson and Eileen Yeo, *The Unknown Mayhew* (1971). In his introduction E. P. Thompson has made available a far wider range of sources dealing with the correspondents than I have done here. It seems unnecessary to repeat what he has already done well.

9. See particularly Chas. Mackay for Angus Reach and E. Yates for Shirley Brooks.
10. Chas. Mackay, op. cit.
11. Ibid.
12. M. H. Spielman, op. cit. For an account of Mayhew's career before he joined the *Chronicle* see: M. H. Bradley and E. P. Thompson, op. cit.
13. Ibid.
14. H. Vizetelly, op. cit., p. 406.
15. The case for Mayhew as a serious sociologist has been well argued by Eileen Yeo in her introduction to *The Unknown Mayhew*. See also Ann Humphreys, *Voices of the Poor* (1971).
16. These reports were republished as: *Claret and Olives* (1852), Angus Reach; *Russians of the South* (1854), Shirley Brooks.
17. Chas. Mackay, op. cit.
18. *Morning Chronicle*, October 18, 1849.
19. Letter I Manufacturing Districts.
20. Quoted Asa Briggs, 'The Language of Class in the Nineteenth Century', *Essays in Labour History* (1961), ed. A. Briggs and J. Saville.
21. Thos Carlyle, *Sartor Resartus*, Bk. 3, Ch. 10.
22. Letter I Rural Districts.
23. Letter I Metropolitan Districts.
24. Letter I Manufacturing Districts.
25. Letter I Metropolitan Districts.
26. Letter XXII Manufacturing Districts.
27. Letter XIII Rural Districts.

The social meaning of pre-marital conception varied from region to region. The locally sanctioned practice whereby marriage followed pregnancy persisted in counties other than Cornwall (see letter XXI Rural Districts), despite the efforts of the Poor Law Commissioners to enforce a stern conformity with the conventional and officially sanctioned conception of the family. The 1834 Poor Law deprived unmarried mothers of the opportunity to make affiliation orders at Petty Sessions, thus disturbing what could quite often be a delicate social balance. In their eagerness to confirm the prejudices of received Malthusianism, the Commissioners of Enquiry for the Poor Law disregarded evidence which might have challenged the devastating simplicity of their conclusions.

For a discussion of the Commissioners' approach to pre-marital conception see: U. R. Q. Henriques, 'Bastardy and the New Poor Law', *Past and Present*, No. 37, September 1967. This touches on the conflict between the traditions of pre-marital conception and the 1834 Poor Law. A neglected source which suggests a variety of enquiries into the regional variations of bastardy is: R. Leffingwell, *Illegitimacy—A study in Morals and The Influence of the Seasons upon Conduct* (1892).

28. Letter VII South Wales.
29. Letter XII Manufacturing Districts.
30. For an evaluation of the criticisms which have been made in relation to Mayhew as a sociologist see Eileen Yeo. She also discusses, in passing, the methods of the provincial correspondents.
31. We agree with E. P. Thompson when he says that "... each was a complementary component of a single process": *The Making of the English Working Class* (1968), p. 288.
32. Letter LXVI Metropolitan Districts.
33. Letter XXXIV ibid.
34. Letter IV Birmingham.
35. Letters XLV and XLVI Rural Districts; Letters XXXII, XXXIII, XXXIV Metropolitan Districts. See also: R. Church, 'Labour Supply and Innovation 1800–1860: The Boot and Shoe Industry', *Business History*, Vol. XII, No. 1, January 1970.
36. Letter VI Liverpool (excluded).

37. Letter LXI Metropolitan Districts. The example of the country painter comes from a part of letter XXVI which has been excluded.

38. E. P. Thompson, *The Making of the English Working Class* (1968), pp. 258–96. For the traditions of London Trades in the eighteenth century and the appearance of garret masters: Dorothy George, *London Life in the Eighteenth Century*, (1966), pp. 158–212.

39. See particularly: letters XXVI, LIX, LX, LXI Metropolitan Districts. Also J. Saville, *Rural Depopulation in England and Wales*, 1957.

40. Letter XLVII Rural Districts. In the rural reports there is no basis for refuting O. R. McGregor's observation on rural housing: "There is no comprehensive history of housing in industrial England. When one comes to be put together, the blackest chapter, paradoxically, will be devoted to the countryside", *English Farming Past and Present*, Sixth ed., 1961, p. cxxi.

41. Letter XV Rural Districts. The system of "open" and "closed" villages and their effects on employment, housing and rents is well described by Dennison in his report of East Anglia in: *The Report of the Assistant Poor Law Commissioners on the Employment of Women and Children in Agriculture*, Parliamentary Papers 1843 (510), XII-I. Of recent research J. P. Shepherd's analysis of East Yorkshire is invaluable. She demonstrates the use of census schedules to measure the excess of "employed" over "resident" labourers in each township. *Agricultural History Review*, Vol. IX, Pt. 1, 1961.

42. For an example of this see: Letter XLVII Rural Districts.

43. Letter III Rural Districts.

44. For a discussion of this see: G. C. Allen, *The Industrial Development of Birmingham* (1929), pp. 151–72; A. Fox, 'Industrial Relations in Nineteenth Century Birmingham', *Oxford Economic Papers* (1955), Vol. 7, No. 1. This is the type of analysis for which *Labour and the Poor* might be used to good effect. It relates the ambivalence in the relationship between employers and workers to sub-contractual types of organisation.

45. Letter VIII Manufacturing Districts.

46. See: Letters XXIV Manufacturing Districts, VI and X South Wales. Also A. J. Taylor, 'The Sub-Contract System in the British Coal Industry', *Studies in the Industrial Revolution*, 1966, ed. L. S. Pressnell, pp. 215–35.

47. Letters XIX, XXII, XXIV, LVIII Metropolitan Districts; Letter IV Liverpool.

48. First Report of the Midland Mining Commission. Parliamentary Papers, 1843 (508), XIII-I, p. 96.

49. Letter XXIV Manufacturing Districts.

50. As a complement to the evidence discussed here see: E. P. Thompson, 'Time, Work and Industrial Capitalism', *Past and Present*, December 1967, No. 38; B. Harrison, 'Religion and Recreation in Nineteenth Century England', *Past and Present*, December 1967, No. 38.

51. Letter VII Manufacturing Districts.

52. Letter XIII ibid.

53. Letter LXVI Metropolitan Districts.

54. Letter XX Birmingham. Patronage by the gentry was an important factor in the existence of the traditional sports. The disintegration of these sports was related to a shift in social relationships experienced by the whole community. We have an example of this process in the village in M. K. Ashby, *Joseph Ashby of Tysoe* (1961), p. 36: "The men said Methodism had killed the sports, because the best sportsmen had been converted. But Jasper said it was due to a change in the church too; the clergy and the gentlemen farmers had ceased to be spectators. Altogether, the matches had lost interest."

55. Letter IX Birmingham.

56. Letter XII ibid.

57. Letter XVIII ibid. See also letter VI South Wales.

Introduction

by P. E. Razzell

The *Morning Chronicle* survey is a unique attempt to describe all forms of
working-class community life in England at a particular point of time. A
large proportion of material has been selected from the original survey in order
to provide information on all major aspects of social life of specific communities, and I hope in this introduction to illustrate how this part of our edited
survey lends itself to sociological analysis. Not only will I attempt to illuminate
the survey through the perspective of sociological ideas, but also in turn evalu-
ate those ideas through the empirical case studies provided by the survey. The
type of analysis that I shall adopt is only one of several to which the material
might lend itself, and my aim is to merely illustrate the value of the survey to
sociological and historical study. The starting point of my analysis is
Lockwood's work on working-class images of society,[1] which takes the variations in the economic structure of community life as given and attempts to
explain associated social and political attitudes as outcome variables.

It is possible to distinguish three types of worker: the traditional deferential, the traditional proletarian and the privatised. The deferential and
proletarian workers both occur in their purest form in closed communities.
The deferential worker typically lives in villages and small towns with a mixture of social classes, whereas the proletarian lives in one occupational communities like mining villages and workingclass town enclaves such as docking and
shipbuilding neighbourhoods. The deferential works in a small workshop or
in service and agricultural occupations where his relationship with his employer is personal and paternalistic; the proletarian worker is to be found in
work situations which isolate him from his employer but unite him with his
workmates. The deferential worker has an hierarchical 'status" conception of
social stratification whereas the proletarian has a conflict "us v. them" power
model of social class. The privatised home-centred worker differs from both
the deferential and proletarian workers in that he is not involved in local
community life—this is a result of his residential mobility and lack of attachment to his workmates through the alienating quality of his factory work. This
type of worker has a money model of social class and an "instrumental"
attitude towards his work which is viewed primarily as a source of income;
he forms the core of "the increasingly large section of the working class
emerging from traditionalism".

Turning to the survey itself, deferential attitudes were found less among
groups such as agricultural labourers, but were found among certain classes of
factory worker: Ashworth's country cotton factory of Egerton, Messrs.
Arrowsmith & Slater's cotton factory on the outskirts of Bolton and Crawshay's
iron-works at Merthyr-Tydfil.[2] Deference in all these cases manifested itself in
respect and admiration for the paternalistic employer, and the absence of industrial conflict in the form of strikes. The key sociological factor in explaining

the deference of these workers appears to have been the residence of the employer in the workers' community, combined with the paternalistic provision of model cottages, free medical provisions and the like.[3] It was possible for the employer to get to know his workers personally even in the context of a large factory work situation because of his prolonged residence in the community in which many of his workers had spent their whole working lives. This of course was not typical of factories in large towns such as Manchester where frequently workers had never even spoken to their employers; for example the Manchester cotton worker who stated that "I have worked in that mill sir, these nineteen years, and the master never spoke to me once".[4] But even in Manchester some of the factory owners were involved in a more personal capacity with their workers through the Sunday School movement, which appears to have helped spread their values of self-help and individual achievement and discouraged radical political activity such as Chartism.[5]

The deference of factory workers is of greater historical importance than most sociologists or even historians have recognised. During Luddite attacks on cotton-factories during the beginning of the nineteenth century it was often the factory workers who helped their employers defend their property and there are examples of factory workers actually firing on and killing Luddite attackers.[6] Many of these early factories were in rural areas where the employers lived in an almost gentry-like relationship with their workers, generating a classical deference situation. Perhaps as important as this social situation though, was the fact that these early factory workers were very highly paid in comparison to their contemporaries such as hand-loom weavers. As well as high income, these factory workers benefited from the sort of paternalistic provision of model cottages etc. discussed above. The influence of paternalistic intervention on behalf of workers is illustrated by the case of the London coal-whippers: the quality of their lives had been dramatically improved through the intervention of the government in legislating against payment of wages in public-houses. They and their wives appear to have been highly appreciative of the government's action, which would go some way in explaining why they "were extremely proud of their having turned out to a man on April 10, 1848, and become special constables for the maintenance of 'law and order' on the day of the great Chartist 'demonstration' ".[7]

The relative absence of deferential attitudes amongst agricultural labourers in the survey can be explained in terms of the fact that they benefited so little from their "personal" relationship with farmers and gentry.[8] The poverty and destitution of the agricultural labourers is more than adequately described throughout the survey, but in order to indicate the unfeeling way they were sometimes treated by farmers I quote the following casual description of their treatment in an area of Norfolk from an unpublished letter:

> It is the usual custom, I was informed in a great many of the adjoining parishes, for the farmers to send their teams in order to convey their labourers with their families to the union workhouse for the winter months, and as many as seventy persons have been seen thus to pass through Trimmingham on their way to the union workhouse.[9]

It is not surprising that rick-burning was a frequent occurrence in East Anglia (where large-scale capitalist farming was most frequently to be found), and in this respect agricultural labourers were solidly proletarian in their attitudes.[10] This reference to rick-burning should however remind the careful reader of Hobsbawm and Rudé's book on the riots of the agricultural labourer in 1830 that in many cases landlords managed to recruit "respectable labourers", "servants and retainers, grooms, huntsmen, game-keepers" as special constables to put down the riot.[11] There is some evidence to show that domestic servants were the most deferential occupational group during this period,[12] and it is unfortunate that the survey was terminated before they were studied (they were about the largest single occupational group in the country). The "respectable labourers" referred to above were presumably labourers who worked on the estates of paternalistic landowners and lived in the "closed" villages attached to these estates. These labourers benefited substantially in economic terms from their relationship with their employers,[13] as did domestic servants particularly those of the aristocratic rich.

Deference arose not only out of a personal relationship with a paternalistic employer but also with other elites such as the clergy. This is illustrated by a description of the religious behaviour of agricultural labourers:

> In small parishes, where the clergyman is frequently brought into personal contact with the labourers, and where, from other causes, he exercises a direct influence over them, they may be found pretty regular in their attendance at church; but generally speaking their attendance is neither large nor constant, most of them moping about on the Sunday, smoking and drinking, and some of them spend nearly the whole day in bed.[14]

This suggests that without the influence of the clergy, labourers had very similar attitudes towards the Church as did their urban proletarian contemporaries. The term influence is rather ambiguous with respect to the analysis of deference, for although there is some evidence that labourers did on occasions genuinely identify with the hierarchical values of the Church, there is even more evidence that many of them attended church in a rather mechanical way as a result of economic pressure.[15] The clergy were often in a position to exercise control because of the desperate economic plight of their parishioners. A labourer's wife living in Cambridgeshire told the rural correspondent in October 1850:

> "I've just put the last twig of wood on the fire. I went to the clergyman this morning, and I asked him for God's sake, to give me sixpence to buy a bit of firing with; and he said he could not afford it, and that he was as bad off as I was."[16]

When the clergy were able and willing to use their wealth they were capable of increasing their congregation significantly. An example of this is when the new vicar of Sutton Courtenay discovered the neglect of church attendance by the labourers living in his parish, partly through the use of his wealth he "got the people into the habit of attending church, which he deemed to be his first duty".[17]

Several communities described in the survey show some sociological features typical of the proletarian worker: the London and Liverpool shipwrights, the Middleton weavers, the Cornish fishermen and miners, the

Swanage stone quarriers, and the London coopers and hatters.[18] However, the fullest description of the proletarian worker in purest form is the account of the Durham and Northumberland miners.[19] The sharing of egalitarian values in these village mining communities took a religious form during this period and most of these miners were members of Methodist congregations. The class basis of Methodism and the linked antagonism towards the Church of England was explicitly recognised, as the manufacturing correspondent revealed:

> The Church of England is, I believe, from what I have seen, regarded by a large proportion of the mining community with feelings of positive and active enmity. They almost invariably class it with the aristocratic institutions and influences which they believe to be hostile to them. The church clergymen, they say take the part of the masters, but the Ranters (Primitive Methodists) take part with the men, addressing their comrades in their own patois, and treating every scriptual subject in the peculiarly technical tone which is common to the whole community.[20]

This class basis of Methodism was expressed during the great strike of 1844:

> A religious feeling came to be strangely mixed up with the movement. The Ranters' chapels were crowded, and the success of the strike was prayed for from the pulpit. The people went to chapel and prayer meetings, as they said, to "get their faith strengthened".[21]

This description of the use of religion as a way of expressing and reinforcing community solidarity is a classic example of what Durkheim conceived as the main function of religious activity, although the religious "rationalisation" of class interests is more akin to a Marxian analysis of social structure.

Unlike the Durham and Northumberland miners, those living in Staffordshire showed little class solidarity amongst themselves. One major reason given for this difference was given by a Staffordshire miner when commenting on the fact that miners in the North were much more active in organising a trade union than those in Staffordshire itself: "They may get it (the union) up again . . . in the North—but we're people from a great many counties here, and we don't trust each other."[22] This is a good illustration of the importance of geographical mobility in determining class solidarity. Two other major reasons for the lack of unity amongst the Staffordshire miners were: (i) they did not live in small separate villages as did the northern miners but inhabited undifferentiated areas of sprawling township shared with iron-workers and others; (ii) they worked in relatively small mines run through middle-men with whom they had some kind of personal relationship —again unlike the north where the mines were run on much more bureaucratic lines. One of the effects of the lack of community solidarity amongst the Staffordshire miners was the absence of any religious consensus such as an attachment to Methodism, and their style of life was characterised by a pub-centred culture and a liking for rough traditional sports.[23]

One of the difficulties in giving a clear-cut theoretical analysis of a survey like that made by the *Morning Chronicle* is its richness of empirical detail. However, this sometimes allows us to extend the analysis by directly using comments reported in the survey; for example the London turner who noted because of the noisy nature of his work "no talk can be carried on, as in a tailor's shop, by which men can pick up a little politics or knowledge".[24] This adds to our understanding about the range of variables to be considered when attempting to account for social facts such as proletarian class consciousness. The noisiness of their work is also stated to be one of the reasons why the "honourable" cabinet-makers were so little interested in politics and might also help to explain their relative indifference to trade unionism—other reasons only implicit in the survey were the absence of any noted concentration of the trade in any particular area of London and perhaps most importantly the fact that most of these London cabinet-makers were "countrymen" in origin.[25] By contrast the London shipbuilders were "mainly natives of the metropolis" who lived "chiefly in Poplar and the adjacent parts"—and presumably these geographical foundations of a closed community life go some way in explaining the fact that "not a few of the shipbuilders have brought up their sons to their own calling". All the three above factors can be seen as contributing to the political awareness of the shipbuilders described as follows:

> The shipbuilders are, I found, great politicians. It is customary during their half hour's luncheon at eleven o'clock, for one man to read the newspaper aloud in the public-house parlour; a discussion almost invariably follows, and is often enough resumed in the evening.[26]

It is not possible to tell from the survey which factor is the most important in determining such political consciousness, a question which could only be settled by a sophisticated methodology of statistical comparison directed at an explicity formulated theoretical proposition. Although the survey has none of this, at least it produces a richness of description which forces us to recognise the complexity of situations to be explained, and the inadequacy of generalisations to account for all the detailed variations. It is for this reason that there is no effective summary substitute for the survey itself.

The privatised worker is more difficult to find in the survey than the deferential and proletarian types and this is what would be expected from the formulation of the privatised worker as belonging essentially to the twentieth century. There are however indications that there was a nineteenth-century equivalent to the privatised worker, particularly where there was an absence of deferential or proletarian community life. For example the London cabinet-makers were not only relatively indifferent to politics and trade unionism but were described by Mayhew in the following terms:

> The great majority of the cabinet-makers are married men, and were described to me by the best informed parties as generally domestic men, living, whenever it was possible, near their workshops, and going home to every meal. They are not much of play-goers, a Christmas pantomine or any holiday spectacle being exceptions, especially where there is a family. "I don't know a card-player", said a man who had every means of knowing, "amongst us. I think you'll find more cabinet-makers than any other trade members of mechanic's institutes and literary institutions, and attenders at lectures."[27]

This was the labouring aristocracy of "respectable" artisans who not only prided themselves on their education and their "rational" amusements, but also on the fact that they could maintain their family without their wives having to work; for example according to a bedstead-maker

"Several of us are house-keepers, and can support our wives and families comfortably. I don't think one of the wives of the members of our society work in any way but for the family."[28]

One of the results of this type of family-centred respectability was that the homes of these artisans were very well furnished; for example in the homes of the "honourable" cabinet-makers

> you have the warm red glow of polished mahogany furniture; a clean carpet covers the floor; a few engravings in neat frames hang against the papered wall; and bookshelves or a bookcase have their appropriate furniture. Very white and bright-coloured pot ornaments, with sometimes a few roses in a small vase, are reflected in the mirror over the mantleshelf.[29]

Given that the privatised worker is not only family-centred but also home-centred (the two are obviously intimately connected), we can take this evidence about the well furnished homes of the "respectable" artisan as a further indication of their relatively privatised state.

The association between a comfortable home and the emotional importance of the family is hinted at by the manufacturing correspondent who implied that "respectability" was not confined to particular occupational groups:

> Before leaving the subject of house and street architecture I may be permitted to observe on the constant recurrence of a phenomenon which I have remarked on in many industrial districts in England. In the houses of the worst class—in those the inhabitants are slatternly and poor—the seldom failing pictorial decoration upon the walls is derived, with significant frequency, from the illustrations of some highwayman novel. In more comfortable dwellings although occupied, perhaps by individuals of the same nominal rank in the social scale, you may find a stiff family portrait or two—probably a crown or half-a-crown's worth—from some vagrant artist; or, perchance, there are engravings of some Chartist or Radical leader belonging to the political school of the pater familias.[30]

The two categories of person described in this passage correspond more or less to the distinction familiar to sociologists between the "roughs" and the "respectables". One of the chief differences between these two groups lay in the focus of their leisure activities: the "roughs" spent most of their spare time in the pub, the "respectables" at home with their family. The survey provides much more evidence about the first than the second, although the constant references to the sobriety of the respectable artisan is indirect confirmation of the latter. An example of this distinction within virtually the same trade is to be found amongst the tanners and the curriers; the London tanners were traditional "roughs" with a pub-centred and prize-fighting sub-culture, as contrasted with the educated home-centred "respectable" curriers. Part of the explanation for this difference lay in the fact that the former all worked in the area of Bermondsey and thus formed a traditional community, whereas the latter worked and lived in different parts of London leading to a degree of privatisation.[31]

There is one problem with using the term privatisation with reference to the mid-nineteenth century period and that is that it assumes a sharp distinction between the work and home situations. Domestic workers by definition worked in the home and where they worked long hours they were effectively privatised; for example the London fancy cabinet-makers were far less political than they used to be. The working singly, and in their own rooms, as is nearly universal with them now, has rendered them more unsocial than they were, and less disposed for the interchange of good offices with their fellow workmen, as well as less regardful of their position and their rights as skilled labourers.[32]

Lockwood however has used the term privatisation to refer to non-work activity, but with these domestic workers non-work activity (leisure) hardly existed. This was not always the case for the small master turners living and working in Spitalfields were

> rare fellows for skittles, cards, and dominoes, and badly as they're off, numbers of them don't work on a Monday.[33]

There are also cases in the survey of workers not working at home but working such long hours that they in effect had no leisure time at all, and perhaps an extreme example of this is the London omnibus drivers and conductors who did not have the time to attend church on a Sunday.[34] Although it is technically correct to apply the term privatisation only to non-work activity, the social and political effects of both work and leisure situations are considered in the analysis, and it is only necessary to add amount of leisure time as a variable in order to extend it to nineteenth-century conditions.

One theme which constantly recurs in the survey is that of wives who had spent their childhood and adolescence as factory workers being less capable of looking after their families than women who had been domestic servants before marriage. One of the results of the lack of domestic competence of ex-factory wives was to discourage husbands from spending their leisure time at home and lead them to spend more time in the local pub. Perhaps even more important than this in creating a pub-centred culture was the lack of elementary domestic comforts such as adequate lighting, heating, furniture, space and cleanliness—all particularly important to make a home an attractive place during a period when fertility and the number of children living was so high. The effect of the lack of lighting and heating in creating a pub-centred culture is beautifully illustrated in a letter on the Liverpool docks where ships were forbidden to have either heat or lighting because of the fear of fire.[35] In this respect the privatisation of the worker can be seen as a function of improvements in the quality of the home, and this was tentatively suggested by the rural correspondent in a discussion of the labourer's home.[36] In fact the home situation is an equally important sociological variable as the work situation, and not only with respect to the comfort of the home but also home situated technology. For example the introduction of running water instead of water from wells increased women's home centredness and eliminated the social relationships based on the communal collection of water.[37]

Although the survey can be interpreted in very general terms as confirming the analysis of different types of working class, the characteristics of nineteenth-century "respectables" do not fundamentally fit into the appropriate classification. This class was not only relatively privatised but also much more aware of itself as a social class with distinct radical political views than the "roughs" who, in spite of their shared community style of life, were not as aware of being a part of the "working class".[38] One of the major reasons for this difference was the greater literacy and education of the "respectables"—and in the nineteenth century working class education was intimately linked with "self-improvement", "temperance" and relative political awareness. In sociological terms "self-improvement" and "temperance" can be translated into privatisation, whereas political awareness can be seen as growing out of the rationality of an educated class. Even the evidence which most appears to support Lockwood's analysis presents contradictions and ambiguities; for example the mining communities of Durham and Northumberland were in some sense both traditional proletarian and privatised. A lot of the leisure time of these miners was spent at home working on and around the house and even their pub-culture had become a residue of its past importance. One of the reasons for their home centredness was that there was no employment available for women in the area and as a result wives were "the great agents in getting the houses as well furnished as they are".[39] Miners also had a relatively short working week which enabled them to spend leisure time at home and they could afford to furnish their houses comfortably because of their relative affluence compared to other working class groups. One probable effect of their home centredness was their Methodism, for it was a religion which emphasised and expressed what for the sake of brevity one might call the domestic virtues: cleanliness temperance, and family respectability.[40]

With reference to the contradictions and ambiguities in the classification of different types of worker it could be argued that the categories are "ideal-types" and that we should not therefore be concerned with empirical exceptions. This type of argument which is popular amongst some sociologists would mean that analytical power of any classification could never be evaluated, nor an analysis refined so as to more adequately explain empirical evidence. An example of how Lockwood's analysis would have to be modified to explain an awkward fact is provided in the survey's account of the relationship between workers and their employers in Oldham.[41] This town was noted for its large number of small employers who rented "floors or small portions of factories . . . dirty, and constructed in the old-fashioned unventilated style". One informant stated that

> "these masters . . . are just the same as if they were the fellow-workmen they employ. They dress much in the same way, they live much in the same way, their habits and language are almost identical, and when they 'go on a spree' they go and drink and sing in low taverns with their own working hands."

These "operative employers" had themselves been ordinary workers before becoming employers, which explains their similar styles of life. On Lockwood's analysis the close relationship between workers and employers would be expected to lead to a sense of community between them, inasmuch as he implicitly assumes a one-to-one relationship between social interaction and social solidarity. In fact the survey informants could not agree on whether the social relationship between the Oldham employers and their workers was more harmonious than that between large capitalists and their workers. The position was summarised by one informant when he stated that "although masters and men often caroused together yet, on occasions of difference arising between them, the masters would get terribly abusive and terribly bad blood would ensue". In extreme cases this "bad blood" led to a complete transformation of the social relationship between employer and employee; for example in Banbury "the workers of one small firm applied to join the union only when this personal relationship had broken down: the boss said to be worse for drink had abused and sworn at them".[42] This type of situation suggests an emotionally ambivalent attitude as characterising the relationship between employer and worker, leading to a mixed deferential/proletarian type of response. The emotional ambivalence is presumably the result of a tension between friendly personal interaction on the one hand and the latent economic conflict between employer and worker on the other.

The use of the term emotional ambivalence is a pointer to the way in which the descriptive analysis employed in this paper can be developed so as to make the assumptions employed theoretically explicit. Implied in this analysis is the assumption that the common theoretical ingredient to all the sociological classifications is a psychological one. This is a position which has most recently been associated with Homans's work, which has increasingly emphasised the importance of rewarded behaviour in determining the effects of social inter-action.[43] In this paper the two main "rewards" of social interaction considered have been economic benefits and friendly personal interaction. Although Homans's analysis would go a long way in explaining the social processes discussed under the various classifications of different types of worker, there are a number of key problems which fall outside of the scope of this type of work. One such problem has already been briefly touched upon in the dis-cussion of labourers' attitudes towards the Church—although they rarely appeared to have identified with the values of the church, they frequently attended it as the result of economic and social pressure of the local gentry etc. This type of behaviour may be seen as socially "defensive" against the the power of controlling elites, and it is possible to find many examples of domestic servants and agricultural labourers presenting a deferential front to their employers, and then giving vent to their true feelings of hostility when amongst themselves.[44] It is therefore necessary to make the distinction between social behaviour and the internalisation of values in order to explain some of these ambiguous and ambivalent situations. The only psychology to attempt an explanation of the internalisation of values in any convincing manner is psychoanalysis,[45] and I will try to develop the theoretical assumptions of the typology of different types of worker by examining the category of deferential worker in the light of psychoanalysis. I will then illustrate how this theoretical development can be applied to the survey in such a way as to further illuminate it, although with the explicit recognition that any sociological generalisation does inevitable violence to the complexity of empirical reality and to that extent must always remain at the level of "ideal-type" analysis.

The attitude of the employer towards the deferential employee has invariably been described as "paternalistic"; an example of this is to be found in Sturt's *Wheelwright's Shop* where he describes how "the men sought his (father's) advice as if they were his trusting children".[46] Psychoanalysis interprets deference as the employee "transferring" his admiration and acceptance of parental authority onto his employer. As well as transference, it is possible to detect the psychological process of identification in the deferential social relationship, with the employee identifying with his employer's social values

xxxviii   THE VICTORIAN WORKING CLASS

and imitating his style of life. Transference and identification are both grounded on the long period of dependency during childhood socialisation, although identification occurs through the child gradually succeeding to a position of equality with its parents (identification can also occur with brothers and sisters—this form of identification plays an important part in the formation of proletarian egalitarian values), whereas transference represents the unconscious residue of childhood dependency. Where a deferential social situation takes the form of a hierarchy with limited social mobility such as that among domestic servants, deference is likely to occur as described by Lockwood and be primarily a question of transference. In this type of situation identification is mostly vicarious, although the literature suggests that the servant imitates aspects of his employer's style of life as well as identifying with him at the level of phantasy.[47] The hierarchical nature of the servant household allows the upper servants to imitate certain features of their employer's authoritative behaviour, which fosters identification through a narrowing of power and status differences. The model that the deferential upper servants has of the hierarchy (and social stratification in general) is likely to be a three status-group one, with himself in the middle and socially superior to the lower servants and the "lower" classes. Lockwood has also mentioned the small workshop as an example of a deferential social situation, and where there is a minimum of social mobility this is likely to be the case.[48] During the nineteenth century however, the small workshop was still associated with the traditional pattern of apprenticeship and journeyman status (to some extent) being preparations for succession to independent master status. Such a social situation fosters identification rather than transference, a point which will be returned to at the end of this introduction.

Identification and transference constitute the key psychological ingredients for distinguishing genuine deferential attitudes from deferential behaviour presented as a defence against the power of the employer. The key sociological factor in producing genuine deferential attitudes (via transference and identification) is the presence of an enduringly rewarding relationship with the employer, particularly with reference to economic benefits and friendly interaction.[49] This rewarding relationship may be seen as producing transference and identification through the reactivation of the experience of being loved as a child by a parent, although psychoanalysis has developed a number of highly complex ideas on this subject which go far beyond this rather simple formulation of the problem (for example Anna Freud's notion of "identification with the aggressor"). It would be possible to extend the present analysis in a number of ways in order to more fully account for the complexities of the social relationships under discussion. Deference can be seen as a "reaction-formation" designed to disguise the unconscious hatred that the powerless feel towards those who exploit and wield power over them—a disguise that the exploited accept through the repression forced on them by their social situation of powerlessness (the classical example of this is of course the "Uncle Tom" syndrome amongst negroes in the American South). The complicating of the analysis in this way leads us away however from the *Morning Chronicle* survey which only provides information sufficient for a simplified form of analysis.

The value of extending the sociological classification of types of worker in a psychological direction may be illustrated by an analysis of religious belief and affiliation. The survey provides us with a starting point through its description of the religious life of various communities. I have already touched on the Methodism of the Northumberland and Durham miners; the survey also suggests that the Cornish miners were also almost exclusively attached to Methodism. Other than the miners, the community which showed the greatest attachment to Methodism were the Cornish fishermen. The common features of these occupational communities were the relative autonomy of the men in their work situations, freedom from an hierarchical relationship with employers, the isolation of the community from other occupational groups and the absence of feminine employment and the resulting home-centredness discussed above. Of these factors, perhaps autonomy and freedom from hierarchical control were the most important in determining religious non-conformity with its emphasis on the ultimate moral responsibility of the individual and the rejection of religious hierarchy.[50] The Cornish fishermen were typical of the social strata of small tradesmen who were the social backbone of religious non-conformity, and they shared in the additional personal freedom associated with the ownership of capital and self-employment. The Cornish miners also shared in the profits of the mine, although they owned little or no capital and were partly subject to the authority of the "captain" of the mine who represented the economic interests of the mine owners. Many of these "captains" had previously themselves been ordinary miners and rose not only to positions of authority within the mine but also in local Methodist chapels where they were frequently lay preachers.[51]

This example of the "captain" lay preachers points to the importance of the psychological mechanism of identification (in this case with the authority of the employer) in spreading the Liberal religious non-conformity of the manufacturing middle class. We have already seen how Manchester manufacturers fostered this identification through the Sunday School movement, and this was particularly effective in the cotton industry because of the very large numbers of owners and managers recruited from the operative ranks.[52] The spread of Liberal self-help values through the identification of workers with their employers probably occurred most frequently in the traditional workshop situation. Small workshop situations have not therefore always been associated with hierarchical Conservatism, but also (and perhaps more frequently) with Liberal individualism. The psychological process of identification was more important in the spread of the latter, transference in the diffusion of the former. With the growth of large-scale industry however, many Non-Conformist manufacturers acquired the same characteristics as their Anglican counterparts, until by the twentieth century it was difficult to distinguish them in terms of their behaviour towards their employees.[53]

January, 1972   P. E. RAZZELL

NOTES

1. D. Lockwood, 'Working Class Images of Society', *Sociological Review*, **14** (1966).
2. Where letters have been included in our edited survey I shall simply state the relevant district and letter number, which in the present instance are *Manufacturing IV* (Manufacturing District, Letter IV) and *Merthyr Tydfil VI* (Merthyr Tydfil District, Letter VI).
3. For other historical examples of deferential factory workers see J. D. Marshall, 'Colonisation as a Factor in the Planting of Towns in North-West England', in Dyos, op. cit., pp. 226–8; C. Townson, *The History of Farington* (1893), pp. 23, 24, 31, 33.
4. *Manufacturing III.*
5. *Manufacturing IX.*
6. The most famous of these incidents is the attack on Cartwright's Rawfolds mill which was defended by a combination of workers and soldiers. See J. L. and B. Hammond, *The Skilled Labourer* (1919), p. 305. More interesting from a sociological point of view is the attack by colliers and weavers on Burton's Middleton factory in 1812 which was exclusively defended by Burton and his workers. The killing of a number of the attackers led to retaliation the next day when Burton's house and his workers' cottages were attacked. See S. Bamford, *The Autobiography: Volume 1* (Class, 1967), pp. 300–5 and the Hammonds, op. cit., p. 289. No scholarly study has ever been made of the defence of factories subject to Luddite attack, but for evidence on the role of factory workers in their defence see the Hammonds, op. cit., pp. 195, 285.
7. *Metropolitan XIX and XXIV.*
8. Physical proximity did not guarantee a "personal" relationship. See *Rural XV* about East Anglian labourers who claimed that it was rare for the farmers "to condescend to speak to them, except in terms of reproach or abuse".
9. *Unpublished Rural XIX.*
10. See *Rural XV* for a description of rick-burnings and the bitterness felt by many East Anglian labourers towards their farmer employers.
11. E. J. Hobsbawn and G. Rudé, *Captain Swing* (1969), pp. 131, 155, 156.
12. For an almost pure case of deference of someone in the position of a servant see H. Mayhew, *London Labour and the London Poor*, Vol. 2 (Dover Publications, 1968), pp. 467–71.
13. For a description of such "respectable labourers" and the model village in which they lived see F. Thompson, *From Larkrise to Candleford* (1948), pp. 274–87.
14. *Rural XIII.*
15. These economic controls did not only involve the administration of charity by the clergy, but also the use of threats about employment and tied cottages coming from farmers and landlords forcing their labourers to church. For a vivid example of the use of a range of economic controls for this purpose see F. Engels, *The Condition of the Working Class in England* (1958), p. 304. For a description of labourers who appear to have genuinely identified with the values of the church see S. Mays, *Reuben's Corner* (1969), pp. 78–88.
16. *Unpublished Rural XXXVIII.*
17. *Unpublished Rural IV.*
18. *Metropolitan LXVIII*; *Liverpool XVII*; *Manufacturing XII*; *Rural X, XI & XIII*; *Metropolitan LXIX & LXXVII*. The London dockers did not form a cohesive community in spite of living in a specific enclave in the East End. The main reason for this was the casual nature of the work and the rapid turnover of the labour force (see *Metropolitan III & IV*). The costermongers of London on the other hand were a highly cohesive class with their own very distinctive sub-culture, in spite of living in different parts of London. The explanation of their cohesion lay in the hereditary transmission of the occupation from father to son and the mobile nature of their work leading to constant contact with each other. For a brilliant description of

this sub-culture see H. Mayhew, op. cit., Vol. 1 (Frank Cass, London, 1967), pp. 4–104.

19. *Manufacturing XVIII to XXII.*
20. *Manufacturing XXI.*
21. *Manufacturing XVIII.* There is some evidence however that Wesleyan Methodist ministers opposed the strike, and that it was the Primitive Methodists that the survey was referring to. See R. F. Wearmouth, *Methodism and the Working Class Movements of England 1800–1850* (1948), p. 189.
22. *Manufacturing XXIII.*
23. It should be pointed out however that there was a residue of this traditional culture among the Durham and Northumberland miners as well.
24. *Metropolitan LXVII.*
25. *Metropolitan LXIII.*
26. *Metropolitan LXVIII.*
27. *Metropolitan LXIII.*
28. *Metropolitan LXIII.*
29. *Metropolitan LXIII.*
30. *Manufacturing XXX.*
31. *Metropolitan LXXVIII.*
32. *Metropolitan LXIV.*
33. *Metropolitan LXVII.*
34. *Metropolitan LXXI.*
35. *Liverpool III.*
36. *Rural XXXIX.*
37. For examples of such communal relationships see *Birmingham II* and *Merthyr Tydfil I.* In our own day, television is by far the most important form of home-situated technology in bringing about privatisation.
38. See the evidence already quoted in this introduction; for the differences between "respectable" artisans and "rough" unskilled labourers see *Metropolitan XIX.* The "working class" discussed by E. P. Thompon in his *The Making of the English Working Class* is mainly made up of skilled artisans and weavers, who in the context of the present discussion were relatively privatised.
39. *Manufacturing XX.*
40. For example, the "sober habits" of the Bilston Methodists led to domestic cleanliness and a relative immunity to the ravages of cholera. *Manufacturing XXIV.*
41. *Manufacturing VIII.* It should be pointed out that the *Morning Chronicle*'s account of social relationships and the nature of industry in Oldham is at complete variance with that presented by Foster in his study 'Nineteenth Century Towns: a Class Dimension', in H. J. Dyos (Ed.), *The Study of Urban History* (1968).
42. M. Stacey, *Tradition and Change: a Study of Banbury* (1960), p. 28.
43. See G. C. Homans, *Social Behaviour: Its Elementary Forms* (1961).
44. See Powell, op. cit., pp. 79–81 for an example of this amongst domestic servants who at times came to expressing amongst themselves proletarian attitudes of "us" opposed to "them". A number of similar examples amongst agricultural labourers can be found in F. Thompson, op. cit., but see especially pp. 50, 51. The "defensiveness" of domestic servants is illustrated in *Rural XIII* which gives a description of the secret language used by servants to hide from their employers meetings with the opposite sex.
45. For an attempt to assess Weber's typology of internalised authority in psychoanalytical terms see Donald McIntosh, 'Weber and Freud: on the nature and sources of authority', *American Sociological Review*, 35 (October 1970).
46. George Sturt, *The Wheelwright's Shop* (1963), p. 55.
47. See for example Margaret Powell, *Below Stairs* (1968), pp. 77–79.
48. Sturt, op. cit., pp. 12, 55, 113, 201.
49. Powell, op. cit., pp. 129, 130.
50. One of the main reasons for the Nonconformist Liberalism of town tradesmen was their freedom from the hierarchical control exercised by the Anglican Tory

gentry. See J. R. Vincent, *Pollbooks: How Victorians Voted* (1967), pp. 15–18. This can be related to the tradition of the "free-born" Englishman which found its most politically effective form in the Leveller movement—and the Levellers rejected the inclusion of servants in the franchise "because they depend upon the will of other men and should be afraid to displease them". See C. B. Macpherson, *The Political Theory of Possessive Individualism* (1962), p. 123.

51. *Rural XI.*
52. S. J. Chapman and F. J. Marquis, 'The Recruiting of the Employing Classes from the Ranks of the Wage Earners in the Cotton Industry', *Journal of the Royal Statistical Society*, **75**, (1912), 293–306.
53. See the *Sunday Times*, May 10, 1970, pp. 3, and May 17, 1970, pp. 54, 55 for the paternalism of the Nonconformist Clark and Pilkington families.

RURAL DISTRICTS

BUCKS. BERKS. WILTS. AND OXFORD

The Labourer's Home

Letter I

... Amongst those not practically conversant with rural affairs, the impression prevails that the bulk of the labourers live in detached residences on the different farms, with a certain tie existing between them and the soil, and, by consequence, between them and its occupiers. In Scotland, and in some portions of the north of England, this is the case to a great extent, although not now to the same extent in Scotland as formerly. The times are past when in the Lowlands, the farmer and his workman were mutually on such a footing that, after toiling together in the same fields, they sat down together at the same table, and in many cases slept under the same roof. But still the bulk of the labourers there live yet upon the farms, accommodation being generally, in such cases, afforded them in the "square", the term frequently applied to the farm buildings. The consequence is, that farm labourers are in Scotland a less distinct and detached class than they are in England, and they are far less frequently to be found, bearing in mind the relative proportions of the two countries as to numbers, clustered together in towns and villages of which they chiefly constitute the population. In England the case is different. Many labourers are hired, with their board included, when accommodation is of course provided them on the farm. But the great bulk of them form a distinct class of society, inhabiting the outskirts of the rural towns and the villages, which they monopolise to themselves having no capital or resource but their labour, no certainty that that will be called into exercise, and no guarantee for its employment, even when it is called into use, beyond a week at a time. . . .

... In some cases, the sites of their villages belong to one proprietor—in others, to several; but it by no means follows that they are employed either on the farm of which a village site may form a part, or even on the property of which the farm may be but a portion. Indeed, it frequently happens that the only connection between them and the proprietor or occupier of the soil on which their habitations are erected, is that of landlord and tenant. Their labour is at the command of any one who bids for it; and as their employment is precarious, and their wages fluctuating, their lives are spent, in the majority of cases, in constant oscillation between their homes and the workhouse, with no alternative beyond but starvation or the gaol. . . .

... As with those of the better order, so there are different grades of cottages amongst those of the inferior description. Some of them, but undergoing considerable alteration, might be rendered habitable with some degree of comfort to the inmates, provided their number was not great; whilst others are in such plight, that no alteration of which they are capable would suffice to make them fitting receptacles for human beings. If the reader will accompany me, I shall lead him into a cabin constituting the abode of some of his contemporaries and fellow-subjects.

The approach to it is by a narrow road, flanked on either side by mouldering banks, crowned with decaying hedge-rows. The road leads down into a vale of rather limited surface, along the bottom of which, having cut a serpentine channel for itself through the deep alluvial deposit, extends a small and sluggish stream—so sluggish, indeed that it seems at a loss to know which way to direct its course. It glides though almost imperceptibly, through rich and well-wooded meadows, with clumps of willows here and there trailing in its muddy waters. At the foot of the descent you have a high stone wall on your left, the bank and hedge-row continuing on the right. It has rained hard for a day or two previously, and the lower part of the wall is immersed in water, which lies to the depth of several inches, and of varying width. Having no visible outlet, it has now been exposed for many hours to the bright sun; and the scum with which it is already, in parts, covered, gleams in the sunshine like so much mother-o-pearl. The air is close and stifling, the spot seeming to have been designed for engendering malaria of the most pestilential description. At the end of the short vista formed by the wall and the bank stands the hovel to which we are directing our steps. It is one of a cluster, two or three being attached to it—the others standing at a little distance apart. They are overhung with foliage, which, in a healthier and more exposed position, would be their ornament, and their shelter, but which here has the effect, by keeping them constantly in the shade, of rendering them cold, comfortless and damp.

The cabin is rude and uncouth and it has less the appearance of having been built than of having been suddenly thrown up out of the ground. The length is not above fifteen feet, its width between ten and twelve. The wall, which has sunk at different points, and seems bedewed with a cold sweat, is composed of species of imperfect sandstone; which is fast crumbling to decay. It is so low that your very face is almost on a level with the heavy thatched roof which covers it, and which seems to be pressing it into the earth. The thatch is thickly encrusted with a bright green vegetation, which, together with the appearance of the trees and the mason-work around, well attests the prevailing humidity of the atmosphere. In front it presents to the eye a door with one window below, and another window—a smaller one—in the thatch above. The door is awry from the sinking of the wall; the glass in the window above is unbroken, but the lower one is here and there stuffed with rags, which keep out both the air and the sunshine. As you look at the crazy fabric, you marvel how it stands. It is so twisted and distorted that it seems as if it never has been strong and compact, and as if from the very first, it had been erected, not as a human abode, but as a humble monument to dilapidation. But let us enter.

You approach the doorway through the mud, over some loose stones, which rock under your feet in using them. You have to stoop for admission and cautiously look around ere you fairly trust yourself within. There are but two rooms in the house—one below and the other above. On leaving the bright light without, the room which you enter is so dark that for a time you can with difficulty discern the objects which it contains. Before you is a large but a cheerless fireplace—it is not every poor man that may be said to have a hearth—with a few smouldering embers of a small wood fire, over which still hangs a pot, recently used for some culinary purpose. At one corner stands a small rickety table, whilst scattered about are three old chairs—one without a back—and a stool or two, which, with a very limited and imperfect washing apparatus, and a shelf or two for plates, tea-cups, etc. constitute the whole furniture of the apartment. What could be more cheerless or comfortless? And yet you fancy you could put up with everything but the close earthy smell, which you endeavour in vain to escape by breathing short and quickly.

As you enter, a woman rises and salutes you timidly. She is not so old as she looks, for she is careworn and sickly. She has an infant in her arms, and three other children, two girls and a boy, are rolling along the damp uneven brick floor at her feet. They have nothing on their feet, being clad only down to the knees in similar garments of rag and patchwork. They are filthy; and on remarking it, we are told whiningly by the mother that she cannot keep them clean. By and by, another child enters, a girl, with a few pieces of dry wood, which she has picked up in the neighbourhood for fuel. Nor is this the whole family yet. There are two boys who are out with their father at work, the three being expected in every moment to dinner. They enter shortly afterwards. The father is surprised, and for a little, evidently somewhat disconcerted at the intrusion, doubtful as to whether it may bode him good or evil. We soon put him at his ease, and the family proceed to dine. The eldest girl holds the child, whilst the mother takes the pot from the fire, and pours out of it into a large dish a quantity of potatoes. This, together with a little bread and some salt butter for the father and the two eldest boys, forms the entire repast. There is neither beef, bacon, nor beer. Bread, potatoes and water form the dinner as well of the growing child as of the working man. They had a little bacon on Sunday last—it is now Thursday—and they will not taste bacon till Sunday again, and perhaps not even then. But whilst they are over their scanty repast, let us take a glance at their sleeping accommodation.

These are above, and are gained by means of a few greasy and rickety steps, which lead through a species of hatchway in the ceiling. Yes, there is but one room, and yet we counted nine in the family! The small window in the roof admits just light enough to enable you to discern its character and dimensions. The rafters, which are all exposed, spring from the very floor, so that it is only in the very centre of the apartment that you have any chance of standing erect. The thatch oozes through the woodwork which supports it, the whole being begrimed with smoke and dust, and replete with vermin. There are no cobwebs, for the spider only spreads his net where flies are likely to be caught. You look in vain for a bedstead; there is none in the room. But there are their beds, lying side by side on the floor almost in contact with each other, and occupying nearly the whole length of the apartment. The beds are large sacks, filled with the chaff of oats, which the labourer sometimes gets, and at others purchases from his employer. The chaff of wheat and barley is used on the farm for other purposes. The bed next the hatchway is that of the father and mother,

The Labourer and his Cottage

from English Peasantry, by F. G. Heath, 1874

with whom sleeps the infant born but a few months ago in this very room. In the other beds sleep the children, the boys and girls together. The eldest girl is in her twelfth year, the eldest boy having nearly completed his eleventh, and they are likely to remain for years yet in the circumstances in which we now find them. With the exception of the youngest children, the family retire to rest about the same hour, generally undressing below, and then ascending and crawling over each other to their respective resting places for the night. There are two blankets on the bed occupied by the parents, the others being covered with a very heterogeneous assemblage of materials. It not infrequently happens that the clothes worn by the parents in the daytime form the chief part of the covering of the children by night. Such is the dormitory in which, lying side by side, the nine whom we have just left below at their wretched meal will pass the night. The sole ventilation is through the small aperture occupied by what is termed, by courtesy, a window. In other words, there is scarcely any ventilation at all. What a den, in the hour of sickness or death! What a den, indeed, at any time! And yet when the sable goddess stretches forth her leaden sceptre over the soft downy couch in Mayfair, such are the circumstances in which, in our rural parishes, she leaves a portion of her slumbering domain.

Let it not be said that this picture is overdrawn, or that it is a concentration for effect, into one point, of defects spread in reality over a large surface. As a type of the extreme of domiciliary wretchedness in the rural districts, it is underdrawn. The cottage in question has two rooms. Some have only one, with as great a number of inmates to occupy it. Some of them, again, have three or four rooms, with a family occupying each room; the families so circumstanced amounting each, in some cases, to nine or ten individuals. In some cottages, too, a lodger is accommodated, who occupies the same apartment as the family. Such fortunately, is not the condition of all the labourers in the agricultural districts; but it is the condition of a very great number of Englishmen—not in the backwoods of a remote settlement, but in the heart of Anglo-Saxon civilisation, in the year of grace 1849....

... Even were the diet of the peasantry good and ample, personal and domestic cleanliness would be indispensable to their health. But, existing as they do, on insufficient food to which they are condemned by the scantiness of their wages, their only chance of preserving health is by keeping clean their persons and dwellings. Soap and soda the chief ingredients in the process of washing, are now cheap, and many keep their cottages, persons, and wearing apparel as clean as possible under the circumstances. But whilst their miserable condition gives many an excuse for the filthiness to which they are prone, it drives others, originally better disposed, into careless and untidy habits. There is a point at which man ceases to struggle with his fate, and resigns himself to the seeming necessities of his condition. Many an English peasant is, in his circumstances, sunk so far below the line of comfort, decency and self-respect, that the effort to reach it seems beyond his power. He convinces himself that he cannot better himself, and ceases the endeavour. At length he does not even cherish the wish, and becomes indifferent. "How can we be clean with eight in a room!" replied one of them, on my alluding to the state of his lodging. Hence the complicated forms of disease with which the small communities in the rural districts are so often afflicted. Diseases of a catarrhal character, dysentery, and fevers, particularly of the typhoid type, are constantly lurking about their wretched habitations . . .

. . . It is not always easy to discern the laws by which epidemic diseases are directed in their course. The pestilence which is now disappearing, whilst it has spared some, has made terrible havoc amongst others of the rural communities. Hearing at Aylesbury of a village named Gibraltar, about five miles distant, on which it fell with terrible severity, I proceeded for the spot to ascertain, if possible, the cause of a visitation so peculiar in its malignity. The situation of the village is suggestive of health, being about half-way between Aylesbury and Thame, on an elevated ridge, looking upon the Chilterns to the south-east. The first thing I inquired into was the state of the drainage, but was told by one of the villagers that there was but little water to draw off. "There is not a pond in the neighbourhood", said he, "and sometimes for weeks we are very ill off for water." The village consists of a very few houses of an inferior description and its whole population did not exceed fifty-six previous to the visitation of the cholera. "How many died here?" I inquired. "Nineteen", replied an old woman, to whom the question was put. "Twenty," said a man in a smock frock standing by. . . .

. . . "I helped to lay out five in one day," said a woman about thirty, who herself lost her husband by the scourge. The population was thus decimated in a day. Sixteen died the first week, and three the second. It then disappeared. One family, consisting of a man and his wife and six children, entirely disappeared, with the exception of one child. The worst feature in the case is that the mortality was chiefly amongst the heads of families. Thirty-seven of the population have been spared, but eleven of them are orphan children. They were almost all sent to the union, but "after having been there a week, and being well cleaned", they were taken out again by their relatives who are now eking out their subsistence by the proceeds of the children's labour in the fields. During the height of the disease the surviving children were kept in a tent some distance from the village. "All that we can say is that it was the work of Providence", said a woman to me who had been a resident on the spot for forty-seven years; "but they were a wicked set", she added, "and perhaps deserved it." "But were they not an underfed, and, from the want of water, a filthy set?" I asked. "Well," said she, "perhaps they were; but they were not that way much worse off than their neighbours". . . .

Wages and Diet of the Agricultural Labourer

Letter III

. . . In inquiring into the condition of the agricultural labourer, there is nothing more important to be considered than his wages, as upon them mainly hinge his physical circumstances. They are characterised by great variety, not only as regards amount, but also in respect of their kind and the time of their payment. The wages in one county do not differ more from those in another than do the wages in one district from those in another district of the same county. To some extent they depend, as to amount, upon the quality and the quantity of the work in return for which they are given; but, generally speaking their amount is determined without any direct relation to the nature of the labour to be performed. There are higher grades of work connected with farming for which superior wages are paid, such as carter's work—that is to say, the work of those who are entrusted with horses in the fields, and the work to be performed by shepherds, who are generally as well paid, because it is indispensable that they should be a trustworthy class. There are also species of work which do not necessarily involve the consideration of trustworthiness, but which, from their acknowledged severity, secure the higher scale of wages to those employed in them. Of this class "breast-ploughing" is an instance—the first, as well as the most laborious, process in the cleaning of foul land. It need surprise no one to find a distinction drawn, as regards wages, between these occupations and the inferior kinds of work connected with tillage. But that which does very naturally excite surprise, is the different rates paid, not only in different counties, but even in different parishes, for the same species of work. The ploughman who gets £12 a year, with his board, in one parish, might not be able to procure more than £10 in that adjoining it; whilst the ordinary farm labourer may have ten shillings a week for doing in one county that which would only bring him eight shillings in the county adjacent to it. It is this discrepancy that strikes one as singular, especially when the circumstances of adjoining districts, between which it may exist, are similar as to the soil to be operated upon, and the skill required, or the labour to be undergone in working it. . . .

. . . If the earnings of a working man are to be taken as indicating the extent to which both he and his family can command the necessaries and comforts of life, what are we to infer as the condition of families whose dependence is here upon nine shillings and there on from seven shillings and sixpence to eight shillings a week? But it may be urged that this is not to be looked upon as their sole reliance, inasmuch as the wife and some of the children, not unfrequently, by their labour in the fields, add considerably to the common stock. . . .

. . . When a married woman goes to the fields to work she must leave her children at home. In many cases they are too young to be left by themselves when they are generally left in charge of a young girl hired for the purpose. The sum paid to the vicarious mother, who is generally herself a mere child, is from eightpence to one shilling per week, in addition to which she is fed and lodged in the house. This is nearly equivalent to an addition of two more members of the family. If, therefore, the mother works in the fields for weekly wages equal to the maintenance of three children for the week, it is, in the first place, in many cases, at the cost of having two additional mouths to feed. But this is far from being all the disadvantages attending out-door labour by the mother. One of the worst features attending the system is the cheerlessness with which it invests the poor man's house. On returning from work, instead of finding his house in order, and a meal comfortably prepared for him, his wife accompanies him home, or perhaps arrives after him, when all has to be done in his presence which should have been done for his reception. The result is, that home is made distasteful to him, and he goes to the nearest alehouse, where he soon spends the balance of his wife's earnings for the week, and also those of his children, if any of them have been at work. A great deal is lost also through the unthrifty habits of his wife. Her experience at out-door labour has been acquired at the expense of an adequate knowledge of her in-door duties. She is an indifferent cook—a bad housewife in every respect; she is also, in numerous instances, lamentably deficient in knowledge of the most ordinary needlework. All that she wants in these respects she might acquire, if she stayed more at home and was less in the fields. In addition to this, her children would have the benefit of being brought up under her own eye, instead of being, as they are utterly neglected and left to themselves; for the party left in charge of them—and it is not always that any one is so— is generally herself a child, having no control whatever over them. . . .

. . . We have seen that in the counties in question there are about 40,000 married couples, who, with their children, numbering about 120,000, depend exclusively upon agricultural labour for support. Of the 40,000 mothers, fully one half stay at home—some being compelled to do so on account of the extreme youth of their children; and others save when their families are somewhat advanced, preferring from calculation to do so, as being the best mode of turning their scanty means to good account. . . .

. . . I had an excellent opportunity at Thame of discovering how things were tending . . . in Bucks and Oxford. It so happened that I was there on the day of the annual fair, when a great many cattle change hands, and servants are hired for the year. The town was very full of booths, travelling shows, whirligigs, jugglers, tumblers, and barrel organs; pigs, horses, and oxen; labourers in clean smock-frocks, and farmers in top-boots. The gaiety and uproariousness of the day were succeeded by the multiform debaucheries of the night. The servants hired at this fair are generally such as are boarded and lodged on the farm, but the wages offered them were a good indication of what was likely to be the rate in vogue, so far as the ordinary farm labourer was concerned. Lower rates were almost invariably offered and accepted. In some parts of Bucks, where eleven shillings a week were paid, ten shillings are now given, and where ten shillings were paid, nine shillings are now taken. Almost throughout the whole of Wilts a reduction has taken place, to a greater or less extent. Even as early as last June, wages in some districts were reduced from eight shillings to seven shillings. It is true there was a temporary rise during harvest, but they have again sunk to seven shillings and apprehensions are everywhere entertained that they will be reduced to six shillings. Indeed in numerous instances, it is known that this has been determined upon by the farmers at their meetings, both in Wilts and Berks. "My master", said one man to me, "is not going to reduce; but what he pays away in one way he saves in another". "How much does he pay?" I asked. "He pays eight shillings," replied he. "And how will he save the difference between eight shillings and six shillings!" I demanded. "Why, sir," said he, "he is going to discharge some that he was in the habit of keeping during the winter. He's going to save in that way; but he has already saved in other ways. I have myself hoed turnips for a third more than I got this year, hoeing them by the job as usual." "You speak", said I, "of your master discharging some of you.

Are you likely to be included in the number?" "I can't say, sire," he answered; "when they discharge, they generally first send off such as have no families, lest, by discharging those that have, a greater burthen should fall on the parish. They then send off those with the smallest families for the same reason. You see, sir, it's made a matter of pounds, shillings, and pence throughout, and not of rewarding them that faithfully serve them." "Are you engaged for any length of time?" I asked. "No," said he, "none but the carters and shepherds are so. They are engaged from Michaelmas to Michaelmas. The rest of us may be sent away on a moment's notice. To be sure, if we are sent away on a Monday, we may demand a whole week's wages. But then, to entitle us to that, we must do nothing else during the week for hire." "Is there any combination amongst yourselves to keep up wages?" I inquired. "None, sir. We are too much in their power for that. If any man complains they call him saucy, and discharge him at once. The employers all understand each other, and won't employ him again until he has learnt better manners, or is punished enough for his impudence." "On what ground", I then asked, "are they lowering the wages around you?" "On the ground that living is cheaper," he replied. "And is it so?" was my next inquiry. "It is," said he; "bread is a good deal cheaper, and so are tea and sugar for such as can buy them. Meat, too, is a little cheaper, but not much." "Are provisions now so cheap, that you could live comfortably with your family on eight shillings and threepence?" "Lord bless you, no," he answered; "we can live better now on eight shillings than before, but not comfortably yet." "What will they do who are reduced to six shillings?" asked I. "I don't know what will become of them," he replied. "As it is, it's wonderful how they get along. The hand of God is in it, sir, or they couldn't do it. But how they can live on six shillings a week, sir, I don't know. They can't do it, sir, they can't do it," he added, with a scowl upon his face, and an asperity in his tone which contrasted strangely with his bearing and utterance throughout. . . .

SOMERSET CORNWALL DORSET AND DEVON

Condition of the Labourer in Devon and Somerset

Letter V

. . . Whilst in many parts of Devon and Somerset, the process of the demolition of cottages has been going on far more rapidly than that of building new ones, the population of the two counties has been fast increasing. "We don't find room, for them", said a farmer, with whom I conversed on this subject, "and they are drafted off to other places." But they are not thus drafted off in all cases; and the real effect of the demolition of cottages is to reduce, if possible, to a still lower point of wretchedness, the physical condition of the labourer. The clergyman of one of the parishes of Devon pointed out to me an addition which had recently been made to the parish church. As it stood, the church was but a small one, but the addition made to it was larger than the original edifice. "Why was the addition made?" I asked. "Because the population of the parish has increased," was the reply. This answer was obvious, and I had anticipated it, but I wished to obtain it in order to base upon it another question. "How comes it", I inquired, "that, if the population has increased so as to require so large an addition to be made to the church, there is not a single new cottage to be found in your parish?" "That is difficult to say," he answered. "It does not appear to me", I added, "that there is a cottage in your whole parish which has been built within the last fifty years." "They all seem to be of that age at least," he replied, "and many much older." . . .

Letter VI

Almost throughout its whole extent the condition of the labourer is one of extreme privation. In parish after parish which I traversed the evidences of this accumulated upon me. But there was one spot in which the complicated misery which I witnessed seemed to culminate. It was the village of Southleigh.

On descending to the road which leads through the village, I found a woman of about fifty years of age engaged with a pitchfork, collecting some straw at the corner of one of the houses. I remarked that the day had been fine—an observation which she seemed to think so commonplace that she scarcely deigned to reply to it. But there was more than this; for both her tone and manner betrayed that she entertained towards me a mingled feeling of suspicion and dislike. I stood looking at her, but she turned her back upon me, and worked all the harder, as if she wished me to understand that the brief interview was over.

"You seem to work very hard," I observed, determined, if possible, to draw her out; "what are you doing that you are so earnest about?"

"Gathering straw," was her categoric reply.

"What are you gathering it for?" I asked her.

"For the pig," she said.

"Do you keep a pig?" was my next query.

"Yes," was all I got by way of an answer.

"What are you going to do with it?" I demanded; "are you going to sell it?"

"We are going to salt it," said she.

I thought her phraseology rather expressive, and ventured upon a smile, at which she did not seem altogether pleased. Resuming my queries, I asked her when she would kill the pig; but to this I received no answer. It apparently occurred to her that she had been altogether too bland and communicative, and so she withdrew once more within herself.

"Whose tenant are you?" I asked; on which she turned hurriedly around, and looked at me with a deep scowl, accompanied by a flourish of the pitch-fork, which reminded me what vulnerable creatures we are. I shrank back a little, so as to be out of arm's reach of her.

"I meant not to offend you by the question," I added; "I merely wished to know if you were one of Mr. Gordon's tenants."

"I be," said she, in a tone and with a hastiness of manner which showed that I had failed to pacify her. She resumed her work, but after a short pause, turned round to me, and said, "Are you the gen'leman that called upon me some time ago?"

"Not I my good woman," said I; "this is the first time that I have ever seen you."

"Didn't you call on me for the key?" she continued.

"I was never here in my life before," I rejoined, somewhat puzzled at the direction taken by her enquiries.

"Didn't you come for the key when I refused to yield it up?" she asked, still endeavouring to identify me with a transaction of which I was profoundly ignorant. I reiterated my former denial, which seemed at last to satisfy her; for leaning on her pitchfolk, she exclaimed, with a loud laugh, and a total change of manner, "Good luck! I took you for the attorney's clerk, who was sent here by the squire to get the key."

This explained to me at once the unwelcome nature of my reception. It appeared that, some time ago, a summary process of ejectment had been attempted against her, in which the clerk of a neighbouring attorney played a rather conspicuous part, and which she stoutly resisted, treating the clerk at the same time, according to her own account, to sundry epithets not very flattering to his vanity. From a similar infliction I was only saved by the timely discovery that I was not the identical individual, or another visiting her under similar circumstances. "Excuse me, sir," said she; "it's some time since he has been here, and we so seldom see strange people here that I thought you might be he."

Once established in her confidence, I proceeded to question her about her domestic circumstances, and found her as garrulous and communicative as she had been taciturn and reserved before. . . .

. . . "Why was the key demanded of you?" I asked her.

"Because we didn't pay no rent," said she. "We didn't pay for a twal'-month."

"And why did you not pay?"

"Because the house isn't fit for a pig to live in, let alone a Christian," she replied, with great indignation.

"Can I see the house?" I enquired.

"I'll show you every bit of it, if you just step down," she rejoined; "and if you think it's a place for Christian people to pay rent for, you ought to be a squire yourself."

"But do you think all the squires bad?" I asked her.

"I can tell you who isn't good," she observed, "and I suppose they are all like him."

"Do you intend to pay no rent?" I enquired.

"I have paid it before, and must pay it again, I suppose," she answered.

"How long have you resided here?"

"Twenty years."

"In the same house?"

"Yes," said she, "in this piggery for twenty years." . . .

. . . I asked her if she was not afraid that the house would come down about her ears. She replied to the effect that her apprehensions had been blunted, as they had been excited by the same cause for the last ten years. I then entered the hovel. . . .

. . . In the deep recess occupied by the window sat the eldest daughter of my guide, working hard at the lace cushion, taking that position as the one which afforded her most light in the room. A good deal of fabric known as Honiton lace is manufactured here. Some years ago it was understood that the Queen had given an order for some, and a portion of that prepared for her Majesty was wrought in the parish of Southleigh. The poor creatures (women exclusively being thus employed) were quite proud of their commission. "They tell we that the Queen is to have it as curtains for her bed," was the information which they frequently conveyed to those enquiring in reference to the subject. The floor of the hovel was of mud. It had never known the covering of quick-lime and sand, and which is to be seen in some of those in the village. Towards the fireplace it descended so as to form a tolerably deep hole, in which water not unfrequently collects, and which had been prevented from deepening still further by a species of rough causeway work with which it was lined. With this exception, you trod nothing, whilst in the lower room, but the cold clay which formed the uneven flooring. I hesitated ere I ventured upstairs. The family was not large, as most of the children were grown up, and were afloat on the world for themselves. But there were still five at home—the father and mother, a young man of twenty-one years of age, a girl of about eighteen, and another girl of about thirteen. The five slept in the room above. In this instance it was more the chamber itself than its furniture that was at fault. It was wretchedly lighted, and the room seemed, in places, to be falling in. To ventilation it was an utter stranger. The crazy floor shook and creaked under me as I paced it.

The bedroom was approached by a few broken steps, which rose to it out of a deep recess opposite the door, and in which were stowed away a few pots and pans, small bundles of faggots, pieces of broken furniture, and a few implements of labour.

"What do you think of it now?" asked my guide, after I had emerged into the light and fresh air; "is it fit for a pig to live in?" With its cracked walls, its clay floor, its imperfect light, and unwholesome atmosphere, I certainly could not say that it was fit to be the abode of a human being.

"What rent do you pay?" I asked. "A shilling a week," she replied—a rent for which, in many places, the labourer has a very comfortable home.

I cannot say that I witnessed anything in Southleigh absolutely worse than what I have met with elsewhere; but nowhere else have I seen a whole community, although it is but small, in so deplorable a plight. Such instances are most likely to be found in close parishes, where the work of cottage clearance is going on, and in districts which at one time contained a focus of manufacturing activity, but the industry of which has since been paralysed. This is the case in the neighbourhood of Axminster, and in the north of Devon, near the lead mines, which have recently become extinct. They are also occasioned by the sudden growth of manufacturing and mining interests in the midst of what was formerly a purely agricultural district, causing the sudden concentration of a large population in a spot where the house accommodation for them is limited, and where, from the policy of the proprietors, it is not increased.

Wages and Diet of the Labourer in Devon and Somerset

Letter VII

. . . I was fortunate in South Devon, stumbling by good luck upon a ploughing match which was taking place in the neighbourhood of Exmouth. It was a grand gala-day for the whole of the neighbourhood, the match being annually got up under the auspices of an agricultural association embracing some half-dozen parishes in the line between Exmouth and Exeter. . . .

. . . After the prize was awarded, the farmers, to the number of about 200, sat down to a hot dinner at two shillings a head—cider included, I believe—in the Globe Inn, Exmouth. I bought a ticket and secured a place. The dinner was soon over, and the cloth being removed, toasts and songs became the order of the day. I heard much conversation, but little or nothing on the subject of wages. The prevailing topic was the price of corn, and the certain ruin which was impending over them all from free trade. . . .

. . . Nor have I as yet made any account of the wages paid to the class of men designated farm servants. These are, in ninety-nine cases out of a hundred, single men resident on the farm, where they are boarded and lodged. In addition to this they receive from eight pounds to ten pounds a year as wages —sometimes higher; but ten pounds would be a high average of the receipts of this class of labourers. In general their fare is very good—far better, at any rate, than that of the ordinary agricultural labourer. They have generally potatoes or bread, and sometimes both, with warm milk for breakfast. In some cases a rasher of bacon is added. For dinner they have meat and potatoes, and for supper such cold meat as may have been left at dinner, with potatoes again. Sometimes they have a meat pie for dinner, the cold remains of which will constitute their supper. When they have no cold meat left, they will sup on warm milk and potatoes, or bread. That is to say the least of it, a substantial bill of fare for the day, and accords with our notions of what a man should eat who has to labour from morning till night and from day to day. They are not in all cases so bountifully provided—much, in this respect, as in the case with wages, depending upon the character or ability, or both, of the employer. But those worst off amongst them are much more favourably situated than the great bulk of those who are best off amongst the agricultural labourers, in the ordinary acceptation of the term. . . .

. . . One of the greatest evils that I find attending the low rate of wages now paid in so many of the rural districts, is the want of a change of clothing for the labourers, both male and female. Most of them wear flannel whilst at work, but few have a change even of that. The consequence is, that they wear the same garment next the skin day and night, although for many hours of the day it may have been soaked with perspiration. . . .

. . . Some days since I was conversing with an old man, near Bridgewater, on the subject of wages. He had been a farm-labourer in his youth, but had abandoned the fields for a trade, at which he had made a little competency, which, he remarked, sufficed to keep him out of the workhouse in his old age. He did not speak very charitably of the farmers, whom he characterised as a very selfish and hard-hearted race of men. I observed to him that they justified the present reduced rates of wages by the prevailing low price of corn. He replied that it was not on the side of wages that the shoe really pinched them. He remembered wages high, when corn was about as low as now. "How came they", I asked, "to keep up the wages, then?" "I tell you what", said he, "they kept them up, and could afford to do so, because they neither lived in such style nor paid such high rents as they do now."

The Fisheries and Fishers of Cornwall

Letter X

. . . Cod, hake, ling, and congor, are caught in considerable quantities off the Cornish coast, but the mackerel and the pilchard are the great source of the fishing industry of the county. Although these are the chief products of the fisheries of Cornwall, they are not the sole objects of a Cornish fisherman's exertions. When he cannot fish on his own coast for the fish frequenting it, he is off to the Irish, and sometimes to the Scotch coast, in search of the herring. The herring fishing, therefore, although the herring is not strictly a Cornish fish, must be included in the annual routine of a Cornish fisherman's vocation. . . .

. . . The boats differ in price according to their class. For boats of the same class, however, the same price is generally paid. A first-class boat will cost, ready for sea, about £180. The price of a second-class one is about £120. This is, of course, in both cases, exclusive of nets and other appliances. But as a man may save money by buying the cloth for his coat, so may a fisherman by buying the wood for his boat, particularly if he can give ready cash for his materials. In that case he might get a first-class boat, ready for sea, for £140, the hull alone costing about £80. But, of course, if he gets credit, which is generally the case, and orders his boat without himself providing the materials, the prices first mentioned are those which he will have to pay, according to its class. The boats are owned in different ways. A few of the wealthier fishermen have a couple of them, but the majority have only one. In some cases the boat is subject to a joint ownership; two, three, or four, as the case may be, having an interest in her. In other cases the boat may belong to one or more parties, whilst the nets, etc., appertain to others. There are others, again, who have no share either in the boats or nets, their only capital being their labour. A boat's crew may thus consist of the owner or owners of the boat, the owner or owners of the nets, and those who have only their labour to bring to the adventure, which is thus a species of copartnery for the time being, each partner's share of the proceeds being determined, of course, by the amount of his interest. But the possession of the boat, whether owned by one or more, is only half the battle. Other and equally expensive appliances are necessary, which I shall now proceed to explain.

The boat is, of course, imperfect without its complement of nets. These, as already seen, are not always the property of the owner or owners of the boat, for the boat and nets may belong to different individuals, or sets of individuals. This is often the case, the nets being so expensive that it requires a fisherman to be a man of some considerable capital to have both boats and nets exclusively for his own. A few have not only one but two boats, with their full complement of nets.

In general the nets are "home-made"—that is to say, at the house of the fisherman for whom they are made. The wages given for making them are very low, which chiefly prevents the men, even when they have spare time on their hands, from frequently employing themselves in their construction. Sometimes they are made by the wife or daughters of the fisherman, when, of course, the wages which would otherwise be paid for them are saved. At other times girls and children are hired for the purpose. A girl, if she works early and late, can work off about two skeins a day. In doing so her fingers fly about as nimbly as do those of a lace-worker over her cushion. Her remuneration is one shilling a week and her food. Sometimes, however, the nets are "put out" to be made, when the "breeder" gets £1 per net, in which case food is not included. When the work is thus given out by the piece, as many as three skeins a day are sometimes worked up; but this requires extraordinary exertions, which could not be long continued. The entire cost of a piece-of-four is about £8. The twine alone costs about £4 11s. There is then the cost of making and of barking, and the expense of the cork and head ropes required. A complete net, therefore, consisting of fifteen pieces-of-four, will cost about £120. . . .

. . . The number of hands to a boat does not vary much, although there is considerable variety as regards their ages and capacities. Some boats have seven men and a boy on board; others carry seven men without the boy; and others, again, but seven in all including a boy. In most of them a boy is to be found, who, although he may take no active part in the fishing, is nevertheless exceedingly useful on board for many purposes, cooking included. He is thus early inured to the undoubted hardships of the life which, in all probability, he will ever afterwards follow. The men go on board well and warmly clad, and frequently with a complete change of dress. His enormous boots form an expensive as well as a prominent item in the fisherman's attire. The poor fellows have generally their names marked upon the breast of their Jersey jackets so that they may be recognised in case of any casualty. . . .

. . . The men never take spirits nor even malt liquor on board with them. Their commissariat generally consists of bread, sometimes potatoes, tea and coffee, a little salt meat, and a supply of freshwater. Thus provided, they set off in January in their small but seaworthy craft for the mackerel fishing off Plymouth Sound. . . .

The division of profits is generally made as follows: One-seventh of the proceeds is laid aside for the boat; the remainder is divided into two equal parts, one of which is appropriated to the nets, the other being divided among the men, share and share alike. If there is a boy on board, he is entitled to half a man's share. If the owner of the boat, or of the nets, is on board, he is entitled to his share as one of the crew, in addition to what is appropriated to the boat or nets. This appropriation is made with a view to keeping them in working order, and of returning a fair percentage upon their original cost.

. . . It follows, from the constant nature of their employment, that the fishermen are comparatively well off as a class. To the great majority of them the whole year is more or less profitable. They are not in the position of the ordinary agricultural labourer, who may be employed today at wages insufficient for his own and his family's comfort, whilst tomorrow he may be entirely out of work, without a penny wherewith to buy bread for his children. There are few pursuits more liable to fluctuation than that of fishing. It may be profitable today and profitless tomorrow; but it has this advantage, that it is sometimes highly profitable, enabling the provident man to provide to some extent against the contingency of profitless adventures. Not so, however, with the agricultural labourer. At the best, his work for the day brings him but a sufficiency for the day. He has no surplus, and can make no accumulation as a resource against a temporary failure of work. The fisherman need never be out of work, though at times his work is profitless. For this, however, he may be prepared; but the agricultural labourer depends upon the continuity of his employment, not only for his comforts, but for the barest necessaries of life.

Although the fishermen are comparatively well off as a class, they are not equally so. They are divisible into three classes—those owning the boats, or the boats and nets; those owning the nets alone; and those having only their labour to bring to the work. These classes differ in their relative proportions at different points of the coast. Those who own the boats and nets, or the boats and nets separately, are the capitalists of their calling. When the fishing is at all prosperous they make a good thing of it, by the appropriations made at the division of the spoils to the boats and nets. You can almost always distinguish a fisherman thus situated by his generally healthy look, and the superior style of his house, family, and dress. His profits may frequently be discouragingly small, but a season must be very unfavourable indeed to reduce him to very straitened circumstances. The loss of a boat or of a net may ruin him, and reduce him to the condition of the lowest class of his calling. The nets are sometimes destroyed by an over-take of fish; at other times they are cut, particularly the mackerel nets, which swim on the surface, by vessels passing to and fro in the Channel. The lowest grade of fishermen are no strangers to privation. It is seldom that they can command much beyond the necessaries of life, and not always even these. After the seventh, and sometimes only the eighth, is laid by for the boat, they get only their share of the moiety which remains, the other moiety going to the nets. Their earnings are neither large, nor regular, although their work is tolerably continuous. In addition to this, they have to submit to great extortion in their purchases of such necessaries as tea, coffee, and sugar. They cannot afford to go to Penzance, and buy in quantities of the retail dealers there, thus paying but one retail profit: they purchase in small quantities from an inferior set of dealers, who charge their own profit over and above the retail profit in Penzance, the poor consumer thus paying two retail profits instead of one. This is one of the penalties of being poor. Poverty is at every disadvantage. This of itself is sufficient to account for the scanty command which this class of fishermen have, even in the best of seasons, of the comforts of life. They are a more emaciated and sickly-looking, whilst they are a less spirited, set of men than their more fortunate brethren, possessed of a little capital in the shape of boats or nets.

For the last few seasons all classes of fishermen have been, more or less, in a depressed condition. Not that the fishing has been unfavourable, or the prices very unremunerative. The great cause of the depression of all, and the privation which has overtaken the lowest class of them, is the failure of the potato. This has been a great blow to the fishermen. Some of them used to raise their own potatoes, but the great bulk purchase them. But few have raised any this year, and fewer still are able to buy them at their present price. Independently of their cheapness when abundant, the potato is the best accompaniment to the pilchard, which forms the staple of the fishermen's food. They will only eat bread to it when potatoes are not to be had. When they do eat bread, that of which they are most fond is the barley bread, which they bake in the form of a loaf. Indeed, this is general throughout Cornwall, barley bread being consumed by the fishers, miners, and agricultural labourers. The labourers of Devon and Somerset would turn up their noses at it; nothing but the finest flour would satisfy them. . . .

. . . Much privation is, of course, averted from the door of the fisherman by his great command of fish. The practice is to salt such fish as cannot readily be disposed of on coming ashore. Pilchards, cod, ling, and hake are thus salted, either for sale, should any demand arise, or for the use of the family during the season. The curing houses, where the fish are dried and salted, are to be seen dotting the hillsides in the neighbourhood of all the fishing ports. They present a singular appearance against the dark hill-sides, overhanging such places as Mevagissy and Polperro.

When the boys are active, too, it often happens, even before they are old enough to be taken to sea, that they cost little or nothing to their parents, so far as their diet is concerned, especially during the busier parts of the fishing season. When a boat goes out for pilchards, it frequently occurs that it brings to shore a quantity of other fish. Of this other fish neither the boats or nets get any share, the whole being divided amongst the men. On coming ashore they pick the best of them for their own use, and leave the rest for such boys as will, in consideration thereof, clean out the boat. They light a fire and cook the fish themselves. At Polperro they cook them at some lime-kilns in the neighbourhood, digging up a few potatoes, perhaps, from a neglected field to eat along with them. They often, in the same way, procure large cray and unsaleable shell-fish, which they cook and eat, without making their appearance at home until bed time.

Again, the privation to which many are subjected is to a great extent attributable to themselves. Some suffer as the consequence of their improvidence and bad habits; others, from being very inexpert at their vocation. Two boats may fish close to each other, one of which may return laden, and the other empty. So much depends on the fishermen. . . .

As regards the house accommodation of the fishermen, there is the same difference to be observed as there is in reference to his wages. The lowest grade are the worst housed; and at some points, such as Looe and Mevagissy, their habitations are of the most straitened and filthy description. There are tenements in West Looe and Mevagissy that may well vie with the cellars of Leeds, or the attics of Rosemary-lane. The same observation might at one time have applied to Polperro, which, when I visited it, was remarkably clean. The whole town had been whitewashed externally, and the floors in almost every house were kept sanded and clean. The rooms were well ventilated, and everything had a neat and tidy appearance about it. Some tenements were, indeed, squalid and miserable enough; but the description here given applies to the great bulk of the town. Polperro has been rewarded for its cleanliness, for it has escaped the visitation of the cholera. So much cannot be said of Mevagissy. This place also underwent a general cleaning, but no sooner was its purification effected than the inhabitants relapsed into their former habits of filthines, and now almost every trace of cleanliness is gone. Here the cholera fell with terrible severity. The people of Mevagissy form, in many respects, a marked exception to those of most of the other fishing towns. The inhabitants of the neighbouring districts stand in dread of them, and hold no communication with them beyond such as is absolutely necessary. At St. Ives there is also much domiciliary wretchedness, but the greatest misery in this respect is to be found in the decaying fishing stations to the north-east of that town. At Mount's Bay they are better off. In Newlyn and Mousehole, the two largest villages, the bulk of the houses are comparatively good. They are not so crowded as elsewhere, and have all at least two bedrooms. They have also two rooms below, one of which, unless the occupant has a covered place behind, is used as a cellar, where fish are cured and salted. A fisherman's house is not complete without his cellar. If he has not one under his roof, he must hire one elsewhere. The evil of filthy and over-crowded dwellings is much enhanced in some of the fishing villages by the number of agricultural labourers, who, by the clearing system, are driven into them from the circumadjacent rural parishes. The rent of a house averages about £4.

The better class of fishermen, and the provident of all classes, have clothing for shore and clothing for sea. That for shore is used when they are at work on land; in addition to which they have generally a Sunday suit.

Whenever butcher-meat figures in their diet, it is almost invariably fresh. They eat too much salt fish to have any relish for salt meat....

... Although but a mile and a half apart from each other, there is a great difference between the character and habits of the people of Mousehole and those of Newlyn. There is much more recklessness in the latter than in the former. The men of Newlyn do not drink on board, but they drink a good deal on shore. A tipsy man is scarcely ever seen in Mousehole. This great reform is the work of the last few years. There were formerly five public-houses in the village; and now, although it has a population of about 1,500, it does not afford sufficient custom to support even one. The habits of the people are in all respects superior to those of Newlyn. No fisherman from Mousehole will take to the sea on a Sunday. Every one of them attends some place of worship or other on that day. They are generally Methodists. They are also very well educated, considering their circumstances. The village school is a very different one.

As indicative of their energy, I may here mention that the fishermen of Mousehole have, at a cost of £1,400, built for themselves a pier, which, with the breakwater built many years ago by the government, forms their little harbour. To construct it they raised £1,200 on their own joint bond, which they are paying off by instalments, each boat being put under a yearly contribution for the purpose. But their harbour is far too small, and they are very anxious that the Government should aid them in enlarging it. The assistance of Government might be much worse bestowed.

The Mines and Miners of Cornwall

Letter XI

... As the main object of the present inquiry is to ascertain the condition and prospects of the labourer, I shall confine myself to a brief account of the practical working of the mines, with a view to the elucidation of the miner's duties, and of the different circumstances which more or less affect his lot and fortunes. Before doing so, it will be as well to premise that the term "miner" exclusively applies to those actually working in the mines—the capitalists, or those employing the miner, being known as adventurers. Each mine is owned by a company of adventurers, the capital being divided into shares, which are marketable and transferable like those of a railway company.

To explain the process of mining, it is advisable to begin with the beginning

—in other words, to follow a mine from its first establishment, until it is in complete and active operation.

The lodes generally manifest themselves, more or less, on the surface. But, even when the indications of ore are greatest, it requires a practised eye to distinguish them, for frequently the richest ores give the least token of their presence to the inexperienced observer. When there is reason to believe that a lode worth trying exists in a place not hitherto worked, a set of adventurers form themselves into a company for the purpose of working it. In doing so, their first business is to apply to the lord of the soil for a licence to work the lode for a given time—sometimes for six months, but generally a year—upon trial; the lord to receive a specified proportion, usually one-fifteenth, of the ore which may be raised during the period of the licence. The lord also comes under an obligation, should the adventurers at the expiration of the licence be disposed to continue the working of the mine, to lease it to them for a certain number of years, generally upon the same terms as those of the licence, so far as his share of the proceeds is concerned. Should the project prove a failure, it may be abandoned at any time before the expiration of the licence. . . .

. . . The course here mentioned is that which is pursued when it is in contemplation to open up an entirely new mine. But it frequently happens that a new mine is opened within bounds already set out to a company of adventurers, and within which they are already working a mine. In such case no new licence is, of course, required. When a new mine is thus opened, the way is generally led by a party of miners, who undertake to try on the "tribute system", which will be immediately explained, either what they believe to be a fresh lode, or a portion of the lode already worked, but which the existing operations are not likely to reach. In the latter case the result, if the experiment is successful, is generally the sinking of some new shafts, which are soon connected with the existing works, whereby the scope of the existing mine is only enlarged. But whether an entirely new mine is to be opened, or the range of an existing mine is only to be enlarged, the operations commence by the sinking of shafts and the construction of levels; these must be done ere the mine is in a workable condition. And this brings us at once in contact with the actual work of the miner.

The miners are divided into two great classes—the surface and the underground men. The latter are by far the most numerous, being fully three to one, as compared with the former. The under-ground men are again divided into two separate classes, known, in mining phraseology, as the "Tutmen" and "Tributers".

The tutmen are those who do "tut" work, which is neither more nor less than simple excavation. In commencing a mine, therefore, the tutmen are first called into requisition. They sink the shaft and run the levels; all the ore which may chance to be raised during the process belonging exclusively to the adventurers, always with the exception of the lord's dues. The work is given out by the fathom; it is regularly bid for, and the parties offering to do it for the lowest price secures the work. It generally happens, however, that one of the captains of the mine ascertains beforehand, as far as can be, the nature of the work, and sets his own price upon it, the price at which it is taken seldom varying much from the captain's price. Both tut and tribute work are usually taken by what is called a "party"; the party, in both cases, consisting of several individuals, their number varying according to circumstances. The party is divided into gangs, which relieve each other in rotation. There are three gangs to a tut party, each gang working eight hours at a time, the whole twenty-four hours being thus turned to account. The gangs employed in tut work are strictly required to relieve each other at the proper time. As their work is chiefly preliminary to the real business of mining, it is, of course, the object of those who employ them to have it done as speedily as possible. Nor are the interests of the tutmen themselves interfered with by this; for, as their work is piece-work, the sooner they get through it the better. A greater degree of discretion is generally given to the tributers as to how long they may work, and when they may relieve each other, it being supposed that they have sufficient inducement to diligence in the share which they have in the proceeds of their own operations. At the poor mines tut work is generally confined to ground which is not metallic, tribute work having reference invariably to metallic ground. At times, however, tut work embraces ground which is metallic, but this is always in the richer mines. When the ore is known to be good, it is raised at so much per fathom, in which case it all belongs to the adventurers. It is generally work of a more speculative kind that is set on the tribute system; and it is because in the poor mines all the work is of this kind, that the whole of the ore is raised on that system. But even when it is raised on the other system—that is to say, by tut work—it is not unusual to give the men employed a small interest in the ore produced. This is done in order to make it their interest not to waste or spoil the ore.

The work of the tutman is, as already said, that of simple excavation, at so much per fathom. He bids for it with a real or presumed knowledge of the nature of the ground to be worked; the same knowledge being possessed, or presumed to be possessed, by the captain assigning him the work. Miscalculations in this respect are not unfrequently made, which are in their results sometimes in favour of, and at others against, the tutman. Although their work has not so much the character of a gambling transaction about it as has that of the tributers, still it is not entirely free from that objection. He may bid for work, and it may be assigned to him on the supposition that the ground is hard and difficult to be operated upon; or the same may be done on the contrary supposition. In the one case it may be found, after a little trial, much easier, and in the other much more difficult, than was anticipated. Thus, by the chance of his work, he may be a gainer to some extent, or a severe sufferer. Thus, after taking work which appears easy at a comparatively low price per fathom, he may, after penetrating for some distance through disintegrated granite, which is easily removed, or soft clay, come to a hard mass of granite, which opposes a serious obstacle to his progress. This the tutman calls a "pebble", and it is a serious question with the party, on discovering it, whether they will change their course to avoid it, if possible, or dash right through it, in the hope that it does not extend to any great depth. There is risk in either case, as the time lost and the expense incurred, in attempting to turn or avoid it, may be much greater than was anticipated. Nor is it always that it can be avoided at any cost. Then, again, if they attempt to go through it, their hopes may be disappointed, as its depth may be very great. Sometimes, after going through it for some distance, they give it up in despair, and attempt to turn it, which they find, to their mortification, after having lost so much labour, that they can rarely do. When the work goes thus against the tutman, he very soon complains, and if his complaint is well founded, a favourable modification is generally effected in the arrangements between him and his employers.

The undertaking of the tutman is to bring to the surface so much matter, whether ore or "stuff", or both together, at so much per fathom. To fulfil it, he requires the use of machinery to raise the matter excavated to the surface. That which he thus employs is, of course, the machinery on the spot, adapted for the purpose, and appertaining to the mine. For this he is usually charged at the rate of fourteen shillings a fathom, which is so much to be deducted from his earnings. There are other deductions also to be made, but, as these are common to both tributors and tutmen, their explanation will be deferred for the present. . . .

. . . It does not necessarily follow that ore has been raised during these operations, although considerable quantities are sometimes brought to the surface in sinking the shafts and running the levels. It is not until these are completed that the real work of mining begins. The levels are then taken possession of by those whose business it is to produce the ore. When the lode is very rich, the tutmen, as already explained, are engaged to work it at so much per fathom. But the production of the ore is generally the work of the tribute man, who is after all the real miner. . . .

. . . Each mine has its own regular setting days, and the process of setting is as follows: At the proper time and place the tributers and the captains of the mine meet together. I may here explain that the captains are invariably men who have risen from the rank of miners. It is their duty to set and superintend the work, to do both of which properly they must frequently descend into the mine. There are three or more of them, according to the extent of the mine, and one or more of them are invariably below. The setting is a species of auction, the captains being the auctioneers, the miners the bidders, and the pitches the subject-matter of the transaction. Since the previous setting-day more pitches may have been opened, either by the further sinking of the shafts and the construction of additional levels, or by the extension of the levels already existing. It frequently happens, too, that pitches already partially worked, but abandoned, may be offered. In such cases they may be taken by different parties, or by the same parties at a higher rate. Both miners and captains are supposed to have a knowledge of the quality of the pitches, and it is upon this knowledge that they proceed to business. The pitches are put up, one after another, not to the highest, but to the lowest bidder. There are maps of each mine, and the pitches, levels, shafts, and winzes are all as well known to the parties concerned as are their streets to the denizens of a town. Pitch so and so is put up, and the bidding commences. The offer, on the part of the captains, is to set the lode to the party that will work it for the smallest share of the proceeds. This explains the position of the tributor, and the character of his work. He does not work for fixed wages, or for so much per fathom, but becomes, *quoad* the portion of the mine which he engages to work, a partner, as it were, in its profits and losses. The share in consideration of which he will work a pitch depends upon his belief as to the quality of the lode at that particular point. Thus, he will offer to work a rich pitch for five shillings in the pound—that is to say, for five shillings out of every pound's worth of ore which he may raise to the surface. This is called his tribute. To work a poor pitch, however, which yields but little ore to a great deal of labour, he may ask as high as thirteen shillings in the pound. Sometimes he will work at a lower rate than five shillings, but when the ore is so rich as to tempt him to go much lower than that, the adventurers generally give it out on tut by the fathom, retaining all the produce to themselves. Between one shilling and thirteen shillings in the pound is the range at which the tribute man generally works. It is seldom that there is any indiscriminate bidding, or any great scramble at the settings. Men who have obtained a footing in the mine have generally the preference over strangers. The captain has generally his price for each pitch, and if it is a new setting for the same pitch, he usually offers it to the party who have already worked it. If they take it, the matter so far is at an end; if not, it is then put up, and the lowest bidders, before a stone which is thrown up falls to the ground receive the work.

The pitches are set for two months at a time, an arrangement advantageous to all parties; for if the tributors find a pitch poorer than they anticipated, they are not obliged to work it for a greater length of time; whereas if it turns out much richer than was expected, the adventurers will be enabled, at the end of that period, to secure their fair share of the produce. The tributors have this further advantage, that, should they find the pitch very poor, they may throw it up at the end of a month, although they have taken it for two; and in such a case it may be reset to them at a higher rate. . . .

. . . When a pitch is set, it is marked down in the books of the mines as set to such and such a party. Their names or marks are all subscribed to the notification. The party varies in number, according to the nature of the pitch, and the quantity of the labour which will have to be extended upon it. Sometimes the party does not exceed four, at other times it consists of six or eight, and occasionally extends to twelve.

The share of the tribute is determined as to its amount by the value of the ore when ready for market. He has therefore not only to extract it from the lode, but also to prepare it for market. This is done on the surface by those whom he employs for the purpose. At every mine there is a large number of surface workers, amongst whom may be seen some men, but the majority of whom are women and boys. They constitute from one-fifth to one-fourth of the whole number employed in and about the mine. These surface workers are almost all in the pay of the tributors or under-ground men. It is their business to take the ore as it comes from the shaft, to have it stamped, cleaned, and washed, and prepared for the smelters. . . .

. . . I one day overtook a tributer making for one of the mines near Redruth. He told me that he worked in the 300 fathom level; that is to say, 1,800 feet below the surface. His engagement was to be on the ladders by six in the morning, and he emerged from the mine about five in the afternoon. Nearly two hours were spent in descending and ascending the ladders. At this period of the year, with the exception of the Sundays, his life is one perpetual night. The temperature was so high in his level, that they all worked naked, ascending every hour or so to several fathoms above them, to dip themselves in some pools which were comparatively cool. He was a tributer, and the tributers look with as great contempt upon the tutmen as the tutmen do upon the surface labourers. Indeed, a tributer will be on the point of starvation before he will take tut-work. Some mines, like the Carn-Brea mine, employ about 1,200 people; others more. The Caradon and other mines, which have recently sprung up in the neighbourhood of Liskeard, afford subsistence to about 10,000 people, including the miners and their families.

It is not very easy to get at the earnings of a miner. The wages of the surface workers are fixed and known, but the earnings of the underground workers depend as to amount upon so many circumstances, that it is difficult to ascertain them. Throughout the midland mining district, particularly around Redruth, which is the centre of the most extensive mining district in the county, they have been receiving for some time past from forty-five shillings to fifty shillings a month. At the Caradon mines the earnings are, on the average, about ten shillings per month higher than those in the west, for whom no adequate house accommodation has since been provided. They are thus not only compelled to huddle together in large numbers, but they have also to pay very high for the wretched accommodation afforded them. Many of them have left their families in the west, and cannot remove them, owing to the scarcity of cottages near Liskeard; they are consequently saddled with the expense of two establishments. In addition to this they have not the advantage of allotments of ground, so common in the west, in cultivating which they could employ their leisure time, of which the miner has a great deal. All these disadvantages have necessitated a higher scale of wages in the east than in the west. . .

. . . One of the greatest evils attending the employment of the miner is the speculative character which it assumes. His whole life is spent in a species of gambling. If his "take", as he calls the proceeds of his pitch, is good, he may make £100 in a month; but, if he has a series of bad takes, he may work for months without earning anything: nay, more than this, he may all the time be getting in debt, not only with tradesmen, but with the adventurers, for the supply of such articles as he uses in mining, and the value of which is deducted from his earnings. It is the fitful character of his earnings that justifies the remark made to me by one very competent to decide, that where one hears of a tributor having fourteen shillings or fifteen shillings a week, it is seldom that he can be put down as so well off as an agricultural labourer with constant work at ten shillings. When men get inured to it, they cling with tenacity to a life of excitement; and such is the life of the tributer. Considering its many disadvantages, the length of time for which it may be worse than unremunerative, and the inroads which it makes upon health, the wonder is that it is pursued at all. The counterbalancing element to all these acknowledged drawbacks, in the tributer's mind, is the great gain that is sometimes made. The circumstances under which the miners thus earn and receive their money impart a general recklessness to their character. Some of them have sufficient forethought and self-control to lay by in their day of prosperity what enables them to meet without difficulty a series of unlucky aventures; but the bulk of them are too apt to spend their money as fast as they get it—sometimes revelling in abundance, and at others suffering the very extreme of privation. As a class, they would be much better off if regular and fixed wages could be given them; but, owing to the difficulties attending the supervision of work in the mines, such a course is deemed impracticable.

The captains must be shrewd, active men, well acquainted with the practice of mining, for the miners are sometimes inclined to be lazy, and at others to play tricks. The amount of work done by the tutman is generally easily ascertained by the quantity of stuff brought to the surface. But if he is not well watched, he is apt to pretend that the ground offers more impediments than were anticipated, with a view to a favourable modifications of their pitches, in order, if possible, to raise the amount of their tribute. Thus, they will send to the surface the poorest part of the lode, representing it as the best, as evidence that their complaint is well grounded. To counteract such devices the captains must be constantly on the look-out. There is a trick called "kitting", to which the tributers sometimes resort. When a pitch supposed to be bad is taken at a high rate of tribute, say thirteen shillings, and one supposed to be good at a low rate, say five shillings, they are apt to transfer a portion of the ore of the rich pitch to the poor one, when it is sent to the surface as coming from a poor pitch, and the high rate of tribute, instead of the low rate, is paid upon it. The gain by this is divided amongst those concerned in the imposition.

The house accommodation of the miners is, generally speaking, of a very inferior description . . . Taking Redruth as a centre, and describing around it a circle with a radius of five miles, there will be found a larger proportion of good cottages amongst the tenements occupied by the miners than elsewhere in the county. Many of these, generally the best of them, have been built by the miners themselves, that is to say, by such of them as have been provident enough to save money for the purpose. The worst tenements in this district are the older cottages, which can be easily distinguished from the others by their mouldy walls, small windows, and thatched roofs. Many of the modern cottages are well built, being two stories high and well lighted. They are usually covered with slate. Their position, too, is better selected, with a view to health, than has been that of the older cottages. But the advantages of room and good position are in too many instances counterbalanced by the numbers which crowd into the best of the cottages as well as the worst. I was told by a member of the local board of health for Camborne, that he knew of a case in which fourteen slept in one room, some of them being members of the family, and the rest lodgers in the house. On my asking him how many beds they had to sleep on, his reply was, that "the room was all bed." The rent generally paid for a cottage is from £3 to £4, exclusive of potato ground. Such as build for themselves can procure a good stone cottage, with four rooms, for from £40 to £50. They have generally a piece of ground attached to it, to occupy them during their spare time. Many such houses have been built by the miners in the neighbourhood of Penzance. Of these, numbers are now deserted and tenantless, their owners having emigrated, some with and others without their families. So anxious were the men to get away, that they have in many cases left the house which they themselves have put up at their sole cost.

The miners, as a class, sacrifice to a great extent their domestic comforts to their inordinate love of dress. This failing has long characterised them, but within the last few years it has greatly increased. The increase in attributable to the greater ease with which they now procure the materials for dress—"tallymen", or peripatetic dealers, perambulating the country in all directions, selling them goods at high prices, but taking payment by weekly or monthly instalments. To see the miners, both men and women, at church on a Sunday, or enjoying themselves at a fair at Redruth, one would not suppose that there was much distress of any kind amongst them. Most of the men are attired in fine broad-cloth, whilst the women parade their finery. But many who come out covered with broad-cloth, or arrayed in flaunting flounces, emerge from holes and dens more resembling pig-sties than human abodes.

I was not prepared to find the diet of the miner so poor as it generally is. I have seen many instances, in all the mining districts of Cornwall, of families living in great comfort, having a good and spacious house to live in, and a sufficiency of nourishing food to consume. The children, too, in such cases, are generally sent regularly to school. But, in all these cases, I found that the husband was a prudent saving man, who kept his small account at the savings-bank, and that the wife was a good manager, thrifty and attentive to her household duties. Much depends upon management. Some families get on very comfortably on fifty shillings a month, with which others cannot manage to escape great privation. The love of dress greatly affects the miner's diet. This is frequently but a coarse unleavened paste, with perhaps a few pieces of turnip, or an apple or two, enveloped in it. Sometimes he has neither the turnip nor the apple in it, having nothing but the heavy paste to eat. Occasionally it is sweetened with a few raisins or currants. Numbers of them seldom taste meat; indeed, many have told me that they have been for weeks together without partaking of it. . . .

As has been shown to have been the case with the fisher, the loss of the potato has also been a great blow to the miner. Whether a tutman or a tributer, he generally works but about eight hours a day, and has thus a great deal of spare time on hand. It is, in more respects than one, of the utmost importance that this spare time should be well employed. So long as the potato succeeded, the spare time of the miner was, in perhaps the majority of instances, well employed. If he had not a garden attached to his house, he generally rented a piece of ground, which he applied to the production of potatoes and other vegetables. These holdings varied from an acre to two or three acres of land, and were generally leased to him for three lives. In some districts, where the land had not been cultivated before, he would have a piece of waste land and inclose it, and thus reduce it to cultivation. A great deal of the surface of Cornwall has been thus reclaimed, and a large proportion of Lord Falmouth's present rental is derived from land originally reduced by the miner. The miner was thus always secure of a good supply of potatoes and other vegetables, for the climate of Cornwall is admirably adapted for the production of vegetables of almost all kinds. The quantity of potatoes which he produced was frequently not only sufficient for the consumption of his family, but also for the feeding of one or two pigs. When he killed his pig, which he generally did about Christmas, he would sell enough of it to enable him to buy another young pig or two, sufficient being still left to supply some animal food to his family. When he killed two pigs, which was not unusual, he would sell enough to enable him not only to buy two other young pigs for the succeeding year, but also to pay the rent of his plot of ground; so that the remainder of the pork, and the potatoes and other vegetables which he had for the use of his family, were all so much clear profit to him. The extent to which this enhanced both his own and the family's comforts may be easily imagined. In addition to the employment of his own spare time, it also gave employment to his wife and children. The chief advantage of this was, that in many cases it enabled the parents to send the children for some part of the day to school; but it was also advantageous to the adventurers and the public. . . .

I was so unfortunate as to stumble upon St. Just when all work was suspended in the parish. This I regretted, as I was anxious to witness the operations carried on in the stupendous mines situated in this district, whose shafts, as it were, overhang the sea, and whose levels project far beneath it. The annual feast of the patron saint of the parish was being observed when I visited it. This ceremony is common to all the western parishes of Cornwall. In this instance it commenced on the Sunday, when the religious part of the ceremony was performed. For the three following days the parish was the scene of a miniature carnival. From 75 to 100 bullocks were slain for the occasion, which gave about 5 pounds of meat for every person—man, woman, and child—in the parish. Of course, during these days no work was done. Thursday would also be a *dies non*. On Friday some would return to work, but the great bulk would make a week of it. After this, the parish would return to labour and sobriety, and think no more of the saint until the next return of his festival. . . .

. . . The present generation of miners are deplorably deficient in education. The number of those who can read or write is very small. But few of the rising generation attend any school but the Sunday school; and a large proportion do not attend even that. There are schools enough in the neighbourhood of the mines; but the children are in most cases put to work as soon as they are able to earn anything. At the Caradon mines I was informed that not one-half of the children could write, whilst not much more than four-fifths of them could read, even imperfectly.

The mining population of Cornwall is generally of the Methodist persuasion. In many of the mines the captains are their preachers. Many of themselves are office-bearers in their respective churches, which has a great effect in keeping the whole body in order. They attend church very regularly. I regret, however, to say that I did not hear the best account of the morals of the miners. Early marriages are very common with them. The number of petty crimes is very great, particularly in the west, but fluctuates very much. It is generally greatest after such orgies as I witnessed at St. Just.

Intellectual and Moral Condition of the Labourer in the Southern and Western Counties

Letter XIII

... The intelligence possessed by the miners and fishermen is the result merely of the education afforded by the peculiar nature of their occupations. As may be supposed, therefore, their range of intellectual activity does not much transcend the sphere of their labours. . . . On conversing with them, one cannot but regret that so much intellectual power as they possess and exhibit should be left to direct itself into but one channel. A very large proportion of them cannot read, and I venture to say that the great bulk of them cannot write. Many of those who read do so with the greatest difficulty, whilst numbers who write can scarcely aspire to any higher achievement, in this respect, than the scrawling of their own names.

Taking the adult class of agricultural labourers, it is almost impossible to exaggerate the ignorance in which they live and move and have their being. As they work in the fields, the external world has some hold upon them through the medium of their senses; but to all the higher exercises of intellect they are perfect strangers. You cannot address one of them without being at once painfully struck with the intellectual darkness which enshrouds him. There is in general neither speculation in his eyes nor intelligence in his countenance. The whole expression is more that of an animal than of a man. He is wanting, too, in the erect and independent bearing of a man. When you accost him, if he is not insolent—which he seldom is—he is timid and shrinking, his whole manner showing that he feels himself at a distance from you greater than should separate any two classes of men. He is often doubtful when you address, and suspicious when you question him; he is seemingly oppressed with the interview whilst it lasts, and obviously relieved when it is over. These are the traits which I can affirm them to possess as a class, after having come in contact with many hundreds of farm-labourers. They belong to a generation for whose intellectual culture little or nothing was done. As a class, they have no amusements beyond the indulgence of sense. In nine cases out of ten, recreation is associated in their minds with nothing higher than sensuality. I have frequently asked clergymen and others, if they often find the adult peasant reading for his own or others' amusement? The invariable answer is, that such a sight is seldom or never witnessed. In the first place, the great bulk of them cannot read. In the next, a large proportion of those who can, do so with too much difficulty to admit of the exercise being an amusement to them. Again, few of those who can read with comparative ease have the taste for doing so. It is but justice to them to say, that many of those who cannot read have bitterly regretted, in my hearing, their inability to do so. I shall never forget the tone in which an old woman in Cornwall intimated to me what a comfort it would now be to her could she only read her Bible in her lonely hours.

... But, in connection with this, as with other subjects, the truth, however startling or disagreeable, should be told. The farmers are now, in many instances, an impediment in the way of education. The church and upper classes are more or less favourable to it; but in the farmers, the employers of labour, is frequently found the great obstacle to its efficient promotion. I do not make this assertion hastily or without proof, for I find abundant evidence of it wherever I go.

To do justice to the farmers, a large proportion of them are insensible to the benefits of education. In many cases you cannot distinguish the children of the farmer, by their dress, demeanour, or intellectual culture, from those of the labourer; and this, too, not only in the case of "smock farmers", as the lowest class of them are termed, but also in that of some tolerably well off in the world. There are others who give their own children the benefit of the best education that they can afford, but who would deny the same boon to the child of the labourer. It is but a few days since I met one of this class. He did not like the present order of things at all. There was too great a tendency in society now-a-days to heave up that which was below to the top. Labourers were anxious to become masters, and so on. To educate the labourer was only to enhance this evil. The child should succeed his father at his toil. His own son was then at the University, and was studying for the church.

Such are, in too many instances, the men who, by becoming guardians of unions, are entrusted with the education of the poor. Some of them speak out openly, and express their disinclination to having them educated. They are obliged to comply with the letter of the law, but they care not for a master or mistress being qualified for the work of instruction. . . .

The truth is, that there is much in our present system of education in the rural districts that is mere sham. We have a varied and tolerably extensive machinery apparently in efficient operation, but it is only when its working is closely inspected that it is found in too many cases to be anything but efficient. . . . It is only here and there that you find efficient schools, particularly in connection with the National Society.

In the parochial union schools geography is now much more generally taught than formerly—the guardians having at length discovered the stimulus which a little knowledge of geography gives to emigration. At first they could discover no use whatever in maps. "Maps!" said they, when it was first propose to introduce them, "you'll be bringing in the dancing-master next." In illustration of the value of geography as regards emigration, the following was related to me: A gentleman, in want of a boy to accompany him to New Zealand, applied at a union school in which geography had not been taught. "Who'll go to New Zealand?" was asked of the whole school, but not one volunteered. The application was next made at a school where geography was taught. "Who'll go to New Zealand?" was again asked, and almost every boy in the school sprang forward, exclaiming, "I'll go!"—"I'll go!" On examining them, it was found that many not only knew its position and other circumstances connected with it, but could also state accurately the different routes by which it could be reached. No sooner was the anecdote known abroad than the guardians of the surrounding unions immediately ordered maps for their respective schools.

Notwithstanding all that has recently been done for the cause of education, the proportion of children growing up utterly uneducated is very great. . . . Even in Cornwall, where, comparatively speaking, so much is done for education by the different sects, this is the case to a very great extent. In treating of the Cornish mines, I have already had occasion to allude to the number of children engaged about them who could not read, and the still greater number who could not write. In a few years, therefore, notwithstanding all the efforts which are being veritably or ostensibly made, a large proportion of those who are now children will be launched into manhood with all the stolidity and ignorance of their fathers. . . .

. . . Having thus glanced generally at the educational system at work in the four counties in question, I now proceed to state the results of my observations as regards the morals of the labouring classes in all the counties which I have hitherto visited. . . .

There are two things which strike every observer, as exercising a most pernicious influence upon the habits and morals of the poor—the straitened character of their house accommodation, and the lowness of their wages. . . .

Let us consider, for a moment, the progress of a family amongst them. A man and woman inter-marry, and take a cottage. In eight cases out of ten it is a cottage with but two rooms. For a time, so far as room at least is concerned, this answers their purpose; but they take it, not because it is at the time sufficiently spacious for them, but because they could not procure a more roomy dwelling, even did they desire it. In this they pass with tolerable comfort, considering their notions of what comfort is, the first period of married life. But, by-and-by, they have children, and the family increases until in the course of a few years, they number perhaps from eight to ten individuals. But all this time there has been no increase to their household accommodation. As at first, so to the very last, there is but the one sleeping-room. As the family increases additional beds are crammed into this apartment, until at last it is so filled with them that there is scarcely room left to move between them . . . But years steal on, and the family continues thus bedded together. Some of its members may yet be in their infancy, but others of both sexes have crossed the line of puberty. But there they are, still together in the same room—the father and mother, the sons and the daughters—young men, young women, and children. Cousins, too, of both sexes, are often thrown together into the same room, and not unfrequently into the same bed. I have also known of cases in which uncles slept in the same room with their grown-up nieces, and newly-married couples occupied the same chamber with those long married, and with those marriageable but unmarried . . . Sometimes, when there is but one room, a praiseworthy effort is made for the conservation of decency. But the hanging up of a piece of tattered cloth between the beds, which is generally all that is done in this respect—and even that but seldom—is but a poor set-off to the fact that a family, which, in common decency, should, as regards sleeping accommodations, be separated at least into three divisions, occupy, night after night, but one and the same chamber. . . . In the illicit intercourse to which such a position frequently gives rise, it is not always that the tie of blood is respected. Certain it is that, when the relationship is even but one degree removed from that of brother and sister, that tie is frequently over-looked. And when the circumstances do not lead to such horrible consequences, the mind, particularly of the female, is wholly divested of that sense of delicacy and shame which, so long as they are preserved, are the chief safeguards of her chastity. She therefore falls an early and an easy prey to the temptations which beset her beyond the immediate circle of her family. . . .

Perhaps, the most striking instance of the demoralisation of a whole com-munity, from over-crowding and other unpropitious circumstances, is that furnished by Sutton Courtney, in Berkshire, formerly alluded to in connection with the subject of education in that county. . . . Chastity is a thing little known in the village, and not at all respected. The want of it is regarded as no stain on a woman's character, nor does it mar her prospects in the slightest degree. Herself a prostitute, and the companion of thieves and prostitutes, she is just as likely to marry and get settled—as people in her class of life are generally settled—as is the honest and virtuous woman in localities possessing a higher standard of morality. I found more than one family of children going by different names. The mother was unmarried, and the different names indicated the paternity of the different children. Again, a whole family has been known to go by different names at different times. Thus, if the mother were living with a man of the name of Smith, the children took his name; but if she changed her paramour, and lived with one named Tomkins, the family would go by the new name. Children have thus been known to give to parties inquiring, one name to-day and a different one to-morrow. . . .

. . . Young girls may be seen at the public-houses, sodden with gin, or drunk with beer. There is, of course, no line drawn by them for the regulation of their conduct, after this. Indeed, they are proficient in licentiousness ere they reach this point. The violence of their tempers, too, leads them into perpetual brawls and fights. I was told by one woman that when she had occasion to send any of them into the fields, she always sent a boy and a girl, because they would not quarrel; whereas, if she sent two boys or two girls, they were sure to disagree and fight. The vicar has at length induced some of them to attend church; but when he first took possession of his charge, he used to find the men, surrounded by nearly all the women and children of the village, playing quoits before the church-door on Sunday morning.

. . . It really seems, in many places, to be taken as a matter of course that a young woman will be found with child before she is married. Many are married as soon as they become pregnant. When marriage does not take place, the child is generally consigned to the care of the mother of the girl, whilst she herself, when she can, goes out in the capacity of wet-nurse. The grandmother will speak as coolly of the whole affair as did both mother and daughter in the case alluded to in a former letter from Cornwall, terming it a "misfortune", but the misfortune being more the necessity of maintaining the child than the stain on the woman's reputation. Indeed, I have reason to believe that in an immense number of cases young people come to a distinct understanding with each other to cohabit illicitly, until the woman becomes pregnant, the man promising to "make an honest woman of her" as soon as that takes place. This they find more convenient than marrying at once, inasmuch as the girl may be of service for herself, and the man elsewhere employed all the time. They meet occasionally, and are thus relieved at least of the responsibilities and the duties of housekeeping, living better on their separate earnings than they could do in a house of their own.

This practice of cohabitation before marriage is almost universal. It is not only a characteristic of low rural life; it is also so with the miners and fishermen. Even in the fishing village of Mousehole, the people of which are in general so orderly, it is the case. And this, too, notwithstanding the extent to which temperance has prevailed amongst them. Total abstinence has not affected much in this respect for society. The miners and pitmen too, are much more under the influence of constant religious teachings than is the rural labourer; and yet they are no better than he is, so far as the practice alluded to is concerned. When a young fisherman passes eighteen he generally gets a man's wages. Immediately thereupon he gets a new suit of clothes and a watch; after which he fancies himself sufficiently set up in the world to commence a courtship, which generally leads to an early marriage by the course mentioned. In some parts of Cornwall the immorality of the females at work about the mines is notorious and proverbial.

It is on the Sunday evening that most mischief is done in this respect. No one can enter or leave a rural town at that time without being convinced of this. It is the time when servants, both male and female, are most generally permitted to go out, and it is therefore that for which they arrange most of their assignations. They have a slang of their own, in which their arrangements are pretty unreservedly made in the presence of those, who, they think, have not the key to it. This, after some time, I became acquainted with, and I have frequently overheard them planning their assignations, which, in nine cases out of ten, were arranged for the first Sunday evening. . . .

Nothing can be more fatal to the young girl, after the training which she has received at home, than the work to which she is early consigned in the fields. She there often meets with associates, even of her own sex, who speedily qualify her for any criminalities in which she may be afterwards tempted to participate. . . .

. . . In small parishes, where the clergyman is frequently brought into personal contact with the labourers, and where, from other causes, he exercises a direct influence over them, they may be found pretty regular in their attendance at church; but, generally speaking, their attendance is neither large nor constant, most of them moping about on the Sunday, smoking and drinking, and some of them spending nearly the whole day in bed.

Another circumstance which powerfully affects the morals of the poor is the lowness of their wages, and the physical privations to which they are thereby subjected. If a labourer has abundance for his family in his cottage, he will crowd them all into a single chamber, and let the other rooms if he can. The evils incident to his position are thus of a complicated nature. In the great majority of cases he has not sufficient house accommodation, whilst in those in which he has, the lowness and uncertainty of his wages, and his consequent scanty command of the necessaries of life, induce him, when he can, to throw away the advantages of it. Thoroughly to elevate him, the work of improvement must be simultaneously pursued from different points.

A large proprietor being asked, when the conversation had turned upon the state of wages, how the poor could live upon the pittances per week which they earned so precariously, turned round, and said, somewhat sternly, "They steal."... Petty theft, on his own and his family's part, may be regarded as part and parcel of a labourer's means ... Ask any one how families can live on seven shillings, eight shillings or nine shillings a week, and the answer almost invariably is, "They can't do so *honestly*." The inference is irresistible that they live dishonestly; and so the great bulk of them do. This is more particularly the case as regards the article of fuel. In general, I find them open, unreserved, and communicative on almost all other subjects; but the moment I touch upon the subject of fuel, their whole demeanour, in most cases, undergoes a change, and their awkward and incoherent statements are often in perfect contrast with their former readiness and consistency in reply. You can see at once, that, whilst they tell you something, there is much that they are keeping back. In some places, furze is raised for fuel, and they are not so ill off in this respect; in others they burn turf, which they sometimes get for the cutting, although at others they have to buy it. When they have to buy their turf, or when there is neither furze nor turf, and they must look for their fuel to coal or wood, the greatest privations are suffered as the consequence of their scanty supply. When they buy their wood, they buy it in faggots—a faggot being frequently little better than a bundle of green twigs. Even this they are not always able to purchase; when, unless they are permitted to take wood, which is very rarely indeed the case, they have to look to theft alone for their supply of fuel. In many parts of Cornwall, Devon, and Dorset, and in some parts of Wilts, they are comparatively well supplied by the furze and turf; but in the other portions of these counties—throughout the greater part of Somerset, and, I may say, the whole of Bucks, Berks, and Oxford—where they have nothing but wood or coal to burn, one universal system of pilfering prevails in respect to fuel. Both as regards themselves and others, this is a perilous alternative to which the poor are driven by the sad necessities of their position. Without expending any of their means in the purchase of fuel, they manage, in most cases, to eke out but a mere existence, generally on an almost exclusively vegetable diet. To buy as much coal, wood, or turf as would serve them, not only for culinary purposes, but also to warm, during the cheerless months of winter, their damp, cold, and desolate homes, would in very many instances, make greater inroads than they could bear into their means of procuring mere edibles. The consequence is, that such fuel as they cannot buy or get in charity they are driven to steal. The evil of this is manifest, for it is generally through the instrumentality of the children that the wants of the household are thus supplied. Petty theft is thus the first positive vice with which they are brought in contact, and in the practice of which they are almost daily instructed. What is the consequence? The child who becomes an adept in stealing wood is soon qualified for robbing a hen-roost. From that, again, to stealing a sheep there is but another step; and in the words of a clergyman with whom I was conversing on this subject, "when a man goes out to steal a sheep, he is ready for anything". Is it any wonder, seeing how many children are thus perniciously instructed, that so large a proportion of those who figure in the statistics of crime are juvenile delinquents? ...

One of the objects of the coal clubs, established in some places, is to check this monstrous evil.

Let me say, in summing up the whole, that a pervading moral apathy is the general characteristic of the peasantry, when positive crime is absent—an apathy which leads, in too many cases, to an utter indifference to the distinction between right and wrong.

In connection with this subject, it is extremely discouraging to find how little good is effected by the education received in the workhouse ... In many instances have cases been pointed out to me of boys entering the gaol soon after leaving the house, and of girls returning pregnant to it a year or two later after they had left it.

The Stone Quarries of Swanage

Letter XXVIII

... Swanage has long been celebrated for its quarries and its quarriers. Almost from time immemorial has stone been extracted from the hills which sweep around the bay, until now the whole country, for miles back, is so perforated and undermined as to resemble one huge catacomb. From the earliest period, too, the quarriers have existed as an organised body—bound together, not only by the tie naturally created amongst those engaged in common pursuits, but also by a number of ancient and revered articles, which they have invariably treated as a charter of incorporation. Indeed, for centuries they were known in their corporate capacity as the Company of Marblers. They still retain the articles, to which even to this day they pay especial reverence, and they still keep up to some extent the organisation of former times. That to which they now cling, however, is more the form than the substance of bygone privileges—the skeleton of their organisation being still perfect, although the flesh and muscle have long since dropped away from it. But much as the general objects of the original association have been departed from, there are still some points in respect to which they are to this day rigidly enforced.

Originally, the body of stone quarriers constituted a species of copartnery—each member being interested in the profits, and liable, pro rata, to make good the losses of the body. When such was the case, wardens were annually elected, under the articles, whose business it was to exercise a general supervision over the interests of the body, to dispose of the produce of its labour, and divide the proceeds amongst its members. The wardens thus chosen by the quarriers were invariably members of their own body; and during their tenure of office, they were relieved from all duties, except such as pertained to the post which they were called upon to fill. Some of these are still performed by wardens—for, to the extent of electing these ancient officers, at least, the old organisation is still kept up. They are not, however, so numerous now as formerly, for the simple reason that their duties are more limited. The number now elected does not exceed two, who, with the secretary (whose position is permanent), constitute the entire official staff of the body. The quarriers have still common interests to watch over and promote; and in the furtherance of these they still act in their united capacity. But the general partnership of past times no longer exists—each, so far as his labour is concerned, being at liberty to promote his own individual interests, whilst it is competent for as many as please to unite in groups for the same object.

One of the main objects of the original association was to secure a monopoly of the quarrying trade of the district. To effect this it was made one of the articles that none but such as were made free of the company should be permitted to enter its works, or to have any share whatever in the business which it pursued. As it scarcely ever happened that any were made free of the company but the children of its existing members, it followed that strangers were effectually excluded, and that the business of stone quarrying, in that neighbourhood at least, remained a complete monopoly in the hands of a certain number of families. If antiquity be an essential element of true mobility, there are families at this moment in Swanage, with unbroken genealogies, extending back far beyond those of half the nobles in the realm. One can understand both the institution and the jealous maintenance of such a provision, so long as the whole body constituted one company with common interests and liabilities. But now that the partnership is effectually broken up, and the business is pursued individually and not as a corporate concern, it may be easier to account for, than to justify, their continued adhesion to the rule for the exclusion of strangers from the quarries. They themselves have free warren of the wide field of competition around them, of which many of them, impatient of labour in the quarries, take advantage, and obtain employment in the metropolis, or wherever else Government works may be in progress—for it is generally to these that they flock. Should they tire of this, or should occupation elsewhere fail them, the quarries at Swanage are open to them on their return—for "once a quarrier always a quarrier" is the rule. It is this that renders so invidious their jealous exclusion of the stranger from their own peculiar field. They avail themselves of the right to compete with him on his ground, but will not suffer him to meet them on theirs. They have, of course, no legal right to exclude him. Any man who chooses may, if he can get a lease from the lord of the soil, take a quarry at Swanage, and work it. But there are a thousand ways in which they could annoy him and put him at a disadvantage; and to remain, under such circumstances, for any length of time amongst them, a man would require to be possessed of some means, and of an uncommon stock of fortitude. They are particularly jealous of the Portland men, who, on the other hand, are equally jealous of them. If a master-quarrier employs any stranger in his quarry, he is liable to a fine of £5—the mode of exacting which will be afterwards alluded to. In some cases there might be a mitigation of the penalty, but the fine would, in all instances, be inflexibly enforced if the interloper could be traced back to Portland. Indeed, the rule is, never to remit, and seldom to mitigate, the fine—a knowledge of which, on the part of the quarriers generally, renders the necessity for its imposition a matter of rare occurrence. An amusing instance of the extent to which the jealousy in question is carried, and particularly as regards strangers of their own order elsewhere, was related to me by a Swanage man who had attempted to smuggle himself into the quarries in Portland. When they find a stranger at work in the latter place they generally permit him to work for a week, at the end of which time they presume that he has earned enough to carry him out of the island. They then, when circumstances will admit of it, present a very ugly alternative to him,—namely to walk a plank, partly projecting over a cliff, or to quit Portland, never to return to it. My informant told me that, for the first week, he was treated with every possible consideration; indeed, he could not conceive of greater kindness than that which he experienced particularly from the man who worked next to him— "Yet that was the very man who laid the plank for me when the week was out," said he; giving me to understand that the alternative alluded to was then quietly, but seriously offered to him. As a sensible man, he preferred quitting the island to walking over a cliff into the sea. "And would you serve a Portland man in the same way?" I asked him. "Well, I am not sure that we would", said he, "but we would lead him such a dog's life of it, that he would soon be glad enough to be off". The system of exclusion is, perhaps, not now so rigidly adhered to in Portland as in Swanage—the Government works which have recently been carried on at the former place having tended more or less, to break it down, from the large and constant influx of strangers which they have occasioned.

A quarrier cannot be made free of the company until he is twenty-one. He may be apprenticed at any age at which he may be found capable of working, but at whatever time that may be, his probation does not cease until he comes of age. It is to his father that he is generally apprenticed, or, if the latter is dead, to his nearest male relative, being a quarrier. It is not necessary, however, that the master should be at all related to the apprentice. It is to the father, however, that in the great majority of cases he is apprenticed, the business regularly descending from father to son. Indeed, the veriest infants, when males, are generally treated by their parents as the raw material for future quarriers. The father is entitled to the whole profits of his son's labour during the entire period of his apprenticeship. Should the father die during the term, the apprentice does not necessarily become his own master. In that case, the mother's interests are provided for—she being conditionally entitled to the profits of his work until he attains the age at which he can be admitted a freeman. The condition on which this right is secured to her is a very simple one, and one easily performed, being neither more nor less than the payment of a shilling into the funds of the company on the day of her marriage. This condition, which is within the reach of every couple, is almost universally complied with. The ceremony of admission takes place but once a year. The grand gala-day of the quarriers is Shrove Tuesday. On that day they meet at Corfe Castle for the admission of new members and the general management of their affairs, so far as they are still regulated in common. The apprentices who have completed their term, and are otherwise unexceptionable are then admitted, and on payment of six shillings and eightpence are enrolled freemen of the company, being thenceforth entitled for life to all the privileges which that honour confers upon them. On this occasion, the quarriers manage to combine festivity and amusement with business. I have already alluded to the condition on which the mother, in case of the father's death, is entitled to her son's earnings whilst he remains an apprentice. The last couple married during the year have to provide a foot-ball, which is regarded as tantamount to the shilling paid by others—the woman who provides the foot-ball being entitled to all the privileges of those paying the shilling. As soon as the young men who are found qualified have been admitted and enrolled members of the company, they are sent out to amuse themselves with a game at foot-ball, in which they very heartily engage. The articles of the company, some of which are supposed to date back as far as the reign of Richard II, are then read by the secretary to the seniors, who remain in conclave behind, the newly-made members not being admitted to so great a privilege until the following year. If there are any matters of general interest to be talked over they are then discussed, after which the elders adjourn to join the young men at their game. The festive board is not a feature overlooked amongst the ceremonies of the day, which generally, however, to the credit of those concerned, closes without riot or disorder. Such is the principal ceremony which has now reference more to the commemoration of past privileges than the maintenance of present ones.

The secretary is a man of no little authority with them. The influence which the present incumbent of that office wields is more of a personal than an official character. His name is Webber. He is at present chief clerk and book-keeper in the office of the Messrs. Pike, formerly alluded to as the principal clay merchants in the neighbourhood of Wareham. His original occupation was that of a stone-mason, which he still occasionally pursues, during his leisure hours, by way of recreation. His labours on such occasions generally take a funereal turn—the carving of gravestones being his forte as regards the chisel. Having received some education in his youth, he has turned it to the best advantage; not only thereby improving his own position, but acquiring an almost unbounded influence over the body to whom he originally pertained. He is not only their chief official, but also their friend and counsellor. "Mr. Webber", they will tell you, "is an understandin' man. He knows more about us than we do ourselves. He keeps us all right. Whenever we get into difficulty, we always go to he." To the qualities of the intelligent observer and shrewd man of business, Mr. Webber superadds some touch of the poetic fire, as the file of the *Poole Herald* can testify.

The quarriers are now divided amongst themselves into two classes—the master-quarriers, and the ordinary quarriers, who give their labour for hire. This classification goes evidently no further back than the termination of their original arrangement, by which all the quarriers were upon an equal footing. The difference between a master and an ordinary quarrier is purely accidental —the two classes not existing as distinct orders amongst them. A master-quarrier is he who takes and works a quarry; and there is nothing to prevent an ordinary workman from taking a quarry if he pleases, and if the lord is willing to give him a lease. Many of the quarries are taken and worked by a single quarrier, all the aid which he receives in his operations being in the shape of hired labour. In other cases, several join together in a kind of partner-ship, working in a quarry between them—being sometimes employed alone, and at others having hired labour in aid of their own. When one or more intend to take a quarry, the first thing to be done is to obtain a lease from the lord. This is generally granted without much difficulty the lessees selecting their own ground, unless some good reasons exist for confining them in their choice. By the terms of the lease the landlord becomes, as it were, a partner in the adventure; his rent depending, as to amount, upon the quantity of stone yielded by the quarry. At Swanage the stone produced is generally of two kinds—the solid block and the flat paving stone. The lord's dues are regulated by the number of superficial feet excavated in the one case, and generally by the number of cubic feet excavated in the other. They amount to a shilling for every hundred superficial feet of paving, and the same for every hundred cubic feet of solid stone. The lord has thus an interest not only in the goodness of the quarry, but also in the industry of the quarriers. One of the conditions of the lease, therefore, is, that the quarry shall be worked—a condition some-times only complied with as regards its letter, when it is not the interest of the lessee or lessees either to work it constantly, or to give up the lease. It is seldom that anything in the shape of a written document passes between the parties, the leases having been verbal ones from time immemorial. And when a lease is once granted, the lessees cannot be dispossessed so long as they comply with the condition already alluded to. As to the scene of operations, too, they are only limited as regards the shaft; but, having sunk the shaft at the point selected when the lease is granted, they are at liberty to work under ground in any direction they please, and as far as they please provided they do not transgress the bounds of the landlord's property, nor come within a hundred feet of another quarry which is being then actually worked. If they go beyond the bounds within which it is competent for the landlord to licence them to work, and trespass upon another man's land, the party thus aggrieved has his remedy, as in ordinary cases. If they go within the forbidden distance of another quarry, the parties whose rights are thus invaded look not for their remedy to the law of England, either common, statute, or ecclesiastical, but to the code peculiar to the locality, and which may be designated as Swanage Law.

For, amongst the other peculiarities of this singular district, it must be borne in mind that its people have their own code of laws, and their own mode of giving them effect. It is possible, no doubt, theoretically, that an English writ might issue into a Swanage quarry; but English law has, generally speaking, very little to do with the practical administration of Swanage justice. When a party is suspected of trespassing in the manner alluded to upon the rights of his neighbours a meeting of the whole body is called, by whom the accusation is heard, and if a prima facie case is made out, a deputation is appointed to descend into the quarry and examine into the real state of the case. This deputation is not a mere committee of investigation, whose simple duty it is to inquire and report—for it is contingently armed with administrative powers, which it is enjoined to put in force, should such a course be necessary, to do justice between the parties. Thus combining ministerial with judicial functions, the deputation descends into the quarry, provided with compasses and other appliances necessary for ascertaining the truth. If there is no ground for the accusation, the charge is dismissed, and the matter goes no further, unless the accusation be repeated; but if there is ground for it, and a trespass has actually been committed, a fine is imposed upon the delinquent party, according to the extent of his transgression. If the trespass is one which is likely to be persevered

in, it is the business of the deputation to take such steps as to render it impossible that it should be so. To effect this, it is armed with very summary powers,
which it invariably exercises, whenever a necessity arises for putting them in
force. The mode of proceeding in such case is to destroy the portion of the
quarry in which the offence is otherwise likely to be continued. This is done by
breaking down the roof, or otherwise destroying the "lane" or level from which
the stone is being excavated. When this process is not likely to answer the
purpose, or when its execution might be attended with considerable risk or
trouble, the end is more speedily effected by walling up the lane with mason
work, and thus preventing the delinquent from having further ingress into it.
It is seldom that the offence is repeated after this, at least in the same direction;
for the culprit is not certain that, should he again be caught trespassing in the
same quarter, he himself might not be walled bodily in as a warning to others.
So tenacious are the quarriers of the privileges which remain to them, that I
am not sure that public opinion in Swanage would not sanction such a mode
of procedure with one who should prove himself incorrigible in their infraction.
One reason for enforcing the rule in question is that, if they approached nearer
each other, they might mutually endanger the stability of their works, as will
be seen when their mode of working is described. One would think that their
interest being thus mutual in the observance of the rule, they would all be
anxious to observe it. And so they are, unless strongly tempted to infringe it.
Thus, a vein of stone which is being worked may be found to be both improving, and getting more and more easy to work, when the prescribed limits are
reached—and then the temptation to transgress them is sometimes too strong
to be resisted. When the rule is being violated, the trespassers sometimes work
at night, so as not to be overheard. An amusing story is told of two parties
who were lately thus trespassing upon each other. They generally worked
within the forbidden limits at night, until at length one of them drove his
crowbar through the thin partition which separated them. The surprise of both
may be imagined at seeing each other's light gleaming through the aperture
which thus unexpectedly revealed them to each other. Mutual recrimination
would have been worse than useless, so for a time the matter was prudently
hushed up between them; but at length it leaked out, to the great scandal of
the whole body.

For all purposes of action as a body, their organization is essentially democratic. They settle nothing by delegates—all matters of common interest being
canvassed and determined in their primary assemblies. It is only when the time
for action comes that they delegate their powers. Whenever a question arises
which it is necessary for them to settle, the two stewards or wardens of the body
go round to all the quarries—not exactly with the fiery cross—but with a
notification to all the members of the body to attend a general meeting thereof
at a time and place then mentioned. Nor is this a notification to be disregarded
with impunity, the attendance being compulsory. The absentee, unless detained
by sickness or other unavoidable cause, is liable, for non-attendance, to a fine
of three shillings and fourpence; and this being more than the average value of a
whole day's work, it is seldom that any who can attend are absent for the sake
of gaining half-a-day, which is the time usually occupied by such meetings. The
place of meeting is generally the neighbourhood of some well-known quarry

in as central a position as possible. At the mouth of most quarries there is a capstan used in drawing the stone out of the mine. The meeting is constituted under the presidency of the session warden, whereupon the business of the day is immediately entered upon. The assembly is usually addressed from the capstan, which is mounted by the different orators in succession. Sometimes the utmost order is preserved; at others, the assembly is somewhat disposed to be disorderly. "At times, sir," said one of them to me, "they do be all talking at once, except the warden, who keeps all the time calling 'silence!'" The matter, whatever it may be, being fully laid before the meeting, the next thing to be done is to come to some resolution respecting it. That being attained, the last business of the meeting is to devise the means of carrying its resolution into action. When the case is one of trespass, the mode of procedure is generally such as has been already described. When the body is called together to adjudicate upon the case of an interloper, the master-quarrier charged with having employed him is regularly put upon his trial. Should he be found guilty, he is condemned, as already intimated, to pay a fine of £5. Should he afterwards refuse to pay the fine, another meeting is convened, at which the whole matter is re-heard—when, if the former judgment is affirmed, the power of levying the fine, per force, if necessary, is delegated to a certain number of the body. These, after having given him sufficient time to reconsider his determination, proceed, if they find him still contumacious, to his quarry—and, without further warrant than the behest of the tribunal which appointed them, seize all the stone they can lay their hands upon, to the value of the fine imposed. A more lawless proceeding can scarcely be imagined—rendering, as it does, every man engaged in it liable to a civil action at least, if not to be criminally indicted, for the part he takes in it. Yet it is generally regarded in Swanage as one of the ordinary channels through which justice takes its course. Again the body may be called together to consider respecting some real or fancied invasion of their privileges, or some nuisance which may have been instituted to their injury. The question then to be determined is, whether they will resist the innovation or abate the nuisance? If the case is one which admits only of passive resistance, the result is a simple resolution to resist; but if it is one calling for active measures, the means for taking them are immediately provided. It is but a short time ago since a case of this kind occurred. The grievance assumed the double aspect of the invasion of a right, and a positive nuisance. The offending object was neither more nor less than a weigh-bridge, which had recently been established upon a road over which the quarriers had long enjoyed the right of conveying as heavy loads as they pleased. They looked with the greatest suspicion upon the appearance amongst them of this appliance of civilised life, and immediately summoned a meeting to canvass its nature and consider its tendencies. The one they soon determined to be at least suspicious, and the other to be indisputably bad; so they resolved, by one and the same act, both to vindicate their right and abate the nuisance. The course determined upon was the very energetic one of demolishing the weigh-bridge, to effect which an executive commission was extemporised on the spot. This commission, armed with sledge hammers, was proceeding in the most orderly manner to the execution of its duty, when it was met by the merchants of Swanage—a set of men who will be afterwards alluded to—who did all in their power to divert it from its purpose. But all their entreaties were of no avail, until they at length pledged themselves that the offending object should be removed. On this the commission desisted, and the weigh-bridge was afterwards removed. The quarriers thus carried their point, and to this day they convey their loads over the road in question without being subjected to the annoyance of having them weighed, and of virtually paying a double toll—one for passing through the gate, in the neighbourhood of which the obnoxious machine was placed, and the other for the purpose of weighing. This may suffice to show how primitive is the state of development which society has as yet reached in Swanage.

When a quarry is taken, whether by one or more lessees, it of course requires several hands to work it. The number generally engaged in and about a quarry varies from six to twelve. When the adventurers themselves are in sufficient force to work it, no hard labour is called for. But it is seldom that you see a quarry where all those at work are master quarriers. It is not uncommon that you find two or three of them working a quarry in partnership, having five or six hired men about them to aid them in the work. The father is frequently found thus in partnership with his grown-up sons. In other cases a man, if his family is pretty numerous, may work his quarry with the aid of his sons alone, who may yet be all in their apprenticeship. The first practical operation is the sinking of the shaft, which is the only portion of the work requiring a little money capital on the part of the adventurer. The expenditure of this capital is, generally speaking, the best guarantee that the lord has that the quarry will be properly worked. The shaft is not sunk perpendicularly, as in most other mines, it being generally constructed at an angle of about forty-five degrees. It presents the appearance of a large hole in the form of a parallelogram, nearly perpendicular at one end, but slanting down at the other, at about the angle named. It is by the slant that access is had to the quarry, and the stone extracted is elevated to the surface. Along one side of this slant, or inclined plane, rude steps are constructed for the ascent and descent of the men. The rest of it is paved with flags, up which a truck is dragged with the stone which is being brought to the surface. Sometimes the motive power is a capstan—at others it is a horse. When the latter, the horse is, in some instance joint property, and does duty at more than one quarry. The depth of the shaft is regulated by that of the vein under the surface. There are three veins of stone lying parallel to, and at pretty regular distances, from each other. To reach the first vein, the shaft, according to circumstances, must be sunk for from forty to seventy feet. It is at the bottom of the shaft, when the vein is reached, and right under the perpendicular end of the shaft, that is to be found the real entrance to the quarry. It looks precisely like what it is— being neither more nor less than the entrance to an artificial cave. A horizontal passage is first driven from the foot of the inclined plane into the vein, from which "lanes" are struck off in different directions, in which lanes the quarry is worked. Generally, to get at the vein, a superincumbent stratus of solid but worthless stone has to be penetrated. Under this, and separated from it by only a very thin layer of clay, lies the first vein, in working which, the stone above forms a safe and substantial roof for the different lanes. They do not trust to it entirely, however, for as the lanes are widened, the roof is propped

up by the rubbish which is accumulated. Thus, if a lane is originally constructed above eight feet wide, it is never permitted to exceed that width, for,
to the extent to which the solid mass is excavated on the one side of it, the
roof is propped up by the rubbish on the other. In some places the vein is six
feet in depth, in which case it is all worked, when the men have sufficient room
to stand at their labour. In others, however, it does not exceed three feet in
thickness, when no more of the mass above or below is removed than is
absolutely necessary to enable the men to work it. Thus, whilst some lanes
are six feet high, others are not more than four, and the smaller the space,
of course, the more laborious the occupation. Whenever they choose they can
sink to the second or third veins. Many have gone to the second, but few to
the third. Such as have done so have their shafts from 100 to 150 feet deep.
The stone is excavated with comparative ease, lying as it does in horizontal
layers, in contact with each other, and having numerous perpendicular frac-
tures, which enable the men to detach it in blocks of different sizes from the
mass. If the layers are thin, the produce is paving instead of block stone. Most
quarries produce both, whilst in some the layers are occasionally found so thin
that a species of slate stone is extracted from them. The stone is brought to
the surface in the rough, where it is dressed and made ready for market by
workmen who seldom descend into the quarry at all. This is frequently also the
work to which apprentices are first put. The highest grade of work is that under
ground. The work below is, of course, all conducted by candlelight; which, as
may be supposed, does not add to the purity of the atmosphere in the lanes.
Sometimes the quarriers complain very much of the "damps", particularly
during the summer season. When the lanes are run very far back—and they
are sometimes so run for hundreds of feet—it becomes advisable, as well for
the additional working facilities which it will afford, as from sanitary considerations, to construct an additional shaft. Sometimes, for the sake of proper
ventilation, a lane will be run through to an old quarry, which may be close
at hand. At others, the owners of two contiguous quarries will agree to run
a lane from one to the other for the same purpose.

When the stone is dressed and ready for market, it is conveyed in waggons
to the harbour. The farmers who lease the surface under which the quarries
are worked, claim the right of carriage between them and the beach. This
claim is acquiesced in, but the result is that the quarriers pay a much higher
freight than they would otherwise do. If in any case the farmer should decline
the carriage, the quarrier can then look where he pleases for his means of
transport.

All the means and appliances of labour about the quarries are of the rudest
description. Main force is the element principally relied upon, but little aid
being derived from machinery. Long as the district about Swanage has been
quarried, and immense as has been the quantity of stone shipped from it, it
does not, even to this day, possess a pier or jetty of any description. The vessels
which receive the stone lie at anchor in the bay. The stone is dragged from the
shore by very tall horses, in carts with very high wheels, as far into the sea
as such an apparatus can venture with safety. From the carts it is consigned
to the vessels, by means of barges, which are constantly plying to and fro.

Could there be a ruder contrivance than this? Yet it is in perfect keeping with everything around.

But the most extraordinary characteristic of this singular social development still remains to be described. The world has long been divided on the subject of the standard of value, and the question of the currency is one that has baffled the most profound statesmen and the most astute economists. In Swanage these questions have received a very easy solution. The virtual standard of value is the article chiefly produced in the district—stone. But as silver is to the only standard of value, gold, in the national currency—so is bread to stone, the recognised and accepted standard in the currency of Swanage. This may be very new to the reader, but is very ancient in this remote nook of Dorset. Stone is virtually in Swanage the standard of value, and the currency is composed of stone and bread. There is scarcely any coin in circulation in the district. All payments which are not made in actual money—those so made being very few—or in goods, are made either in stone or in bread. The workmen in the quarries are paid in stone, and it is for stone that they receive in exchange such articles as they consume. It is quite true that there is a money value put on everything, but stone is almost the universal substitute for money. Thus when a master quarrier takes a quarry, and hires workmen to assist him in his operations, a money value is put upon their labour, and they are engaged at so much per day, or so much per week. But when the time of payment comes, no money passes between the master and his workmen, but a portion of the stone produced, equal in value (taking its current value for the week) to the sum at which the workmen were in each case hired, is set apart for them. Thus, if a man was hired at the rate of three shillings a day, instead of getting eighteen shillings at the end of the week, he would get eighteen shillings worth of stone. The stone so apportioned to him would in that case constitute his sole means for commanding the necessaries of life for himself and family. Sometimes, instead of the stone, the quarrier gives his workmen orders upon the merchant with whom he has credit. But still it is the stone that does it all, for it is upon the credit of the stone that the orders are executed. The course of dealing between the master quarrier and the merchant will serve to explain the whole system.

It is necessary to premise that the word merchant has, in Swanage, a peculiar local signification. There are here two classes of merchants in the ordinary acceptation of the term. There is, in the first place, the class of independent dealers who sell their goods for ready money, when they can get it, or for bread, which they afterwards convert into money, but who never deal in transations having the transfer of stone for their basis. There is, in the next place, the class to whom the term merchant is exclusively applied, who keep a general assortment of goods, which they exchange for stone. Each merchant has a bakehouse attached to his establishment, the bread baked at which is one of the chief articles which he exchanges for the stone. His shop is thus, in one sense, a bank of issue; for he manufactures in it that which forms half the currency of the district—and its entire currency, in the way of small change. Every quarrier must have his merchant, as every man of business elsewhere has his banker. To establish a credit with a merchant, the quarrier must deposit stone with him, and the extent of the credit is regulated by the quantity of stone deposited. The merchant has what he calls his bankers, which is neither more nor less than the spot of ground on which the stone left with him is deposited. The banker is like the vault, and the stone like the bullion deposited in it. The quarrier may make his deposits in the banker when he pleases and to what extent he pleases, until the merchant, for reasons of his own, refuses to receive any more. An account is kept by both parties of the quantity deposited, as well as of the goods taken by the quarrier, or on his order, from the shop. When he wants to know how he stands he takes an account, and the balance, in the shape of stone, which remains to his credit in the banker, indicates the extent of his worldly means. When the stone is deposited a money value is set upon it, according to the current price of the day, that price being now about twenty-one shilling and sixpence per hundred superficial feet of paving stone. The goods are also sold at a money value, so that the accounts between the parties are, as elsewhere, kept in money. When the quarrier pays his men in stone, they must have their merchant, as he has, to turn it to account. When he pays them by order on his merchant, he of course, takes all the stone and deposits it, to his own account, in his merchant's banker. The merchants dispose of it as they best can, Southampton being one of their best and most accessible markets.

So far as the system savours considerably of transactions based on credit. But there are, as it were, ready money transactions, in which stone figures as currency. A pair of boots, for instance, is sometimes paid for at once in stone. At some of the public-houses they take stone in deposit; at others, if a man wants a pint of beer, he must wheel a barrowful of stone to the house to pay for it. But in the great majority of transactions of the ready money kind, bread is the currency in vogue. Although the merchants keep a pretty varied stock, it is generally in the shape of different articles of food, bread being the principal. If a quarrier therefore, wants a coat, a pair of shoes, or anything else for himself or family which his merchant has not got, he has to go to one of the independent dealers who can supply him. But they not dealing in stone, and he having no credit with them, he is obliged to procure from his merchant that which they will take in exchange for what he wants. This is generally—in fact almost invariably—bread. He, therefore, draws for so much bread upon his merchant, which he carries to his clothier or his shoemaker, and gives in exchange for what he procures. It is in transactions like these that the system works with peculiar hardship to him. The result of the whole system is to make almost every necessary of life fifteen to twenty per cent dearer in Swanage than elsewhere in the neighbourhood. Thus the loaf which can be got for fivepence in Poole, is valued at 6½d. in Swanage. But it is only so valued to the quarrier when he takes it from his merchant. When he exchanges it for anything else, at the independent dealer's, he can only get 3½d. for it, or 5½d.'s worth. He thus loses a penny on every loaf which he turns to the purposes of currency. A quarrier in whose house I was seated, conversing on the subject, sent, during the interview, for some ale. His wife took with her a 6½d. loaf, and brought back 5½d.'s worth of beer. The stranger, ignorant of the purpose to which bread is thus applied, would be utterly at a loss to account for the quantity which he would see carried about in all directions. If a woman wants a piece of ribbon she must take a loaf with her to the shop.

The dealers afterwards convert the bread into money at the price at which they receive it—those who ultimately consume it thus getting it at a penny a loaf less than the value at which it was originally issued from the merchant's establishment, and all at the cost of the poor quarrier. But this is not the only disadvantage under which he labours, for whilst his stone is taken from him at the lowest—and the bread and other articles which he receives from his merchant are given to him at the highest—possible rate, such commodities as he afterwards purchases from the dealers, by means of his bread, are highly overcharged; whilst that in which he pays for them is reduced at the counter fully sixteen per cent in value. Thus although the wages of a quarrier may nominally be three shillings a day, they are virtually reduced to two shillings by the series of peculations to which he is subjected. But even of the master quarriers, few can be said to average three shillings nominally a day. The average nominal wages of the working men, as contradistinguished from the masters, are from two shillings and threepence to two shillings and ninepence a day. This, in reality, is but from one shilling and sixpence to one shilling and tenpence a day. They are also subjected to another great inconvenience by the length of time which sometimes elapses ere the merchants will balance their accounts with them. Some are careful to have a balance struck every year, but there are cases in which years elapse without any settlement of accounts. This leads some of them astray as to their real standing, whilst it begets reckless habits in the more thoughtless of them. These latter, so long as they have credit at their merchants, care little how they stand, so long as the day of reckoning is postponed. Others again, meaning to stand well, find themselves at last unexpectely in debt, when they thought they had a balance in their merchant's hands.

There is little money in circulation in town and district; house rents are exacted in money, and so are the lord's dues. To enable the quarriers to meet these demands, and also the rates which are levied upon them, the merchants, instead of goods, allow a certain sum of money to be drawn each week by their depositors. It is seldom that this sum exceeds two shillings and sixpence per week to each depositor. This enables them to meet the demands in question, and also occasionally to buy a little fresh meat, which they do not often enjoy, and for which they have invariably to pay money.

They bitterly complain of the inconvenience and losses to which they are subjected from the almost total absence of money from their ordinary every-day transactions; and they are most anxious that some merchants would come amongst them, who, taking their stone at even a lower valuation than now, would pay them money instead of giving them goods for it. In this respect matters do not seem to be improving with them, the more advanced in life amongst them saying that there is less money in circulation now than formerly. But their universal desire is, at any reasonable sacrifice, to commute their present earnings into money. If a money system were established amongst them, instead of the present system of limited barter, not only would the price of the necessaries of life fall, and their physical comforts be thus increased, but the habits of some of them would be greatly improved.

Taking their condition throughout the year, they are, on the whole, considerably better off than the agricultural labourers throughout the country.

Their houses are, generally speaking, vastly superior as regards accommodation, and consequently as regards cleanliness and healthiness, to those of the labourer in the fields. There is an abundance of the best material for constructing them at hand, and they are in many cases provided with four or five rooms. With the exception of Hop-about-lane, the houses in which are of a very inferior description, the dwellings of the quarriers in Swanage may be characterised as spacious, clean and comfortable. Their furniture and bedding are also abundant and clean. They generally pay from £4 to £4 10s. in the shape of rent, in addition to which they pay rates amounting to nearly £1 more. Their diet, too, is also, in the main, better than that of the farm-labourer. They seldom eat fresh meat, but they consume more bacon than he does. But even of this they have a very insufficient supply, considering the laborious character of their occupation.

They are generally very ignorant, and in the majority of cases almost entirely illiterate. If any of them attend school, they are sent too early to work to derive much benefit from it. The boys, at about nine years of age, become useful about the quarry, and they are sent below as soon as they become strong and skilful enough for underground work. The bulk of the quarriers adhere to the Church, the rest being chiefly divided amongst the Methodists and Independents. On the whole, they are considered an orderly and well-regulated set of men.

But few, perhaps, of those who read this account were aware, before perusing it, that so rude and primitive a state of society is to be met with within a few hours' ride of the metropolis.

EASTERN AGRICULTURAL DISTRICTS

NORFOLK SUFFOLK AND ESSEX

Letter XV

I propose in the present letter to enter somewhat more in detail into the condition of the agricultural labourers as regards his work and his wages, and to point out a few of the evils in connection with these subjects which tend to produce that feeling of sullen discontent which is so generally prevalent among them—particularly in those portions of this district where of late so many incendiary fires have taken place.

I shall first deal with the question of wages. In my previous letter I stated that the wages of the labourer averaged from seven shillings to nine shillings per week. Nothing, however, could be more erroneous than to suppose that the actual amount paid to the labourer is equal to that sum, or, on the other hand, that it is his good fortune to receive such a sum during the entire year. The system of hiring the labourer by the week is one which is comparatively rarely adopted in Suffolk; when, therefore, we are told that the wages of the labourer are eight shillings per week, it is, so far as the great body of agricultural labourers are concerned, a perfect delusion. Labourers are paid by the day, not by the week—and only for the number of days during which they are actually at work. If, in consequence of wet or unfavourable weather, they are unable to work, the wages for such days are deducted from what, by courtesy, are called their weekly wages. If a day's sickness or domestic affliction keeps the labourer at home, the same principal is acted upon. In fact, upon the day which was set apart from the General Thanksgiving the wages of great numbers of the labourers were stopped, on the plea that no work was done by them. I am happy, however, to state that the instances of such hardship, and of such total disregard to the comforts of the poor, which came under my own notice, were comparatively rare. Those of the farmers who acted in so ungenerous a manner towards the labourers were principally confined to a small district in the western division of the country, to which I shall presently have occasion more particularly to refer.

The full wages of eight shillings, or even nine shillings per week, are little enough to keep body and soul together; but when from that sum are deducted the wages of every day, or of every portion of a day, upon which the labourer is unable to work, the manner in which he exists becomes a mystery indeed. "There's some weeks," said a poor fellow to me, "that we only get four shillings—sometimes less than that—and in very wet weather we gets nothing at all." "How, then," said I, "do you manage to subsist, and pay one shilling and sixpence a week for that cottage of yours?" "We can't do it on our wages, you may be sure," he said; "the truth is, master, that we're often driven to do a many things those times that we wouldn't do if we could help it. It is very hard for us to starve; and we sometimes pull some turnips, or p'raps potatoes, out of some of the fields, unbeknown to the farmers." ...

... Most unfortunately, however, for the comforts of the labourer, there is a very large proportion of the farmers of Suffolk who have gone on making additions to the size of their farms, without increasing in the same proportion the amount of capital with which to cultivate them. The difficulty and embarrassment in which they are consequently placed, prevent them from employing the number of hands which they would otherwise require on their farms, or from sufficiently remunerating those whom they do employ ... Although the principal of the Poor-law is to give relief to the able-bodied, except in the workhouse, still there are many cases in which the boards of guardians relax a little the stringency of the rules. An instance of this kind came under my notice a short time since. A labourer applied to the board for relief; he was asked, of course, the usual questions as to the state of health of his family: he had six children. There was an evident desire on the part of the guardians to afford some slight relief, which they knew would be only of a temporary character, rather than be burdened with the expense of maintaining the whole family for an indefinite period in the workhouse. They accordingly strove hard to make out a "case." The applicant stated that his family were all well, and that he only wanted a little assistance to help him in the meantime, as he hoped to get something to do in the ensuing week. The guardians pressed the poor man still more closely. "Is not your wife poorly?" "No," replied the honest applicant. "Are you quite well yourself?" "Yes, I'm pretty well myself." "Is there none of your children ill?" "'No." "Not one?" "No." "None of them got the ringworm, or anything the matter with their heads?" "No" was still the answer of the applicant, evidently not perceiving the design of the board. "Have any of them," at last suggested a member of the board, "had the ringworm lately?" "Why, yes" said the poor man, "a little time ago Billy caught it somewhere." The applicant was ordered to withdraw. The consciences of the board were sufficiently elastic—one of his children had had the ringworm—it was a case of illness, and the man was ordered out-door relief. The following week the man was in work again. Repeated instances of this kind take place among the guardians, and they are generally considered rather liberal towards the poor ... There are, however, many labourers, who, when unemployed, refuse to apply for relief, as they are aware that, if able-bodied, the workhouse would be the only relief offered them; and sooner than subject themselves to such restraints as would be there imposed upon them, they endeavour by some means, fair or foul, to support themselves until they are enabled to get employment ...

Another of the causes of complaint which I have frequently heard among the labourers, is the hardship of having to walk some ten or a dozen miles in the course of the day, in going to and from their work. The necessity for this has arisen from the practice which exists in the neighbourhood of some of the larger towns—upon the part of some of the close parishes, or of the owners of the extensive estates—of endeavouring to evade the operation of the law of settlement, by pulling down the cottages, or turning out the tenants just before the expiration of the term which would make them irremovable.

Upon several properties in the neighbourhood of Bury, for instance, I have been informed of cases where, upon the slightest possible pretext, a whole family has been driven off the estate. The poor people thus driven away are unable to obtain accommodation in the village in the immediate neighbourhood, for owners of property there not wishing to run the risk of having any burden thrown upon their parish; and they accordingly seek shelter in some of the wretched back streets and lanes of the larger towns. In several instances I was told by the labourers themselves that they had to walk one, two, three or four miles to work on the very estate from which, as tenants, they had but a short time since been removed. I was informed of the case of one family which had been driven off an estate situated a few miles from Bury, under circumstances of the greatest hardship; though, it must be added, that there are few gentlemen who have devoted more time and attention to the improvement of the cottages and the condition of their tenantry than the owner of the estate in question. The plea for the removal of this family was, that the mother had been seen to pick up a few small potatoes, which had been left upon the surface of the field after the bulk of the crop had been removed. After having been turned out of the house, the whole family took up their abode within the porch of the church for two days, determined that they would not be driven out of the parish, although they might be evicted from their dwelling. From the church, however, they were finally removed as vagrants, and, travelling on to Bury, they obtained lodgings in the wretched place to which I referred in my former letter, viz., Hogg's-lane.

Several other instances like this came to my knowledge as having occurred in the neighbourhood of Bury. In the various other parts of the county through which I have travelled, I have made it my business to inquire into the existence of such a practice, and I feel bound to state that the result of my inquiries was such as to lead me to the opinion that it is not carried on to so great an extent as I was led to suppose, except in some comparatively few cases, where close parishes exist in the immediate neighbourhood of large towns. I found upon inquiry that in a great number of cases, where cottages had been pulled down, others had been erected in their stead, of a more commodious character, and in some cases nearer to the farms. Taking the whole country, I do not believe that the number of cottages pulled down has exceeded the number of new ones that have been built. The insufficiency of cottage accommodation remains, however, still as great.

Another complaint on the part of the labourers is founded on the unfeeling manner in which they consider that they are almost invariably treated by their employers. They feel—to use their own words—that "they are treated like slaves." It is seldom, they say, that the farmer will condescend to speak to them, except in terms of reproach or abuse. There is no display of anything like kindly feeling towards them, nor any desire shown to improve their condition. . . .

I have heard an opinion expressed that a great number of incendiary fires were traceable to boys. After the age of sixteen the boys became paupers in their own right. The parents begin to think that it is time that the boys should earn something for themselves; the boys also think that they ought to assume the habits of men, and they wish to become independent of their parents;

they accordingly endeavour to get work; but they are boys in the eye of the
farmer, and they have not the requisite qualification for high wages; they are
unmarried; they are not able to earn more than two shillings and sixpence to
three shillings and sixpence a week. They soon get tired of working for so
small a sum; they spend a short time in the workhouse; becoming dissatisfied
there, they meet with other boys of the same age who are similarly situated,
they talk over their grievances, and become sullen and discontented with
everybody and everything; they leave the house literally with their hands
against every man, and avail themselves of the first opportunity of indulging
their feelings upon the property of those who may or may not have done
them some real or imaginary wrong. . . .

. . . Referring to individual cases of incendiarism, it is curious to observe how,
in the great majority of cases, the fires occur in districts where either a low
rate of wages is paid, or where the labourers deem themselves improperly
treated. Speaking to many of the labourers upon the subject, they have not
unfrequently made use of expressions towards those whose property had been
destroyed, such as—"Oh, sarve him right;" "He was a grinder;" "He was
very hard upon his men," and other terms of similar character. On the other
hand, some of the fires have happened in cases where the farmer bore the
highest possible character. . . .

But while, on the one hand, some farmers who bear a good character among
the labourers have suffered, there are many instances in which they have been
spared, although fires have been constantly taking place around them. A large
farmer, residing five or six miles from Bury, and farming upwards of 1,000
acres, was a singular instance of this. "He is a good man—a good fellow,"
said a labourer to whom I was speaking; "he is one of the best men we have
around here, and he hasn't had so much as a hay-rick or barley-stack set on
fire. Aye! A better man never trod shoe leather than he. The poor men all
like him. He isn't ashamed to speak to 'em when he sees 'em, and he's always
glad to help a poor fellow when he's in want." . . .

But although there are cases in which the farmers who bear a high character
have suffered, and likewise cases in which they have escaped, there are also
many in which farmers who are very generally disliked by the labourers, who
give very low wages and afford but insufficient employment, have escaped
injury. You may frequently hear the poor people speak in terms of almost
unmeasured abuse of some of the farmers; and, in looking over the list of
fires, you expect to find some of their farms included. Such, however, in a
great many instances, is not the case. Any theory which may be set up on the
subject is, therefore, liable to be immediately overthrown by some case or
cases which may be cited, and which it is impossible to reconcile with any
preconceived opinions. Difficult as it may be to explain many individual cases,
we have, however, the broad facts before us, that in the northern and eastern
parts of the county fires are comparatively unknown, and that the rate of
wages is higher there than in the other portions of the county; and that in the
southern and western parts of the county, where fires are constantly taking
place, the rate of wages is, generally speaking, lower. In the former case, wages
average from eight shillings to nine shillings per week; in the latter, from six

shillings to seven shillings per week. How far low wages may tend to produce this state of things is a question upon which the reader will form his own opinion.

Letter XX

. . . The cottage accommodation of the labourer is in many parts of Norfolk lamentably deficient. . . . In point of fact, it is impossible to obtain a piece of ground, for building purposes, in any of the villages within eight or ten miles of Norwich. Many of the estates have been entirely cleared of tenantry. To such an extent has the system been carried on, that there are at present in Norwich not less than 500 agricultural labourers, who have to walk to their work distances varying from three to seven miles. Every expedient to prevent the labourers obtaining a settlement in the rural parishes is resorted to by the occupiers. In Wackton parish, one of the modes of removing the paupers was, to set a number of persons, principally weavers, who had some claim on the parish, and who, in all probability, had never had a spade in their hands before, to dig up a common in the middle of January, the snow at the time lying upon the ground several inches deep. The poor wretches were told that they must dig a certain portion of the common before they could obtain any relief. The first thing which they did was to dig in the snow what they called "the grave" of the magistrate who had given the order. So far as the experiment was concerned, it was perfectly successful for after two or three days the greater proportion of the persons left their employment and contrived to settle themselves, by one means or other, in the city of Norwich or in some of the surrounding open parishes. The effect of this conduct, in addition to the injury inflicted upon the paupers, has been most materially to enhance the rates of the adjoining parishes. In Long Sutton, for instance, a number of small cottages have been built; they are crowded by the evicted of the other parishes and the rates are six shillings in the pound, while in the parish of St. Michael, which adjoins it, and where the cottages have been been pulled down, the rates are only two shillings and sixpence in the pound. This system is not, however, confined to Norwich; for it has been carried on to a great extent in the neighbourhood of Castle Acre, which is an open parish, the consequence being that whilst Castle Acre is overstocked with inhabitants, and the cottages there are densely crowded, there are not in the surrounding parishes anything like sufficient hands to cultivate the land. It is owing to the excess of labourers in one district, and the great want of them in the neighbouring parishes, that the custom has sprung up within the last few years of employing the people in what are termed "gangs", a system which, there can be no doubt whatever, is attended with a considerable amount of evil to the person employed.

The principle upon which this "gang system" is carried on is the following. A farmer residing in or near the Castle Acre may wish to have some particular piece of work done, the performance of which will require a considerable number of hands. In such a case he would apply to a gang-master at Castle Acre, who would contract to do the work, and to supply the labour. The gang-master would accordingly get together as many hands as might be necessary and they would be sent in a gang to the place of work. In cases where the work can be done by women and children as well as men, the gang is composed of persons of both sexes and of all ages. During the time they are at work, they are superintended by an "overseer", whose duty it is to see that they are steady to their work, and to prevent the use of any bad language or the occurrence of any misconduct. The overseer generally accompanies the gang both to and from the place of work. This system, although it works well for the employer, has in many cases a directly contrary effect upon the workpeople. The farmer gets his work done well, quickly, and cheaply; and the prospect of work to be obtained in the gangs at Castle Acre has drawn together a vast number of labourers from the surrounding districts, till at length, to use the language of one of the overseers, of the gangs, published a few years since, the parish has become "the coop of all the scrapings in the country; for if a man or a woman do anything wrong, they come here, and they think by getting among them here they are safe". The employer is not only benefited by the system, but also the gang-master, inasmuch as it has the effect of raising him in some degree to the position of a master instead of labourer, and as such affords him great local power and an indefinite kind of patronage. But the system operates most injuriously upon the employed. In the first place, it is a mode of getting them to do the largest possible amount of work for the smallest amount of pay. The gang-master contracts for the work by the piece, and the labourers are compelled to work as hard as though they were working by piece-work for themselves; while, in point of fact, they are only receiving day labourers' wages. It not unfrequently happens also, that after the gang has walked some four or five miles to the place of work, wet or unfavourable weather may prevent them from performing the task for which they were employed, and they thus have to walk there and back without receiving any remuneration. . . .

. . . The system of granting allotments to the labourer has been attended with an incalculable amount of good in the counties of Norfolk, Suffolk, and Essex. The effect of giving the labourer a small piece of land upon which he can grow his own vegetables, and perhaps a coomb or two of wheat, has been to wean him from the ale-house, from the ill example of bad company, and to give him something akin to a feeling of independence, while it has taught him to feel that he has a small stake in the country. Generally speaking, the farmers are opposed to the system. There are, however, many exceptions to the contrary; they consider that the labourers will be apt to husband their strength for their own allotments, and that they will not be able to get a fair amount of work out of them. In many cases the farmers expressly prohibit the labourers from growing any wheat on the allotments. The reason given to me for this prohibition was, that the labourer might frequently be able "to make free with my corn, and sell it along with his own to the miller; but if the miller knows that the men don't grow corn when they come to him to sell any, they'll know at once that they haven't come by it fairly". If suspicions of this kind were allowed to prevail generally, the obvious effect would be to prevent the labourer producing anything whatever upon his allotment. From all that I have seen of the labourers themselves, I think that suspicions of this kind are generally unfounded. In many cases the farmer, suffering himself to be actuated by his suspicions, also forbids the labourer from keeping either pigs or poultry, lest they should be kept at his expense. When once, however, the labourer is in possession of his allotment, and is able to procure a few things from it, his condition becomes at once improved, and the temptation to dishonesty is removed; and so far as experience goes, it entirely supports this view of the case. . . . Since the introduction of the system, the minds of the labourers have been greatly improved, and throughout the whole hundred, consisting of thirty-four parishes, they have not had a single prosecution for felony during the last twelve months. . . . Many of the labourers to whom I have spoken upon the subject have said that, without their allotments, they do not know whatever they should have done last winter when out of work. One of them stated that he had lived almost entirely during the winter months on the produce of his "bit of ground". "When I comes home", said he, "at night, my missus always has something ready for me out of the garden, and I fancy my taturs and cabbage, and everything is ever so much sweeter and better off my own ground than if we'd got to buy 'em. I growed eight bushels of taturs last year, and they served us nearly all the winter. Then this here little bit I keeps for radishes, inguns, and them sort of things, and in the summer it's very nice to have a few of 'em with your tea—it relishes it like. Then in the little bit of ground at home we grows a few flowers, and they look very pretty, you know. Sometimes my missus cuts a few, and puts 'em in a mug with some water to 'em, and then we can see 'em in the room without going into the garden, and then you know, sir, it does you good to look at 'em, and know that you growed 'em yourself." I have met with several instances in which the labourers have given expression to their feelings in almost the same words. Many of them have informed me that they have been enabled to pay the rent of their cottages out of their allotments. . . .

. . . As an invariable rule, the agricultural labourer commences his career as a weekly labourer; and, whatever may be his talents and industry, he must inevitably end his days as a labourer, or, when unfitted through old age to continue his work, die as a pauper.

Letter XXI

. . . When speaking to several of the farmers I have always been told the condition of the labourer is not so bad as would at first sight appear. . . . A large farmer in Clavering informed me that "a man with a family of five children will be nearly able with six shillings a week to buy bread enough, if he buys the coarsest flour; his rent he generally pays out of his harvest money; his clothes he gets by some means or other—people sometimes give them to him—and then, when he is unoccupied why we keep him in the workhouse. So you see, sir, he is amply provided for, even with wages at six shillings per week." . . . The statement given above is one that I have heard from the farmers, not once, but many times, and it affords a key to the whole system of paying the agricultural labourer. . . .

. . . It is not at all an uncommon complaint to hear among the farmers that the pauper children are receiving too much education. A few days since I met with one who said that he was opposed to all the new-fangled education that they were giving to the paupers. "I am", said he, "one of the guardians of our union; and I just happened to go into the schoolroom, and there if the master wasn't telling the boys to point out with a stick, on some big maps that were hanging up, where South Amerikey was, and France, and a lot of other places; and they did it too. Well, when I went home, I told my son of it, and asked him if he could tell me where them places was; and he couldn't. Now, is it right that these here pauper children should know more than the person who will have to employ them?" . . .

. . . Complaints have not unfrequently been made to me—not by the labourers, but by those above them—that the pauper children are receiving a better education than those of the labourer. It is one of the anomalies of the poor-law, that the pauper is better fed, better clothed, and better lodged than the labourer; and the same person who would find fault with the pauper receiving a better education than the child of the labourer, must also in justice complain that he is better fed, clothed, and lodged, and that he is so there can be no doubt. Let those who are able to adjust the inequality. In the case of the labourer, as of the farmer, the real cause of complaint is, not that the child of the pauper is educated well, but that his own is not. . . .

. . . One species of immorality which is peculiarly prevalent in Norfolk and Suffolk is that of bastardy. With the exception of Hereford and Cumberland there are no counties in which the per centage of bastardy is so high as it is in Norfolk—being there 53.1 per cent., above the average of England Wales; in Suffolk it is 27 per cent. above, and in Essex 19.1 per cent. below the average. In the two first-named counties, and even in the latter one, though not to the same extent, there appears to be a perfect want of decency among the people. "The immorality of the young women", said the rector of one parish to me, "is literally horrible, and I regret to say it is on the increase in a most extra-ordinary degree. When I first came to the town, the mother of a bastard child used to be ashamed to show herself. The case is now quite altered; no person seems to think anything at all of it. When I first came to the town there was no such thing as a prostitute in it; now there is an enormous number of them. When I am called upon to see a woman confined with an illegitimate child, I endeavour to impress upon her the enormity of the offence; and there are no cases in which I receive more insult from those I visit than from such persons. They generally say they'll get on as well, after all that's said about it, and if they never do anything worse than that, they shall get to Heaven as well as other people." Another clergyman stated to me that he never recollected an instance of his having married a woman who was not either pregnant at the time of her marriage or had had one or more children before her marriage and a third clergyman told me that he went to baptize the illegitimate child of one woman, who was thirty-five years of age, and it was absolutely impossible for him to convince her that what she had done was wrong. "There appears", said he, "to be among the lower orders a perfect deadness to all moral feeling upon this subject." Many of the cases of this kind which have come under my knowledge evince such horrible depravity that I dare not attempt to lay them before the reader. Speaking to the wife of a respectable labourer on the subject, who had seven children, one of whom was then confined with an illegitimate child, she excused her daughter's conduct by saying "What was the poor girls to do; the chaps say that they won't marry 'em first, and then the girls give way. I did the same myself with my husband". There was one case in Cossey, in Norfolk, in which the woman told me, without a blush crimsoning her cheek, that her daughter and herself had each a child by a sweep who lodged with them, and who promised to marry the daughter. The cottage in which these persons slept consisted of but one room, and there were two other lodgers who occupied beds in the same room; in one of which "a young woman occasionally slept with the young man she was keeping company with". The other lodger was an old woman of seventy-four years of age. To such an extent is prostitution carried on in Norwich, that out of the 656 licensed public-houses and beer-shops in the city, there are not less than 220 which are known to the police as common brothels. And although the authorities have the power of with-holding the licenses, nothing is done to put a stop to the frightful vice. "At Bury", said one of the guardians of the poor to me, "there is, I believe, a larger amount of prostitution, in proportion to the size of the place, than is to be found in any town or city in England." Harwich appears to be remarkably free from this vice, "There are not", I was informed by the police, "more than six prostitutes in the town, and there is not a single brothel".

Letter XXII

... Although the Burial Clubs have been brought prominently before the notice of the public in connection with the county of Essex, they are by no means peculiar to that county. Great numbers of them exist in various other parts of the country, in the manufacturing districts, and in the metropolis. The clubs for the labouring classes in Essex are almost invariably got up by an undertaker and by the publican at whose house their meetings are generally held; and in passing along the streets the passenger may frequently see placards in the windows of the public-houses, bearing such headings as, "All flesh is grass", "In the midst of life we are in death", and other texts or mottos. Beneath these may also occasionaly be seen a ghastly-looking death's head and bones. In cases where the clubs are the joint speculation of the publican and the undertaker, mutual agreements appear to be entered into for the promotion of their respective interests. Provision is made in the rules of the society that the "box" shall not be removed from the publican's house—the publican being almost invariably appointed the treasurer; and the undertaker is guaranteed the exclusive right to the performance of his professional duties for such members of the club as may require it....

... The contributions to these societies, and the amount derived from them in cases of death, vary considerably in different clubs. In some cases the subscriptions are one penny per week, and twopence or fourpence per quarter for expenses; in others the payments are fourpence per quarter for expenses, and sixpence at the time of a death, from each member; in a few of them the amount of subscriptions is regulated according to the age of the party, and the amount paid upon death is dependent upon the class to which the member may belong; while in others, persons of all ages admitted into the club pay a like sum, and the survivors or nominees receive an equal amount upon the death of the member.

The reason which I have most frequently heard assigned for the existence of these clubs is, the great desire felt by the poor of procuring decent interment. There appears to be nothing more repugnant to the feelings of great numbers of the labouring population than the idea of being buried as a pauper by the parish. Several old persons in the different workhouses, have, after telling me that so far as their present existence was concerned they were tolerably comfortable, added, with evident emotion "But I suppose I shall be buried by the parish". "There", said another to me, pointing to a small enclosed spot, which the small green mounds marked as the paupers' burial ground—"There will be my home at last, and it's not a pleasant thought neither—is it!—to be buried like a pauper". Another person, who was employed as an agricultural labourer, said to me, when speaking of the hard struggle which he had to maintain for an existence, "So as I can but rub through, master, and pay up the club, and be buried decently after all, I don't mind working hard". The enormously high price which the labourer has to pay for the gratification of this, the almost only object of his ambition, forces him to become a member of one or more of the numerous clubs which hold out to him the prospect of a realisation of his wishes; and he will endure almost any amount of privation, and subject himself to any inconvenience, in order to pay up his "death money", or the subscription to his benefit club. So strongly does this desire for decent interment prevail among the working classes, that many of them who are in a condition to do so will leave deposits in the savings banks, or in provident institutions, for the purpose of ensuring the object of their wishes; and in not a few cases it has happened that upon the death of the party he has been found to have died an inmate of a poor house, and destitute of every kind of property save the little fund which he had set apart for his funeral. There is nothing perhaps which has tended more to the establishment and growth of these badly constituted clubs, than the enormous expense to which the poor are invariably put at the time of a funeral. The expenses upon these occasions are seldom less than £4, and they not unfrequently exceed £6....

... A working man, who is the secretary to one of these societies, stated that he had known drink to be given to such excess, that the undertaker's men were frequently unfit to perform their duty, and sometimes even reeled while carrying the coffin. "The men", he says, "who stand as mutes at the door, as they stand out in the cold, are supposed to require most drink, and receive it most liberally. I have seen these men reel about the road, and after the burial we have been obliged to put these mutes and their staves into the interior of the hearse, and drive them home, as they were incapable of walking. After the return from the funeral, the mourners commonly have drink again at the houses". In the case of a death, the publican at whose house the club is held claims that a certain portion of the "funeral allowances" should be spent with him....

... When treating of the wages of the labourer, it was shown that it was impossible for him to do more than merely obtain a bare sufficiency of food for himself and family with the amount which he usually received. The means by which he obtains his clothing is admitted by almost every one to be a mystery. So impressed have many of the more wealthy persons residing in the neighbourhod of small towns been with the utter impossibility of the labourer obtaining clothing for himself and his family, that they have formed in many places what are called "clothing clubs". These clubs are conducted on the principle of allowing the labourer to contribute one penny or more per week, according as he can afford it, and at the end of the year the person so contributing receives an order upon some tailor or draper in the town, to the amount of ten shillings or fifteen shillings for every three shillings which he may have subscribed himself; the increased sum being made up from the contributions of charitable individuals in the town, some of whom are contributors to the extent of £1, £2, and £3 each. In the town of Halesworth, upwards of £200 is thus annually distributed for clothing for the labourers in the immediate neighbourhood. In many other parts of the country, clubs of a similar character abound. The supply of coals, too, is not unfrequently obtained through the same agency by the labourers.

Without these associations for enabling the labourer to obtain fuel, clothing, relief in sickness, and burial at his death, his condition would be, if possible, far worse than it is at present. Even from the friendly and burial clubs, badly constructed as they are, an enormous amount of assistance is afforded to the poor man, but under an improved system of management the benefits would be increased tenfold. Unfortunately the present state of the labourer, in the absence of any material improvement in his condition, imperatively demands the assistance of associations of this kind. His whole life appears to be constantly wavering between toil and charity. The parish doctor attends at (in all probability) his illegitimate birth; he is swathed in linen provided for him by the hands of some charitable individual, or benevolent association. A charity school doles out to him his scanty education in the irregular intervals of his youthful labour; as he advances in years the subscriptions of the more affluent are necessary to provide him with clothing; when unemployed, or unable through old age or infirmity to do a fair day's work, the workhouse is his refuge; in sickness the parish doctor attends him, and his club supports him; in death, if his club be in existence, the funds for his burial are provided by a portion of the hard earnings of his club-mates—for many of whom, who may have passed away before him, he had been called upon to perform the like act of self-denying charity. If his club be closed, as is frequently the case, the parish will find him a shell; four of his neighbours, perhaps poorer than himself, sacrifice their half-day's wages to bear him gratuitously to the spot which the guardians of the poor have appointed as the pauper's final resting-place, and in which his ancestors and some of his offspring were perhaps laid before him. The clergyman waives his burial fees, or the union chaplain consigns him to the ground which for half a century, in seed time and in harvest he had moistened with his sweat and enriched by his toil.

NORTHERN COUNTIES

DURHAM

Letter XXIV

... In the county of Durham there were by the last census rather more than 10,000 agricultural labourers, male and female, of all ages; 7,886 of these were males of twenty and upwards; 1,203 were males under twenty. The former, supposing nine-tenths of them to be married, would of course represent a population of about 28,000. There are three classes of agricultural labourers in this county, the case of each of which I shall now proceed to lay before you—the hind, the farm servant, and the ordinary labourer by the day or the week, or, as he is expressively called here, the daytillman. I put aside women, who, when regularly employed, are almost always inmates of the farmhouse, their occupation partaking equally of the nature of the domestic attendant and the farm servant, and boys—as the instances of their working independently apart from the families of husbands or fathers are extremely rare. Confining myself for the present to male labourers, I begin with the hind. He is the farmer's righthand man of all-work, acting also as a man of authority among the labourers. He is almost always married, with a family generally of moderate numbers, for Scottish household maxims are as rife here as north of the Tweed. His cottage, which he holds rent-free, is either near the grange, or forms a portion of the garth or farm-inclosure (gard is a Norse word, still existing among us in the forms of garth and yard, and connected also with gird). There is no precise limitation of his hours of labour, for he is understood to be ever ready at the farmer's behest, and works occasionally both late and early, tending the cattle at even and night, and repairing to the threshing-floor or his mill with lanthorn alight in the early winter's morning. . . . The hind's wages, as I have learned from themselves, are from ten shillings to twelve shillings a week; he is entitled, besides a cottage rent-free, to other "privileges", as they are styled, which generally consist of twenty bushels of potatoes in a year, and his fuel carted; if he gets the milk and butter of one cow for himself and family, this is reckoned at four shillings weekly. . . . The hind may be paid by the week, but the agreement is generally by the year, though sometimes by the half-year. The hind's cottage, from its locality, is sometimes without a garden, for which he has less occasion than other labourers. On a farm of two hundred acres there are generally two hinds, but, of course, other labour is required. This class of labourers, except when they forfeit position and character by misconduct, are rarely in distressed circumstances; yet the last few years have somewhat modified their status, and the new law of settlement introduced by the passing of the Poor Removal Act, which confers irremovability after five years' residence, has seriously affected their interests in some instances. To evade the operation of the law, and obviate the possibility of the hind ever acquiring a chance of settlement by residence, some farmers will not keep them longer than four years, at the utmost, and have new hinds every year or two. This course shows but a mean spirit, and I should hope is not often taken by respectable farmers.

The denomination of farm servant is applied to unmarried men, oftenest youths, who are lodged and boarded at the farm, and hired by the year. The wages of adults in this situation vary from £10 to £18, or even £20, according to the work of the workman, and the duties required of him; this year, however, has left few at the latter standards, and a common rate even for smart hands is £14. Boys and very young lads obtain only their clothes, or a sum of £3 or £4 in addition to their board. . . .

. . . I now come to the daytillman, or ordinary day-labourer, the most numerous class of all, and, it must be added, the most precariously situated. It is here where the shoe really pinches; not but that a large proportion, I may say the largest proportion, are comfortably enough situated, but it is a class which includes all, from the man in receipt of regular wages at twelve shillings and sixpence a week, to him whose employment is the most temporary or uncertain . . .

. . . Fully the half, I should say, of the labouring people with whom you converse are merely denizens, not natives, of the locality, having immigrated into it in search of employment; very frequently they will tell you that they are strangers in the neighbourhood, having only been there a few weeks or months. This is the case more or less all over England, for the habits of our labouring population are no longer stationary, but migratory—nowhere, however, so much so as in the north. . . .

. . . The in-door work of a farm is generally done by female servants, who are the daughters of agricultural labourers, in conjunction with the wife and daughters of the farmer; but women thus employed speedily marry, and their savings go rather to find clothing and furniture for themselves than to eke out the necessities of the paternal household. In out-door work, the wife and children of the labourer are employed in hoeing turnips, weeding, or "couching", as it is sometimes called, clearing the ground from stones, manuring it, tending cattle, etc. . . . the great branch of occupation for the youngest is in scaring birds from the corn, at which they will earn one shilling and sixpence a week, or for other things two shillings.

NORTHERN COUNTIES

NORTHUMBERLAND

Letter XXVI

... The lot of the tiller of the soil in Northumberland, though far from being exempt from hardship and vicissitude, is yet one of comparative comfort on the whole. I have already given you an account of the "hind" or as it is commonly called, the "bondage" system, as partially prevailing in Durham; it is much more widely spread in Northumberland, where it may be considered as the general condition of the labourer. But this difference is to be noted—that whereas in Durham the hind generally receives the greater portion of his wages in money, in Northumberland he is paid chiefly, and sometimes wholly, in kind. There are many degrees of variety in the condition of hinds; perhaps the best paid men—as they are those of greatest trust and mark—are the drovers employed on the large cattle-farms and sheep-walks, and charged with the care of the numerous and valuable flocks and herds which roam on the upland pastures. The drover, or head of the herdsmen, is, in fact, part holder of the stock; he has sixty sheep for every six hundred he tends, and pasturage for two horses and his cow, together with his wheat, oats, and potatoes. . . .

... There is one peculiarity in the aspect of Northumberland to which I may here advert. Villages are rare, and the eye is not offended by those aggregations of rickety hovels so common in some districts of the south. Small towns, from 1,000 to 3,000 inhabitants, are comparatively numerous—clean, pleasant-looking places, well and substantially built, generally of the whin or freestone, plentifully found in the north of England and the south of Scotland. This feature of the social arrangements of the district arises, no doubt, from the insecurity of life and property caused in old times by the turbulent and predatory habits of the border population, and which admitted of safety only under the shelter of the feudal castle, or in the streets of the walled town. This, doubtless, has its effect in maintaining the old-fashioned system of lodging the farm-servants and labourers in or about the homestead. The extended cultivation of the soil is here of comparatively recent date; a great portion of the county consists of reclaimed moorland, which has been enclosed and brought under tillage within the last hundred years. The district under the Cheviots naturally was the last to receive cultivation, both from the poorness of the soil and from the memories of ancient ravage and depredation. Some most excellent farms have been created here within fifty years—the farm-steadings being on such a large scale as to be in fact hamlets, and the buildings of a very superior description. The cottage accommodation in many localities was formerly indifferent, from the fact of the dwellings being held rent-free, and therefore, often neglected, and left without repair; and in some places it still continues to be so, but in no respect has the march of improvement been so rapid as in this. This result is to be ascribed, I am informed, to the excellent example set by the Duke of Northumberland and Sir Walter Riddell, a magistrates and proprietor of the county, who also presides in the duke's court-leets. It is doubtful, indeed, whether in some cases improvement is not being pushed to extremes. New cottages are now almost always built with four rooms (some of the old cottages had but one); the consequence is, that the labourer cannot, for some considerable time at least, furnish them, and this leads to the temptation of subletting.

I come now to consider the condition of the hinds, who in Northumberland constitute the mass of the agricultural labourers. Hinds do not work for weekly wages, but are hired by the year or the half-year. Each of the married men is provided with a cottage and small garden on the farm for himself and family, several of whom are in many cases engaged by the year as well as himself. The wages of the hind, as I have said, are paid chiefly in kind; those of his sons, either in money, or partly in money and kind. He is bound also to find the services of a woman, who, of course, is almost always one of his family. The conditions of the engagement vary somewhat in different parts of the county, and will best be illustrated by taking a series of particular instances. The first I shall take is that of a hind employed on the Greenwich Hospital estates, once belonging to the Derwentwater family, near Hexham, in the south-western district of the county; he receives 36 bushels of oats, 24 of barley, 12 of peas, 3 of wheat, 3 of rye, 36 to 40 bushels of potatoes, and 24 lbs. of wool; he has besides a cottage and garden, a cow's keep for the year, carriage of coals from the pit, and £4 in cash. The next is that of one employed on a farm near Morpeth, in the central district; he receives 10 bushels of wheat, 30 of oats, 10 of barley, 10 of rye, and 10 of peas; he has besides the potatoes grown on 800 yards of ground, a cow's keep for a year, a cottage and gardens, his coals led, three hens, or two bushels of barley as an equivalent, and £3 10s. in cash. The next case I take from the neighbourhood of Wooler, in the northern part of the county; this hind receives 36 bushels of oats, 24 of barley, 12 of peas, and 6 of wheat, with the potatoes grown on 1,000 yards of ground, a cow's keep, a house and garden, coals led, and £3 in cash. A pig also is kept in most cases, and is a source of considerable profit, being killed for the market in winter; at 20 stone it will bring (at the present price of pork) a sum of £5 to £5 10s. The conditions of the agreement are in writing— sometimes, indeed, a printed form is used. It is to be observed that the recent reduction in the price of grain has partially affected the money value of the hind's earnings. Of course, the greater part of the whole of what he receives is consumed in his own house, when he is married and has a tolerably numerous family. There is, however, often a considerable surplus, and this will fetch less in the market than it did three years ago. Hence the reduction of prices has in some cases affected them; and I heard a husbandman employed in the midland district of the county (an unmarried man, however, which is not frequently the case) regret the tenor of his bond, and express an opinion that the condition of the hinds and other labourers near Newcastle, where the payment is made chiefly in money (fourteen shillings and fifteen shillings a week, with cottage and garden, potatoes and fuel carted) was now preferable. In some cases, as I have stated, the hind is paid wholly in kind; he then receives 12 bolls, or 24 bushels, of wheat, with the other articles in pretty nearly the same proportion as above; in cases where his cow is not kept, he receives five shillings a week instead, which thus appears to be considered the money value of a cow's keep. I have thus given you the average wages of the hind; of course, however, these do not include the earnings of his wife and family. The latter will often amount to a sum of £20 in the year—sometimes considerably more, sometimes less. The female bondager, who is the hind's wife, or eldest daughter, is paid tenpence a day for what is called small-work, and one shilling a day in harvest. This is the stipulated price, in cases where where the employment of the woman is regular during the year; but when she is only casually employed, in harvest time, the amount is from two shillings to two shillings and sixpence a day. Children's earnings are very various in their nature and amount; they run from fourpence to sixpence a day, and one shilling in harvest time. In one case of which I had cognizance, the man's family consisted of six persons, including his father; the half-yearly earnings of all these persons were £19 7s. None of the three daughters was employed in domestic service.

It will be admitted, I think, that in such a state of things as I have described, the condition of the hinds is one of general comfort. The system is one well adapted to a simple rural population, and especially to the Northumbrian character. It has not, however, escaped censure or condemnation, though upon no very rational or intelligible grounds. The name of the "bondage" system, as it is commonly termed, seems to have been the chief objection brought against it. Cobbett, towards the close of his life, attacked it, and his example has once found imitators, who have denounced it as a species of serfage, which it in no respect resembles. It surely argues a confusion of ideas, amounting almost to imbecility, to speak of a voluntary engagement for a year, upon specified terms, as a sort of slavery; yet this has been done. I have explained in a former letter that the true meaning of the word "bondage" if we recur to its original sense—and no doubt it is in this sense that a people of Danish descent continue to use it—is simply husbandry; bonde signifying to this day, in the Swedish, Danish, and Norse tongues a free peasant, or yeoman. An outcry, however—on this ground chiefly or solely—was raised some years back against the system, and many of the hinds were led away by it. Mr. Jobson, of Chillingham Newton, one of the largest farmers in the northern district, yielded to the wishes of his men, and hired them at certain wages, with regular employment for the year, but before the year was out they unanimously desired to be replaced on their original footing. In fact, as has been well remarked, there can be no doubt that, owing to the thinness of the population, the great farmers who have suddenly sprung up on the borders found some such system necessary in order to carry on their agricultural operations, and the labourers receive an equivalent for submitting to tie themselves by the year. One of these farmers estimated to me the yearly value in money of the earnings of his hinds—not including, of course, their families—at £35 to £36 a year, which I am far from thinking an over-estimate. Unmarried farmservants, who are lodged in the farm-house or (now more generally) in some cottage adjoining were paid till lately £10 for the summer half-year, and £8 for the winter half-year. There has however, I am sorry to say, been a reduction in the recent hirings, and the general rate for the past year was £8 or £9 for the summer half, and £5 or £6 for the winter. The daytillmen, or husbandmen at weekly wages, regularly employed in Northumberland, are comparatively few; but there is always a class of labourers whose exact occupation is not easily definable, and who generally work on a farm during a portion of the year. The rate is two shillings and sixpence a day, or by the week twelve shillings to thirteen shillings.

NORTHERN COUNTIES
CUMBERLAND AND WESTMORLAND

Letter XXVII

... I now come to the condition of agriculture and of the class dependent on it; and with reference to this subject I find more diversity of circumstances prevailing in Cumberland than in any other case which has yet come under my notice.... Farms in this county are extremely various in size; but the proportion of those of 500 acres or upwards is very small, though in the lake district a farmer may have moorland pasture almost ad lib., to add to his tilled land. There is a class of landowners in this country, who, if not absolutely peculiar to it, far exceed in number and relative importance the ordinary proportion; I allude to the small proprietors or yeomanry, who are here known by the appellation of "statesmen", that is, men of estate. Most of these occupy estates, worth from ten to fifty pounds a year, either freehold, or held of the lord of the manor by customary tenure. It is said that this class has been decreasing in numbers during the last seventy years; they are still estimated, however, at nearly 7,000. There is also a large class of small farmers not proprietors, whose holdings are from forty to 100 acres. ...

... The numerous class of small proprietors and tenants, alluded to above, in some degree restricts the employment of agricultural labourers in this county; the extra labour required on a small farm, beyond that of the occupier and his family, being inconsiderable—at least upon the very imperfect system of culture which universally obtains in such cases, except where the tenant is a man of ample means, who keeps the farm chiefly as an amusement or hobby. Generally, in this county, the labourers are lodged in or near the farm-steading, where they are boarded also, is in a large proportion of instances the case. Their present wages are from seven to eight guineas for the half-year, which is a reduction on the rates prevailing three or four years back, when they were from nine to ten. The wages of day-labourers are in general two shillings a day, but it is customary in this county for this description of labourers to receive their daily dinner at the farm-house, and in this case the wages given do not exceed one shilling and threepence, and are in many cases not higher than one shilling. The advantages of this arrangement are very questionable inasmuch as, though the labourer may thereby obtain a better dinner than he would eat at home, the amount disposable for household expense, when the man is married and has a family, is materially lessened. This arrangement, however, subsists by the consent of both parties; and I am bound to say that I have not heard it complained of by the one principally concerned.

HERTS. BEDS. HUNTS. CAMBRIDGE

The Straw-plait and Lace-making Districts

Letter XXXIV

... Pillow lace, straw-plaiting, malting, and agriculture form the chief sources of employment for the people. . . .

... The straw-plait affords employment, however, not only to the adults of both sexes, but to children of the most tender age. From the age of three years many of them are sent to the straw-plait school, where they are taught to plait; but in very few of them is there anything else taught. Probably, the worst feature in connection with this kind of work is that it affords employment to children so young. As soon as they are able to earn a few pence during the week by their exertions, they are almost certain to be kept constantly to it, and no opportunity is afforded for giving any education to the children. "I've got", said one woman to me, "four children; three of 'em— that's all but Tommy and he's too young yet—work at the plait, and they can't get much schooling. The three of 'em arnes about three shillings and sixpence a week, and you know that's a great help to poor people like we". . . . So generally is the straw plait carried on in those parts of the counties of Beds and Herts to which allusion has been made, that you can scarcely meet a child walking along the road that is not engaged in plaiting. This employment has the effect of relieving to a great extent the pressure which would otherwise rest upon the agricultural labourer. . . .

... One other great source of employment for the people of Bedfordshire consists in making pillow lace. The trade in this article was once very considerable, but the introduction of machinery, and the extensive manufactures of Nottingham and other places, have reduced it so low that it has ceased, almost as if by common consent, to be considered as a means of subsistence. . . .

... "This is the real British lace, pillow lace—all made with the bobbins; there's not a bit of machinery in the town; no, and I wish there never was none nowhere else—that I do. Now I can't make more than six yards in a week, do all I can; and that is a shilling—that's just what it is. If I can save it till it comes to a dozen yards, I should be able to get $2\frac{1}{2}$d. a yard, that is two shillings and threepence a dozen. They won't give us more than twopence a yard for less than a dozen yards, because they've got to pay something to the lace-joiners, who join the pieces when they're less length than that". . . .

... Another person who lived in a small village, a few miles from Bedford, said that she was usually employed on "point ground edging". "The last time I went", says she, "to Mr. ——, to sell my lace, I saw one poor woman a crying in the streets, and I asked her what was the matter, and she said that when she went to sell her lace Mr. —— had bated her, and had got off six shillings from what she ought to have had fifteen shillings for. He wouldn't give her more than nine shillings for her lot. The poor woman said, she had depended on the money to pay her rent with, but they saw that she had got a good lot of it, and so they made her take what they liked for it. Mr. —— won't turn nothing away; he'll buy anything, if you'll only take his price for it." . . . "There isn't nobody that works at the lace as hasn't got a husband to bring 'em home something as they can live upon what they arnes. The girls as isn't married, and works at the lace, are obliged all of 'em to have something from the parish to keep 'em from starving—or else they're not virtuous, and goes in the streets."

Letter XXXVIII

. . . Throughout the greater part of the counties of Bedford and Cambridge, the average wages may be taken to be about eight shillings for married, and from five shillings to seven shillings for single men. . . .

. . . Upon the farm of the Duke of Bedford, at Woburn, the wages generally given are about nine shillings a week for farm labourers, and from ten shillings to eleven shillings for horsemen. In the fen lands of the Isle of Ely and Huntingdon the wages are about eight shillings per week. In the Linton union, in Cambridgeshire, there are several parishes conspicuous for the wretchedness of the condition of the labourer, and the low rate of wages. In more than one of the parishes in this union the whole of the cottages have been pulled down, and the labourers, being compelled to live in Linton, have to walk considerable distances in going to and returning from their work. There appears to be a great desire on the part of some of the farmers to avoid giving the labourer more work than is absolutely necessary. I was informed of the case of a man, who was known to be one of the most notorious poachers in the district, and five of the farmers actually subscribed together three shillings a week to assist him in obtaining a livelihood, and to prevent him coming to the board of guardians; they at the same time well knowing that, as they would not give him work, he would make up the deficiency by poaching. "They're screwin', close-fisted, hard set of fellows—that's what the farmers are all about here", said an old labourer to me. . . . Upon one occasion of a meeting of the Board of Guardians, there was a farmer present who was notorious for the small amount of employment which he afforded to the people in his parish. While at the board it so happened that three families came up for relief who belonged to his parish, one with seven, a second with eight, and a third with nine children. What was to be done with them was the question put by the chairman. "Send 'em to the house", was the reply of the farmer. Orders for their admission were accordingly made out by the clerk. The farmer in question was the principal rate-payer in the parish to which the families belonged. "What will be the weekly expense to the parish of these thirty persons?" inquired the chairman of the clerk. "About five pounds a week", was the reply. "My share of the poor-rate won't be less than three pounds of that", said the farmer. "I can get 'em to work for me for eight shillings a week; that'll be only twenty-four shillings a week. Call 'em in."

Letter XXXIX

The injurious effects of insufficient and unsuitable cottage accommodation for the agricultural labourers, referred to in my last letter, are to be seen not only in the wretchedness of their mode of living, but in many other phases of their physical, social and moral condition. ... In the agricultural districts of these counties, cases of incest are of frequent occurrence, and numerous cases have come under my own knowledge in which mother and daughter have claimed for their children one and the same father. ... Speaking to several of the unfortunate females who obtained their livelihood by prostitution, as to the causes which had led them to the adoption of their wretched life, I have been struck with the fact that in many cases they belonged to large families, the members of which were in the habit of sleeping together in one crowded apartment. "I had four sisters and three brothers," said one of them to me, "when I left home; my eldest brother was seventeen; there were but two beds on the floor for the children and we used all to sleep there together, and it is to that more than anything else, that I can trace my ruin." Another said, "there were four of us, not counting father and mother, that had but one room to sleep in, and we had two lodgers with us for two or three weeks in harvest time, and that was the beginning of wrong with me, though I was only fourteen at the time." A third said, "If it hadn't been that we were all forced to undress ourselves before one another, and five of us to sleep in the same room, I do think—though perhaps that wasn't the only reason—that I should not have been leading the life I now am. If there had been no one else sleeping in the same room, I might perhaps have fallen into this way, but I don't think I should have gone wrong so soon". In several other cases similar statements were made, and in more than one the fearful depravity disclosed was such that I will not shock the reader by stating it.

The vast majority of the evils inseparable from the constant attendance on ale-houses and beer-shops are also in a great measure traceable to the comfort-less condition of the labourers' dwellings. It not unfrequently happens that at the close of the day the agricultural labourer betakes himself to the neighbour-ing pot-house, rather than return to his own home. In these places of resort he has a comfortable fire provided for him; he meets with companions for whom, unfortunately, in too many instances, he feels a greater sympathy than for the members of his own family; idle and dissolute habits are contracted, and many a nocturnal depredation upon the hen-roosts and game-preserves is planned within the precincts of such places. ...

... The effluvia from the dung heap, the drain, or the adjoining privy, or the closeness of the room, appear to give them no concern; they will sit, together with their families, unmolested by a stench which, in many cases, has com-pelled me either to apply my handkerchief to my nose, or hastily to retreat to the door for fresh air. In one case I inquired whether the smell of a dung heap, the steam from which was reeking through the windows, was not offensive to them—the answer I obtained was, "Oh, no, we be used to it". There is also too often, an utter want of cleanliness in their dwellings. There are, it is true, exceptional cases in which the places are kept surprisingly clean and neat, but of the vast majority of them it may be said that they are dirty and wretched in the extreme. "It is useless to try to keep the place clean", said one person to me, "the damp comes up through the floor and in at the door, and mucks everything all over as soon as you've made it a bit tidy; it puts you quite out of heart with the miserable hole, and then when it rains, it all comes down the walls—thick, black, mucky stuff, enough to poison you". . . .

. . . The chairman of the Bedford Union, whose statement fully and entirely coincides with all that I have heard and seen among the labourers, says, when speaking of the moral effects upon the labourer of improved tenements, "I have much pleasure in saying that some cases of the kind have come under my own observation, and I consider that the improvement has arisen a good deal from the parties feeling that they are somewhat raised in the scale of society. The man sees his wife and family comfortable, he has a better cottage and garden, he is stimulated to industry, and as he rises in respectability of station, he becomes aware that he has a character to lose. Thus one important point is gained. Having acquired certain advantages, he is anxious to retain and improve them, he strives more to preserve his independence and becomes a member of benefit, medical and clothing societies, and frequently besides this, lays by a certain sum quarterly or half-yearly in the savings bank. Almost always attendant upon these advantages we find the man sending his children to be regularly instructed in a Sunday school, and, where possible, in a day school, and himself and family are more constant in their attendance at some place of worship. I know of more instances than one, where, in consequence of encouragement of the kind above-mentioned to the father of a poor family, the children were regularly sent to school, and there became so much improved in character and learning that they are now filling situations of high respectability (one a confidential clerk in a large mercantile house in London) and are assisting to support their parents in a manner as delightful as it is creditable. A man who comes home to a poor and comfortless hovel, after his day's labour, and sees all miserable around him, has his spirits more often depressed than excited by it. He feels that, do his best, he will be miserable still, and is too apt to fly for a temporary refuge to the ale-house or beer-shop. But give him the means of making himself comfortable by his own industry, and I am convinced by experience that in many cases he will avail himself of it."

Letter XLI

. . . There is, probably, no habit which, in any part of these counties, has taken a deeper root among the labouring classes than has that of opium-eating in the districts where it prevails. This practice is at present confined almost exclusively to the fen districts of the county of Hunts and the Isle of Ely; in the high lands of those parts the custom prevails but to a very limited extent.

The practice is one which has grown up within a comparatively short period —the principal reason which I have heard assigned for it being the great extent to which persons are afflicted with rheumatic affections in the fen districts. In order to procure some little alleviation, numbers of the poor have had recourse to opium as a means of dulling or making them insensible to their pain. From those who had recourse to the drug medically as it were, the practice of taking opium has gradually spread to others who were anxious only to enjoy the temporary stimulant which it afforded.

The trade in opium is one which has increased very rapidly during the last few years, and the price has also fallen very considerable. A few years since, the price of laudanum was sixpence per ounce, and of opium two shillings and threepence. The present price of laudanum is in Ely threepence per ounce, in St. Ives fourpence, of opium, one shilling and fourpence per ounce in Ely, and one shilling and sixpence in Wisbeach. One great cause of the extent to which the drug is used is its comparative cheapness as compared with ardent spirits; the same effects may be obtained, I was informed, from a penny-worth of opium as from a shilling's worth of spirituous liquors. Indeed there is very little spirits drunk in these parts, for the opium appears to have almost entirely superseded it and so deeply has the practice taken root among the people that the drug has come to be considered by them almost as an article of necessity. The more respectable of the labouring classes adopt as much secrecy as possible with respect to opium eating. It is a solitary vice, and is indulged in for the pure love of the effects which the narcotic drug produces. Many of the labourers or their wives, when they go to the shops to purchase it, state "that it is for the pigs, as they fat better when they're kept from crying". One plan very usually adopted by them to avoid its being known what quantity they are in the habit of taking, is that of going to different shops to purchase it. In too many cases, however, all sense of decency is entirely destroyed. While I was in one of the druggists' shops in Ely, a woman came in and asked for a penny-worth of laudanum. The quantity was weighed out, and she drank it off with the utmost unconcern. I was informed that many persons are in the habit of going to the shop, taking their pennyworth of opium or laudanum, and then calling for a pennyworth of alcohol, which is fifty-six degrees above proof; and this they swallow immediately after, to take away, as they say, the taste of the laudanum. The usual quantity taken by elderly women—who are principally the greatest opium-eaters— is thirty grains per day, that being a pennyworth. Many of them, however, will take considerably more than that. . . .

But the consumption of opium is not confined to the adult portion of the population, nor is it merely in its crude state, or as laudanum, that this drug is taken. The quantity of opium which is consumed in the shape of Godfrey's Cordial is incredible. "How many ounces of Godfrey do I sell in a week? Ask how many gallons of it are sold", said a druggist with whom I was conversing on the subject; "it is sold by the pailful about here". "If you want to reduce the rate of infant mortality in Ely", said another druggist, "you must make a common sewer to drain the place of Godfrey and paregoric, which are given to the little creatures to a frightful extent. . . .

When under the influence of this mixture, the children lie in a perfectly torpid state for hours together. "The young 'uns all lay about on the floor", said one woman to me who was in the habit of dosing her children with it, "like dead 'uns, and there's no bother with 'em. When they cry we gives 'em a little of it—p'raps half a spoonful, and that quiets 'em; sometimes when they're hungry, and the victuals isn't ready for 'em, we gives 'em a drop too".

A sufficient dose of Godfrey for a child of three or six months old "to begin with", would be, I was told, "about fifteen minims". About harvest time the quantity of this mixture which is sold is considerably more than at any other season of the year; it is then given to the children to keep them quiet while the parents are at work, many of whom are in the habit of leaving a number of children in the care of some person while they are absent. "I always take care", said a young girl of about fourteen, who had been employed on several occasions to take charge of a number of children in the absence of their parents, "that they leave me plenty of 'stuff', 'cause then, when they begins to cry, or gets troublesome, I shoves some of it in their mouths, and that stops 'em." During the period of gleaning the quantity sold is even greater than during the time of the harvest, as every person who is able to glean is anxious to get out into the fields. The children are then in many cases left without any person in charge of them, a sufficient quantity being given by the parents to keep them in a state of stupor till they return home. It appears that the habit, once commenced with children, is rarely or never discontinued; the moment the child recovers from its temporary stupefaction, it feels uneasy, and begins to cry; recourse is again had to the deleterious compound—the state of torpor again succeeds, to be followed again by the same treatment to the almost total neglect of proper and nourishing diet—till nature can bear up no longer against the barbarous practice. "It is my firm belief", said a medical gentleman of St. Ives, "that hundreds of children are killed in this district by the quantities of opium, which are administered to them in the shape of Godfrey's and other cordials." The practice of taking the drug is one that is never adopted by the Irish labourers who arrive in these parts to assist in the harvest. Several of the druggists informed me that they never remembered a single instance in which Irish labourers had purchased either opium, laudanum, paregoric, or "Godfrey"—but of tobacco they consumed large quantities.

Another practice, which almost by necessity in many cases exists among the labourers, is that of frequent attendance at the beer-shop. Vast numbers of them take their meals in the middle of the day in these places, in consequence of the great distance which they would have to walk to their own homes. But in addition to those who resort to the beer-shops to have their meals, there are great numbers who have not the excuse of distance from their dwellings to account for their very frequent attendance at such places.

As showing the extent to which attendance at the beer-shop is indulged in by the labourers, I may state that in the county of Bedford, which consists of 120 parishes, while there are 188 butchers' shops, and 259 bakers, there are not less than 883 public-houses and beer-shops. The Chaplain of the Bedford County Gaol says "To drunkenness and attendance at the beer-shop, directly or indirectly, I may safely say crime, in a great measure, in the county, owes its origin. Destitution, no doubt, occasionally leads to theft and fraud. But to what is the destitution in too many cases owing? Generally to drunkenness. This conclusion has been drawn from the statements of the prisoners themselves, and the vast number of public-houses and beer-shops throughout the county go to confirm it."

There exists, also, among the labourers a very general propensity to theft, when employed in the barns of their employers. For years past they have been in the almost constant habit of taking home with them at night in their pockets, or in small baskets, small quantities of wheat or barley. They seem to imagine that they have obtained a prescriptive right to these pilferings, and many a labourer who has been punished for the theft has indulged in the same offence for several years. It was informed of the case of one labourer, who had been punished for it, who stated that he had been in the constant practice of taking home small quantities of grain for the last twenty years; and that he always considered this as his perquisite. Many of the labourers consider it as almost amounting to a case of hardship, when a farmer, who happens to have his suspicions aroused, causes the men to be watched and apprehended by the police. They think that if he were to give his men fair warning of his intention not to allow such proceedings, it would have the effect of putting a stop to the practice. Sack stealing, also, is another custom of which the farmers complain sadly. Several who have spoken to me, have stated that they lose every year from forty to fifty sacks. These articles, it appears, are almost universally taken by the labourers, either for the purpose of coverings for their beds, or for nailing up, to keep the wind out of their cottages. How far these practices might be put a stop to by a more liberal treatment of the labourers, and by improvements in their dwellings, is a question which might not be unworthy of the consideration of the employers of labour. . . .

. . . With the class of professional beggars, the counties of Hertford and Cambridge are almost overrun; and to the absence of a constabulary force in the county of Cambridge, is, no doubt, mainly to be attributed the large number of beggars who resort thither; and the proximity of Hertford to the metropolis may probably account in some measure for the large number in that county. At Cambridge, during term time, the beggars usually reap a rich harvest; indeed it is, in their vernacular, "a crack town". It is the head quarters for the beggars in the Midland and surrounding districts. It is also the grand centre for the Irish who come over to this country as reapers . . . There are in the town of Cambridge thirteen lodging-houses, to which more or fewer of this class of persons resort at the close of the day; but there is one in particular, well known to every beggar within the British seas. Among the other lodging-houses of the town which I visited, was this favoured place of resort, or "boozing ken" of the professional mendicant.

The room in which the "company" were assembled might be, from its position, justly designated a cellar. A descent of about a dozen steps from the level of the ground conducted you to a small passage, having upon one side a door leading to the beer-cellar, which contained about twenty-four barrels of beer. The other door opened into a room of about 14 feet by 20, in which were assembled a group of the most miscellaneous characters which it could be supposed possible to collect together in one focus. There were 46 persons in all—men, women, and children of all ages. There was the member of the Spanish Legion, whose services were still unrequited by the Government for whom he would tell you he had fought; there were three who were on the "sea lurk;" two decent-looking artisans, with clean white shirts, their unfortunate "companions in distress, and their dear children, who had done nothing to deserve it". Close by stood a widow woman, who had been "trying to get a bit of bread by the sale of tattens and driz—(threads and tapes), and her companion, who went the same rounds, with her, with a huge bandage round his head, and his arm in a sling, both of which were now laid aside. He had now recovered from "the fall which he received when engaged in building the new Houses of Parliament". There were the shoeless, the ragged, the dirty, the clean, the lame, and even the blind, young and old—one and all in their 'varied characters suited to call forth sympathy or to impose upon the charitable and humane . . . . .

. . . Among those present were one or more of each branch of the begging professions. There were "high-flyers", "slummers", "nakes", "dreary nakes", "shallow go nakers", "sea lurks", "croakers", "sucaks", "tattens and drizzers", "common frizzlers", "dreary grizzlers", "dance bloaks", and others, to one or more of each of which class I was introduced by a friend who accompanied me. From several of them I succeeded in obtaining some account of their mode of life. The first to which I will refer was the statement of an Irishman, whose appearance was altogether deplorable. He had no shirt, and his breast was almost entirely uncovered; as for his coat, it is an abuse of words to call the rags that hung together on him a coat; his knees protruded through his trowsers, which hung in fringed tatters from below his knees, and his feet were, of course, bare. "Sure then", said he, "it's thirty years I've been on the cadge, and it's a long day, too. I never had a home of my own since I came to this counthry. I have slept in the boozing-kens in the counthry, many's the time; maybe it's been in the prison I have, and in the workhouse, bad luck to 'em. It's five days since I came to Cambridge; last week I made fourteen shillings but there was two days that I didn't go out, it was so cold. To-day I only got 10½d. and some grub (victuals). Sometimes I work a little in the summer at raping, but not much; in the winter I always 'pad the hoof'. Sure it's little money we'd get if it wasn't for that, and it's better than staleing any day—they'd transport a man for that—but they only 'lumber' you for a moon (a month's imprisonment) for t'other. I always work the 'nake', sometimes the 'dreary nake' (a naker is one who begs in a ragged or ill-clothed condition; 'a dreary naker' being one who carries on his operations without shoes or stockings, and this is called 'padding the hoof', or 'padding it on the shallows'). I never did nothing with a 'slum' in my life, since I haven't the larning for that. When I beg I tells the people anything that comes in my mouth. 'Sure it's a cowld day, yer honner,' I says sometimes; 'For the love of God give us a thriffle, sometimes.' When I can make ten or fifteen shillings a week I'm satisfied. One good gintleman gave me ten shillings a few days ago, another gave me seven shillings and sixpence and one gintelman heaved a savereign out of his carriage and said 'There, Pat, go and buy a coat'. Indeed I didn't buy one, for this one does very well, but I wouldn't tell the gintleman so. Sure, we're every bit as honest among ourselves as the rich folks are. I come from Tuam, in county Galway; I don't know how many times I've been 'jigged'; the last I had was two 'moons". The last four days I was on the cadge I made ten shillings and ninepence. I got a lump of bread to-day, but its too hard for an ould man like me to ate; sure I put it in the scran-pot when I don't want it, and the pigs gets it". . . .

. . . After I had remained in this apartment some time, and the dinners and suppers of the various parties had been disposed of, it was suggested that they should have some singing. Accordingly a number of songs were sung, many of which, by a more select audience, might be considered objectionable; but the more obvious and indecorous the allusions, the more general were the marks of approbation of the company, males as well as females. On another occasion nearly the whole of the evening was occupied by the trial of a prisoner for murder—the company having formed themselves into a criminal court for that purpose. Seated in an elevated position on one of the tables sat the judge; he had on a woman's red cloak, a white collar turned over about his neck, an old grey Welsh wig upon his head, and a pair of woman's duffs tied round his wrists. There was a small table with writing materials before his lordship, who conducted himself throughout with all the gravity peculiar to the high and important station which he filled. The prisoner was arraigned at the foot of the table, but was accommodated with a stool. On each side of the table sat the learned counsel, each of whom was robed in a woman's black dress, with white collars round their necks. On one side of the room sat the twelve jurors; opposite to them were the forms for the accommodation of those present who represented the public. The door was guarded by one who acted as policeman, and there was an usher of the court, with a wand of considerable dimensions, who kept silence while the proceedings were going on. I did not hear the opening address of the counsel for the prosecution, but from what I could gather, the unfortunate transaction arose out of a quarrel at a beer-shop. The prisoner and the deceased had been engaged in a quarrel, they had both left the house together, and the last time the deceased was seen alive was in the company of the prisoner. Witnesses were called who deposed to these facts, and the case for the prosecution being closed, several witnesses were called for the defence, who stated that the witnesses previously called were not to be believed on their oath. A policeman proved the former convictions of two of them. A witness who represented himself as a Jew, and who refused to be sworn as a Christian, and was directed to take the oath as a Jew, also gave it as his opinion that others of the witnesses were undeserving of credit. The prisoner's counsel, "oppressed with the importance of his duties, and having the life of a fellow-creature placed in his hands", pointed out with considerable ability several discrepancies in the evidence, dwelt at some length on the "hardship of hanging a fellow on merely circumstantial evidence", and concluded by impressing on the minds of the jury, "the saying of a learned judge, which could not be too often repeated in a criminal court, that it was better for a hundred guilty men to escape than for one innocent soul, like his client, to be hanged". The counsel for the prosecution having addressed the jury, the judge, in the mose solemn manner, proceeded to charge the jury— pointed out discrepancies in the evidence, and several contradictions in the statements of the witnesses—told them to weigh well the evidence on both sides, and if they had a doubt upon their own minds "to be sure to give it in favour of the prisoner;" and he expressed his "perfect concurrence in what had fallen from his 'learned brother' as to the injustice and hardship of hanging an innocent man". The jury, after some consultation, found the prisoner guilty. The judge put on the black cap, and passed sentence upon him according to the regular form. The court broke up, and preparations were immediately made for carrying the sentence into execution. The crowd of gazers to witness the execution were assembled in the lower end of the room— the procession was formed in the adjoining beer cellar—the clergyman, the sheriff, the hangman, and other officials were all represented—the culprit was led to a chair upon which he stood—the rope was adjusted and made fast to a hook in the ceiling. Everything was in readiness for drawing away the chair from under the man, when a loud knocking was heard at the door, and a messenger arrived with a reprieve, the announcement of which was received with rapturous applause, and the mock tragedy, with all its revolting features, ended by an order for an abundant supply of warm ale and gin, and other beverages.

COUNTIES OF NORTHAMPTON LEICESTER RUTLAND NOTTINGHAM AND DERBY

The Boot and Shoemakers of Northampton

Letter XLV

... The leather having gone through its various stages at the currier's passes into the hands of the shoe manufacturers or factors, where the services of a class of persons called "clickers or cutters" are next required. Their duties consist in "casting", or cutting up the skins of leather into pieces of various sizes for the shoemakers. The earnings of the "clickers" vary in some of the establishments from twelve shillings to eighteen shillings per week, the work-men usually being employed on the premises of the manufacturers. The leather having been cut into the required shapes and sizes, undergoes the process of "blocking".... Blocking is almost always done at the house of the workpeople.

After blocking, the next stage is that of "closing". The persons employed in this department are generally very young, the better description of work requiring excellent eyesight. The labour is particularly trying to the eyes, and impairs the eyesight very greatly. Lads and young men are frequently com-pelled to wear spectacles of great magnifying power, and I was informed of several cases where the workmen "used two pair of spectacles at once". Children are put to this kind of work at a very early age, some of the "closures" employing great numbers of them. The reason the children are more generally sent to the "closing" than to the "making up" branch is that they will be "out of hand sooner" at the one than at the other. At many of the closers they kept what is called "a factory of children". "At these places," said a shoemaker to me, "the poor little creatures go to work, many of 'em as early as four years old. They are so afraid of being late that they'll jump out of bed at four or five o'clock and run to look at the church clock. They give the poor little children very little wages, too—very often not more than a shilling a week—although they get through a deal of light kind of work in the day; and as they give 'em so little for their work, they are able to compete with other men, who won't have anything to do with the factory plan, but who work single-handed." The children do not receive anything for the first six months; after that period they received from one to two shillings per week, and gradually rise to eight shillings. One young man informed me that he was eight years at work before he got as high as seven shillings and sixpence per week, and he was then seventeen years of age.

The first closer that I called upon was employed in closing "best patent

Wellingtons, morocco legs and patent frouts;" for which he would receive four shillings per pair; for short Wellingtons, of the same description, the price paid was three shillings. Out of the sum which he received for closing the best patent Wellingtons, done in white silk, he would have to find the silk. It would take him and his wife "fourteen hours, without any 'hobbling' to close a pair of boots of this sort, such as the aristocracy appeared at in their balls". "I don't think they know," said he, "all the sweat and blood which is spent upon their fine boots—they don't know all the aching heads and aching hearts endured by those whose fingers perform the labour for them; if they did, they would soon make the Legislature tell a different tale from what it has ever done.". . . This person complained very bitterly of the system pursued by the manufacturers, of limiting the time for receiving and giving out work to the hours of nine and ten in the morning. The workmen are, he said, obliged to attend at that hour to take in their work, and receive other work in return. If they are after that time, they are not able to get any work for that day; they are locked out sometimes to the half-minute; and even when punctual, they not unfrequently have to wait a couple of hours before they can obtain their supply of work. I was informed, however, by several of the manufacturers, that it was absolutely indispensable that some certain time in the day should be fixed for taking in and giving out work, and that no more delay took place than could be expected where so large a number of workpeople were to be attended to. . . .
. . . The leather having gone through these several stages of "blocking and closing", is now ready for the maker. The first person of this class upon whom I called was employed in making Wellingtons. His statement was as follows: "The usual mode of giving out the work to the men is this—they give you out the stuff for half-a-dozen pair, that is for the bottoms, and then, when they are at all slack, they will give you out the tops, one pair at a time, and make you go and dance upon 'em every time you want 'stuff'. Then, when they're at all slack they have a custom of changing nearly all their hands—at least two thirds of them are discharged and fresh ones taken on; this is done to see if they can't get some superior article produced to what was produced before by those who were employed because it is thought that, when men get on fresh, they will do their best to keep their situations. This is a system that ought to be put a stop to, for in my opinion, if it is not, it will not only be the ruin of Northampton but of all England. There is no such thing as middle-men in our trade. We get the work direct from the manufacturers and take it home to them. Some time since they used to make you take some of the wages out in bread or flour or such like, but it is only with the smaller and lower manufacturers that that plan is adopted now."

Letter XLVI

A practice, which during the last few years has sprung up in connection with the boot and shoe trade of Northampton, is very generally complained of by the numerous class of artisans employed in that trade, and is one which, if not checked, would, I was informed, prove the ruin "not only of Northampton, but of the whole country". In this case, at all events, it is not the large capitalists of whom they complain, but persons of their own condition, who, by their petty and oppressive conduct, prove the truth of the adage that "servants generally make bad masters". It appears that a somewhat numerous class among the shoemakers of Northampton, who, either from drunken and disorderly habits, or from inability properly to perform their work, have been refused employment at the principal manufacturers of the town, have set up for themselves as small masters and employers of labour; and, encouraged in too many instances by the less respectable of the manufacturers and boot vendors of Northampton and London, they have introduced into the town, though not exactly in the same mode, all the mischiefs and injustice of the sweating system which exists in connection with the slop-sellers of the metropolis. The evils thus introduced among the shoemakers of the town are not, however, solely attributable to members of their own craft; but in a great number of cases these petty masters know nothing whatever of the trade, their occupation being that of keepers of small provision and chandlery shops, who endeavour to eke out their weekly profits by the high prices which their unfortunate workmen pay for the provisions which they are virtually compelled to purchase of them. These small tradesmen are in the habit of getting the work done at prices less than those usually paid by the respectable manufacturers; and, unfortunately, the helpless condition of many of the shoemakers, owing to their intemperate and improvident habits, makes them fall an easy prey to the rapacity of this class of persons, for, in the first moment of slackness of trade among the manufacturers, having no resources whatever upon which to fall back, they eagerly catch at anything in the shape of employment, heedless of the remuneration which they may receive, or of the injury which they thus inflict upon their more sober and industrious brethren. These small and unprincipled tradesmen, too, finding that there is then an abundance of labour in the market, regardless of the ability of the workman, take the opportunity of grinding all applicants for work down to the lowest possible scale. The position in which such a person is placed, between the factor on the one hand who purchases his articles, and the workman on the other who produces them, renders it absolutely necessary for him, if he would continue to carry on his trade, to get the work done at the lowest price; and thus, upon the producer, as is too often the case, falls the greatest and the most crushing part of the burden. . . .

. . . "There are also some men", said one of the shoemakers to me, "who cannot get work from the manufacturers, and who will get a bit of leather and make two or three pairs of boots and sell them then and there for ready money. They will often sell Wellington boots right out for six shillings and sixpence a pair to the manufacturers, all ready for the feet; aye, and some of the boots are good ones too. I could buy some made with really good leather and French town lasts for that price. This practice prevails to a great extent throughout the town, and causes great injury to the regular trade; for the manufacturers are always ready to buy them, because it saves them the trouble of giving out the work, and they can get 'em done cheaper too that way. Another shoemaker, speaking upon the same subject, said "Sometimes they get two or three men to help 'em to make the boots, and so make up the boots and shoes at lower prices than the regular employer can get them made for.

Some of them will buy the split kip and offal leather, get the blocking, closing, and everything done, and sell a pair of Bluchers for 2s 6d or Clarences for 3s 6d and Wellington boots they will get up and sell as low as 6s. The large manufacturers besides get an extra profit on the leather which they sell, as the workman has to take a good part of his charge for the boots out in that material. The work which is got up in this way is of the worst description, and anything does in the shape of leather, for they are only meant for the cheap London markets. Mr. —— and Mr. —— of London, send down their leather, and get nearly all their stock made up in this way.". . .

. . . The physical condition of the shoemakers in the country parts is far superior to that of those who reside in Northampton and the larger towns. They have nearly all of them small plots of ground, in which they spend some portion of their time, and during the harvest great numbers of them go out to work in the fields. They are also, generally speaking, more healthy, sober and contented than the shoemakers of the larger towns.

It is almost impossible to convey an adequate idea of the utter wretchedness and dirty appearance of the places in the larger towns in which many of the shoemakers live and carry on their operations. There is a great resemblance throughout the whole of them; and, although the details may differ in most cases, a description of one or two of them will suffice for all. On opening the door, which almost invariably leads directly into the room, the first thing that meets the eye is a quilt or coverlid, rarely clean and mostly ragged, which is stretched across that portion of the room adjoining the door. Arriving at the termination of this drapery, and looking round on the other side, will be seen, sitting in the recess between the window and the chimney, upon a low stool, an individual with a face as black as the presence of dirt and a long absence of soap and water can make it. It is, however, but a small portion of the face of this personage that can be seen; his hair generally covers his forehead, or hangs down the sides of his face, when not confined, as in some cases it is, by a band which is worn round the head: his chin, upper lip, and the lower part of his cheeks are almost completely concealed beneath the exuberance of his beard and mustachios, the crop of which is seldom, if ever, disturbed more than once a week; indeed several whom I saw had a three weeks' growth. Among the shoemakers it will be found, almost as a general rule, that where there is an excessive development of beard, there will be found a corresponding diminution in the completeness of the attire. The elbows protrude out of the coat, the knees through the trowsers and leather apron, and the toes out of the boots. The remaining parts of the man's person are covered with a quantity of rags, which originally were of divers colours, but which, through the constant application of grease, paste, ink, heelball, and other articles, which are included under the head of "grindery", have in some cases become a polished jet, and in others a dirty black, only exceeded in intensity of dye by the flesh of the wearer. By the side of this lugubrious specimen of humanity will be found his small table, containing his various articles of grindery and tools—a miscellaneous collection, consisting of broken awls, pieces of glass, blades of knives, pieces of brown wax, ends of candles, small brads, paste, bristles, wax-ends, and other articles of a similar kind,

which constitute the stock of a working shoemaker. Thus equipped, the son of
Crispin, with his head bent low over his work—giving him the appearance
of a person doubled up into the smallest possible compass—and a pair of
huge spectacles before his eyes, pursues his avocation, accompanying the
blows of his hammer by some fragment of a song which he picked up at the
last meeting of his "free and easy" or which he may have under rehearsal for
one of those vocal entertainments in which the genius of the great body of
Northampton shoemakers delights to revel. On the other side of the fire-place,
if he is a married man, will frequently be seen a female, who, in point of
cleanliness and tidiness, has no pretensions to the title of his "better half". She
will be found at work either at the "closing" or "binding". If not engaged in
either of those occupations, she will most likely be employed in washing a few
articles of clothing, in a pan or small tub, which is mostly placed upon a chair,
or upon the table, amid the articles of the breakfast service which have not
yet been removed, even though it be past noon. Indeed, so highly do many
of the shoemakers' wives appear to value time, that, in order to avoid any
unnecessary waste of that precious commodity, the tea and dinner services are
usually allowed to remain from one meal to another. If there are any children
at home, they will be certain to be found—whether male or female—occupied
in some department of the shoe trade; and it is scarcely necessary to state that,
in point of cleanliness and decency of attire, their condition is not many degrees
superior to that of their parents. The apartments of the shoemakers may
generally be classed under two heads—they are either scantily furnished, or
filled with the wrecks of broken furniture. Under the former class, an inventory
of the goods and chattels would include an old small round table, a couple of
chairs, and, if there are children, perhaps, as many stools as there are
occupants for them. In several instances that came under my notice there was
no table—the stool or table containing the tools and various articles of
grindery being used as the dining-table of the family, and an old teaboard
placed upon a chair containing the articles of crockery used at the meals.
In one place a dish with some potatoes and turnips was placed upon the floor,
the wife and chidlren sitting round, eating out of the dish with spoons, and
the father taking his portion of the meal in his usual place in the chimney
recess. A great proportion of the homes of this class of workmen bear witness
to the dissipated habits of their occupiers, and, in the ruinous condition of the
furniture, tell too plainly that the owners were "quarrelsome when in their
cups". In such places as these the chairs are without bottoms, and many
without backs; the face of the Dutch clock in the corner is broken, the looking-
glass on the wall contains about a tithe of its original quantity, and portions
of its frame are gone. Shakespeare and Milton are headless as they stand
upon the mantel-piece; the fragments of crockery which abound in the place
are varied in their character, and in the amount of injuries which they may
have sustained, but all have suffered more or less in these "clashes of arms",
which, upon various occasions, have disturbed the propriety of peaceful
neighbours and called for the intervention of the police.

There are, however, to be found among the shoemakers of Northampton,
cases which contrast most favourably with the condition of many of their
fellow labourers. Where temperate and provident habits have been formed,

there the home of the shoemaker will be found to present features of domestic comfort, for which we may search in vain the dwellings of his improvident and intemperate neighbour. In such a place will be found a small collection of books—thumb-worn, it is true, and not so clean, perhaps, as many a more fastidious person might desire, but showing that their contents have been well perused. Indeed, the whole appearance presents a scene of order and decency, as complete and as perfect as could be expected under the circumstances in which he is placed.

Politics generally run somewhat high among the great body of the shoemakers. In times of political excitement, if accompanied by slackness in trade, the shoemakers generally occupy a prominent position, "We are the most radicallest set of fellows, and Northampton is the most radicallest town in the kingdom", said one of the craft to me. Of cheap literature also they are great patrons, about two hundred dozen of penny weekly publications being usually sold in the town during the week. It is one of the great boasts of the shoemakers that their trade has produced more celebrated characters than any other trade in existence. Whitier, the celebrated American shoemaker-poet, has written some verses which are particularly popular with the shoemakers. One person upon whom I called, when enlightening me upon the antiquity and mysteries of the craft, and the number of its celebrated heroes, recited, with evident feeling, the following lines, as near as I was enabled to collect them :

> Let foplins sneer, let fools deride,
>   We heed no idle scorner;
> Free hands and hearts are still our price,
>   And duty done our honour.
> We dare to trust for honest fame
>   The jury time empanels,
> And leave to truth each noble name
>   Which glorifies our annals.
>
> Thy songs, Hans Sach! are living yet
>   In strong and hearty German.
> And Bloomfield's lay, and Gifford's art,
>   And the rare good sense of Sherman.
> Still from his book a mystic seer
>   The soul of Behmen teaches,
> And England's priestcraft shakes to hear
>   Of Fox's leathern breeches.

The principal source of amusement to the shoemakers appears to be the "Free and Easy", or the "select concerts", usually held at some public-house or beer-shop. The prices of admission to these species of entertainment usually range from twopence to threepence, for which sum a ticket is usually given, by virtue of which, in addition to the right of admission, the holder becomes possessed of a title to "refreshments during the evening". Each person present at the Free and Easy, is expected to "favour the company with a song" when called upon by the chairman for the time being to do so, and the great point of ambition with those who frequent these convivial meetings is "to give something new". The demand which this species of emulation among them produces for "Vocal Gems", "Minstrel's Companions", and a host of other cheap song books is very considerable. One bookseller in the town informed me that he sold on an average about twenty dozen of penny and two-penny song-books in the week. A demand has lately sprung up for a sixpenny song-book, on the ground of its containing more new songs than the cheaper editions; and he who is disposed to invest sixpence may be almost certain of finding something new with which he can astonish at the next meeting of his less fortunate compeers. I was informed by one of the shoemakers that it not infrequently happened that, after the vocalist had spent a week or more in the rehearsal of "something new", a more fortunate competitor for the honours of the club obtained the precedence in point of time, "and took the identical song out of his mouth". Actuated by a laudable desire to discharge the important duties of his office impartially, the chairman, upon such occasions, decides upon "hearing both sides"; and the company are thus afforded an opportunity of pronouncing an opinion upon the merits of the respective parties.

The material condition of the shoemakers might be equal to that of any body of operatives in the kingdom if they only paid a little more regard to their own best interests. The money which they spend in drink, and the time which they uniformly waste in each week, would go far to increase their comforts and to mitigate their distress. Monday is a day which they invariably devote to idleness and to the honour of their tutelary saint; and many a worshipper of St. Monday, after having spent the night at the station-house, loses the following day in explaining to the authorities the cause, and paying the penalty, of his intemperance or riot. The number of shoemakers taken by the police during the year ending December 31, 1849, on charges of being "drunk" and "drunk and disorderly" in the town of Northampton, was 211; of these a proportion of three out of seven were taken on Monday nights. The total number of charges of all sorts in the town of Northampton for the same period was 583. Deducting from these the number of "drunk" and "drunk and disorderly", the number remaining for other offences would be 372; and of these the greater number was furnished by shoemakers, and consisted mainly of charges arising out of drunkenness, such as assaults, embezzling of leather and boots, and other minor offences.

Letter XLVII

Rutland is the smallest of all the English counties, its area being but 97,500 acres, and its population amounting only to 21,302. With the exception of a small manufacture of parchment and glue at Barrowden, there are no manufacturers carried on within it, the employment of the people being exclusively agricultural. . . .

. . . Probably there is no county in England in which the injurious effects of the present law of settlement are more severely felt. The fact of the county being so purely agricultural in its character, and there being no manufactures upon which the labourers can fall back, render more striking than they would otherwise be the mischiefs produced by the operation, or rather the abuse, of the present law. It is impossible to describe the injuries inflicted upon the agricultural labourer under the present law of settlement. The due cultivation of the land is impeded by the restrictions which it places upon labour. The difficulties thrown in the way of obtaining labour prevents the application of capital for the improvement of the land, and the consequent employment of the labourer. By increasing the expenses connected with the relief of the poor, it tends to swell the amount of poor rates, places an additional burden upon the farmer, and in the same proportion deprives him of the power of employing a fair amount of labour. The social and moral evils caused by the influx of large numbers of labourers into towns and villages, where there is no sufficient accommodation for them, and where they are compelled to crowd together in large numbers, are not the least of the evils produced by the existing law. The scenes of contention and confusion continually arising in this and in the other counties which I have visited, and which, in accompanying the relieving officer in his visits, I have had frequent occasions of witnessing, are almost impossible to describe. Most undignified contests ensue between the representative of the authorities and the recipients of the relief, as to the parish to which they belong, and from their heap of straw or wretched sick-beds, they not unfrequently vent the most horrid curses upon the administrators of the law. In the five counties the names of which stand at the head of this letter, there are not less than 1,284 parishes; and the labourer has to contend, hopelessly and unfriended, against the constant manoeuvres of interested parties in these parishes who strain every nerve, and have recourse to every expedient, to send him over the country in quest of a home and a settlement. While the number of parishes is 1,284, the number of unions, however, is only forty-four. The labourer thus has, in these parishes, 1,284 enemies, who have an interest more or less in banishing, or otherwise placing obstacles in the way of his comfort and happiness. The substitution of union for parochial rating and chargeability, such as exists in one of the unions of Norfolk, would in these counties, if not entirely remedy this state of things, at least reduce the number of the conflicting interests against which the labourer has to contend in the proportion of 1,284 to forty-four. "So long", said a gentleman to me, who has been a county magistrate upwards of twenty years, and had had considerable experience in the working of the poor law, "as this parochial chargeability exists, and the power of removing English poor is vested in the parties whose interest it is to remove and banish them from their homes; the scenes of suffering and distress which have been constantly brought under your notice in these counties will continue to exist." The mode in which the labourer most usually suffers from this law is by landowners, or cottage proprietors, getting the poor man out of his dwelling and out of the parish before the expiration of the five years which would give him a legal settlement, if not already possessed of one. Having thus driven, the poor man out of the parish, and being relieved from all fear of his becoming a burden upon them, they will still, if they have need of his services, give him employment and in order to perform which he will have to walk frequently very long distances. There are also many of the landowners who will not allow any increase in the number of cottages upon their estates, and others who destroy what few do really exist, and others who, more slowly, but not less effectually, accomplish the object of clearing their estates of labourers and paupers, by allowing all their cottages to sink into decay, without making the least exertion to prevent their ruin, and when, through age and neglect, the wretched hovels fall down, no new ones are erected in their stead.

One labourer, whose cottage had been pulled down in an adjoining parish, had been forced to seek a residence in Oakham, for which he was compelled to pay £8 a year; and as he could not get employment out of the parish from which he had been evicted, he was, at the time of my visit, compelled to walk four miles every day to his work. Another poor man, in the same union, was receiving out-door relief, on account of the large number of his family, and of his bad state of health, brought on by not having, as the medical officer informed me "adequate support to enable him to go through the labour which he had to perform; he lived at a distance of four miles from his work, not being able to procure a residence nearer. He was driven out of his parish, as a considerable number of other labourers were, in consequence of the reduction of the number of tenements; a system which is still carried on to a great extent by the landlords, in order to prevent, as much as possible, settlements being effected in their parishes". In the parish of Exton, I was informed that a very large reduction had also been made in the number of cottages, and the expelled inhabitants resorted to Greetham parish, about two miles distant, in which there are a number of small freeholds. This influx of labourers from the adjoining parish is most injurious to the parish of Greetham; "the foreigners", said one of the occupiers, "don't get so regularly employed as the natives and it's quite natural that we should not feel much interest in them; we think that they might as well go a little further as settle upon us". The occupier, however, is not, unfortunately, the only party who has cause to complain of this state of things; neither does the mischief stop with the unfortunate evicted labourer. By causing in one parish a large surplus of labour, an opportunity is afforded to parties so disposed to effect a considerable reduction in the wages of the labourers and thus the selfishness of one or more unprincipled proprietors may produce an incalculable amount of distress; first, by destruction of the health of the labourer consequent upon increased fatigue in going to and returning from work; and, secondly, by a reduction of wages in those districts to which the unfortunate victims of his selfishness are compelled to resort. Another precaution is also taken in the parish of Exton to prevent any additional settlements being made. If the occupier of one of the houses upon the estate has a son or a daughter married, and is unable to obtain a residence in the parish, he is strictly prohibited from taking them to live with him, although he may have ample means of accommodating them. It appears to be an understood rule in this and in some other parishes, that if any person affords an asylum to a new comer, or to a newly-married couple, he is not to receive employment from any farmer in the parish; and if he should succeed in obtaining employment from one over whom control cannot be exercised, he is threatened with ejectment from his dwelling. "The consequence of this conduct", said my informant, "is, that persons thus situated are compelled to live together in any hole or corner they can find, and some of the wretched hovels which they inhabit are so crowded that they are compelled to live together like pigs."

When a man is once expelled from his parish "he might as well", said a gentleman to me, "ask for the teeth of the employers, in other parishes, as for work, the answer invariably given being 'we have enough to do to employ our own labourers—go to your own parish' ". An instance of this came under my knowledge in the case of a labourer who had resided for twenty-six years in the parish of Whissendine, and had been unemployed scarcely a day during that period. The poor man had a large family, and was considered, therefore, a fit object for transference, if possible, to some other parish. He received notice accordingly to quit, left the parish in which he had resided upwards of a quarter of a century, and had to establish his character and obtain employment in some other place, where the employers would no doubt be equally as anxious as the people of Whissendine to avoid the risk of becoming burdened by additional labourers.

Having by this means reduced the amount of pauperism in any given parish, the only expense which will fall upon it will be its portion of the establishment charges, which include the expense of management of the union workhouse, salary to the schoolmaster, and charges for irremovable poor and for vagrants. In the Uppingham Union these establishment charges for the half year ending September 29, 1849 were £453, the total expenditure for the same period being £2,384. The proportion of the establishment charges to be borne by each parish is decided in the following manner: As the total average expenditure for any three years is to the total amount of the establishment charges, so is the average for each particular parish to the amount required, which in many cases is a mere trifle—in one parish in the county of 1,530 acres, and another of 840 acres, not being more than £1. It is in order to obtain this minimum amount of rating in other parishes that so much injury is constantly inflicted upon the honest and industrious labourer.

Another practice adopted by many of the farmers to prevent the poor from obtaining relief, is by promising the applicant that they will give him work upon their farms. The applicant, deceived by this offer, and barred by it from obtaining relief, has one or perhaps two days' work given him, when he is discharged, to do the best he can till the next board day, when he is handed over to the tender mercies of another of the guardians of the poor. "I've been at work", said a poor man to me, "for the last twenty years. My master discharged me, as he said he could not afford to keep me any longer. I've got five children, and I was obliged, for the first time in my life, to go to the board. While I was there, one of 'em said to me that, sooner than I should go to the workhouse and be parted from my family, he would find some job for me. I went to him after the board was over. I asked him what I could do, and he told me that he should be glad to employ me, but he had not got the means. I told him how he had promised to give me work, and at last he gave me a day's threshing and discharged me, so I had one shilling and twopence to live on till next board day; and they've served me two or three times since that." Another poor fellow, who was out of work, and who had occasion to apply for relief, was ordered to receive four loaves of bread, on the ground of illness of his family. Some members of the board, who chanced to be absent when the order was made, heard of this order for relief having been given, and they insisted that work should be found for the man by some of the occupiers in the parish. He applied again the next board day, and was told that he must go and look for work. He stated that he had already been unsuccessful in his application for work. He was referred to several persons, and told to go and inquire for work there, and if he could not get any to return to the board. The poor man had to walk two miles to the residence of the persons mentioned, and when he returned, as might almost have been expected, the meeting of the board had broken up. He contrived to subsist until the next board day, when he again presented himself, and was told by one of the guardians that he should have some work upon his farm. He went accordingly, had two days' work and was discharged. In this manner he had been bandied about through nearly the whole list of guardians, and when, nearly worn out with this treatment, he applied to the relieving officer, who had no power whatever in the matter, he was told that nothing could be done for him so long as work was offered to him.

METROPOLITAN
DISTRICTS

Demonstration of Trade Unionists in Copenhagen Fields
by W. Summers

Letter III

. . . The dock labourers are a striking instance of mere brute force with brute appetites. This class of labour is as unskilled as the power of a hurricane. Mere muscle is all that is needed; hence every human "locomotive" is capable of working there. All that is wanted is the power to move heavy bodies from one place to another. Mr. Stuart Mill tells us that labour in the physical world is always and solely employed in putting objects in motion; and assuredly, if this be the principal end of physical labour, the docks exhibit the perfection of human action. Dock work is precisely the office that every kind of man is fitted to perform, and there we find every kind of man performing it. Those who are unable to live by the occupation to which they have been educated can obtain a living there without any previous training. Hence we find men of every calling labouring at the docks. There are decayed and bankrupt master butchers, master bakers, publicans, grocers, old soldiers, old sailors, Polish refugees, broken-down gentlemen, discharged lawyers' clerks, suspended Government clerks, almsmen, pensioners, servants, thieves—indeed every one who wants a loaf and is willing to work for it. The London Dock is one of the few places in the metropolis where men can get employment without either character or recommendation; so that the labourers employed there are naturally a most incongruous assembly. Each of the docks employs several hundred "hands" to ship and discharge the cargoes of the numerous vessels that enter; and as there are some six or seven such docks attached to the metropolis, it may be imagined how large a number of individuals are dependent on them for their subsistence. At a rough calculation, there must be at least 20,000 souls getting their living by such means. . . .

Letter IV

. . . "It's an ill wind", says the proverb, "that blows nobody any good"; and until I came to investigate the condition of the dock labourer, I could not have believed it possible that near upon two thousand souls, in one place alone, lived, chameleon-like, upon the air; or that an easterly wind, despite the *wise* saw, could deprive so many of bread; . . .

. . . We have shown that the mass of men dependent for their bread upon the business of only one of the docks, are by the shifting of the breeze occasionally deprived in one day of no less than £220—the labourers at the London Docks earning, as a body, near upon £400 today, and tomorrow scarcely £150. . . .

. . . But where the means of subsistence occasionally rise to fifteen shillings a week, and occasionally sink to nothing, it is absurd to look for prudence, economy, or moderation. Regularity of habits are incompatible with irregularity of income—indeed, the very conditions necessary for the formation of any habit whatsoever are, that the act or thing to which we are to become habituated should be repeated at frequent and regular intervals. It is a moral impossibility that the class of labourers who are only occasionally employed

The Docks – Night Scene   from *London, A Pilgrimage*, by Gustave Doré and Blanchard Jerrold, 1872

should be either generally industrious or temperate; both industry and temperance being habits produced by constancy of employment and uniformity of income. Hence, where the greatest fluctuation occurs in the labour, there of course will be the greatest idleness and improvidence; where the greatest want generally is, there we shall find the greatest occasional excess; where, from the uncertainty of the occupation, prudence is most needed, there strange to say, we shall meet with the highest imprudence of all! "Previous to the formation of a canal in the north of Ireland," says Mr. Porter, in the Progress of the Nation, "the men were improvident even to recklessness. Such work as they got before came at uncertain intervals; the wages, insufficient for the comfortable sustenance of their families, were wasted at the whisky-shop, and the men appeared to be sunk in a state of hopeless degradation. From the moment, however, that work was offered to them which was constant in its nature and certain in its duration, men who before had been idle and dissolute were converted into sober, hard-working labourers, and proved themselves kind and careful husbands and fathers; and it is said that, notwithstanding the distribution of several hundred pounds weekly in wages, the whole of which must be considered as so much additional money placed in their hands, the consumption of whisky was absolutely and permanently diminished in the district." . . .

. . . Moreover, with reference to the dock labourers, we have been informed upon unquestionable authority, that some years back there were near upon 220 ships waiting to be discharged in one dock alone; and such was the pressure of business then, that it became necessary to obtain leave of her Majesty's Customs to increase the usual time of daily labour from eight to twelve hours. The men employed therefore earned 50 per cent more than they were in the habit of doing at the briskest times; but so far from the extra amount of wages being devoted to increase the comforts of their homes, it was principally spent in public-houses. The riot and confusion thus created in the neighbourhood were such as had never been known before, and indeed were so general among the workmen, that every respectable person in the immediate vicinity expressed a hope that such a thing as "overtime" would never occur again. . . .

. . . from St. Katharine Docks . . . it should be observed, that no labourer is employed without a previous recommendation; and indeed it is curious to notice the difference in the appearance of the men applying for work at this establishment. They not only have a more decent look, but they seem to be better behaved than any other dock labourers I have yet seen. The "ticket" system here adopted—that is to say, the plan of allowing only such persons to labour within the docks as have been satisfactorily recommended to the company, and furnished with a ticket by them in return this ticket system, says the statement which has been kindly drawn up to expressly for me by the superintendent of the docks "may be worth notice at a time when such efforts are making to improve the condition of the labourers. It gives an identity and locus standi to the men which casual labourers cannot otherwise possess; it connects them with the various grades of officers under whose eyes they labour, prevents favouritism, and leads to their qualifications and conduct being noted and recorded. It also holds before them a reward for intelligence, activity, and good conduct, because the vacancies in the list of 'preferable' labourers which occur during the year are invariably filled in the succeeding January by selecting, upon strict inquiry, the best of the 'extra' ticket labourers—the vacancies among the permanent men being supplied in like manner from the list of 'preferable' labourers, while from the permanent men are appointed the subordinate officers, as markers, samplers,"...

... The business of this establishment is carried on by 35 officers, 105 clerks and apprentices, 135 markers, samplers, and foremen, 250 permanent labourers, 150 preferable ticket labourers, and a number of extra ticket labourers, proportioned to number the amount of work to be done. The average number of labourers employed, "permanent", "preferable" and "extras" is 1,096; the highest number employed on any one day last year was 1,713, and the lowest number 515, so that the extreme fluctuation in the labour appears to be very nearly 1,200 hands....

... As we said before, uncertain employment destroys all habits of prudence; and where there is no prudence, the present affluence cannot be made to provide for the future want. Since it is the very necessity of those who depend upon their daily work for their daily food, that if such work is not to be obtained, they must be either paupers, beggars, or thieves, it cannot be wondered at that the great majority of the population round about the port of London, where work is of such a precarious nature, should consist principally of these three classes. That such was the fact we had been assured by those whose long residence in the neighbourhood had made them acquainted with the condition of the lower classes abounding in the purlieus of Rosemary-lane and the Minories....

Letter IX

... In my present communication I purpose laying before the public the intelligence I have gathered respecting the Stay-stitchers.... Here I procured an introduction to one of the largest wholesale stay-makers in the City, in the hopes of obtaining some account of the trade. But I soon found that my time was wasted in so doing. The gentleman assured me that there were scarcely any stay-stitchers resident in London. He could get his work done so cheap in the agricultural districts, owing to the number of people out of employ in those parts, that he had scarcely any done in town; and indeed he was loth to make the least communication to me on the subject and object of my visit.

Accordingly, finding it useless seeking for any information from the employer in this particular branch of business, I made the best of my way to two work-people, who had been engaged at the business for upwards of twenty years.

The following are their statements:

"I work at stay-stitching. I've worked at it these thirty years; yes, that I have.... It's eighteen year ago since I worked at Portsmouth for a party who is now one of the largest wholesale dealers in London, and all he gave me was two pence a pair.... The party as I spoke of, who is in the City, got on, I know, in this here way. He got a number of the poor people to work for him, and made 'em all put down five shillings each before they had a stitch of work. Before you got work you must raise the five shillings somehow. Well, the five shillings laid in his hands until such time as you wanted to leave him; if you worked for him for ten years it would be in his hands all the time. . . . Well, it was by the number of five shillings that he got from the people in this manner he was able to launch and take a large establishment. He didn't care how many hands he took on so long as he had the five shillings and of course he had the interest of it all. Why, he had as many as three hundred poor people; aye, more. It was said he had as many as seven hundred in his employ working out of doors, and from each he had five shillings, and that was the cause of his uprising—that it certainly was. The downfall of the stay business was all through him and another as lived close to him. They were the first to cut down the prices of the workpeople. They sent the work into the country, to get done in the cheapest way they could, and have always been lowering the prices of the poor people. Thirty years ago I have made as much as seventeen shillings and five pence for my week's work. At the very commonest I could have made from twelve to fourteen shillings a week; and now the most I can make is three shillings and six pence.". . .

The Operative Tailors

Letter XVI

I now give the views of an intelligent Chartist . . .: "I am a Chartist, and did belong to the Chartist Association. My views as to the way in which politics and Government influence the conditions of journeymen tailors are these— Government, by the system now adopted with regard to army and police clothing, forces the honest labouring man, struggling for a fair remuneration for his labour, into a false position, and makes him pay extra taxes to those paid by other branches of the community; they force him into this false position by disposing of Government work at such contract prices that no man can make a decent livelihood at it. One of the best workmen, employed the whole week, cannot earn more than twelve shillings weekly on soldiers' or police-men's clothing, out of which he must pay for all the sewing trimmings, except twist; and having to make the articles at his own place, of course he must find his own fire, candles, &c. Tailors in prison are put to work by the Government at clothes that come into the market to compete with the regular trader employing the regular artisan. The public pays the taxes from which prisons are supported, and the smallest amount, even a penny a pair, is regarded by the authorities as a saving on the cost of prisons; and, indeed, they keep the prisoner at work, if he earns nothing, as the public pays all the expenses of the prison. The working tailor pays *his* quota of the taxes out of which the tailor put to work in prison is maintained, and the prisoner so maintained is made to undersell the very tax-payer who contributes to his support. My opinion is, that if tailors in gaol were not employed by Government, it would leave the market more open to the honourable portion of the trade, and there would be no discreditable employing of a felon—for felons *are* so employed—to diminish the small earnings of an honest man. At Millbank, they teach men to be tailors, who are always employed, while the honest operative is frequently subjected to three month's compulsory idleness; six weeks, towards the close of the year, is a very common period of the tailor's non-employment. I think that if the Charter became law, it would tend to improve our (the journeymen tailors) condition, by giving us a voice in the choice of our representatives, who might be so selected as thoroughly to understand the wants of the working man, and to sympathise with his endeavours for a better education and a better lot altogether."

Letter XVII

I now proceed in due order to give an account of the cheap clothes trade in the East-end of London. . . .
. . . If we wish to see the effect of this system upon the physical, intellectual, and moral character of the workpeople, we should spend a week in visiting the homes of the operative tailors connected with the honourable part of the trade, and those working for the slop-trade. The very dwellings of the people are sufficient to tell you the wide difference between the two classes. In the one you occasionally find small statues of Shakespeare beneath glass shades; in the other all is dirt and foetor. The working tailor's comfortable first-floor at the West-end is redolent with the perfume of the small bunch of violets that stands in a tumbler over the mantelpiece; The sweater's wretched garret is rank with the stench of filth and herrings. The honourable part of the trade are really intelligent artisans, while the slopworkers are generally almost brutified with their incessant toil, wretched pay, miserable food, and filthy homes.

Nor are the shops of the two classes of tradesmen less distinct one from the other. The quiet house of the honourable tailor, with the name inscribed on the window blinds, or on the brass plate on the door, tells you that the proprietor has no wish to compete with or undersell his neighbour. But at the show and slop shops every art and trick that scheming can devise, or avarice suggest, is displayed to attract the notice of the passer-by and filch the customer from another. The quiet, unobtrusive place of business of the old-fashioned tailor is transformed into the flashy palace of the grasping tradesman. Every article in the window is ticketed—the price cut down *to the quick*—books of crude, bald verses are thrust in your hands, or thrown into your carriage window—the panels of every omnibus are plastered with showy placards, telling you how Messrs.—defy competition.

The principal show and slop shop at the East-end is termed the —, and now occupies the ground of several houses. The windows are of rich plate glass—one window, indeed, is nearly thirty feet high—and it is said, that at the time of the attack upon the house by the mob, the damage done by breaking two of the windows amounted to £150. The business is not confined to tailor's work. The proprietors are furriers, hatters, and bootmakers, hosiers, cutlers, trunk-sellers, and milliners. They keep six horses and carts constantly employed in their business, and, I am told, pay above £1,000 a year for gas.

The show-rooms are lighted by large ormolu chandeliers, having thirty-six burners each. . . .

. . . An offer was made to introduce me privately into the workshop of a large show and slop-shop at the East-end of the town, where I might see and interrogate the men at work on the premises; but to this I objected, saying I did not think it fair that I should enter any man's premises with such an object, unknown to him. I was then told that several of the workmen would willingly meet me, and state the price they received for their labour, and the unjust system upon which the establishment was conducted. This statement I said I should be very glad to listen and give publicity to. . . . "We all three of us work at coat-making. . . . We are not always fully employed. We are nearly half our time idle. Hence our earnings are, upon an average, throughout the year, not more than five shililngs and sixpence a week." "Very often I have made only three shillings and fourpence in the week," said one. "That's common enough with us all, I can assure you," said another. "Last week my wages was seven shillings and sixpence," declared one. "I earned six shillings and fourpence," exclaimed the second. "My wages came to nine shillings and twopence. The week before I got six shillings and threepence." "I made seven shillings and ninepence;" and "I, seven shillings or eight shillings, I can't exactly remember which." "This is what we term the best part of our winter season. "The reason why we are so long idle is because more hands than are wanted are kept on the premises, so that in case of a press of work coming in our employers can have it done immediately. Under the day-work system no master tailor had more men on the premises than he could keep continually going; but since the change to the piece-work system, masters make a practice of engaging double the quantity of hands that they have any need for, so that an order may be executed 'at the shortest possible notice,' if requisite." . . . "We all make for ——, the 'poor man's friend', said they, satirically. We used to have to make for him frequently; but now he has shifted to another slop-shop near London bridge, where the same starvation prices are paid. We have also made garments for Sir ——, Sir ——, Alderman ——, Dr. ——, and Dr. ——. We make for several of the aristocracy. We cannot say whom, because the tickets frequently come to us as Lord —— and the Marquess of ——. This could not be a Jew's trick, because the buttons on the liveries had coronets upon them. And again, we know the house is patronised largely by the aristocracy, clergy, and gentry, by the number of court suits and liveries, surplices, regimentals, and ladies' riding-habits that we continually have to make up. There are more clergymen among the customers than any other class, and often we have to work at home upon the Sunday at their clothes, in order to get a living. The customers are mostly ashamed of dealing with this house, for the men who take the clothes to the customers' houses in the cart have directions to pull up at the corner of the street. We had a good proof of the dislike of gentlefolks to have it known that they deal at that shop for their clothes, for when the trowsers buttons were stamped with the name of the firm, we used to have the garments returned daily, to have other buttons put on them; and now the buttons are unstamped. Formerly an operative tailor's wife never helped him. He worked at the shop— brought his weekly wages home—from thirty shillings to thirty-six shillings a week; and his wife attended to her domestic duties, and lived in ease and comfort. This was the case twenty years ago, but since that time prices have come down to such an extent, that now a man's entire family, wife and daughters, all have to work, and, with the whole of the family's work, the weekly income is not one-half what the operative could get by his own labour some years back."...

Letter XIX

The transition from the Artisan to the Labourer is curious in many respects. In passing from the skilled operative of the West-end to the unskilled workman of the Eastern quarter of London, the moral and intellectual change is so great that it seems as if we were in a new land among another race. The artisans are almost to a man red-hot politicians. They are sufficiently educated and thoughtful to have a sense of their importance in the State. It is true they may entertain exaggerated notions of their natural rank and position in the social scale, but at least they have read and reflected, and argued upon the subject, and their opinions are entiled to consideration. The political character and sentiments of the working classes appear to me to be a distinctive feature of the age, and they are a necessary consequence of the dawning intelligence of the mass. As their minds expand they are naturally led to take a more enlarged view of their calling, and to contemplate their labours in relation to the whole framework of society. They begin to view their class not as a mere isolated body of workmen, but as an integral portion of the nation, contributing their quota to the general welfare. If PROPERTY has its duties as well as its rights, LABOUR, on the other hand, they say, has its rights as well as its duties. The artisans of London seem to be generally well informed upon these subjects. That they express their opinions violently, and often savagely, it is my duty to acknowledge; but that they are the unenlightened and unthinking body of people that they are generally considered by those who never go among them, and who see them only as "the dangerous classes", it is my duty, also, to deny. So far as my experience has gone, I am bound to confess that I have found the skilled labourers of the metropolis the very reverse, both morally and intellectually, of what the popular prejudice imagines them.

The unskilled labourers are a different class of people. As yet they are as unpolitical as footmen. Instead of entertaining violently democratic opinions, they appear to have no political opinions whatever; or, if they do possess any, they rather lean towards the maintenance "of things as they are", than towards the ascendancy of the working people. I have lately been investigating the state of the *coal-whippers*, and these reflections are forced upon me by the marked difference in the character and sentiments of the people from those of the operative tailors. Among the latter class there appeared to be a general bias towards the six points of the Charter; but the former were extremely proud of their having turned out to a man on April 10, 1844, and become special constables for the maintenance of "law and order" on the day of the great Chartist "demonstration". As to which of these classes are the better members of State, it is not for me to offer an opinion. I merely assert a social fact. The artisans of the metropolis are intelligent and dissatisfied with their political position; the labourers of London appear to be the reverse; and, in passing from one class to the other, the change is so curious and striking that the phenomenon deserves at least to be recorded in this place.

The labourers, in point of numbers, rank second on the occupation list of the metropolis. The domestic servants, as a body of people, have the first numerical position, being as many as 168,000, while the labourers are less than one-third that number, or 50,000 strong. They, however, are nearly twice as many as the boot and shoe makers, who stand next upon the list, and muster 28,000 individuals among them; and they are *more* than twice as many as the tailors and breeches makers, who are fourth in regard to their number, and count 23,500 persons. After these come the milliners and dress-makers, who are 20,000 in number.

According to the Criminal Returns of the Metropolis (for a copy of which I am indebted to the courtesy of a gentleman who expresses himself most anxious to do all in his power to aid the inquiry), the labourers occupy a most unenviable pre-eminence in police history. One in every twenty-eight labourers, according to these returns, has a predisposition for "simple larceny;" the average for the whole population of London is one in every 266 individuals; so that the labourers may be said to be more than nine times as dishonest as the generality of people resident in the metropolis. In drunkenness they occupy the same prominent position. One in every twenty-two individuals of the labouring class was charged with being intoxicated in the year 1848; whereas the average number of drunkards in the whole population of London is one in every 113 individuals. Nor are they less pugnaciously inclined; one in every twenty-six having been charged with a "common assault" of a more or less aggravated form. The labourers of London are therefore nine times as dishonest, five times as drunken, and nine times as savage as the rest of the community. Of the state of their education as a body of people, I have no similar means of judging at present; nor am I in a position to test their improvidence or their poverty in the same conclusive manner. Taking, however, the Government returns of the number of labourers located in the different unions throughout the country at the time of taking the last census, I find that one in every 140 of the class were paupers, while the average for all England and Wales was one in every 159 persons; so that while the Government returns show the labourers generally to be extraordinarily dishonest, drunken, and pugnacious, their vices cannot be ascribed to the poverty of their calling, for, compared with other occupations, their avocation appears to produce fewer paupers than the generality of employments. . . .

The coalwhippers, previously to the passing of the act of Parliament in 1843, were employed and paid by the publicans in the neighbourhood of the river, from Tower-hill to Limehouse. Under this system none but the most dissolute and intemperate obtained employment—in fact, the more intemperate they were the more readily they found work. The publicans were the relatives of the northern shipowners; they mostly had come to London penniless, and being placed in a tavern by their relatives, soon became shipowners themselves. There were at that time seventy taverns on the north side of the Thames, below bridge, employing coalwhippers, and all of the landlords making fortunes out of the earnings of the people. When a ship came to be "made up"—that is, for the hands to be hired—the men assembled round the bar in crowds, and began calling for drink, and outbidding each other in the extent of their orders, so as to induce the landlord to give them employment. If one called for beer, the next would be sure to give an order for rum; for he who spent most at the public-house had the greatest chance of employment. After being "taken on", their first care was to put up a score at the public-house, so as to please their employer, the publican. In the morning, before going to their work, they would invariably call at the house for a quartern of gin or rum; and they were obliged to take off with them to the ship "a bottle" holding nine pots of beer—and that of the worst description, for it was the invariable practice among the publicans to supply the coal whippers with the very worst article at the highest prices. When the men returned from their work they went back to the public-house, and there remained drinking the greater part of the night. He must have been a very steady man indeed, I am told, who could manage to return home sober to his wife and family. The consequence of this was, the men used to pass their days and the chief parts of their nights drinking in the public-house; and I am credibly informed that frequently, on the publican settling with them after clearing the ship, instead of having anything to receive, they were brought in several shillings in debt; this remained as a score for the next ship: in fact, it was only those who were in debt to the publican who were sure of employment on the next occasion. One publican had as many as fifteen ships; another had even more; and there was scarcely one of them without his two or three colliers. The children of the coalwhippers were almost reared in the tap-room, and a person who has had great experience in the trade tells me he knew as many as 500 youths who were transported, and as many more who met with an untimely death. At one house there were forty young robust men employed about seventeen years ago, and of these there are only two living at present. My informant tells me that he has frequently seen as many as 100 men at one time fighting pell-mell at King James's-stairs, and the publican standing by to see fair play. The average money spent in drink by each man was about twelve shillings to each ship. There were about 10,000 ships entered the Pool every year, and nine men were required to clear each ship. This made the annual expenditure of the coalwhippers in drink £54,000, or £27 a year per man. This is considered an extremely low average. The wives and families of the men at this time were in the greatest destitution: the daughters invariably became prostitutes, and the mothers ultimately went to swell the number of paupers at the union. This state of things continued till 1843 when, by the efforts of three of the coalwhippers, the Legislature was induced to pass an act forbidding the system, and appointing commissioners for the registration and regulation of coalwhippers in the port of London, and so establishing an office where the men were in future employed and paid. . . .

. . . "Our children under the old system were totally neglected (they said); the public-house absorbed everything." Under that system as many as 500 of the children of coalwhippers were transportèd; now that has entirely ceased; those charged with crime now were reared under the old system. "The Legislature never did a better thing than to emancipate us (said the man): they have the blessings and prayers of ourselves, our wives, and children."

. . . I then proceeded to take the statement of some of the different classes of the men. The first was a coalwhipper whom the men had selected as one knowing more about their calling than the generality. He told me as follows:

"I am about forty, and am a married man with a family of six children. I worked under the old system, and that to my sorrow. If I had been paid in money, according to the work I then did, I could have averaged thirty shillings a week. Instead of recieving that amount in money I was compelled to spend in drink fifteen shillings to eighteen shillings a week (when work was good), and the publican even then gave me the residue very grudgingly, and often kept me from eleven to twelve on a Saturday night before he would pay me. The consequences of this system were that I had a miserable home to go to. I would often have faced Newgate as soon. My health did not suffer, because I didn't drink the liquor I was forced to pay for. I gave most of it away. The liquours were beer, rum, and gin; all prepared the night before, adulterated shamefully for our consumption, as we durst'nt refuse it, and durstn't even grumble. The condition of my poor wife and children was then most wretched. Now the thing is materially altered, thank God; my wife and children can go to chapel at certain times, when work is pretty good, and our things are not in pawn. By the strictest economy I can do middling well—very well when compared with what things were. When the new system first came into operation, I felt almost in a new world. I felt myself a free man. I wasn't compelled to drink. My home assumed a better aspect, and keeps it still. . . ."

An Asylum for Vagrants

Letter XXVI

. . . Of the class of distressed tradesmen seeking shelter at this asylum, the two following may be taken as fair types. One was a bankrupt linen-draper, and appeared in a most destitute state. When he spoke of his children his eyes flooded with tears:

"I have been in business in the linen-draper line—that's five years ago. I had about £600 worth of stock at first starting, and used to take about £65 every week. My establishment was in a country village in Essex. I went on medium well for the first two or three years, but the alteration of the poor-laws, and the reduction of the agricultural labourers' wages destroyed my business. My customers were almost all among the working classes. I had dealings with a few farmers, of whom I took butter, and cheese, and eggs, in exchange for my goods. When the poor-laws were altered, and out-door relief was stopped, and the paupers compelled to go inside the house. Before that, a good part of the money given to the poor was expended at my shop. The over-seers used to have tickets for flannels, blankets, and shirtings, and other goods; with these they used to send the paupers to my house. I used to take full £8 or £10 a week in this manner; so that when the poor-laws were altered, and the previous system discontinued, I suffered materially. Besides, the wages of the agricultural labourers being lowered, left them less money to lay out with me. On a market day they were my chief customers. I would trust them one week under the other, and give them credit for seven shillings or ten shillings, if they wanted it. After their wages came down, they hadn't the means of laying out a sixpence with me; and where I had been taking £65 a week, my receipts dwindled to £30. I had been in the habit of keeping two shopmen before, but after the reduction I was obliged to come down to one. Then the competition of the large houses in other towns was more than I could stand against. Having a larger capital, they could buy cheaper and afford to take a less profit, and so of course they could sell much cheaper than I could. Then to try and keep pace with my neighbours I endeavoured to extend my capital by means of accommodation bills, but the interest I had to pay on these was so large, and my profits so little, that it soon became impossible for me to meet the claims upon me. I was made a bankrupt. My debts at the time were £300. This is about six years ago. After that I took a public-house. Some property was left me. I came into about £1,000; part of this went to my creditors, and I super-seded my bankruptcy. With the rest I determined upon starting in the publican line. I kept at this for about ten months, but I could do nothing with it. There was no custom to the house. I had been deceived into taking it. By the time I got out of it all my money was gone. After that I got a job as a referee at the time of the railway mania, and when that was over I got appointed as a police-man on the Eastern Union line. There I remained two years and upwards, but then they began reducing their establishment, both in men and in wages. I was among the men who were turned off. Since that time, which is now two years this Christmas, I have had no constant employment. Occasionally I have got a little law-writing to do; sometimes I have got a job as under waiter at a tavern. After I left the waiter's place I got to be very badly off. I had a decent suit of clothes to my back up to that time, but then I became so reduced I was obliged to go and live in a low lodging-house in Whitechapel. I was enabled to get along somehow; I knew many friends, and they gave me a little money now and then. But at last I had exhausted these. I could get nothing to do of any kind. I have been to Shoreditch station to try to pick up a few pence at carrying parcels, but there were so many there that I could not get a crust that way. I was obliged to pawn garment after garment to pay for my food and lodging, and when they were all gone I was wholly destitute. I couldn't raise even two pence for a night's lodging, so I came here and asked for a ticket. My wife is dead. I have three children; but I would rather you would not say anything about them if you please, because I have told all the truth, and if the gentle-man was to see my statement it might hurt his feelings." I assured the man that his name would not be printed, and he then consented to his children being mentioned. "The age of my eldest child is fourteen, and my youngest nine. They do not know of the destitution of their father. They are staying with one of my relations, who has supported them since my failure. I wouldn't have them know of my state on any account. None of my family are aware of my misery. My eldest child is a girl, and it would break her heart to know where I am, and see the state of distress I am in. My boy, I think, would never get over it. He is eleven years old. I have tried to get work carrying placard boards about, but I can't. My clothes are now too bad for me to do anything else. I write a good hand, and would do anything, I don't care what, to earn a few pence. I can get a good character from every place I have been in."

The other tradesman's story was as follows:

"I am now thirty-three, and am acquainted with the grocery trade, both as master and assistant. I served a five years' apprenticeship in a town in Berkshire. The very late hours and the constant confinement made me feel my apprenticeship a state of slavery. The other apprentices used to say they felt it so likewise. During my apprenticeship I consider that I never learnt my trade properly. I knew as much at the year's end as at the five years' end. My father gave my master £50 premium; the same premium, or more, was paid with the others. One, the son of a gentleman at ——, paid as much as £80. My master made an excellent thing of his apprentices. Nearly all the grocers in the part of Berkshire I'm acquainted with do the same. My master was a severe man to us in respect of keeping us in the house, and making us attend the Methodist chapel twice, and sometimes thrice, every Sunday. We had prayers night and morning. I attribute my misfortunes to this apprenticeship, because there was a great discrepancy between profession and practice in the house, so there could be no respect in the young men for their employer, and they grew careless. He carried on his business in a way to inspire anything else but respect. On the cheesemongery side we were always blamed if we didn't keep the scale well wetted, so as to make it heavier on one side than the other— I mean the side of the scale where the butter was put—that was filled, or partly filled with water, under pretence of preventing the butter sticking, and so the customer was wronged half an ounce in every purchase. With regard to the bacon, which, on account of competition, we had to sell cheap—at no profit sometimes—he used to say to us, 'You must make the ounces pay'; that is, we were expected to add two or more ounces, calculating on what the customer would put up with, to every six odd ounces in the weight of a piece. For instance, if a hock of bacon weighed 6lb. 7oz., at $4\frac{1}{2}$d. per lb., we were to charge 2s. 3d. for the 6lbs., and (if possible) adding two ounces to the seven which was the actual weight, charge each ounce a halfpenny, so getting 2s. $7\frac{1}{2}$d. instead of 2s. 5d. This is a common practice in all the cheap shops I'm acquainted with. With his sugars and teas inferior sorts were mixed. In grinding pepper a quantity of rice was used, it all being ground together. Mustard was adulterated by the manufacturers, if the price given showed that the adulterated stuff was wanted. The lowest-priced coffee was always half chicory, the second quality one-third chicory; the best was 1lb. of chicory to 3lb. of coffee, or one-fourth. We had it either in chicory-nibs, which is the root of the endive cultivated in Yorkshire, Prussia, etc.; or else as spurious chicory powdered, twopence or threepence per pound cheaper, the principal ingredient being parsnips and carrots, cut in small pieces, and roasted like chicory. A quart of water is the allowance to every twenty-eight pounds of tobacco. We had to keep pulling it so as to keep it loose, for if left to lie long it would mould and get a very unpleasant smell. In weighing sugar, some was always spilt loose on the scale opposite the weight, which remains in the scale, so that every pound or so is a quarter of an ounce short. This is the practice only in 'cutting' shops. Often enough, after we have been doing all these rogueries we were called in to prayers. In my next situation, with an honourable tradesman in Yorkshire, I found I had to learn my business over again, so as to carry it on fairly. In two or three years I went into business in the town where I was apprenticed; but I had been subjected to such close confine-ment, and so many unnecessary restrictions, without any opportunity of improving by reading, that when I was my own master, and in possession of money, and on the first taste of freedom, I squandered my money foolishly and extravagantly, and that brought me into difficulties. I was £150 deficient to meet my liabilities, and my friends advanced that sum, I undertaking to be more attentive to business. After that, a man started as a grocer in the same street, in the 'cutting' line, and I had to compete with him, and he sold his sugar a halfpenny a pound less than it cost, and I was obliged to do the same; the preparing of the sugar for the market day is a country grocer's week's work, and all at a loss. That's the ruin of many a grocer. My profits dwindled year by year, though I stuck very close to business, and in eighteen months I gave it up. By that time other 'cutting' shops were opened—none have done any good. I was about £100 bad, which my friends arranged to pay by instal-ments. After that I hawked tea. I did no good in that. The system is to leave it at the working men's houses, giving a week's credit, the customers often taking more. Nothing can be honestly made in that trade. The Scotchmen in the trade are the only men that can do any good in it. They charge six shillings for what's four shillings in a good shop. About nine months ago my wife—I had been married seven years—was obliged to go and live with her sister, a dressmaker, as I was too poor to keep her or myself either. I then came to London to try for employment of any kind. I answered advertisements, and there were always forty or fifty young men after the same situation. I never got one, except for a short time at Brentford. I had also a few days' work at bill delivery—that is, grocer's circulars. I was at last so reduced that I couldn't pay for my lodgings. Nobody can describe the misery I felt as I have walked the streets all night, falling asleep as I went along, and then roused myself up half frozen, my limbs aching, and my whole body trembling. Sometimes, if I could find a penny, I might sit up in a coffee-shop in Russell Street, Covent-garden, till five in the morning, when I had to roam the streets all day long. Two days I was without food, and determined to commit some felony to save me from starvation, when, to my great joy—for God knows what it saved me from, as I was utterly careless what my fate would be—I was told of this Refuge by a poor man who had been there, who found me walking about the Piazzas in Covent-garden as a place of shelter. I applied, and was admitted. I don't know how I can get a place without clothes. I have one child with my wife, and she supports him and herself, very indifferently, by dressmaking."

A soldier's wife, speaking with a strong Scotch accent, made the following statement. She had altogether a decent appearance, but her features—and there were the remains of prettiness in her look—were sadly pinched. Her manners were quiet, and her voice low and agreeable. She looked like one who had "seen better days"—as the poor of the better sort not unfrequently say in their destitution, clinging to the recollection of past comforts. She wore a very clean checked cotton shawl and a straw bonnet tolerably entire. The remainder of her dress was covered by her shawl, which was folded closely about her, over a dark cotton gown: "I was born twenty miles from Inverness (she said), and have been a servant since I was eleven. I always lived in good places—the best of places. I never was in inferior places. I have lived as a cook, housemaid, or servant of all work, in Inverness, Elgin, and Tain, always maintaining a good character—I thank God for that. In all my distress I've done nothing wrong; but I didn't know what distress was when in service. I continued in service until I married; but I was not able to save much money, because I had to do all I could for my mother, who was a very poor widow, for I lost my father when I was two years old. Wages are very low in Scotland to what they are in England. In the year 1847 I lived in the service of the barrack-master of Fort George, twelve miles below Inverness. There I became acquainted with my present husband, a soldier; and I was married to him in March 1847, in the chapel at Fort George. I continued two months in service after my marriage—my mistress wouldn't let me away; she was very kind to me; so was my master: they all were. I have a written character from my mistress." This, at my request, she produced. "Two months after, the regiment left Fort George for Leith, and there I lived with my husband in barracks. It is not so bad for married persons in the artillery as in the line (we were in the artillery) in barracks. In our barrack rooms no single men were allowed to sleep where the married people were accommodated. But there were three or four married families in one room. I lived two years in barracks with my husband, in different barracks. I was very comfortable. I didn't know what it was to want anything I ought to have. My husband was a kind sober man. (This she said very feelingly.) His regiment was ordered abroad, to Nova Scotia. I had no family. Only six soldiers' wives are allowed to go out with each company, and there were seventeen married men in the company to which my husband belonged. It's determined by lot. An officer holds the tickets in his cap, and the men draw them. None of the wives are present. It would be too hard a thing for them to see. My husband drew a blank." She continued: "It was a sad scene when they embarked at Woolwich, last March. All the wives were there, all crying and sobbing, you may depend upon that; and the children too, and some of the men; but I couldn't look much at them, and I don't like to see men cry. My husband was sadly distressed. I hoped to get out there and join him, not knowing the passage was so long and so expensive. I had a little money then, but that's gone, and I'm brought to misery. It would have cost me £6 at that time to get out, and I couldn't manage that. So I stayed in London, getting a day's work at washing where I could, making a very poor living of it; and I was at last forced to part with all my good clothes after my money went;" . . .

Of the Vagrants of London

Letter XXVII

. . . Another class of vagrants consists of those who, having been thrown out of employment, have travelled through the country seeking work without avail, and who consequently have lived on charity so long that the habits of wandering and mendicancy have eradicated their former habits of industry, and the industrious workman has become changed into the habitual beggar. . . .

. . . A cotton-spinner (who had subsequently been a soldier), whose appearance was utterly abject, was the next person questioned. He was tall, and had been florid-looking (judging from his present complexion). His coat—very old and worn, and once black—would not button, and would have hardly held together if buttoned. He was out at elbows, and some parts of the collar were pinned together. His waistcoat was of a match with his coat, and his trowsers were rags. He had some shirt, as was evident by his waistcoat, held together by one button. A very dirty handkerchief was tied carelessly round his neck. He was tall and erect, and told his adventures with heartiness.

"I am thirty-eight," he said, "and have been a cotton-spinner, working at Chorlton-upon-Medlock. I can neither read nor write. When I was a young man, twenty years ago, I could earn £2 10s. clear money every week, after paying two piecers and a scavenger. Each piecer had seven shillings and sixpence a week—they are girls; the scavenger—a boy to clean the wheels of the cotton-spinning machine—had two shillings and sixpence. I was master of them wheels in the factory. This state of things continued until about the year 1837. I lived well and enjoyed myself, being a hearty man, nowadays a drunkard, working every day from half-past five in the morning till half-past seven at night—long hours that time, master. I didn't care about money as long as I was decent and respectable. I had a turn for sporting at the wakes down there. In 1837 the 'self-actors' (machines with steam power) had come into common use. One girl can mind three pairs—that used to be three men's work—getting fifteen shillings for the work which gave three men £7 10s. Out of one factory four hundred hands were flung in one week, men and women together. We had a meeting of the union, but nothing could be done, and we were told to go and mind the three pairs, as the girls did, for fifteen shillings a week. We wouldn't do that. Some went for soldiers, some to sea, some to Stopport (Stockport), to get work in factories where the self-actors wer'n't agait. The masters there wouldn't have them, at least some of them. Manchester was full of them; but one gentleman in Hulme still won't have them, for he says he won't turn the men out of bread. I listed for a soldier in the 48th. I liked a soldier's life very well until I got flogged—100 lashes for selling my kit (for a spree), and 150 for striking a corporal who called me an English robber. He was an Irishman. I was confined five days in the hospital after each punishment. It was terrible. It was like a bunch of razors cutting at your back. Your flesh was dragged off by the cats. Flogging was then very common in the regiment. I was flogged in 1840. To this day I feel a pain in my chest from the triangles. I was discharged from the army about two years ago, when the reduction took place. I was only flogged the times I've told you. I had no pension and no friends. I was discharged in Dublin. I turned to, and looked for work. I couldn't get any, and I made my way to Manchester. I stole myself aboard of a steamer, and hid myself till she got out to sea, on her way from Dublin to Liverpool. When the captain found me there he gave me a kick and some bread, and told me to work—so I worked for my passage, twenty-four hours. He put me ashore at Liverpool. I slept in the union that night—nothing to eat, and nothing to cover me—no fire; it was winter. I walked to Manchester, but could get nothing to do there, though I was twelve months knocking about. It wants a friend and a character to get work. I slept in unions in Manchester, and had oatmeal porridge for breakfast, work at grinding logwood in the mill, from six to twelve, and then turn out. That was the way I lived chiefly; but I got a job sometimes in driving cattle, and three-pence for it—or twopence for carrying baskets in the vegetable markets—and went to Shoedale union at night. I would get a pint of coffee and half a pound of bread, and half a pound of bread in the morning, and no work. I took to travelling up to London, half-hungered on the road—that was last winter—eating turnips out of this field, and carrots out of that, and sleeping under hedges and haystacks. I slept under one haystack, and pulled out the hay to cover me, and the snow lay on it a foot deep in the morning. I slept for all that, but wasn't I froze when I woke? An old farmer came up with his cart and pitch-fork to load hay. He said, 'Poor fellow! Have you been here all night?' I answered 'Yes.' He gave me some coffee and some bread, and one shilling. That was the only good friend I met with on the road. I got fourteen days of it for asking a gentleman for a penny; that was in Stafford. I got to London after that, sleeping in unions sometimes, and begging a bite here and there. Sometimes I had to walk all night. I was once forty-eight hours without a bit, until I got hold of a Swede turnip, and so at last I got to London. Here I've tried up and down everywhere for work as a labouring man, or in a foundry. I tried London Docks, and Blackwall, and every place, but no job. At one foundry the boiler-makers made a collection of four shillings for me. I've walked the streets for three nights together—here, in this fine London. I was refused a night's lodgings in Shoreditch and in Gray's-inn-lane. A police-man, the fourth night, at twelve o'clock, procured me a lodging, and gave me twopence. I couldn't drag on any longer. I was taken to a doctor's in the city. I fell in the street, from hunger and tiredness. The doctor ordered me brandy and water, two shillings and sixpence, and a quartern loaf, and some coffee, sugar, and butter. He said what I ailed was hunger. I made that run cut as long as I could but I was then as bad off as ever. It's hard to hunger for nights together. I was once in 'Steel' (Coldbath-fields) for begging. I was in Tothill-fields for going into a chandlers' shop, asking for a quartern loaf and half a pound of cheese, and walking out with it. I got a month for that. I have been in Brixton for taking a loaf out of a baker's basket, all through hunger. Better a prison than to starve. I was well treated because I behaved well in prison. I have slept in coaches when I had a chance. One night on a dunghill, covering the stable straw about me to keep myself warm. This place is a relief. I shave the poor people and cut their hair on a Sunday. I was handy at that when I was a soldier. I have shaved in public houses for halfpennies. Some landlords kick me out. Now in the days I may pick up a penny or two that way, and get here of a night. I met two Manchester men in Hyde Park, on Saturday, skating. They asked me what I was. I said 'A beggar.' They gave me two shillings and sixpence, and I spent part of it for warm coffee and other things. They knew all about Manchester, and knew I was a Manchester man by my talk."

Letter XXVIII

... I now come to the characteristics of vagrant life, as seen in the casual wards of the metropolitan unions. ...

Previously to entering upon my inquiry into this subject, I consulted with a gentleman who had long paid considerable attention to the question, and who was, moreover, in a position peculiarly fitted for gaining the greatest experience and arriving at the correctest notions upon the matter—I consulted, I say, with the gentleman referred to, as to the Poor-law officers from whom I should be likely to obtain the best practical information; and I was referred by him to Mr. Knapp, the master of the Wandsworth and Clapham Union, as one of the most intelligent and best informed upon the subject of vagrancy. I found that gentleman all that he had been represented to me as being, and obtained from him the following statement—which, as an analysis of the vagrant character, and a description of the habits and propensities of the young vagabond, has, perhaps, never been surpassed:

He had filled the office of master of the Wandsworth and Clapham Union for three years, and immediately before that he was the relieving officer for the same union for upwards of two years. He was guardian of Clapham parish for four years previously to his being elected relieving officer. He was a member of the first board of guardians that was formed under the new Poor-law Act, and he has long given much attention to the habits of the vagrants that have come under his notice or care. He told me that he considered a casual ward necessary in every union, because there is always a migratory population, consisting of labourers, seeking employment in other localities, and destitute women travelling to their husbands or friends. He thinks a casual ward is necessary for the shelter and relief of such parties, since the law will not permit them to beg. These, however, are by far the smaller proportion of those who demand admittance into the casual ward. Formerly they were not 5 per cent. of the total number of casuals. The remainder consisted of youths, prostitutes, Irish families, and a few professional beggars. The youths formed more than one-half of the entire number, and their ages were from twelve to twenty. The largest number were seventeen years old—indeed, he adds, just that age when youth becomes disengaged from parental control. These lads had generally run away either from their parents or masters, and many had been reared to a life of vagrancy. They were mostly shrewd and acute youths; some had been very well educated. Ignorance, to use the gentleman's own words, is certainly not the prevailing characteristic of the class: indeed, with a few exceptions, he would say it is the reverse. These lads are mostly distinguished by their aversion to continuous labour of any kind. He never knew them to work—they are, indeed, essentially the idle and the vagabond. Their great inclination is to be on the move, and wandering from place to place, and they appear, he says, to receive a great deal of pleasure from the assembly and conversation of the casual ward. They are physically stout, healthy lads, and certainly not emaciated or sickly. They belong especially to the able-bodied class, being, as he says, full of health and mischief. When in London they live in the day time by holding horses, and carrying parcels from the steam-piers and railway

---

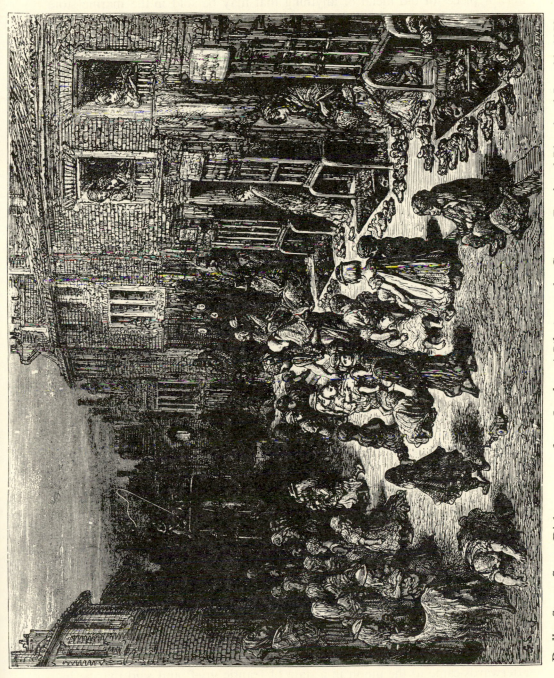

Dudley Street, Seven Dials

from London, A Pilgrimage, by Gustave Doré and Blanchard Jerrold, 1872

termini. Some loiter about the markets in the hope of a job, and others may be seen in the streets picking up bones and rags, or along the water-side searching for pieces of old metal or anything that may be sold in the marine store shops. They have nearly all been in prison more than once—and several a greater number of times than they are years old. They are the most dishonest of all thieves, having not the least respect for the property of even the members of their own class. He tells me he has frequently known them to rob one another. They are very stubborn and self-willed. They have often broken every window in the oakum-room rather than do the required work. They are a most difficult class to govern, and are especially restive under the least restraint; they can ill brook control, and they had great delight in thwarting the authorities of the workhouse. They are particularly fond of amusements of all kinds. My informant has heard them often discuss the merits of the different actors at the minor theatres and saloons. Sometimes they will elect a chairman and get up a regular debate, and make speeches from one side of the ward to the other. Many of them will make very clever comic rations; others delight in singing comic songs, especially those upon the workhouse and gaols. He never knew them love reading. They mostly pass under fictitious names. Some will give the name of "John Russell", or "Robert Peel", or "Richard Cobden". They often come down to the casual wards in large bodies of twenty or thirty, with sticks hidden down the legs of their trowsers, and with these they rob and beat those that do not belong to their own gang. The gang will often consist of 100 lads, all under twenty, one-fourth of whom regularly come together in a body; and in the casual ward they generally arrange where to meet again on the following night. In the winter of 1846 the guardians of Wandsworth and Clapham sympathising with their ragged and wretched appearance, and desirous of affording them the means of obtaining an honest livelihood, gave my informant instructions to offer an asylum to any who might choose to remain in the workhouse. Under this arrangement about fifty were admitted. The majority were under seventeen years of age. Some of these remained a few days—others a few weeks—none stopped longer than three months; and the generality of them decamped over the wall, taking with them the clothes of the union. The confinement, restraint, and order of the workhouse were especially irksome to them. This is the character of the true vagrant, for whom my informant considers no provision whatever should be made at the unions, believing as he does that most of them have settlements in or around London. The casual wards, he tells me, he knows to have been a great encouragement to the increase of these characters. Several of the lads that have come under his care had sought shelter and concealment in the casual wards after having absconded from their parents. In one instance the father and mother of a lad had unavailingly sought their son in every direction; he discovered that the youth had run away, and he sent him home in the custody of one of the inmates, but when the boy got within two or three doors of his father's residence, he turned round and scampered off. The mother afterwards came to the union in a state of frantic grief, and said that he had disappeared two years before. My informant believes that the boy has never been heard of by his parents since. Others he has restored to their parents, and some of the young vagabonds who have died in the union have, on their

death-beds, disclosed the names and particulars of their families, who have
been always of a highly respectable character. To these he was sent, and on
their visits to their children scenes of indescribable grief and anguish have
taken place. He tells me he is convinced that it is the low lodging-houses and
the casual wards of the unions that offer a ready means for youths absconding
from their homes immediately on the least disagreement or restraint. In most
of the cases that he has investigated, he has found that the boys have left home
after some rebuke or quarrel with their parents. On restoring one boy to his
father, the latter said that, though the lad was not ten years old he had been
in almost every workhouse in London; and the father bitterly complained of
the casual wards for offering shelter to a youth of such tender years. But my
informant is convinced that, even if the casual wards throughout the country
were entirely closed—the low lodging-houses being allowed to remain in their
present condition—the evil would not be remedied, if at all abated. A boy
after running away from home generally seeks shelter in one of the cheap
lodging-houses, and there he makes acquaintance with the most depraved of
both sexes. The boys at the house become his regular companions, and he is
soon a confirmed vagrant and thief like the rest. The youths of the vagrant
class are particularly distinguished by their libidinous propensities. They
frequently come to the gate with a young prostitute, and with her they go off
in the morning. With this girl they will tramp through the whole of the country.
They are not remarkable for a love of drink—indeed, my informant *never* saw
a regular vagrant in a state of intoxication, nor has he known them to exhibit
any craving for liquor. He has had many drunkards under his charge, but
the vagrant is totally distinct—having propensities not less vicious, but of a
very different kind. He considers the young tramps to be generally a class of
lads possessing the keenest intelligence, and of a highly enterprising character.
They seem to have no sense of danger, and to be especially delighted with such
acts as involve any peril. They are likewise characterised by their exceeding
love of mischief. The property destroyed in the union of which my informant
is the master, has been of considerable value, consisting of windows broken,
sash frames demolished, beds and bedding torn to pieces, and rugs burnt. They
will frequently come down in large gangs on purpose to destroy the property
in the union. They generally are of a most restless and volatile disposition.
They have great quickness of perception, but little power of continuous attention or perseverance. They have a keen sense of the ridiculous, and are not
devoid of deep feeling. He has often known them to be dissolved to tears on
his remonstrating with them on the course they were following—and then they
promise amendment; but in a few days, and sometimes hours, they would
forget all and return to their old habits. In the summer they make regular tours
through the country, visiting all places that they have not seen—so that there
is scarcely one who is not well acquainted with every part within 100 miles
of London, and many with all England. They are perfectly organized, so that
any regulation affecting their comforts or interests becomes known among the
whole body in a remarkably short space of time. As an instance, he informs me
that on putting out a notice that no able-bodied man or youth would be
received in the casual ward after a certain day, there was not a single application made by any such party, the regular vagrants having doubtless informed

each other that it was useless seeking admission to this union. In the winter the young vagrants come to London and find shelter in the Asylum for the Houseless Poor. At this season of the year the number of vagrants in the casual wards would generally be diminished one-half. The juvenile vagrants constitute one of the main sources from which the criminals of the country are continually recruited and augmented. Being repeatedly committed to prison for disorderly conduct and misdemeanour, the gaol soon loses all terrors for them; and, indeed, they will frequently destroy their own clothes, or the property of the union, in order to be sent there. Hence they soon become practised and dexterous thieves, and my informant has detected several burglaries by the property found upon them. The number of this class is stated, in the Poor-Law Report on Vagrancy, to have been, in 1848, no less than 16,086, and they form one of the most restless, discontented, vicious, and dangerous elements of society. At the period of any social commotion they are sure to be drawn towards the scene of excitement in a vast concourse. During the Chartist agitation, in the June quarter of the year 1848, the number of male casuals admitted into the Wandsworth and Clapham Union rose from 2,501 to 3,969, while the females (their companions) increased from 579 to 1,388.

Of the other classes of persons admitted into the casual wards, the Irish generally form a large proportion. At the time when juvenile vagrancy prevailed to an alarming extent, the Irish hardly dared to show themselves in the casual wards, for the lads would beat them and plunder them of whatever they might have—either the produce of their begging or the ragged kit they carried with them. Often my informant has had to quell violent disturbances in the night among these characters. The Irish tramp generally makes his appearance with a large family, and frequently with three or four generations together—grandfather, grandmother, father and mother, and children—all coming at the same time. In the year ending June, 1848, the Irish vagrants increased to so great an extent that, of the entire number of casuals relieved, more than one-third in the first three-quarters, and more than two-thirds in the last quarter were from the sister island. Of the Irish vagrants, the worst class—that is the poorest and most abject—came over to this country by way of Newport, in Wales. The expense of the passage to that port was only two shillings and sixpence; whereas the cost of the voyage to Liverpool and London was considerably more, and consequently the class brought over by that way were less destitute. The Irish vagrants were far more orderly than the English. Out of the vast number received into the casual ward of this union during the distress in Ireland, it is remarkable that not one ever committed an act of insubordination. They were generally very grateful for the relief afforded, and appeared to subsist entirely by begging. Some of them were not particularly fond of work, but they were invariably honest, says my informant—at least so far as his knowledge went. They were exceedingly filthy in their habits, and many diseased.

These constitute the two large and principal classes of vagrants. The remainder generally consist of persons temporarily destitute, whereas the others are habitually so. The temporarily destitute are chiefly railway and agricultural labourers, and a few mechanics travelling in search of employment. These are easily distinguished from the regular vagrant; indeed, a glance is sufficient to the practised eye. They are the better class of casuals, and those for whom the wards are expressly designed, but they form only a very small proportion of the vagrants applying for shelter. In the height of vagrancy they formed not 1 per cent of the entire number admitted. Indeed, such was the state of the casual wards that the destitute mechanics and labourers preferred walking through the night to availing themselves of the accommodation. Lately the artisans and labourers have increased greatly in proportion, owing to the system adopted for the exclusion of the habitual vagrant, and the consequent decline of their number. The working man travelling in search of employment is now generally admitted into what are called the receiving wards of the workhouse, instead of the tramp room, and he is usually exceedingly grateful for the accommodation. My informant tells me that persons of this class seldom return to the workhouse after one night's shelter; and this is a conclusive proof that the regular working man seldom passes into the habitual beggar. They are an entirely distinct class, having different habits, and indeed different features, and I am assured that they are strictly honest. During the whole experience of my informant he never knew one who applied for a night's shelter commit an act of dishonesty, and he has seen them in the last stages of destitution. Occasionally they have sold the shirt and waistcoat off their backs before they applied for admittance into the workhouse, while some of them have been so weak from long starvation that they could scarcely reach the gate. Such persons are always allowed to remain several days to recruit their strength.

Letter XXXI

. . . A meeting of unprecedented character was held at the British Union School-room, Shakspeare walk, Shadwell, on Monday evening last. The use of the school-room was kindly granted by Mr. Fletcher, the proprietor, to whose liberality we stand indebted for many similar favours. It was convened by our Metropolitan Correspondent, for the purpose of assembling together some of the lowest class of male juvenile thieves and vagabonds who infest the metropolis and the country at large; and though privately called, at only two days' notice, by the distribution of tickets of admission among the class in question at the various haunts and dens of infamy to which they resort, no fewer than 150 of them attended on the occasion. The only condition to entitle the parties to admission was that they should be vagrants, and under twenty years of age. They had all assembled some time before the hour for commencing the proceedings arrived, and never was witnessed a more distressing spectacle of squalor, rags, and wretchedness. Some were young men, and some were children; one, who styled himself a "cadger", was six years of age, and several who confessed themselves "prigs" were only ten. The countenances of the boys were of various characters. Many were not only good looking, but had a frank, ingenuous expression that seemed in no way connected with innate roguery. Many, on the other hand, had the deep-sunk and half-averted eyes which are so characteristic of natural dishonesty and cunning. Some had the regular features of lads born of parents in easy circumstances. The hair of most of the lads was cut very close to the head, showing their recent liberation from prison; indeed, one might tell by the comparative length of the crop, the time that each boy had been out of gaol. All but a few of the older boys were remarkable, amidst the rags, filth, and wretchedness of their external appearance, for the mirth and carelessness impressed upon their countenances. At first their behaviour was very noisy and disorderly: coarse and ribald jokes were freely cracked, exciting general bursts of laughter; while howls, cat-calls, and all manner of unearthly and indescribable yells threatened for some time to render the object of the meeting utterly abortive. At one moment a lad would imitate the bray of a jackass, and immediately the whole 150 would fall to braying. Then some ragged urchin would crow like a cock, whereupon the place would echo again with 150 cock-crows. Then, as a black boy entered the room, one of the young vagabonds would shout out "swe-ee-op". This would be received with peals of laughter, and followed by a general repetition of the same cry. Next, 150 cat-calls of the shrillest possible description would almost split the ears. These would be succeeded by cries of "Strike up, you catgut scrapers", "Go on with your barrow", "Flare up, my never-sweats", and a variety of other street sayings. Indeed, the uproar which went on before the meeting began will be best understood if we compare it to the scene presented by a public menagerie at feeding time. The greatest difficulty, as might be expected, was experienced in collecting the subjoined statistics of their character and condition. By a well-contrived and persevering mode of inquiry, however, the following facts were elicited:

With respect to their *ages*, the youngest boy present was six years old. He styled himself a "cadger", and said that his mother, who is a widow, and suffering from ill-health, sends him into the streets to beg. There were 7 of 10 years of age, 3 of 12, 3 of 13, 10 of 14, 10 of 15, 11 of 16, 20 of 17, 26 of 18, and 45 of 19.

Nineteen had *fathers and mothers* still living; thirty-nine had only one parent; and eighty were orphans in the fullest sense of the word, having neither father nor mother alive.

Of professed beggars there were fifty, and sixty-six who acknowledged themselves to be *habitual thieves*. The announcement that the greater number present were thieves pleased them exceedingly, and was received with three rounds of applause. . . .

. . . As to the *causes of their vagabondism*, it was found that twenty-two had run away from their homes, owing to the ill-treatment of their parents; eighteen confessed to having been ruined through their parents allowing them to run wild in the streets, and to be led astray by bad companions; and fifteen acknowledged that they had been first taught thieving in a lodging-house.

Concerning the vagrant habits of the youths, the following facts were elicited: seventy-eight regularly roam through the country every year, sixty-five sleep regularly in the casual wards of the unions, and fifty-two occasionally slept in tramper's lodging houses throughout the country.

Respecting their *education*, according to the popular meaning of the term, 63 of the 150 were able to read and write, and they were principally thieves. 50 of this number said they had read "Jack Sheppard", and the lives of Dick Turpin, Claude du Val, and all the other popular thieves' novels, as well as the "Newgate Calendar" and "Lives of the Robbers and Pirates". Those who could not read themselves, said they'd had "Jack Sheppard" read to them at the lodging-houses. Numbers avowed that they had been induced to resort to an abandoned course of life from reading the lives of notorious thieves and novels about highway robbers. When asked what they thought of "Jack Sheppard", several bawled out "He's a regular brick"—a sentiment which was almost universally concurred in by the deafening shouts and plaudits which followed. When asked whether they would like to be Jack Sheppards, they answered "Yes, if the times was the same now as they were then." Thirteen confessed that they had taken to thieving in order to go to the low theatres; and one lad said he had lost a good situation on the Birmingham Railway through his love of the play.

Twenty stated they had *been flogged in prison*—many of them two, three, and four different times. A policeman in plain clothes was present; but their acute eyes were not long before they detected his real character notwithstanding his disguise. Several demanded that he should be turned out. The officer was accordingly given to understand that the meeting was a private one, and requested to withdraw. Having apologised for intruding, he proceeded to leave the room—and, no sooner did the boys see the policeman move towards the door, than they gave vent to several rounds of very hearty applause, accompanied by hisses, groans, and cries of "throw him over." . . .

Letter XXXII

I now return to my investigations into the condition of the artisans of London. The present letter will be the first of a short series upon the state of the Metropolitan Boot and Shoe Makers. . . .

I must now allude to the measures that have been resorted to by the workmen in order to effect an increase, or to prevent a decrease, in the rate of their remuneration—viz., *the strikes*. Many of the older workmen make these their epochs. "It was before (or after) the great strike of 1812"—or, "It was before the change in 1830", are not uncommon phrases. The strike of 1812, I am informed by an intelligent bootman, was for a rise of sixpence a pair on the wages both for closing and making, "all round"—that is, on every description of work in boots and shoes, together with certain allowances for "extras". The masters, at that time, after holding out for thirteen weeks, gave way, yielding to all the demands of the men. "The *scabs* had no chance in those days," said my informant, "the wages-men had it all their own way; they could do anything and there were no slop-shops then. Some scabs went to Mr. Hoby *'occasioning'* (that is, asking whether he 'had occasion for another hand'), but he said to them, 'I can do nothing; go to my masters (the journeymen) in the Parr's Head, Swallow-street' (the sign of the public-house used by the men that managed the strike)." This was the last general strike of the trade; for in 1830, though the shoemakers joined the grand union of all the trades, walking with them in procession with a petition of behalf of the Dorchester labourers—the procession, six deep, extending from Copenhagen-fields to Kennington-common—

they did not "strike" for an advance, but only resisted the attempt of the masters to lower their wages. . . .

Letter XXXIII

. . . To enable the reader to contrast the present rate of the workman's income with the past, and so to judge of the earnings of a *bootman* in the palmy days of the trade, I give the statement of a first-rate workman employed by the late Mr. Hoby. My informant is now a small master on his own account. He was what is called a *ready man*; that is, one who can work at his trade with more average celerity.

"I got work at Mr. Hoby's", he said, "not long after the battle of Waterloo, in 1815, and was told by my fellow-workmen that I wasn't born soon enough to see good times; but I've lived long enough to see bad ones. Though I wasn't born soon enough, as they said, I could earn and did earn £150 a year, something short of £3 a week; and that for eight years, when trade became not so good. Mr. Hoby used to send out returned boots (misfits) to America, and in a slack time kept his regular hands going, making boots for the American market, and paying his bootmen seven shillings and twopence a pair for them. I never sat still for want of work until he dropped this foreign trade. One week a shopmate of mine had twenty pairs to take pay for. The regular wages was eight shillings and twopence for the ground-work of Wellingtons with three-quarter heels, and liberal extras. I could then play my £1 a corner at whist. I *wouldn't* play at that time for less than five shillings. I could afford a glass of wine, but never was a drinker; and, for all that, I had my £100 in the Four per Cents. for a long time (I lent it to a friend afterwards), and from £40 to £50 in the savings bank. Some made more than me, though I *must* work. I can't stand still. One journeyman, to my knowledge, saved £2,000; he once made thirty-four pairs of boots in three weeks. The bootmen then at Mr. Hoby's were all respectable men; they were like gentlemen—smoking their pipes, in their frilled shirts, like gentlemen—all but the drunkards. At the trade meetings, Hoby's best men used to have one corner of the room to themselves, and were called the House of Lords. There was more than 100 of us when I became one; and before then there were even a greater number. Mr. Hoby has paid £500 a week in wages. It was easy to save money in those days; one could hardly help it. We shall never see the like again."

Letter XXXIV

. . . The *general rate of wages in the Stepney district to women's-men in society* are from sixpence for sew-round boots, up to one shilling and twopence for single-sole boots and shoes. A single-handed man working at sew-round boots will make about four pair at sixpence per pair in a day of fourteen hours. At the lowest rate of wages a man will earn about twelve shillings a week, out of which he will have to pay one shilling and sixpence for grindery and light, making his clear earnings ten shillings and sixpence. These prices are given by the warehouse. The workman will not be more than half employed during five months in the year. Throughout the year the average earnings of a society man in the Stepney district will be about nine shillings a week. The wages for plain pumps, for society men, are eightpence, ninepence, tenpence, elevenpence, and one shilling. The ninepence, tenpence, elevenpence, and one shilling work is for the retail shops in the Stepney district, and the eightpence work is for the warehouses. For welts or double soles the wages are from one shilling up to one shilling and sixpence, the higher price being for the retail shops. Throughout the year the society men earn twelve shillings a week, or ten shillings clear, on the heavy description of work; and about nine shillings a week on the lighter. The reductions have been very considerable within the last ten years, certainly to the extent of fivepence a pair upon an average. The work has, moreover, been made a great deal better lately, and that is a very serious loss to the men, as more time must be given to each pair. The cause of the reduction is the system of chamber-mastering, which allows the employers to buy their goods cheaper than they can manufacture them. There is a shop in the Commercial-road that supplies country orders, and purchases them of the chamber-masters at two shillings and threepence per pair for patent enamel shoes, single sole. The party of whom he buys them will give about eightpence or ninepence per pair for the making; whereas the employer, if he made them himself, would have to give elevenpence per pair. These shoes he sells wholesale at thirty-six shillings a dozen, so that he clears a good percentage, and is saved all trouble and expense of clickers into the bargain. This is the main cause of the reduction of wages in the women's trade, and especially in the Stepney district. The same system extends, however, all through the City, and indeed through a good part of the West-end. It is this that throws the whole of the women's men out of work every day. The system is fast running through the whole country. The eastern portion of London is the great hotbed of this evil. Employers at the East-end, who buy of the chamber-masters, supply some of the best shops at the West-end, and many of the better kind in the country parts. The reason why the chamber-masters are able to get up goods at a less price than the usual rate, is on account of the number of boys, and girls, and women, and all kinds of cheap labour they employ. "The great evil of our trade," said a shrewd Stepney women's-man, "I consider to be the chamber-master system—the importation of foreign goods, I think, is a minor injury to us. . . . There is a system of obtaining apprentices from the workhouses at the East-end of London; the journeyman takes the apprentices in the first instance, because the wages are so reduced by the employer that he cannot obtain a living by his own labour. After having got one or two, he generally commences cutting for himself—that is, he starts as a small manufacturer, and begins hawking his goods to the warehouses, and retail shops, and, in some cases, to private families. As his work increases, he obtains either more apprentices or employs girls and women, as well as any kind of cheap labour that he can lay hold of. If he takes a man into his employ that party again is compelled to employ another boy to assist him, and so it goes on until our trade is completely over-populated; for these boys, as soon as they get out of their time, or upon their own hands, again employ more boys, adopting the system to which they have been brought up.". . .

Letter XLIV

... An experienced gentleman, to whom I was referred as a person who could give me information as to the influence of the Ragged Schools on the criminal juvenile population of Westminster, was of the opinion that they tended to increase the evil which benevolent persons, through the agency of such schools, sought to check. The congregating of so many boys, he considered, must be full of harm, as it was known that vicious boys were of the number, and they were sure to make acquaintanceship with poor boys who were not corrupted, and the consequence was an increase of thievery. As far as his observation went, those schools had done harm, and were doing it, as one schoolmaster, however good, could not check the propensities of boys inured to thieving to corrupt other boys. He told me of the school having been robbed by the boys (as was believed), but that it was not brought before the public. Another gentleman, whose peculiar calling gave him an equal opportunity for judging of the effects of the Ragged Schools, expressed an unhesitating opinion that they were bad schools—for a small proportion of bold, vicious boys would corrupt the better-disposed boys far more readily than the schoolmaster could inculcate principles of honesty into them. The young thieves in a Ragged School knew, he said, very well how to appeal to the spirit of daring and emulation in honest poor boys whom they met in the school and talked with afterwards. Many young thieves, my informant said, went to the Ragged School just for what might be described as "a lounge", and to see if they could in any way form a connection with boys unknown to the police there.

In the course of my inquiries I heard that several boys who had been to the Ragged Schools, had subsequently been in prison, and that some were there now. I therefore called upon Lieut. Tracy, the governor of the Tothill-fields prison, to inquire into this subject. He expressed an opinion—cursorily given he said—that Ragged Schools were not adapted to the reformation of the juvenile criminals of London who resorted there; inasmuch as the great evil to be guarded against, to arrest the progress of criminality, was the *congregating* of criminals. Evil always resulted, and must result, from that; and criminal offenders met in Ragged School, and congregated afterwards. He summoned one of his principal officers who was familiar with the habits and character of juvenile offenders, and the latter expressed an opinion—unequivocally—that the boys in prison from Ragged Schools were generally worse than boys who had not been so educated. He had known above a dozen boys in that prison who had been in Ragged Schools within a recent period. He attributed great evil to vicious boys associating together, under any circumstances, at the Ragged Schools, or elsewhere. The schoolmistress of the prison stated that the girls who had been in Ragged Schools, and afterwards in prison, were neither better nor worse than other girls in prison. Through the courtesy of Lieut. Tracy, I am enabled to give two statements from children then in prison. The first was an intelligent-looking boy (who had an impediment in his speech), and declared his anxiety to speak nothing but the truth—the governor and officer being convinced that his statement might be relied on. He said:

"I am twelve, and have been three times in prison once for stealing cigars, once for a piece of calico, and once for some pigs' feet. I have been twice whipped. I was twelve months at the Exeter-buildings Ragged School, Knightsbridge. I learned reading, writing, and Church of England there. I was brought up there to the Church of England. I know I was, because I went to church with the schoolmaster. I know it was a church. A church is bigger than a chapel, and has a steeple. I learned sums, too, and the commandments, and the catechism. I can't read well." (He was tried on an act of Parliament as to his ability to read. It began "whereas the laws now existing". "Whereas" he could not make out anyhow, and "the laws now" he called "the lays no". He was unable to read any word of two syllables.). At the Ragged School, there were forty or fifty boys. We went at nine, left at twelve, and went back at two. Between twelve and two I was out with the other boys, and we often made up parties to go thieving. We thieved all sorts of things. We taught one another thieving. We liked to teach very young boys best; they're pluckiest, and the police don't know them at first. I knew good boys at the Ragged School— good when they went there—and we taught them to thieve. If we could get a good boy at the Ragged School we taught him to thieve, for he's safe some time from the police, and we share with him. At the Ragged School I was taught that I was to keep my hands from picking and stealing, but I thought it fun to steal. The schoolmaster didn't know I ever stole. God is a spirit in heaven, and is everywhere. If I do wrong I shall be burnt in fire. It frightens me to think of it sometimes. I was first taught and tempted to steal by a boy I met at the Ragged School. He said 'Come along, and I'll show you how to get money'. I stole some cigars, and the other boy, a little boy, kept watch. I was nailed the first time. I shouldn't have been a thief but for the Ragged Schools, I'm sure I shouldn't."

The other boy, a healthy-looking child, said:

"I am ten, and have been twice in prison, and once whipped. I was in prison for 'a fork' and 'some lead'. I sold them in rag-shops. I was three months in Pye-street Ragged School, Westminster. I was a month at the St. Margaret's National School (Westminster). At the Ragged School I learned reading, writing, tailoring, shoemaking, and cleaning the place. (He then read a verse in the Bible imperfectly, and by spelling the words, but quite as well as could be expected). There were forty or fifty boys at the Ragged School; half of them were thieves, and we used to go thieving in gangs of six. When we were away from school we went thieving. We taught any new boy how to thieve, making parties to do it. We would teach any good boy how to thieve. I know four or five good boys at the Ragged Schools taught to thieve by me and others. We got them to join us, as we got afraid ourselves, and the police don't so soon 'spect new boys. Thieving is wrong. Some boys where I lived taught me to thieve. They did not go to a Ragged School, that I know of."

Of the Labourers at the Timber Docks

Letter LVIII

... The Working Lumpers, as I before explained, are the labourers employed to discharge all wood-laden vessels except foreign ships, which are discharged by their own crews. The vessels unladen by the lumpers are discharged sometimes in the dock, and sometimes (when too heavily laden) in the river. ... When a vessel is unladen in the river, the landed goods are discharged by lumpers, who also load the lighters; whereas, in dock, the lumpers discharge them into the company's barges, which are loaded by them as well. With smaller vessels, however, which occasionally go alongside, the lumpers discharge directly to the shore, where the "goods" are received by the company's porters. The lumpers never work upon shore. Of the porters working on shore, there are two kinds, viz., deal and stave porters, whose duty is to receive the landed goods, and to pile and sort them, either along the quay or in the bonding ground, if duty has to be paid upon them. ...

... *A deal porter at the Surrey Canal Dock* stated—

"I have worked a good many years in the Surrey Dock. There were four contractors at the Surrey Canal, but now there's one, and he pays the publican, where we gets our beer, all that's owing to us deal porters, and the publican pays us every Saturday night. I can't say that we are compelled to take beer—certainly not when at our work in the dock; but we're 'expected' to take it when we're waiting. I can't say either that we are discharged if we don't drink; but if we don't we are kept waiting late on a Saturday night on an excuse of the publican's having no change, or something like that; and we feel that somehow or other, if we don't drink, we'll be left in the background. Why don't the superintendent see us paid in the dock? He pays the company's labourers in the dock—they're corn-turners and rafters—and they are paid early, too. We now have four shillings and fourpence a day of from eight to four, and five shillings and eightpence from six to six. It used to be, till four months back I think, four shillings and tenpence and six shillings and fourpence. In slack times, say six months in the year, we earns from ten shillings to twelve shillings a week; in the brisk times, thirty shillings, and sometimes more, but thirty shillings is about the average. We are all paid at the public-house. We gathers from after five or so every Saturday night. We are kept now and then till twelve, and after twelve, and it has been Sunday morning before we've got paid. There is more money spent, in course, up to twelve than up to ten. To get away at half-past nine is very early. I should say that half our earnings, except in our best weeks, goes to the publican for drink—more than half oft enough. If it's a bad week all our earnings, or more. When it waxes late, the wives, who've very likely been without Saturday's dinner or tea, will go to the publican's for their husbands, and they'll get to scold very likely, and then they'll get beaten very likely. We are chiefly married men with families. Pretty well all the deal porters at the docks are drunkards; so there's misery enough for their families. The publican gives credit two following weeks, and encourages drinking in course, but he does it quietly. He'll advance any man at work one shilling a night in money, besides trusting him for drink. I don't know how many we are—I should say from 50 to 200. In old age or accident, in course, we comes on the parish."

Other men whom I saw corroborated this statement, and some of their wives expressed great indignation at the system pursued in paying the labourers. None of them objected to their husbands having four pints of beer when actually at their work in the dock; it was against the publican's temptations on Saturday and other nights that they bitterly inveighed.

At the earnest entreaty of a deal porter's wife, I called on Saturday evening at the public-house where the men were waiting to be paid. I walked into the tap-room as if I had called casually, and I was then unknown to all the deal porters. The tap-room I found small, dark, dirty, and ill-ventilated. What with the tobacco-smoke and the heat of the weather, the room was most disagreeably close and hot. As well as I could count—for, though it was a bright summer's evening, the smoke and gloom rendered it somewhat difficult—there were twenty-four men in this tap-room, which is fitted up in boxes, and the number completely filled the apartment. In the adjoining room, where was a small bar, there were some six or eight more deal porters, lounging about. These numbers, however, fluctuated, for men kept coming in and going out; but all the time I was there thirty men might be stationary in the two hot, dirty, little rooms. They were strong-looking men enough, and all sunburnt; but amongst them were some with pinched features and white lips. There they sat, each man with his beer before him. There was not the slightest hilarity among them; there was not the least semblance of a convivial Saturday night's gathering. The majority sat in silence. Some dozed—others drank or sipped at their pint measures, as if they must do it, or to while away the time. These deal porters were generally dressed in corduroy, fustian, or strong coarse blue woollen jackets, with trowsers of similar material, open big woollen waist-coats, and with coloured cotton handkerchiefs rolled round some thick substance in the way of a stock, and tied loosely round their necks over a striped cotton or coarse linen shirt. All had rough bristly beards, intimating that their shaving was confined to the Saturday mornings. With respect to the system pursued at this dock in the payment of the deal porters, it is right that I should state that I heard from many deal porters praises of the superintendent, though certainly not of the contractor or the publican. I am glad to be able to state, however, that it is the determination of the company to attempt—and that, indeed, they are now attempting—the abolition of the system of public-house paymen. Mr. M'Cannan, the superintendent of these docks, to whom I am indebted for many favours and courtesies, informs me that an arrangement was once made for the payment of the deal porters in "an old box" (a sort of wooden office) within the dock; but the impatience and struggling of the men who had to wait a little while for their week's earnings almost demolished the frail timbers of the old box, and the attempt was abandoned. Within the dock the supply of beer is now limited to three times a day, with a "vend" of half-a-pint a man each visit. . . .

Of the London Sawyers

Letter LIX

The majority of London sawyers, I am informed by some of the most intelligent and experienced members of the trade, are countrymen. They are generally the sons of village carpenters or wheelwrights, though some have been "bred and born" in the trade, as they say. As a body of men they are essentially unpolitical. I could not hear of one Chartist among them; and, although suffering greatly from machinery, I found few with what may be called violent or even strong opinions upon the subject. They spoke of the destruction of Richardson's Saw-mill as one of the follies and barbarisms of past days, and were quite alive to the importance of machinery as a means of producing wealth in a community. They also felt satisfied that it was quite out of their power to stop the progress of it. As a body of men I found them especially peaceable, and apparently of very simple and kindly dispositions. They are not what can be called an educated class, but those whom I saw were certainly distinguished for their natural good sense. They are usually believed to be of intemperate habits, and I am informed that in the palmy days of the trade there was good reason for the belief. But since then work has declined, and they have become much more sober. There are many teetotallers now among them; it is supposed that about one in ten has taken the pledge, and one in twenty kept it. The cause of the intemperance of the sawyers, say my informants, was their extremely hard labour, and the thirst produced by their great exertion. Moreover, it was the custom of their employers, until within the last fifteen years, to pay the men in public-houses. Since then, however, the sawyers have received their wages at the counting-houses of the timber merchants; and this, in connection with the general advance of intelligence among the body, has gone far to diminish the intemperance of the trade. The coffee-shops, again, I am assured, have added greatly to the sobriety of the operative sawyers. The large reduction which has taken place in the earnings of the sawyers has not been attended with any serious alteration in their habits. As a general rule, neither their wives nor their children "go out to work;" and since the decline of their trade no marked change in this respect has occurred. The majority of the men are certainly beyond the middle-age—many that I saw were between sixty and seventy years. Cooper's stave-sawyers, however, are younger men. This is accounted for by the fact that since the decline of the trade of the "general sawyers", very few fresh hands have been brought into the trade, while many of the younger men have emigrated or sought some other employment—whereas the old men have been not only loath to leave the country, but unable to turn their hand to a new business. . . .

The first steam-mill for the sawing of planks was established . . . about thirty-six years ago, by Mr. Smart, near Westminster-bridge. For perhaps twenty years before that period horses had been employed to supersede men's labour. The principle on which these horse-mills were constructed was not dissimilar to that now in use in the steam saw-mills. The horses then did the work of the engine now—working nine saws at once, but with perhaps only half the motive power of steam as regards velocity. About forty-five years ago a party of sawyers one night walked abruptly into the largest of these horse saw-mills—that of Mr. Richardson, of Limehouse—and with sledge-hammers and crow-bars utterly demolished the whole apparatus, which was the work of but a few minutes. The men did not carry a single fragment away with them after the work of demolition had been done, and they studiously abstained from any other act of violence, and even from any act or words of insult. Their plea was, that these horse-mills would bring them and their families to the parish, by making beasts do the work of men, and that they had a right to protect themselves the best way they could, as no man, they said, merely for his own profit, had any right to inflict ruin upon a large body. So I was assured, and such feelings were at that period not uncommon among the ruder class of labourers. These horse-mills were but little remunerative, and Mr. Richardson did not think it worth his while to replace his machinery. It lay scattered about his yard until within twenty or thirty years ago. Another horse-mill, that of Mr. Lett, was demolished in the same way, not long after, by a party of sawyers; and the other proprietors of such places—there were perhaps about six in all—either discontinued the use of horse through fear, or the working of their mills became less remunerative, and they were gradually done away with. I had these particulars from a very intelligent man, now engaged in the sawing business. They were beyond his own recollection; but he had often heard his father, who passed a long life in the capacity of a sawyer, relate the circumstances. My informant was not altogether positive as to dates—he gave them to the best of his recollection. Yet, without this precipitate violence, horse saw-mills would have been discontinued, "for a very sufficient reason", said my informant, "because they didn't pay, I feel pretty well satisfied. Horses, you see, sir, must eat their oats of a night, or whether they are at work or not, but steam consumes coals only when at work."...

Of the London Carpenters and Joiners

Letter LX

... It is with the carpenters and joiners of the metropolis that I have specially to deal. These, as I said before, numbered in 1841 as many as 18,321 individuals, of whom 16,965 were males, and 83 females, of twenty years of age and upwards—and 1,273 males below the age. But among the 18,000 individuals given in the census of 1841, both masters and working men are included, so that to arrive at a correct estimate as to the number of operatives in the metropolis we must take the number of London carpenters who are in business for themselves (and these, according to the "Post-office Directory", are 1,239), and deducting them from the 18,321 individuals cited in the census, we shall come to the conclusion that there were somewhere about 17,000 operative carpenters resident in the metropolis nine years ago; and presuming the trade to have increased since that period at the same rate as it did in the ten years previous, it follows that there are at this present time upwards of 20,000 operative carpenters in London.

Numerically considered then, the carpenters rank amongst the most important of the working classes of the metropolis. The domestic servants, the labourers, the boot and shoe makers, the tailors, the dressmakers, and the clerks, alone take precedence of them in this respect.

About three-fourths or four-fifths of the carpenters working in the metropolis, I am informed are from the country; for it is only within the last fifteen or twenty years that the London masters have taken apprentices. Before that time apprentices were taken—with but few exceptions—only in the City, and those who served their time there did so solely with the view of "taking up their freedom" afterwards. Large masters in London would not then be troubled with lads, though small jobbing masters generally took one or two. Now, however, there is scarcely a master in London but what has some youths in his employ, and many of the large builders have as many lads and "improvers" as they have men, while some of them have even more. All these are used as a means of reducing the cost of men's labour. "When I first came to town, twenty years ago," (said one of the carpenters whom I saw), "I never knew a lad to be employed in any of the large firms in which I worked." As a proof of this, he told me, he never worked at that time but with one "Cockney", that is to say with a person who had been regularly brought up to the carpenter's business in London. Twenty years ago it was usual for the country carpenters to come up to London immediately after having served their apprenticeship; some did this to better their condition, the wages in town being double what they were in the west of England, and some come up to improve themselves in the business and then to return. At that time one-third at least of the number that came to London would go back into the country to settle after two or three years' practice in town. At the present time, however, it is estimated that not one in twelve who come to town from the country ever return. A great number of country carpenters are still attracted to London under the belief that the wages here maintain their former rate. When they arrive in the metropolis they find to their cost that they can obtain employment only among the speculative builders and petty masters, where but two-thirds of the regular wages of the trade are given; and once they take to this kind of work, it becomes impossible for them, unless very prudent indeed, ever to get away from it. This, I am informed, is one of the principal reasons of the over population of the London trade—for the work in the metropolis is now sufficient to give employment only to two-thirds of the hands. Another cause of the trade being over stocked is the reduction of wages that has taken place among those working for the speculative builders and petty masters, for I have before shown that the necessary consequences of under-pay is over-work—that is to say, if the wages of the "non-society" carpenters and joiners have been reduced one-third, then each man will endeavour to do one-third more work in his struggle to obtain the same amount of income as he previously did. Again, it will be found that a new race of employers has sprung up in the metropolis of late years, who are known among the trade as "strapping masters", from the fact of their forcing the men to do double as much work in a day as was formerly expected of them. Hence it is clear, that though the London carpenters have increased 4 per cent less than the general population of the metropolis, still each of the operatives has been compelled of late years, either by the strapping masters, or a reduction of wages, to get through twice or three times as much work as formerly, and thus the trade has become as overstocked by each hand doing double work, as it would have been if the hands themselves had been doubled.

The carpenters and joiners that work for the low speculating builders are, generally speaking, quite a different class of men to those who are in "society". As a rule, to which, of course, there are many exceptions, they are men of dissipated habits. What little they get I am assured is spent in beer and gin, and they have seldom a second suit to their backs. They are generally to be seen on a Sunday lounging about the suburbs of London with their working clothes on, and their rules sticking from their side pockets—the only difference in their attire being, perhaps, that they have a clean shirt and a clean pair of shoes.

The great majority of the hands that work for the speculating builders are young men who have come up from the country, hoping to better their condition. About one-fourth of those who work for the speculative builders are, it is said, men of depraved and intemperate habits, and have scarcely a tool amongst them. The better class of workmen would rather part with the clothes off their backs and the beds from under them, than make away with their tools; so that it is only in cases of the most abject distress that a skilful joiner seeks to raise money upon the implements of his trade. When this is the case, I am told, it is usual for the operatives in "society" to club together, and lend a person so circumstanced, some one tool and some another, until a sufficient "kit" is raised for him to go to work with.

The majority of carpenters who are settled in London are married men with families, and mostly live in lodgings; many of the working men, however, are householders, paying as much as £70 per year rent, and letting off apartments, so as to be wholly or nearly rent free. In London there are several of what may be termed colonies of working carpenters. A great many reside in Lambeth, a large number in Marylebone, in the vicinity of Lisson-grove, and a considerable proportion are to be found in Westminster. This is to be accounted for by the fact that several of the principal firms are established in these quarters. The carpenters who live in lodgings mostly occupy a floor unfurnished, and pay from five to ten shilling rent; but men with large families generally contrive to be householders, from the fact that children are usually objected to in respectable lodgings, so that they must either live in some low neighbourhood or else pay an exorbitant rent for their residences in a better district. The more respectable portion of the carpenters and joiners "will not allow" their wives to do any other work than attend to their domestic and family duties, though some few of the wives of the better class of workmen take in washing or keep small "general shops". The children of the carpenters are mostly well brought up, the fathers educating them to the best of their ability. They are generally sent to day schols. The cause of the carpenters being so anxious about the education of their children lies in the fact that they themselves find the necessity of a knowledge of arithmetic, geometry, and drawing in the different branches of their business. Many of the more skilful carpenters, I am informed, are excellent draughtsmen, and well versed in the higher branches of mathematics. A working carpenter seldom sees his children except on a Sunday, for on the week day he leaves home early in the morning, before they are up, and returns from his work after they are in bed. Carpenters often work miles away from their homes, and seldom or never take a meal in their own houses, except on a Sunday. Either they carry their provisions with them to the shop, or else they resort to the coffee-shops, public-houses, and eating-houses for their meals. In the more respectable firms where they are employed, a "labourer" is kept to boil water for them, and fetch them any necessaries they may require, and the meals are generally taken at the "bench end", under which a cupboard is fitted up for them to keep their provisions in. In those shops where the glue is heated by steam the men will sometimes bring a dumpling or pudding and potatoes with them in the morning, and cook these in a glue-pot which they keep for the purpose. In firms where the glue is dissolved by means of hot plates small tins are provided, on which they cook their steaks, rashers of bacon, red herrings, or anything else they may desire. These arrangements, I am informed, are of great convenience to the men, and in those shops where such things are not allowed they are mostly driven to the public-houses for their food. . . . In some shops as many as from 200 to 300 men are employed, and one of my informants, who worked in as large a shop as any in London, says that among the 300 benchmen employed at his master's, there were not more than six drunkards, and these men were held in general disrepute among their fellow-workmen. Before the men leave their work in the large shops, it is usual for them to change their working clothes for others which they keep in a little cupboard under their bench. Their appearance in the street is as respectable as that of any tradesman.

Letter LXI

. . . I shall now proceed to set forth the effects of each of these several causes of low wages *seriatim*—beginning with the means used by the more honourable masters, and concluding with an account of the practices pursued by the speculative builders. First, of the "*strapping*" system. Concerning this I received the following extraordinary account from a man after his heavy day's labour; and never in all my experience have I seen so sad an instance of overwork. The poor fellow was so fatigued that he could hardly rest in his seat. As he spoke he sighed deeply and heavily, and appeared almost spirit-broken with excessive labour:

"I work at what is called a strapping shop," he said, "and have worked at nothing else for these many years past in London. I call 'strapping', doing as much work as a human being or a horse possibly can in a day, and that without any hanging upon the collar, but with the foreman's eyes constantly fixed upon you, from six o'clock in the morning to six o'clock at night. The shop in which I work is for all the world like a prison—the silent system is as strictly carried out there as in a model gaol. If a man was to ask any common question of his neighbour, except it was connected with his trade, he would be discharged there and then. If a journeyman makes the least mistake, he is packed off just the same. A man working at such places is almost always in

fear; for the most trifling things he's thrown out of work in an instant. And
then the quantity of work that one is forced to get through is positively awful;
if he can't do a plenty of it, he don't stop long where I am. No one would
think it was possible to get so much out of blood and bones. No slaves work
like we do. At some of the strapping shops the foreman keeps continually
walking about with his eyes on all the men at once. At others the foreman is
perched high up, so that he can have the whole of the men under his eye together. I suppose since I knew the trade that a man does four times the work
that he did formerly. I know a man that's done four pairs of sashes in a day,
and one is considered to be a good day's labour. What's worse than all, the
men are everyone striving one against the other. Each is trying to get through
the work quicker than his neighbours. Four or five men are set the same job
so that they may be all pitted against one another, and then away they go
everyone striving his hardest for fear that the others should get finished first.
They are all tearing along from the first thing in the morning to last at night,
as hard as they can go, and when the times comes to knock off they
are ready to drop. It was hours after I got home last night before I could
get a wink of sleep; the soles of my feet were on fire, and my arms ached to
that degree that I could hardly lift my hand to my head. Often, too, when we
get up of a morning, we are more tired than we went to bed, for we can't sleep
many a night; but we mustn't let our employers know it, or else they'd be
certain we couldn't do enough for them, and we'd get the sack. So, tired as we
may be, we are obliged to look lively somehow or other at the shop of a morning. If we're not beside our bench the very moment the bell's done ringing,
our time's docked—they won't give us a single minute out of the hour. If I
was working for a fair master, I should do nearly one-third less work than I
am now forced to get through, and sometimes a half less; and even to manage
that much, I shouldn't be idle a second of my time. It's quite a mystery to me
how they do contrive to get so much work out of the men. But they are very
clever people. They know how to have the most out of a man, better than any
one in the world. They are all picked men in the shop—regular "strappers",
and no mistake. The most of them are five foot ten, and fine broad shouldered,
strong backed fellows too—if they weren't they would not have them. Bless
you, they make no words with the men, they sack them if they're not strong
enough to do all they want; and they can pretty soon tell, the very first shaving
a man strikes in the shop, what a chap is made of. Some men are done up at
such work—quite old men and grey with spectacles on, by the time they are
forty. I have seen fine strong men, of six-and-thirty, come in there and be bent
double in two or three years. They are most all countrymen at the strapping
shops. If they see a great strapping fellow who they think has got some stuff
about him that will come out, they will give him a job directly. We are used
for all the world like cab or omnibus horses. Directly they've had all the work
out of us we are turned off, and I am sure after my day's work is over, my
feelings must be very much the same as one of the London cab horses. As for
Sunday, it is *literally* a day of rest with us, for the greater part of us lays a bed
all day, and even that will hardly take the aches and pains out of our bones
and muscles. When I'm done and flung by, of course I must starve.". . .

. . . I now come to treat of the system pursued by the speculating builders of the metropolis. Of all the slop-trades that I have yet examined there appear to be greater evils connected with cheap building than with any other. It will be seen that from this the public derive *no benefit whatsoever*—house rent not even being reduced by it, while the journeymen are ground down to the same state of misery and degradation as in all other trades where the slop system flourishes. Of the 18,000 men working for the dishonourable portion of the building trade, it should be remembered that not one belongs to a society, and consequently they have no resource but the parish in case of sickness, accident, or old age. Consequently, as one of the more intelligent journeymen said to me, it is the master alone, who, by reducing the wages of the workmen, is benefitted, for though the house is built cheaper, the public have not only to pay the same rent, but to support the workmen out of the poor-rates. More-over, it is by means of this system that the better, the more skilful, and more provident portion of the trade are being dragged down to the same wretched abasement as the unskilful and improvident workmen. In order, however, that I might not be misled by the journeymen, I thought it my duty to call upon some master builders of the "honourable trade"—gentlemen of high char-acter—as well as upon architects of equally high standing. I found the same opinion entertained by them all as to the ruinous effects of the kind of com-petition existing in their trade to a master who strives to be just to his cus-tomers and fair to his men. This competition, I was assured, was the worst in the contracts for building churches, chapels, and public institutions generally. "Honesty is now almost impossible among us," said one master-builder. "It *is* impossible in cheap contract work, for the competition puts all the honourable trade out of the field; high character, and good materials, and the best work-manship are of no avail. Capitalists can command any low-priced work, by letting and subletting, and all by the piece. Most of these speculating and contracting people think only how to make money; or they must raise money to stop a gap (a bill perhaps to be met), and they grasp at any offer of an advance of money on account of a building to be erected. Their proceedings are an encouragement to every kind of dishonesty. They fail continually, and they drag good men down with them." Strong as these opinions are, I heard them fully confirmed by men who could not be mistaken in the matter. "Advertise for contracts work," said another gentleman, "and you'll soon have a dozen applicants at all sorts of prices; and all tradesmen like myself, who calculate for a contract at a rate to pay the regular wages, and not to leave either the timber-merchant or anybody else in the lurch, and to yield us the smallest possible percentage for our risk and outlay, are regarded as a pack of extortionate men."

The system of contract work was known forty years ago, or earlier, among the tradesmen employed in the erection of houses of the best class; but it was known as an exception rather than as an established system. It was long before that, however, not unfrequent as regards the erection of public buildings. A customer would then obtain "estimates" of the probable cost from well-known firms, and so ascertain the lowest price at which a private house could be erected. Thirty years back this system had gained a strong hold on all building capitalists, and it has gone on increasing within these ten or twelve, or more years. No mansion is built otherwise than by contract, except in the rare instance of an old connection of an old firm. The introduction of stuccos, cements, etc., within these twenty-five years, has further encouraged the contract system, by supplying a low-priced exterior for our houses—while the introduction of cheap paper, and of cheaper wood-work, by means of machinery, supplied the materials of a cheap interior; and a tradesman of little skill or probity can speculate in a building where he is not called upon to make heavy outlays for superior stone or timber, and can employ under-paid labour.

. . . "Unless," said one architect to me, "some check is given to this dishonest system, the honourable masters must be dragged down towards the level of the others, and the best artisans must sink with them. The low-priced builders of the worst class cannot possible do their work in any way but by cheating the tradesmen and robbing the artisan."

Such are the opinions of the honourable masters in connection with the building trade, as to the ruinous effects of the slop or contract system. I shall now subjoin the statements . . . of the foreman . . . in connection with this part of the trade:

"I am a foreman to a speculating builder. My employer is not in a very large way: he has about ten carpenters and joiners. He does not let the work, he employs all the men by the day. The highest wages he gives is twenty-eight shillings a week; this sum he pays to three of his men. He gives twenty-four shillings to three others; and two more have £1 a week. Besides these he employs two apprentices. To the oldest of these he gives fifteen shillings a week, and to the youngest six shillings. The men who have twenty-eight shillings are superior hands—such men as at either of the C—'s would get their six shillings a day. The twenty-four shillings men are good skilful carpenters, fairly worth thirty shillings; and those in the receipt of £1 are young men fresh from the country—principally from Devonshire. The wages in the west of England are from twelve shillings to fifteen shillings, and these low wages send a lot of lads to town every year, in the hope of bettering their condition. They mostly obtain work among the speculating builders. I suppose there are more carpenters in London from Devonshire and Cornwall than from any other counties in England. At least half of the carpenters and joiners employed by the speculating builders here are lads fresh up from the country. Apprentices are not employed by the speculators as a rule. Most of the speculators have no fixed shops. Their work is carried on chiefly in, what we term, camp shops —that is in sheds erected in the field where the buildings are going on, and that's one reason why apprentices are not generally taken by speculating builders. The speculators find plenty of cheap labour among the country lads. A hand fresh up from the West of England can't get employment at the best of shops, unless he's got some friends, and so, after walking all London, he generally is driven to look for a job among the speculators at low wages. What few good hands are employed by the speculators are kept only to look after the countrymen. As a rule, I think young hands are mostly preferred, because there is more work in them. It is one of the chief evils of the carpenter's trade, that as soon as a man turns of forty masters won't keep him on. The master whom I work for pays much better prices than most of the speculators. The average wages of the inferior hands employed in building is about fifteen shillings; that is, I think, one-half of the hands don't receive more than that, and the other about twenty-four shillings. But day-pay is the exception with the speculators. The way in which the work is done is mostly by letting and sub-letting. The masters usually prefer to let work, because it takes all the trouble off their hands. They know what they are to get for the job, and of course they let it as much under that figure as they possibly can, all of which is clear gain without the least trouble. How the work is done, or by whom, it's no matter to them, so long as they can make what they want out of the job, and have no bother about it. Some of our largest builders are taking to this plan, and a party who used to have one of the largest shops in London has within the last three years discharged all the men in his employ (he had 200 at least), and has now merely an office, and none but clerks and accountants in his pay. He has taken to letting his work out instead of doing it at home. The parties to whom the work is let by the speculating builders are generally working men, and these men in their turn look out for other working men, who will take the job cheaper than they will, and so I leave you, sir, and the public to judge what the party who really executes the work gets for his labour, and what is the quality of work that he is likely to put into it. The speculating builder generally employs an overlooker to see that the work is done sufficiently well to pass the surveyor. That's all he cares about. Whether it's done by thieves, or drunkards, or boys, it's no matter to him. The overlooker, of course, sees after the first party to whom the work is let, and this party in his turn looks after the several hands that he has sub-let it to. The first man who agrees to the job takes it in the lump, and he again lets it to others in the piece. I have known instances of its having been let again a third time, but this is not usual. The party who takes the job in the lump from the speculator usually employs a foreman, whose duty it is to give out the materials, and to make working drawings. The men to whom it is sub-let only find labour, while the 'lumper', or first contractor, agrees for both labour and materials. It is usual in contract work, for the first party who takes the job to be bound in a large sum for the due and faithful performance of his contract. He then in his turn finds out a subcontractor, who is mostly a small builder, who will also bind himself that the work shall be properly executed, and there the bidding ceases —those parties to whom the job is afterwards let, or sub-let, employing foremen or overlookers to see that their contract is carried out. The first contractor has scarcely any trouble whatsoever; he merely engages a gentleman, who rides about in a gig, to see that what is done is likely to pass muster. The subcontractor has a little more trouble; and so it goes on as it gets down and down. Of course I need not tell you that the first contractor, who does the *least* of all, gets the *most* of all; while the poor wretch of a working man, who positively executes the job, is obliged to slave away every hour night after night to get a bare living out of it; and this is the contract system. The public are fleeced by it to an extent the builders alone can know. Work is scamped in such a way that the houses are not safe to live in. Our name for them in the trade is 'bird cages', and really nine-tenths of the houses built now-a-days are very little stronger. Again, the houses built by the speculators are almost all damp. There is no concrete ever placed at the foundation to make them dry and prevent them from sinking. Further, they are all badly drained. Many of the walls of the houses built by the speculators are much less in thickness than the Building

Act requires. I'll tell you how this is done. In a third-rate house the wall should be, according to the Act, two bricks thick at least, and in a second-rate house, two bricks and a half. The speculators build up the third-rates a brick and a half thick, and the second-rates only two bricks, and behind this they run up another half brick, so that they can throw that part down immediately after the surveyor has inspected it. Many of the chimney breasts, too, are filled up with rubbish, instead of being solid brickwork. The surveyor is frequently hand in hand with the speculator, and can't for the life of him discover any of these defects—but you know there's none so blind as those that *won't* see. And yet, notwithstanding, and starving of the workmen, rents in the suburbs do not come down. . . .

Concerning ground rents, I had the following account from one well acquainted with the tricks of the speculators:

"The party for whom I am foreman has just taken a large estate, and he contemplates making some thousands of pounds by means of the improved ground rents alone. There are several with him in the speculation, and this is the way in which such affairs are generally managed. A large plot of ground (six or seven meadows, may be) somewhere in the suburbs is selected by the speculators as likely to be an eligible spot for building—that is to say, they think that a few squares, villas, and terraces about that part would be likely to let as soon as run up. Then the speculators go to the freeholder or his solicitor, and offer to take the ground of him on a ninety-nine years' lease at a rent of about £50 a year per acre, and may be they take as many as fifty acres at this rate. At the same time they make a proviso that the rent shall not commence until either so many houses are built, or perhaps before a twelve month has elapsed. If they didn't do this the enormous rent most likely would swallow them up before they had half got through their job. Well, may be, they erect half or two-thirds of the number of houses that they have stipulated to do before paying rent. These are what we term 'call-birds', and are done to decoy others to build on the ground. For this purpose a street is frequently cut, the ground turned up on each side, just to show the plan, and the corner house, and three others, perhaps, are built just to let the public see the style of thing that it's going to be. Occasionally a church is begun, for this is found to be a great attraction in a new neighbourhood. Well, when things are sufficiently ripe this way, and the field has been well mapped out into plots, a board is stuck up, advertising 'THIS GROUND TO BE LET, ON BUILDING LEASES'. Several small builders then apply to take a portion of it, sufficient for two or three houses, may be, for which they agree to pay about five guineas a year (they generally make it *guineas* these gentlemen) for the ground-rent of each house. And when the parties who originally took the meadows on lease have got a sufficient number of these plots let off, and the small builders have run up a few of the carcases, they advertise 'a sale of well-secured rents will take place at the Mart on such a day'. Ground-rents, you must know, are considered to be one of the safest of all investments now-a-days; for if they are not paid, the ground landlord, you see, has the power of seizing the houses; so gentle-men with money are glad to lay it out in this way, and there's a more ready sale for ground-rents than for anything else in the building line. There's sure to be strong competition for them, let the sale be whenever it will. Well, let us see now how the case stands. There are fifty acres taken on lease at £50 an acre a year, and that is £2,500 per annum. Upon each of these fifty acres fifty houses can be erected (including villas and streets, taking one with the other upon an average). The ground-rent of each of these houses is (at the least) £5, and this gives for the 2,500 houses that are built upon the whole of the fifty acres £12,500 per annum. Hence you see there is a clear net profit of £10,000 a year made by the transaction. This is not at all an extraordinary case in building speculations."

The subjoined supplies information concerning some other tricks of the speculators:

"For the last fifteen months I have been at work on the estate. You had better not say what estate, or I shall be known. My master was a bankrupt some time back. Since his bankruptcy, he has started in business again. His friends have taken him by the hand, and a speculating builder has no need of any capital. The agents and lawyers find whatever cash is required to pay the workmen, on the Saturday night, and the builder makes a smash of it for the materials—as a matter of course. I'll tell you, sir, how this dodge is worked. A party of gentlemen who wishes to put their money into some building specula-tion that seems to promise well, agree with a builder to find him all the cash to pay the workmen with, provided he will make himself answerable for the material, and for this they agree to give him a share in the profits if the spec turns out well. If, however, it should turn out bad, he is to be the party to go into the Gazette, for whatever may be owing. Of course everything is kept snug and secret among 'em, and if the builder goes to pieces, and doesn't let out who was his backers, why, directly he gets his certificate, they don't mind starting him again on the same terms. This is one of the ways in which building is carried on at the present time, on a large scale. The master I'm speaking of never gives a carpenter or joiner, if they are at day work for him, less than five shillings a day; he takes it out of the timber merchant and brickmaker, instead of the journeymen.". . .

Of the Moulding, Planing and Veneering Mills

Letter LXII

. . . The veneer-mill sawyers are paid five shillings, six shillings, and seven shillings a-day; but for that payment the saw is "taxed" to perform 5,000 feet in a week, and for all beyond that the veneer mill-sawyer receives seven shil-lings per 1,000 feet—his average the year through is £2 15s. a week. There is no society among these men, and their number in London—where there are eight mills with twenty-eight saws—does not exceed forty. The labourers at the veneer mills are paid three shillings and three shillings and sixpence a day, and the men who pile the timber, known in the trade as "gangers", earn six shillings, seven shillings, and eight shillings a day. These gangers, however, are a very small body, only four being employed at the great mill in question. In packing and tying the matches twenty girls are usually employed.

To this it is but fair that I should append the statement of one of the most intelligent of the operative carpenters, concerning the influence of machinery upon his trade. I wish it, however, to be distinctly understood that the opinions expressed below are those of the working men, and they are given here merely in order that the public should be made acquainted with them:

"The opinion of the journeymen generally is, that machinery cannot but make the trade worse and worse every year. The public, I know, generally believe it to be the greatest of blessings to have work done as cheap as possible, and as machinery does work cheaper than human beings, of course it is looked upon as a great benefit to society. The reason why the work can be done cheaper by machinery is, because a steam-engine only wants coals, and we require victuals—besides, masters can keep their steam-engines working night and day, and human beings *must* rest. The longer a master can keep his machinery going, the oftener, of course, he turns his capital over. You see directly they get a large quantity of machinery together, so as to keep it going continually, they will work at any price. I'm certain if they was tied to time as we are, we could beat them in our trade, for there's only particular parts that they can do effectually, and the great portion of these is the most laborious. To produce work as cheap as possible is certainly a great benefit to all those who have money to buy with; but to the working classes—that is to those who have no money but what they earn by their labour—machinery cannot but be a curse, since the object of it is to displace the very labour by which they live. Of course, the capitalist gets ultimately a greater amount of profit by machinery, because he does more work with it, and so increases the returns on his capital, even though he sells at a less rate; it's by small profits and quick returns that all the fortunes are made in the trade. But, only let us have machinery carried out to its full extent and then we shall soon know whether it is really a blessing or a curse to society as at present constituted. No working man that ever I heard but did not admit that machinery might be a benefit in another state of things, but that at present it must do an inconceivable amount of harm. If carried out to its full extent, of course it would displace human labour *altogether* (except the few children that would be required to tend upon it, and the few makers of it)—and when *all* labour is displaced, what is to become of the working men? But there is another point connected with machinery that also requires to be attended to. Suppose, I say, that *all* human labour is done away by it, and the working men are turned into paupers and criminals, then what I want to know is, who are to be the customers of the capitalists? The capitalists themselves, we should remember, spend little or none (comparatively speaking) of the money *they* get; for, of course, it is the object of every capitalist to save all he can, and so increase the bulk of money out of which he makes his profits. The working men, however, spend *all* they receive —it's true a small amount is put into the savings bank, but that's a mere drop in the ocean; and so the working classes constitute the great proportion of the country. The lower their wages are reduced of course the less they have to spend, and when they are entirely superseded by machinery, of course they'll have nothing at all to spend, and then, I ask again, who are to be the capitalists' customers?"

Of the Furniture Workers

Letter LXIII

The cabinet-makers find all their own tools, a complete set of which is worth from £30 to £40. They all work on the master's premises, which, in establishments where many men are employed, are, with a few exceptions, spacious and well-ventilated rooms, open to the skylighted roof. Valuable timber is generally placed along the joists of the workshop, and there it remains a due time for "seasoning". When the men are at work there is seldom much conversation, as each man's attention is given to his own especial task, while the noise of the saw, the plane, or the hammer, is another impediment to conversation. Politics, beyond the mere news of the day, are, I am assured by experienced parties, little discussed in these workshops. I am told, also, that the cabinet-makers, as a body, care little about such matters.

The operative cabinet-makers of the best class are, to speak generally, men of a very high degree of intelligence. I must be understood to be here speaking of the best paid. Of the poor artisans of the East-end I have a different tale to tell. I was told by a cabinet-maker—and, judging by my own observations, with perfect correctness—that of all classes of mechanics the cabinet-makers have the most comfortable abodes. The same thing may be said also, if in a less degree, of the joiners and carpenters; and the reason is obvious—a steady workman occupies his leisure in making the articles for his own use. Perhaps there are not many stronger contrasts than one I have remarked in the course of my present inquiry—that between the abode of the workman in a good West-end establishment, and the garret or cellar of the toiler for a "slaughter-house" at the East-end. In the one you have the warm, red glow of polished mahogany furniture; a clean carpet covers the floor; a few engravings in neat frames hang against the papered wall; and bookshelves or a bookcase have their appropriate furniture. Very white and bright-coloured pot ornaments, with sometimes a few roses in a small vase, are reflected in the mirror over the mantelshelf. The East-end cabinet-maker's room has *one* piece of furniture, which is generally the principal—the workman's bench. The walls are bare, and sometimes the half-black plaster is crumbling from them; all is dark and dingy, and of furniture there is very little, and that, it must be borne in mind, when the occupant is a furniture-maker. A drawer-maker whom I saw in Bethnal-green had never been able to afford a chest of drawers for his own use; "besides," he added, "what do I want with drawers? I've nothing to put in them." What is meant by a "slaughter-house" will be seen in my account of the non-society cabinet-makers in Spitalfields and the adjacent districts. The same establishments in the West-end are generally described as "linen-drapers"; they are indeed the drapers who sell every description of furniture and upholstery, but the workmen from whom they receive their goods are the "East-enders". These "linendrapers", and indeed all masters who employ non-society men, are known in the trade as "black" masters. "He's nothing but a black" is a sentence expressive of supreme contempt in a cabinet-maker's mouth.

"Within my recollection," said an intelligent cabinet-maker, "there was much drinking, very much drinking, among cabinet-makers. This was fifteen years back. Now I'm satisfied that at least seven-eighths of all who are in society are sober and temperate men. Indeed, good masters won't have tipplers now-a-days." According to the Metropolitan Police returns, the cabinet-makers and the turners are two of the least criminal of all the artisans; I speak not of any one year, but from an average taken for the last ten.

The great majority of the cabinet-makers are married men, and were described to me by the best informed parties as generally domestic men, living, whenever it was possible, near their workshops, and going home to every meal. They are not much of play-goers, a Christmas pantomime or any holiday spectacle being exceptions, especially where there is a family. "I don't know a card-player", said a man who had every means of knowing, "amongst us. I think you'll find more cabinet-makers than any other trade members of mechanics' institutes and literary institutions, and attenders at lectures." Some journeymen cabinet-makers have saved money, and I found them all speak highly of the advantages they, as well as their masters, derive from their trade society." The majority of the cabinet-makers in London are countrymen. There are some very good workmen from Scotland. One who has been an apprentice to a good London master is, however, considered to rank with the very highest as a skilful workman.

Bedstead making is, as I have stated, a distinct branch of the cabinet-maker's business. . . .

. . . From a well-informed man, a member of "society", I had the following statement, which embodies information (which I found fully corroborated) of the social conditions of the men, and the fashions of the trade. I am informed that in the society of bedstead-makers there is not one unmarried man.

"When I first knew the business, forty years ago, I could earn at bed-stead making, by hard work, fifty or sixty shillings. I have heard men brag in a public-house that they could make more than sixty shillings, and masters got to hear of it, and there was great dissatisfaction. We always work by piece, and did so when I was an apprentice in London. The prices paid to society men are, on the whole, the same as in 1811. We all find our own tools, and a good kit is worth £30. I consider the bedstead-makers an intelligent, sober, class. I'm speaking of society men—gentlemen I may call them. I don't know much of the others. The majority of us are members of literary institutions, and some of us have saved money. There is great improvement since I first knew bedstead makers, in point of temperance. There used to be hard drinking and less working. In 1810, when we met for society purposes, our allowance of fourpence a night per man that had to attend was drunk in an hour; now it's not consumed in the course of the meeting. Several of us are house-keepers, and can support our wives and families comfortably. I don't think one of the wives of the members of our society work in any way but for the family. I have brought up seven children well, and now five are working at other trades, and two girls at home. Very few good hands now earn less than thirty shillings a week, and some eight or nine shillings more. I do that, and I've been very rarely out of work. . . .

Of the Fancy Cabinet-Makers of London

Letter LXIV

... The fancy cabinet-makers are, I am informed, far less political than they used to be. The working singly, and in their own rooms, as is nearly universal with them now, has rendered them more unsocial than they were and less disposed for the interchange of good offices with their fellow-workmen, as well as less regardful of their position and their rights as skilled labourers. "Politics, sir," said one man, in answer to my inquiry, "what's politics to me, compared to getting my dinner—and what's getting my dinner, compared to getting food for my children?"

The amusements of the cabinet-makers, I was told by one of the older workmen, used to be principally the play. Some were very fond of going to the Polytechnic Institution. "Now, however," he said, "few comparatively can afford the shilling, or sixpence that's wanted, and they go to penny concerts, and get to think that 'Sam Hall', or some nigger thing is very prime indeed. In my own case I've seen Liston play *Paul Pry*, and Farren play the *Colonel*, and Mrs. Glover the *Housekeeper*. I think that was the cast at the start, but I'm not quite sure. I went to see it, sir, at least eight times at my own expense. Latterly I've been to the play only once these three years, and then I had an order." Card-playing, dominoes, and games that are carried on without bodily exertion, seem now to be the chief recreations of the fancy cabinet-makers. The fancy cabinet trade has of late years almost entirely sunk into low prices and inferior workmanship. There are still five or six West-end masters who give good wages—six times as much as I have detailed—but none of the masters employ more than two or three hands, and for these hands there is not, at the fancy cabinet trade, half employment, so they become general workmen. ...

... The person from whom I received the following narrative was an elderly man, and a workman of great intelligence. He resided in a poor and crowded neighbourhood. His wife was a laundress, and there was a comfortable air of cleanliness in their rooms. I give this man's statement fully, as it contains much that has been repeated to me by others in different branches:

"I've known the London fancy cabinet trade", he said, "for forty-five years, as that's the time when I was apprenticed in London. My father was a button-maker in Birmingham, and gave a premium of fifty guineas with me. But he failed, and came to London, and was for some time a clerk with Rundell and Bridge, the great jewellers. My master was a tyrannical master; but he certainly made a workman of me and of all his apprentices. I don't recollect how many he had. I think that now even a little master treats his apprentices middling well; for if he don't they turn sulky, and he can hardly afford their being sulky, as he depends on them for work and profit, such as it is. I got work in a good shop immediately after I was out of my time. No good hand need, then, be a week out of work. Masters clamoured for a good man. I have made £3 3s. a week, and one week I made £3 15s. For twenty years after that I didn't know what it was to want a job. I once during that time had three letters altogether in my pocket from Mr. Middleton, the great fancy cabinet-maker—you may have heard of Middleton's pencils, for he was the first in that line too—pressing an engagement upon me. Then I prided myself (and so did my mates) that I was a fancy cabinet-maker. I felt myself a gentleman, and we all held up our heads like gentlemen. I was very fond at that time of reading all that Charles Lamb wrote, and all that Leigh Hunt wrote. As to reading now, why, if we have a quarter of cheese or butter, I get hold of the paper it's brought in, and read it every word. I can't afford a taste for reading if it's to be paid for. I got married twenty-five years ago, and could live very comfortably then without my wife having to work to help me. We had two houses towards the West-end, and let them out furnished. But twenty years ago, or less, I resisted reductions in our wages, and fought against them. I fought against them for $3\frac{1}{2}$ years, and things went wrong—uncommon wrong —and I had to sacrifice everything to meet arrears of rent and taxes, and I was seized at last; for it wanted a weekly lift through a man's earnings to keep all prosperous. I've done all sorts of work in my time, but I'm now making desks 'ladies' school', or 'writing'—of mahogany, rosewood, and satin-wood. Those are the principal; though every now and then another fancy wood is used. Walnut sawn solid makes a beautiful desk or box. I think walnut's coming into fashion again for that work. Twenty years ago I made thirty-five shillings at the least a week the year through. My family then, and for five, six, or seven, or more years after that time, had the treat of smelling a real good tasty Sunday dinner of beef, or pork, or mutton, as it came hot from the baker's, steaming over the potatoes. And after smelling it we had the treat of eating it, with a drop of beer to wash it down. On week days, too, we had the same pretty regular. I've had six children. Now we have still the smell and the taste of a Sunday meat dinner, but there it stops. We have no such dinners for week days. I'm forced now-a-days to work on Sundays too, and almost every Sunday. People may talk as they like about Sunday labour; I know all about it; but an empty cupboard is stronger than everything. If I have the chance I may make fifteen shillings a week at present prices. I work, as we mainly do, at my own bench, in my own place, and find my own tools, glue, glass-paper, candles, and et ceteras; so that my fifteen shillings a week sometimes falls down to twelve shillings clear. I work for masters, but not always, that find their own materials; but a great many of us have to find material and all. When our work's taken in, if the key breaks, the foreman—and the foreman is often the master's very convenient tool—fines a man twopence, or he may take back the work, and make it good, if he's found the material—that's called 'stopping'. Locks for the low-priced works are paltry, infamous things. Good locks used to be put to good work; they cost tenpence and one shilling for inferior, and averaged two shillings for better, and from five shillings to seven shillings for desks and boxes, where security was wanted. Now locks cost twopence and $2\frac{1}{2}$d.—slop things, that's no safeguard. What was reckoned, and indeed was, inferior box-locks, was sixpence and is now $1\frac{1}{2}$d. Work's huddled together any how. How it'll all end with me is a poser. I suppose in the workhouse. I almost always worked at piece-work, and don't object to it when wages are fair; indeed, piece-work is better for a good hand, and he's more independent. If a man was on by day he would be expected to do so much work a week, and that would come to about the same thing. In 1825 or 1826 I had four shillings for making a lady's workbox if it was ordered to be first rate, as the customer was very particular; three shillings and sixpence was the regular wages, and I could make ten or eleven, or, in long days, twelve, in a week. Candlelight isn't well adapted for our trade; and when a man works in his own room, as I've mostly done, and has been and is the custom of our trade, he don't think of gas. Cheap provisions is a great blessing. No one knows what we suffered in '47, when bread was elevenpence to one shilling; and when it was at the highest our wages were reduced. When I was first a journeyman I had ten shillings for making a twenty-inch desk, and it fell to eight shillings, and seven shillings, and six shillings, and by littles and littles down to what it is now, four shillings; and it's pretty well two days' work to make it properly, but it ain't made properly nineteen times out of twenty. It can't be done at the money. Perhaps a scamping hand might make five such things in a week, or six if he worked on Sundays, and if he was kept regularly at it, but he never is, or very seldom. In my young days an inferior hand couldn't get work in London; now he has a better chance. I think that machinery has been a benefit to us; it increases the material for our work. If there wasn't so much veneering there shouldn't be so much fancy cabinet-work. To show how wages have fallen, I'll mention this. A month back I walked through the Lowther-arcade, and saw fancy boxes, made of different kinds of wood, marked two shillings and sixpence, and I've had twenty years ago—aye, and fifteen years ago, but not so often—three shillings for the mere making of them, and found nothing at all. The material couldn't cost less than one shilling or from that to one shilling and sixpence altogether. Such boxes are plastered together by boys—or most likely by girls, if a man has sharpish girls in his family, and works at his own bench. Hawkers have sold such boxes so that they didn't get 1½d. a piece for making them. The French goods, in my opinion, don't harm us now; they did at one time. I fancy that little masters sprung up twenty years ago, and have gone on increasing. How many of them there are I don't know; Lord knows there's too many. I'm satisfied that a scamping hand will do his work in one quarter of the time that a good hand will. I can't scamp. A man must be brought up to do it." . . .

Of the Slop Cabinet Trade

Letter LXV

The cabinet-makers, socially as well as commercially considered, consist, like all other operatives, of two distinct classes; that is to say, of "society" and "non-society men", or, in the language of political economy, of those whose wages are regulated by *custom*, and those whose earnings are determined by *competition*. The former class numbers between six and seven hundred of the trade, and the latter between four and five thousand. As a general rule, I may remark that I find the "society men" of every trade comprise about one-tenth of the whole. Hence it follows, that if the non-society men are neither so skilful nor so well conducted as the others, at least they are quite as important a body, from the fact that they constitute the main portion of the trade. The transition from the one class to the other is, however, in most cases, of a very disheartening character. The difference between the tailor at the West-end, working for the better shops at the better prices, and the poor wretch slaving at "starvation wages" for the sweaters and slop-shops at the East-end, has already been pointed out. The same marked contrast was also shown to exist between the society and non-society boot and shoemakers. The carpenters and joiners told the same story. There we found society men renting houses of their own —some paying as much as £70 a year—and the non-society men overworked and underpaid, so that a few weeks' sickness reduced them to absolute pauperism. Nor, I regret to say, can any other tale be told of the cabinet makers—except it be that the competitive men in this trade are even in a worse position than any other. . . .

. . . Here we shall find that the wages a few years since were from three to four hundred per cent better than they are at present—twenty shillings having formerly been the price paid for making that for which the operatives now receive only five shillings, and this notwithstanding that the number of hands in the London trade from 1831 to 1841 declined thirty-three per cent relatively to the rest of the population. Nor can it be said that this extraordinary depreciation in the value of the cabinet-maker's labour has arisen from any proportionate decrease in the quantity of work to be done. The number of houses built in the metropolis has of late been considerably on the increase. Since 1839 there have been 200 miles of new streets formed in London—no less than 6,405 new dwellings having been erected annually since that time; and as it is but fair to assume that the majority of these new houses must have required new furniture, it is clear that it is impossible to account for the decline in the wages of the trade in question upon the assumption of an equal decline in the quantity of work. How, then, are we to explain the fact, that while the hands have decreased 33 per cent and work increased at a considerable rate, wages a few years ago were 300 per cent better than they are are present? The solution of the problem will be found in the extraordinary increase that has taken place within the last twenty years of what are called "garret masters" in the cabinet trade. These garret masters are a class of small "trade-working masters", supplying both capital and labour. They are in manufacture what "the peasant proprietors" are in agriculture—their own employers and their own workmen. There is, however, this one marked distinction between the two classes—the garret master cannot, like the peasant proprietor, *eat* what he produces; the consequence is that he is obliged to convert each article into food immediately he manufactures it, no matter what the state of the market may be. The capital of the garret master being generally sufficient to find him in materials for the manufacture of only one article at a time, and his savings being but barely enough for his subsistence while he is engaged in putting those materials together, he is compelled, the moment the work is completed, to part with it for whatever he can get. He cannot afford to keep it even a day, for to do so is generally to remain a day unfed. Hence, if the market be at all slack, he has to force a sale by offering his goods at the lowest possible price. What wonder, then, that the necessities of such a class of individiuals should have created a special race of employers, known by the significant name of "slaughter-house men"—or that these, being aware of the inability of the "garret masters" to hold out against any offer, no matter how slight a remuneration it affords for their labour, should continually lower and lower their prices until the entire body of the competitive portion of the cabinet trade is sunk in utter destitution and misery. Moreover, it is well known how strong is the stimulus among peasant proprietors, or, indeed, any class working for themselves, to extra production. So it is, indeed, with the garret masters; their industry is almost incessant, and hence a greater quantity of work is turned out by them, and continually forced into the market, than there would otherwise be. What though there be a brisk and a slack season in the cabinet-maker's trade as in the majority of others—slack or brisk, the garret masters must produce the same excessive quantity of goods. In the hope of extricating himself from his overwhelming poverty he toils on, producing more and more—and yet the more he produces the more hopeless does his position become; for the greater the stock that he thrusts into the market, the lower does the price of his labour fall, until at last he and his whole family work for less than half what he himself could earn a few years back by his own unaided labour.

Another cause of the necessity of the garret master to part with his goods as soon as made, is the large size of the article he manufactures, and the consequent cost of conveying them from slaughterhouse to slaughterhouse till a purchaser be found. For this purpose a van is frequently hired; and the consequence is that he cannot hold out against the "slaughterer's" offer, even for an hour, without increasing the expense of carriage, and so virtually reducing his gains. This is so well known at the slaughter-houses, that if a man, after seeking in vain for a fair remuneration for his work, is goaded by his necessities to call at a shop a second time to accept a price that he had previously refused, he seldom obtains what was first offered him. Sometimes, when he has been ground down to the lowest possible sum, he is paid late on a Saturday night with a cheque, and forced to give "the firm" a liberal discount for cashing it.

For a more detailed account, however, of the iniquities practised upon this class of operatives, I refer the reader to the statements given below. It will be there seen that all the modes by which work can be produced cheap are in full operation. The labour of apprentices and children is the prevailing means of production. I heard of one small trade working master, who had as many as eleven apprentices at work for him; and wherever the operative is blessed with a family, they all work, even from six years old; for it is generally in the worst paid trades that the labour of children is valuable, and hence a premium is given for the over population of a business that is already too fully stocked with hands. The employment of any undue number of apprentices—a system which I find is invariably adopted in those trades and where the remuneration has fallen below the standard of men's labour—also tends to increase the very excess of hands from which the trade is suffering; and thus it is that the lower wages become, the lower still they are reduced. There are very few—some told me there were none, but there are a few—who work as journeymen for "little masters"; but these men become little masters in their turn, or they must starve in idleness, for their employment is precarious. There is among the East-end cabinet makers no society, no benefit or sick fund, and very little communion between the different classes. The chair-maker knows nothing of the table maker next door, and cannot tell whether others in his calling thrive better or worse than he does. These men have no time for social intercommunication. The struggle to live absorbs all their energies, and confines all their aspirations to that one endeavour. Their labour is devoted, with the rarest exceptions, to the "slaughter-houses", "linen-drapers", " 'polsterers", or "warehouses". By all these names I heard the shopkeepers who deal in furniture of all kinds, as well as drapery-goods, designated. These shopkeepers pay the lowest possible prices, and in order to insure a bare livelihood under them, the cabinet-makers must work very rapidly. This necessity has led the men to labour only at one branch, at which an artisan becomes expert; but he can do little or nothing else, and that again makes him more dependent on the warehouses. The loo table maker only makes loo tables; the cheffonier maker, only cheffoniers. The men find their own material, and hawk the article when completed to the different warehouses. Even a wet Saturday is a disadvantage to the poor artisan, for his goods become either damaged, or lose their freshness of appearance if they get wet, and the man is unwilling to subject them to a further wetting by exposing them still further to the weather, so that often enough, rather than take his goods back or hawk them to another warehouse, the poor fellow accepts the first warehouseman's paltry offer. "One Saturday afternoon, sir," said a respectable artisan to me, "I happened to hear a slaughter-house keeper say, 'I hope to God it'll rain hard tonight, that'll put £20 into my pocket.' " The necessity of raising money on a Saturday night, to buy materials on Monday morning for the next week's toil, is often an irresistible motive for accepting the very worst offer, if it be but barely the price of the material.

Of the Ship and Boat Builders

Letter LXVIII

According to the last census the number of "ship-builders, carpenters, and wrights" (terms between which it is not easy to distinguish, the builder, carpenter, and wright being, according to my informants, one and the same individual), were in 1841 20,424 throughout Great Britain. Of these 17,498 were resident in England and Wales, and 2,926 in Scotland. The number located in the metropolis—with whom I have more particularly to deal—was then 2,309. Since that period the number appears to have increased nearly one-fifth, . . .

. . . In the principal, and, indeed, in nearly all the ship-building yards, the men work by contract—a system which has been pursued for the last fifty years at the least. A shipwright contracts to do all the wright's work, or a portion of it, and employs men under him. In these cases no day-work is performed; all is done by the piece. In some yards, however, there is occasional day-work, and the payment for it is six shillings and seven shillings a day. I am assured, moreover, that on piece work, in a good establishment, good workmen earn an equivalent amount at least, as the proprietors will not allow them to be ground down to swell the profits of the contractors. Nor, in the best yards of which I am now writing, are there any middlemen (beyond the contractor), or any sub-letting. The same system is pursued in the departments of the joiner and the caulker. Under the best management, however, and with all the checks adopted against abuse, the system of contract leads to the following grievance. Each contractor can employ his own men, or "mates" as they are termed, and of course he gives the preference to his own friends and relatives, who may be young men, while wrights or joiners who have spent half a lifetime in working, "off and on", for the same firm, may stand by idle. . . .

. . . The hours of labour are from six in the morning in summer, and from daylight in winter, until six at night, or until dusk. Out of this term of labour half an hour is allowed for breakfast, half an hour for tea; so that the entire term of labour is at the utmost nine hours and a half. . . .

. . . In point of intelligence, the ship-builders must be ranked high—quite as high as their fellow labourers of the best class (I now allude to none other) ashore. One shipwright, however, thought that many of his fellows did not avail themselves so freely as they might of the munificent means for the education of children which an eminent shipbuilder has so generously provided —I allude to Mr. Green. I was assured, notwithstanding, that every shipbuilder, . . . —could, at the very least, read and write.

The shipbuilders are, I found, great politicians. It is customary, during their half hour's luncheon at eleven o'clock, for one man to read the newspaper aloud in the public-house parlour; a discussion almost invariably follows, and is often enough resumed in the evening. The men for the most part go home to their dinners. The earnings of the shipwrights of the best class are, while at work, from forty shillings to fifty shilings a week; and those of the joiners and caulkers from 10 to 15 per cent less; but it must be borne in mind that the average employment of the general body does not exceed nine months in the year. The majority of the shipbuilders are married men with families, residing chiefly in Poplar and the adjacent parts. Some of whom I called upon had very comfortable homes, and in their apartments there was no lack of books—a very fair test, it may be said, of the intelligence and prudence of a working man. Not a few of the shipbuilders have brought up their sons to their own calling, or to some other branch of ship-building, or else to a seafaring life. Within these twenty years the shipbuilders generally were hard drinkers—now, I am assured, there are fifty steady men to one tippler.

In some yards the workmen are paid once a fortnight, the money being disbursed to them out of the counting-house on a Friday evening, the payment being for all that was due up to the previous Tuesday night. In other yards they are paid at four p.m. on the Saturday. I was informed that it is common enough for a shipbuilder, with his wife and children, to enjoy his Saturday evening in some suburban excursion. Payment in public-houses, or anything approximating to the truck system is unknown. . . .

. . . The shipbuilders in London are—as regards the majority—natives of the metropolis. The others are principally Scotchmen, and west of England men, with a small proportion of north countrymen, and a very small proportion of

Irishmen. In one large yard there was but one Irishman. All whom I saw, no matter from what part of the country, spoke of the London built ships, in the good yards, as being the best in the world.

There are two other classes of operatives connected with ship-building to whom I need only allude, as my present inquiry is confined to the workers in wood—viz., the workers in iron. These are the ship's smiths (called blacksmiths in the trade), who make the bolts, knees, and other iron work of the ship, and who are a highly respectable class; as well as the iron shipwrights, or men employed in constructing the iron steam-boats. Between these last-mentioned workers in ship iron and the workers in ship wood, there is no cordiality. The iron workers are called "boiler-makers" by the regular shipwrights, who describe them as an inferior class to themselves, made up from all descriptions of workers in iron, and including many boys and unskilled labourers. . . .

. . . A *ship-joiner*, whom I found in a very comfortable room with his wife and family, gave me the following account:

"My father was in the busines, and I was brought up to it by a friend of his. That's often reckoned a better way, as fathers are too severe or too indulgent. I was regularly apprenticed, and have never worked anywhere but in London, except once. I have always worked under the contractors, and have made my thirty-three shillings, thirty-six shillings, and thirty-eight shillings, a week when at work, according to the piece work—it's all piece work—that I get through. There is no fixed price—so much for the job, whatever it may be—and I've done all parts, I think. There's an understanding as to the pay. We know that we can make our living out of it. I may work rather more than nine months in the year altogether. In a good yard, after a ship is finished, there may be a slack of two or three months before we are wanted on a new ship. We are not kept going regularly at any one yard—only as long as a ship's in hand. We look out at all the yards. I'm a society man, and wish everybody was. I earn as much now as I did twelve or thirteen years back, when I first worked as a journeyman, and as provisions are cheaper I'm better off, or I could not give my children—there's three of them—good schooling as I do. I don't know that I can do better than bring up my boy—the others are girls—to my own trade, if he grows up sharp and strong; it's no use without. I know of no grievances that we have. I worked, not long since, in the joinering of an iron ship. There's more joinering in them than in wood ships, as there's a lining of wood to back the iron work. I don't mix with the 'boiler-makers'. I seldom stir out of a night, as I'm generally well tired after my day's work. I live near my work, and take every meal at home, except my luncheon, and that's a draught of beer, and sometimes a crust with it and a crumb of cheese, that I now and then put in my pocket." . . .

. . . The London boat-builders are not now a numerous class—numbering only about 120, independently of the builders of wherries, who are not more than thirty-five. Three-fourths of these operatives are London men; the majority of the others being from Deal and the north of England, especially from Whitby. They are a sober and far from ignorant class. "I really don't know one drunkard among us," said one of them to me, "and I think we can all read and write; but we are a downcast lot to what we were once." Another man, whose information I found corroborated, said, "I think the men in my trade are steady and domestic. Most of us have wives and families. I don't know a gambler among us, and there's only a few youngsters that care for a hand at cards. Generally of a Saturday night, if we've had a middling week in the yard, we pay sixpence a piece, and enjoy ourselves quietly over our beer or ale, or whatever we like, and our pipes, and our talk, and when the money's out we go away." . . .

. . . Another boat-builder, employed at present in the building of ships' boats, gave me the following statement. He resided in a crowded neighbourhood, not far from the river-side. His room was small and dark, but fully furnished, and a few numbers of cheap periodicals lay on the table. He was a grave, good-looking man :

"I have been a boat-builder fourteen or fifteen years," he said, "and served an apprenticeship in London. My father was a waterman, and I wish he had brought me up to some better business; but they say no businesses are as good as they were once. He's been dead some years. There's no reduction in the wages paid me since I was out of my time, but I must do more work for less money. . . . I lived with my mother until she died, four or five years back, and all I'd saved went to bury her. I don't think I could very well afford to keep a wife, though it's very lonesome having nobody to care about one. No doubt I could get a wife, but to keep her is another thing. I shouldn't like two to be in poverty instead of one, and I wouldn't like any decent girl I might marry to have to do work for the sweaters, to help us to make both ends meet when work's scarce. Some have to do it, though, to my knowing; and don't the girls find out the difference between that and being in good service, as some of them have been! I'm not employed—and very few of us are—three quarters of my time; and, take the year through, I don't earn more than a guinea a week. I may be hard at work this month and having nothing to do for the next fortnight, but go from yard to yard and be told I'm not wanted. Now, suppose I've twenty-one shillings a week, and I'm a single man. I pay two shillings a week for this room, with a recess there for my bed. They're my own sticks. Then say eightpence a week for my washing, as I can't bear to be dirty. Well, then, I often work a good way off, and must live out. I can potter on cheaper at home. My breakfast, at the very lowest, is 3½d., and that's only 1½d. for half a pint of coffee, penny loaf, and penny butter. Properly, for a working man, it should be sevenpence—pint of coffee, threepence, penny loaf, and penny butter, and twopence for a rasher; but say 3½d. When one's hard at work one requires some refreshment before dinner time, and you can't have anything cheaper than half a pint of beer—a pint's not too much; the half pint's a penny. Then for dinner, half a pound of steak is 3½d.; if you get it cheaper it's tough and grisly, and no good. I get it cooked for nothing at a public-house if I take a pint of beer with it, and that's twopence, and a penny for potatoes, and a halfpenny for bread; altogether the lowest for a decent dinner, anything like satisfying, is sevenpence. Tea is a halfpenny more than breakfast; for it's tea instead of coffee, you see, sir. Then there's a pint of beer, and a penn'orth of cheese and a penn'orth of bread for supper, that's fourpence. I know there's plenty of working men who go without supper; but I'm hearty myself, and I feel I want it. That's 1s. 7½d. for a day's keep, and a boat-builder's is hard work, and we require good support. Seven times 1s. 7½d.—

and indeed Sunday should be reckoned more, for if I have a good dinner off a joint with my landlord and his family, as I have every now and then, I pay him a shilling—but, say seven times 1s. 7½d. that's how much?—11s. 4½d. Well, then, there is my club money, and I pay threepence a week for papers; and I go to chapel on a Sunday pretty regular, and there's often a collection, and I can't pass the plate without my threepence, and, indeed, I oughtn't; and I sometimes get a letter from a brother, a mason, I have in Australia, and I sometimes write to him: and besides there's fourpence a week for tobacco, at the very least, as a pipe's a sort of company to a lone man; and for such like things we can't pay less than two shillings a week; indeed not less than two shillings and sixpence. Now, sir, what's that altogether? (I told him 16s. 6½d.) Then there's four shillings and sixpence a week, he continued, left for clothes, and for any new tool I may want, and for everything else; and I couldn't keep a wife, let alone a family, on that." (He seemed to enter with great zest into these explanations.) "Besides, this is the most favourable way to put it; for when I have a good week's work, and make thirty-three or thirty-four shillings, or as much as thirty-six shillings, I want more support, and my living costs me more, though I keep it as square as I can for a rainy day or a slack time. If I ask for work, and say I'm quick at clinch boats (ship's boats), a master will say, 'Now here's a long boat I want building, how much will you do it for? Don't tell me about prices, I can't get my price, and if you won't come down a peg, another will.' If I ask £4, he'll bid £3 3s., and will bargain, perhaps, for £3 10s., and it's from eight to ten days' work. I can't very well pass an offer, as I may not very soon have another. I have worked ten months and more in Mr. —'s yard; but that was only once. I know men and families live on twelve shillings a week. It's not living, though; it's only tea and bread and butter, or no butter. There can't be any strength in that." ...

Letter LXVI

... Concerning the motives for men to become small masters, I had the following statement from one of the most intelligent workmen belonging to the craft:

"One of the inducements", he said, "for men to take to making up for themselves is to get a living when thrown out of work until they can hear of something better. If they could get into regular journeywork there a'n't one man as wouldn't prefer it—it would pay them a deal better. Another of the reasons for the men turning small masters is the little capital that it requires for them to start themselves. If a man has got his tools he can begin as a master-man with a couple of shillings. If he goes in for making large tables, then from thirty to thirty-five shillings will do him, and it's the small bit of money it takes to start with in our line that brings many into the trade, who wouldn't be there if more time was wanted to begin with. Many works for themselves, because nobody else won't employ them, their work is so bad. Many weavers has took to our business of late. That's quite common now— their own's so bad; and some that used to hawk hearthstones about is turned Pembroke table-makers. The slaughterers don't care what kind of work it is, so long as it's cheap. A table's a table, they say, and that's all we want. Another reason for men turning little masters is because employment's more certain like that way; a man can't be turned off easily, you see, when he works for himself. Again, some men may prefer being small masters because they are more independent like; when they're working for themselves, they can begin working when they please, and knock off whenever they like. But the principal reason is, because there an't enough work at the regular shops to employ them all. The slaughterers have cut down their prices so low that there aint no work to be had at the better houses, so men must go on making up for the 'butchers' (slaughterers) or starve. Those masters as really would assist the men couldn't do it, because they're dead beat out of the field by the slaughter-houses. There was a large house lately as used to employ sixty men at fair living wages was broke up owing to the master going to the Cape of Good Hope, and then the whole of the men was turned adrift. Well, what was to be done? Some was lucky enough to get into a job, but a good part was obliged to buy a bit of stuff for themselves, and to set to working on their own account. Half a loaf you know is better than no bread at all, and nobody knows that so well as the slaughterers."

Of the Turners of London

Letter LXVII

... The number of turners of twenty years of age and upwards who were resident in London in 1841 amounted to 1,320; in 1831, however, there had been 150 more hands in the metropolis—that is to say, according to the census of that date, the London turners of the same age amounted to 1,470. Here, then, was a decrease in the number of hands, very nearly equal to 10 per cent; so that, allowing the quantity of work to have remained stationary during that time, wages ought to have risen 10 per cent from 1831 to 1841. But, strange to say, the quantity of work actually increased—for it was during that period that it became the fashion to have several articles, such as door-knobs, curtain poles and rings, etc., made of wood which had before been manu-factured of brass—and yet, notwithstanding the augmentation of the ordinary amount of turning work, and the decrease in the quantity of hands in the trade, wages were 400 per cent better in 1831 than they were in 1841.

The turners themselves, it will be seen, attribute the decline in their wages to the same causes as that in the cabinet trade—viz., to the competition of the small masters in reducing the prices of the articles they produce. . . .

... The operatives in this trade are nearly all married, the very young being the only exceptions. Some of their wives work for the slop tailors, under whose employ sevenpence a day (less by the expense of thread, candle, etc.), is con-sidered good earnings. The best class of workmen average about eighteen shillings a week wages, nearly the whole being payments for piece work. (In the country the payment is almost always by the day). The very inferior workmen, the East-enders, earn, it appears, from three shillings to five shillings a week less than the West-end men. Among the turners at the East-end there are few journeymen; they are nearly all little masters, and do their work in the hastiest and roughest manner, so as to gain payment for the largest possible quantity. They dispose of this work to the little masters in the cabinet trade and to the iron mongers. They or their wives hawk ball feet and small nobs, and feet of every kind, to cabinet makers as well as to their own trade. They are subject to the usual distress of the underpaid classes, being kept waiting (the women more especially) before receiving any decisive answer until a Saturday night is almost spent, and the necessity of having *something* for a Sunday dinner allows a customer to purchase upon his own most niggardly terms. . . .

. . . I met a few intelligent men among the turners, but intelligence is not the characteristic of the great mass of them. The poverty of the little masters tempts them, as I have stated, to take numbers of apprentices, who in their turn become little masters, and boys reared as I have described cannot be expected to attain tastes beyond such as can be gratified in the tap-room or the skittle-ground. Their ordinary amusements are skittles, cards ("all fives" being their usual game), and dominoes, played in the taprooms for beer. Nor is there any distinction between the journeyman and the little master, except that the journeyman may be better off. Drunkenness is far less common among them than it used to be, but that I found to be mainly attributed to the scantiness of their means. "Most turners in small wares", said a fringe turner to me, "amuse themselves in the public-houses near where they work. I amuse myself with reading the papers or anything when I have a little spare time; but the Spitalonians (Spitalfields men) are rare fellows for skittles, cards, and dominoes, and, badly as they're off, numbers of them don't work on a Monday. I like a game at knock-'em-downs (skittles) now and then myself. It's good exercise, and good for trade, as skittles is turners' work, but I hate cards without it be a hand at cribbage, and cribbage is a cut above the Spitalonians."

A highly intelligent man gave me an account of what he knew to be the state of his calling:

"I have known the trade upwards of forty years; and as soon as I was out of my apprenticeship, I could make £2 to £2 10s. a week on the average the year through. Some made more. I know one man who made £2 in one day, in turning 'pateras' for billiard tables, but that was an exception. Pateras were were six shillings a gross then; they're now three shillings and sixpence. Wages have been falling gradually these last twenty years. They fell long before provisions did. Now there's hardly a job we do, but there's a reduction or an attempt at it. 'If you won't do it,' the masters say, 'there's plenty will.' 'Well, then,' I say, 'you'd better get them; I'll take no less'; for I know, you see, sir, that I'm a skilful hand, and that makes a man independent. I turn bed-posts, tables and chair legs, and everything required in the furniture line, door knobs, and all those sort of things included. I average the year through eighteen shillings a week, or hardly that; and them's the best earnings in the trade, excepting the turners employed by the best cabinet-makers, who have their own lathes and turners, and employ the men on their own premises. There may be seven cabinet-makers who do this, and their men may average from thirty-two shillings to thirty-six shillings a week. The reduction in the wages paid to us since I have known the trade, amounts to between one-third and two-thirds of what we formerly received, and there are still attempts to lower our wages further. We feel the want of a society, but it's no use to raise one, as the men won't stick to it, and on the whole, the main body of us turners are not so intelligent as other mechanics. Our work is noisy, too, and no talk can be carried on, as in a tailor's shop, by which men can pick up a little politics or knowledge. We are now like the bundle of sticks after it was opened, and masters know that, and know we have nothing to fall back upon, and they treat us accordingly. I am married, but have no family, and have the good fortune to have a careful wife, and a comfortable bit of home, but that can only be done by my being abstemious, for I often suffer from sickness, and that brings such a heavy expense that I can't save anything." ...

... Concerning the "little masters", I had the following information. There were very few little master turners in the general branch of the trade before 1823. The operative turners were, prior to that time, generally journeymen working for the respectable master turners, who were then four times as numerous as now. Each of these masters employed from three to half a dozen men on their premises, having very rarely more than one or two apprentices. The wages of the journeymen ranged from £5 to £2, the average earnings being between fifty shillings and sixty shillings per week. After the year 1823 the cabinet-makers by whom the master turners were employed, finding that they could not get their work done owing to the drinking habits of the journeymen turners, determined on reducing the prices paid to the masters, on the plea that they gave too much money to their men; and no sooner were the masters' prices reduced than they lowered the wages of the men. The journymen, however, knowing that it was the custom of the masters to charge one-third as profit upon the amount paid to the journeymen for their labour, determined not to submit to the reduction, and accordingly several started in business for themselves. These journeymen then solicited the custom of the cabinet makers who had employed their former masters, offering to do their work at a lower rate. The more respectable masters, finding themselves undersold by the journeymen who had left their employ, then went to work to reduce the prices of the men that still remained with them, and thus sought to get their work back again from the cabinet-makers. This further reduction, however, caused more journeymen still to leave their masters' employ, and to start in business for themselves, seeking to obtain work at a lower rate still. And thus matters have been going on to the present time—journeymen trying to cut under the masters, and the masters, partly in self defence and partly in revenge, trying to cut down the wages of the men.

There are now, I am told, four principal reasons for turners becoming little masters. First, says my informant, the men are generally so fond of drink that a large master won't employ them. Then they commence business themselves, and work for little master cabinet-makers. Another cause is, that it takes but a few pounds to commence operations on their own account. A third reason is, because they don't like to be under the control of an employer. And the fourth, because, when working for themselves, they begin when they like, and leave off and have "a spree" when they please.

The little masters in the turning trade work the same long hours as the garret masters in the cabinet trade. When a man begins for himself he gets a boy to tread the lathe, clean up the articles with sand-paper, and chop up the wood ready for turning. I heard of no boys working at a lathe who are less than twelve years of age. "You see, sir," I was told, "the work is so heavy that it requires a strong boy to do it." . . .

Of the London Coopers

Letter LXIX

As a body the coopers are an intelligent class of mechanics. I met among them some superior men, and heard of several who had saved a little money. Hard drinking, I regret to say, though not drunkenness, prevails among the majority of the men employed in large cooperages. "I seldom see them drunk," said one cooper to me, "and I think it's not in the drink to intoxicate some of the seasoned hands." This addiction to continuous drinking, rather than to drunkenness—and the coopers drink principally beer—was accounted for to me by their work being very laborious, while the heat is often so great that they acquire a distaste for solids during the hours of labour, and stay the cravings of the appetite with draughts of beer. In a shop where "large work" is made, and where the timber is the stoutest and the fire the hottest, a moderate drinking cooper, as he is accounted, drinks two pots of beer a day; some will drink three pots and upwards, but in such circumstances two pots is the average drinking. The most moderate coopers, I am told, expend not less, on the average, than four shillings a week upon beer. The coopers become prematurely old, suffering greatly from pains in the chest and across the back, attributable to their bending over their hot work. "A cooper at large work is an old man, sir, at forty," said one of them to me; "his physical energies then are nearly exhausted."

Coopers are generally fond of manly exercises, such as cricket. There are very few skittle-players among them. Cards are played sometimes in the public-house on Saturday night, but not generally. "Had the coopers a taste for cards, it would be very easy to introduce them into the workshops," said one of them to me, "by making a card table on a barrel head. Often for days together a master never enters a shop, and the foreman, when he has given a man the stuff, leaves him almost entirely to himself." The theatre and the public gardens, I am told, are, however, the principal recreations of the coopers.

The coopers are mostly married men, living in unfurnished lodgings (generally two rooms), at about four shillings a week rent. They usually reside as near to their work as possible; consequently the majority are to be found in Whitechapel, where the largest sugar-houses are situate; whilst some of the men, for the same reason, are located in St. George-in-the-East. A few have houses at £25 a year rent, letting off part of them, but this is the exception rather than the rule. The operatives have generally from two to five or six in family, and only some of the children are put to school. "I don't consider", said an intelligent member of the trade to me, "that coopers' children are properly looked after, or that they are as well educated as they ought to be. I believe that it is owing to the drinking habits of our trade that the men's families are neglected as they are; perhaps another reason for this is, because during the slack season it takes all the men can earn to procure even food for their families. Upon an average in the slack season, which lasts about four months in the year, I think the coopers' earnings are not above ten shillings a week. In the brisk, however, they make about thirty shillings a week; and I have no doubt it is this great fluctuation in their incomes that makes the men less provident and less attentive to their homes than they otherwise would be. I think the majority of the operative coopers' wives take in slop-work, and many of their daughters do so. This has been the custom as long as I can remember. Some of the wives were formerly employed in winding silk for the Spitalfields weavers; but now that's all knocked on the head. The cause of the coopers' wives taking to slop-work is partly owing to the slackness of the trade at certain times and partly to their living in the neighbourhood of the slop-sellers. Lately there has been a great reformation in the drinking habits of the men. There are two causes for this, in my opinion. One is the closing of the public-houses at twelve o'clock on Saturday night, and not allowing them to be opened until after church time on Sunday; and the other is the cheapness of railway travelling, so that the men are induced to go a little way into the country on a Sunday, instead of wasting their money and ruining their health in taverns." The usual time of labour among the coopers is from six in the morning till eight o'clock at night (fourteen hours a day). This is generally considered in the trade to be two hours too much, and is looked upon as a great evil, it being considered one of the the principal reasons why so many are out of employment. The hours of labour, however, have always been the same. The coopers are not very partial to piecework, though this is their usual mode of payment. They consider it makes men do more work than they ought, and thus deprives others of their fair share of employment. They are never employed at day work in shops, but I am assured that they would prefer this mode of working to all others. Most coopers are London men, having served their time in the metropolis. About half, I am told, are the sons of former workmen.

The coopers in large establishments work in lofty brick sheds, with large open frontages; these are usually well ventilated, which indeed is indispensable, on account of the fires, where there is the slightest regard for the health and comfort of the workmen. They work singly, each man being engaged on his own cask. When it is finished, it is rolled into an adjacent yard, and there awaits the testing or inspection of the foreman or master.

Nearly all the working coopers can read and write, and some are educated men. Their moral standard is quite equal to that of the generality of trades. They were described to me as rough but manly. Some years ago, "strikes" were common among the coopers, and tended to promote idleness and foster the love for drink; but within the last twenty years strikes have been few and partial, and the men are now opposed to them as to a bad policy.

Of the London Omnibus Drivers and Conductors

Letter LXXI

The driver is paid by the week. His remuneration is thirty-four shillings a week on most of the lines. On others he receives twenty-one shillings and "his box", that is, the allowance of a fare each journey, for a seat outside if a seat be so occupied. In fine weather this box plan is more remunerative to the driver than the fixed payment of thirty-four shillings, but in wet weather he may receive nothing from the box; the average the year through being about thirty-four shillings a week, or perhaps rather more, as on some days, in sultry weather, he may make six shillings, "if the bus do twelve journeys", from his box.

The omnibus drivers have been butchers, farmers, horsebreakers, cheese-mongers, old stage coachmen, broken down gentlemen, turfmen, gentlemen's servants, grooms, and a very small sprinkling of mechanics. Nearly all can read and write, the exception being described to me as a singularity, but there are such exceptions, and all must have produced good characters before their appointment. The majority of them are married men with families, their residences being in all parts, and on both sides of the Thames. I did not hear of any of the wives of coachmen in regular employ working for the slop tailors, "We can keep our wives too respectable for that," one of them said in answer to my inquiry. Their children, too, are generally sent to school, frequently to the national schools. Their work is exceedingly hard, their lives being almost literally spent on the coachbox. The most of them must enter "the yard" at a quarter to eight in the morning, and must see that the horses and the carriage are in a proper condition for work, and at half-past eight they start on their long day's labour. They perform, I speak of the most frequented lines, twelve journeys during the day, and are so engaged until a quarter past eleven at night. Some are on their box till past midnight. During these hours of labour they have twelve "stops", half of ten, and half of fifteen minutes duration. They generally breakfast at home—or at a coffee-shop, if unmarried men—before they start, and dine at the inn where the omnibus almost invariably "stops", at one or other of its destinations. If the driver be distant from his home at his dinner hour, or be unmarried he arranges to dine at the public-house; if near, his wife or one of his children brings him his dinner in a covered basin, some of them being provided with hot water plates to keep the contents properly warm, and this is usually eaten at the public-house with a pint of beer for the accompanying beverage. The relish with which a man who has been employed several hours in the open air enjoys his dinner can easily be understood, but if his dinner is brought to him on one of his shorter stops, he often hears the cry before he has concluded the meal, "Time's up", and he carries the remains of his repast to be consumed at his next resting place. His tea, if brought to him by his family, he often drinks within the omnibus, if there be an opportunity. Some carry their dinners with them, and eat them cold. All these men live "well", that is, they have sufficient dinners of animal food every day, with beer. They are strong and healthy men, for their calling requires both strength and health. Each driver (as well as the time-keeper and conductor), is licensed at a yearly cost to him of five shillings. From a driver I had the following statement:

"I have been a driver for fourteen years. I was brought up as a builder, but had friends that was using horses, and I sometimes assisted them in driving and grooming, when I was out of work. I got to like that sort of work, and thought it would be better than my own business, if I could get to be connected with a bus; and I had friends, and first got employed as a time-keeper; but I've been a driver for fourteen years. I'm now paid by the week, and not by the box. It's a fair payment, but we must live well. It's hard work is mine, for I never have any rest but a few minutes, except every other Sunday, and then only two hours, that's the time of a journey there and back. If I was to ask leave to go to church, and then go to work again, I know what answer there would be, 'You can go to church as often as you like, and we can get a man who doesn't want to go there.' " ...

... The conductor, who is vulgarly known as the "cad", stands on a small projection at the end of the omnibus, and it is his office to admit and "set down" every passenger, and to receive the amount of fare, for which amount he is, of course, responsible to his employers. He is paid four shillings a day, which he is allowed to stop out of the moneys he receives. He fills up a way-bill each journey with the number of passengers. I find that nearly all classes have given a quota of their numbers to the list of conductors. Among them are grocers, drapers, shop-men, barmen, printers, tailors, shoemakers, clerks, joiners, saddlers, coach-builders, porters, town travellers, carriers, and fish-mongers. Unlike the drivers, the majority of conductors are unmarried men, but perhaps only a mere majority. As a matter of necessity every conductor must be able to read and write. They are discharged more frequently than the drivers, but they require good characters before their appointment. From one of them, a very intelligent man, I had the following statement:

"I am thirty-five or thirty-six, and have been a conductor for six years. Before that I was a lawyer's clerk, and then a picture dealer, but didn't get on tho' I maintained a good character.... I never get to a public place—whether it's a chapel or a play house—unless indeed I get a holiday, and that is not once in two years. I've asked for a day's holiday and been refused. I was told I might take a week's holiday if I liked, or as long as I lived. I'm quite ignorant of what's passing in the world, my time's so taken up. We only know what's going on from hearing people talk in the bus. I never care to read the paper now, though I used to like it. If I have two minutes to spare I'd rather take a nap than anything else. We know no more politics than the backwoods-men of America, because we haven't time to care about it. I've fallen asleep on my step as the bus was going on, and have almost fallen off. I have often put up with insolence from vulgar fellows that think it fun to chaff a cad, as they call it. There's no help for it. Our masters won't listen to complaints. If we're not satisfied we can go. Conductors are a sober set of men. We must be sober. It takes every farthing of our wages to live well enough and keep a wife and family. I never knew but one teetotaller on the road. He's gone off it now, and he looked as if he was going off altogether. The other day a teetotaller on the bus saw me take a drink of beer, and he began to talk to me about its being wrong, but I drove him mad with argument, and the passengers took my part with me. I live one-and-a-half mile off the place I start from. In summer I sometimes breakfast before I start. In winter I never see my three children only as they're in bed, and I never hear their voices, if they don't wake up early. If they cry at night it don't disturb me, I sleep so heavy after fifteen hours work out in the air. My wife doesn't do anything but mind the family, and that's plenty to do with young children." ...

Of the London Carmen and Porters

Letter LXXIII

... The London carmen are of two kinds, public and private. The private carmen approximate so closely to the character of servants, that I purpose dealing at present more particularly with the public conveyers of goods from one part of the metropolis to another. The Metroplitan public master carmen are 207 in number, of whom fifteen are licensed to ply on the stands in the City. The carmen here enumerated must be considered more in the light of the owners of vans and other vehicles for the removal of goods than working men. It is true that some drive their own vehicles, but many are large proprietors and belong to the class of employers rather than operatives. ...

... A new van costs from £50 to £80. The average price of a good van-horse is from £16 to £18. The harness, new and good, costs £5 to £5 10s. for two horses. The furniture van of the latter end of the week is the pleasure van of the Sunday, Monday, and Tuesday, those being the days devoted to excursions, unless in the case of a club or society making their "annual excursion", and then any day of the week is selected except Sunday; but Sunday, on the whole, is the principal day. The removal of the seats and of the apparatus for the awning converts the "pleasure" into the "furniture" van. The uses to which the same vehicle is put are thus many a time sadly in contrast. On the Saturday the van may have been used to convey to the broker's or the auctioneer's the furniture "seized" in some wretched man's dwelling, leaving behind bare walls and a wailing family—and on the Sunday it rings with the merriment of pleasure-seekers, who loudly proclaim that they have left their cares behind them.

The owners usually, perhaps I might say always, unite some other calling along with the business of van-proprietorship. They are for the most part greengrocers, hay and corn dealers, brokers, beershop keepers, chandlers, rag and bottle-shop keepers, or dairymen. Five-sixths of them, however, are green-grocers, or connected with that trade. It is not unusual for these persons to announce, that besides their immediate calling of a greengrocer they keep a furniture van, go pleasure excursions, beat carpets (if in the suburbs), and attend evening parties. Many of them have been gentlemen's servants. They are nearly all married men or widowers, with families, and are as a body not unprosperous. Their tastes are unexpensive, though some drink pretty freely, and their early rising necessitates early going to bed, so there is little evening expenditure. I am told that their chief enjoyments are a visit to Astley's, and to the neighbouring horse-races. Their enjoyment of the turf, however, is generally made conducive to their profits, as they convey vans full to Hampton, Egham, and Epsom races. A few van-men, however, go rather further in turf business, and "bet a little", but these, I am assured, are the exceptions. The excursions are more frequently to Hampton-court than to any other place. The other favourite resorts are High Beech, Epping Forest, and Rye House, Hertfordshire. Windsor is but occasionally visited, and the shorter distances such as Richmond, are hardly ever visited in pleasure vans; indeed, the superior cheapness of the railway or the steamboat has confined the pleasure excursions I am speaking of to the longer distances, and to places not so easily accessible by other means.

The vans will hold from twenty to thirty grown persons, "twenty, you see, sir," I was told, "is a very comfortable number, not reckoning a few little 'uns over; but thirty, oh, thirty's quite the other way." The usual charge per head for a "comfortable" conveyance to Hampton Court and back, including all charges connected with the conveyance, is two shillings, "children going for nothing, unless they're too big for knees, and then sometimes half price." Instead of two shillings, perhaps the weekly payment speculator receives two shillings and sixpence or two shillings and threepence, and if he can engage a low priced van, he may clear ninepence or one shilling a head, or about £1 in all. On this subject, and on that of "underselling", as it was described to me, I give the statement of a very intelligent man, a prosperous van proprietor, who had the excellent characteristic of being proud of the kindly treatment, good feeding, and continued care of his horses, which are among the best employed in vans.

The behaviour of these excursionists is, from the concurrent testimony of the many van proprietors and drivers whom I saw, most exemplary, and perhaps I shall best show this by at once giving the following statement from a very trustworthy man:

"I have been in the van trade for twenty years, and have gone excursions for sixteen years. Hampton Court has the call for excursions in vans, because of free trade in the Palace. There's nothing to pay for admission. A party makes up an excursion, and one of them bargains with me, say for £2. It shouldn't be a farthing less with such cattle as mine, and everything in agreement with it. Since I've known the trade vans have increased greatly. I should say there's five now where there was one sixteen years ago, and more. There's a recommendable and a respectable behaviour among those that goes excursions. I have known some bother from drunkenness when excursions first came up, fifteen years back or so, but nothing much to talk about. It's not your drinkers that go excursions. But now on an excursion there's hardly ever any drunkenness, or, if there is, it's through the accident of a bad stomach, or something that way. The excursionists generally carry a fiddler with them— sometimes a trumpeter, or else some of them is master of an instrument—as they goes down. They generally sings, too. Such songs as 'There's a good time coming', and 'The brave old Oak'. Sometimes a nigger thing, but not so often.

They carry always, I think, their own eatables and drinkables, and they takes them on the grass very often. Last Whit-Monday I counted fifty vans at Hampton, and didn't see anybody drunk there. I reckoned them earlyish, and perhaps ten came after, at least, and every van would have twenty and more. (Sixty vans would, at this moderate computation, convey 1,200 persons.) They walk through the Palace at Hampton, and sometimes dance on the grass after that; but not for long. It soon tires, dancing on the grass. A school often goes, or a club, or a society, or any party. I generally do Hampton Court in three hours, with two horses. I reckon it's fourteen miles, or near that, from my place. If I go to High Beech, there's the swings for the young ones, and the other merry-makings. At Rye House it's country enjoyment, mere looking-about the real country. The Derby Day's a great van day. I'm sure I couldn't guess to one hundred nor perhaps to twice that, how many pleasure vans go to the Derby. It's extra charge, £3 10s. for the van to Epsom and back. It's a long distance, but the Derby has a wonderful draw. I've taken all sorts of excursions, but it's working-people that's our great support. They often smoke as they come back; tho' it's against my rules. They often takes a barrel of beer with them." . . .

. . . before the railway-trips, there were 225 pleasure excursions by vans every week during five months in the year, or 4,000 such excursions in the course of twelve months, and only 1,640 since that time. This is exclusive of those to Epsom races, at which there were nearly 200 more.

When employed in the removal of furniture, the average weight carried by these vans is about two tons, and they usually obtain about two loads on an average per week. The party engaged to take charge of the van is generally a man employed by the owner, in the capacity of a servant. The average weekly salary of these servants is about eighteen shillings. Some van proprietors will employ one man, and some as many as nine or ten. These men look after the horses and stables of their employers. . . .

. . . The privileged *porters* of the city of London were at one period, and until within these thirty years, a numerous, important, and tolerably prosperous class. Prescriptive right and the laws and by-laws of the corporation of the city of London have given them the sole privilege of porterage of every description, provided it be carried on in the precincts of the City. The only exception to this exclusive right is that any freeman may employ his own servants in the porterage of his own goods, and even that has been disputed. . . .

. . . The number of the ticket porters was, twenty years ago, about 600. At that time, to become free of the company which has no hall, but assembles at Guildhall, costs upwards of £40, but soon after, this expense was reduced to £6 3s. 4d. By a resolution of the Common Council, no new ticket porters have been appointed since 1838. Previously to becoming a ticket porter, a man must have taken up his freedom, no matter in what company, and must produce certificates of good character, and security of two freemen householders of good credit, each in £100, so that the owner of any articles entrusted to the ticket porter may be indemnified in case they were lost. The ticket porters are not the mere labourers people generally imagine they are, but are, or were, for their number does not now exceed 100, decayed tradesmen, who resorted to this means of livelihood, when others had failed. They are also the sons of ticket porters. Any freeman of the City, by becoming a member of the Tackle-house and Ticket Porters' Company, was entitled to act as a ticket porter. They are still recognised at the markets and the wharfs but their privileges are constantly, and more and more infringed. From a highly intelligent man of their body I had the following statement:

"It may be true, or it may not, that ticket-porters are not wanted now; but fifteen or sixteen years ago a committee of the Common Council—the market committee, I believe it was—resolved that the ticket-porters ought to be upheld, and that £50 should be awarded to us, but we never got it; it was stopped by some after resolution. Put it this way, sir. To get bread for myself and my children I became a ticket porter, having incurred great expense in taking up my freedom and all that. Well, for this expense I enjoyed certain privileges, and enjoy them still to some extent, but that's only because I'm well known, and have had great experience in porterage, and quickness at it is as much art as strength. But supposing that railways have changed the whole business of the times, are the privileges I have secured with my own money, and under the sanction of all the old laws of the City, to be taken from me? If the privileges, tho' they may not be many, of the rich City companies are not to be touched, why are mine? Every day they are infringed. A railway waggon, for instance, carries a load of meat to Newgate-market. Ticket-porters have the undoubted right to unload the meat and carry it to its place of sale, but the railway servants do that, though only freemen employ their own servants in porterage, and that only with their own goods, or goods they are concerned in. I fancy that railway companies are not freemen, and don't carry their own property to market for sale. If we complain to the authorities, we are recommended to take the law of the offenders, but we can only take it of the person committing the actual offence; and so we may sue a beggar, whom his employers may send down their line, an hour after, to Hull, or Halifax, as the saying is. . . .

Of the Journeymen Hatters of London

Letter LXXVII

The hat manufactures of London are to be found in the district to the left of the Blackfriars road (as the bridge is crossed from the Middlesex side), stretching towards and beyond the Southwark-bridge-road to the High-street, Borough, and to Tooley-street. There are, moreover, no inconsiderable number of hat factories in Bermondsey. Hat making is almost entirely confined to the Surrey side of the Thames, and until within the last twenty years, or there-abouts, it was carried on chiefly in Bermondsey. In Bermondsey, however, there are still many large "hatteries"; one of them, the property of a wealthy Quaker firm, ranks among the largest in London, rarely employing, in the slackest seasons, fewer than 90 or 100 men, and sometimes as many as 300, with, of course, a proportionate number of the women who are employed in the trade. . . .

... The hatters and hat manufacturers of the metropolis in 1841 were 3,500 in number, of whom 2,600 were males of twenty years of age and upwards, the other 900 being composed of nearly 600 women, and upwards of 300 children. ...

... These workmen carry on their trade in large rooms, generally well ventilated, and comodious, but in some employs dirty, dark, and confined. Each workman has his own "plank", or "bench", as it is called in other trades, for certain stages of his work; but the men, when engaged in working their "proofs", stand around a large tub, or open vat, the "liquor" in it steaming freely. In summer the heat is often excessive, as in so many stages of the manufacture the workmen require fires. The men work in trowsers, flannel shirts, and slippers, or wooden clogs, their arms being bared above the elbows. Notwithstanding the exposure to heat, I am assured that the hatters' is not an unhealthy calling, as their lives are of the average duration, and men of sixty-five are now working efficiently in the business. These operatives used to drink great quantities of beer when at work—two pots, or even ten pints, a day being a frequent consumption by a man not accounted a "fuddler"' There is now a great change in this respect, few drinking more than a pot a day whilst at work. In the larger shops, however, it is still the practice for a new comer to pay his "footing", which in this trade is called "garnish". A workman refusing to join in this conviviality is stigmatised as a "straight stick". A first rate workman informed me that eighteen or nineteen years ago he regularly spent eighteen shillings a week in drink, but at that time he earned as much as £4 in a week, and very frequently £3. The same workman told me that at the Wheatsheaf, a public-house near the Borough-market, twenty years back, the hatters used to be "dancing and footing it, and drinking, of course", all the week long, but that now there is nothing of the kind.

In the London houses from twelve to twenty journeymen are more frequently employed in the "fair" trade than any larger or smaller number. The majority of these journeymen, perhaps three-fourths of them, are countrymen, chiefly from Cornwall, Gloucestershire, and Lancashire, with a few Scotchmen, and a very few Irishmen. A great number of hats, principally of the cheaper sorts, used to be sent from the country to London until eleven or twelve years ago, when the substitution of silk hats for stuff put an end to the trade, or nearly so, as the country hat-makers were not sufficiently skilled in the new manufacture. ...

The way in which a hat-maker acquires a knowledge of his craft is by apprenticeship. In the strictest branch of the "fair" trade no man is admitted as a member of "society" who has not served a seven years apprenticeship; and no master, employing society men, can have more than two apprentices at one time besides the members of his own family whom he may choose "to put in the trade", and they must be regularly "bound". The number of apprentices is not influenced, as in the printers' and some other businesses, by the number of journeymen employed. Whether a master hatter employ one journeyman or 100, he is alike limited to two apprentices. Small as this number of apprentices may appear, it ensures a full supply of skilled labourers.

In the "foul" or slop trade, no regulations of the kind I have described exist. The workers in this trade are the men who have served no apprenticeship,

or who, from drunkenness or other causes, have not kept up their payments to the society, and have ceased to be members of it—or who have left
other callings, such as that of weaving, to work as hatters; a course which is
facilitated by the silk hat manufacture being a much easier or less skilled
process than that of the stuff hat. I was told, indeed, that sweeps and costermongers had "turned foul hatters". These men are somewhat equivalent to
the garret masters in the cabinet-making business; but with this distinction,
that the hatters do not *complete* the articles of their manufacture as does the
slop cabinet maker for the "slaughter houses;" the "foul" hatter makes only
"bodies". They are to be found about Brick-lane, Whitechapel, in Spitalfields,
and in Lock's-fields, Walworth. They work in their own rooms—which the
operatives in the fair trade never do—and have to find their own irons and
material. They are thus "little masters", as they nearly all work on their own
account. . . .

The "foul" hatters are many of them young men, with a smaller proportion
of married men among them than is common, perhaps, among handicraftsmen. When they are married, the wives have usually some slop employment.
They very rarely finish a hat, unless when they avail themselves of a practice
known in the trade as "malokering". A maloker, frequently a Jew, collects
old hats from door to door, and sells them to the dealers in Rosemary-lane.
The slop hatter buys them off the dealer at from one shilling and sixpence to
five shillings a dozen. If any of the silk be tolerably good, he strips it off, and
puts it upon a new body, or "cougles in" the old body (as the restiffening
of it is called) and sells the hat new lined, re-dyed, and "trimmed up", to the
dealers in secondhand attire, or hawks it to public-houses, sometimes "swop-
ping" it for an old hat and a shilling.

I heard the number of these little masters (who were unknown in the trade
ten years ago) computed at 1,000 in the present time, and their earnings at from
ten shillings to twelve shillings a week, taking the year's average. Previously
to ten years back the little masters in the trade supplied the general public, or
worked to order, as "out-door hands", for the greater houses. A man "taking
up the trade" has generally to pay for instruction about £2, and to supply
three weeks' or a month's labour gratuitously to his instructor. A working
hatter told me that in a fortnight's time he could teach a quick lad how to make
calico bodies for common silk hats well enough for the slop trade.

The working hatters in the honourable trade generally take some interest
in politics, and are for the most part Protectionists, as they think protection
would have "kept out the French hats". Indeed, I did not meet with one Free-
trader. I did not hear of their being more inclined to one particular amusement
than to another, but a game at cards is common with them in the public-house
when the day's work is over. They are generally married men, and reside in
the neighbourhoods of the hatteries. Some of their wives are employed as hat
binders and liners, but none, I am informed, work at slop-work. Among the
hatters I found many intelligent men, but as a body they are certainly less
advanced than some other classes of handicraftsmen. Some of them have saved
money. . . .

Of the London Tanners, Curriers, etc.

Letter LXXVIII

... The several workers in the preparation of leather—the curriers being an exception—are not an educated class. There need be no stronger proof of this than the fact, as I was informed by an intelligent workman from his own knowledge, that in their societies not one man in three can write his name legibly, or spell it correctly. I found a working tanner, to whom I was directed, in a public-house, reading to two of his trade, who regretted their inability to read an account of a prize fight. Among tanners, I was told, there was still a strong "hankering after a prize fight", and that some noted boxers had sprung from them—among others "Ned Turner", who was brought up as a tanner, but was afterwards a *frizer,* or a man who divided the grain of sheep-skin for hat linings and other purposes from the flesh, to be manufactured into "chamois". The operation is now done unerringly by machinery, and the frizer's occupation is extinct. The workmen in this trade are generally married men. They reside in Bermondsey or its immediate vicinity, occupying one room at about one shilling and sixpence, or sometimes two rooms (according to their means) at from two shillings and sixpence to three shillings a week. There is still a good deal of drinking prevalent among them, and little inclination for working on Mondays, but in both these respects there has been within these twelve years a decided improvement. The workers not *in* but *on* leather, now rarely drink more than a pot of beer a day when at work; from twelve to twenty years ago they consumed twice that quantity. On Father Matthew's visit to Bermondsey, six or seven years ago, a great number of the men in this trade took the pledge, but, with the exception of about one in twenty or twenty-five, they have all broken it. "I took the pledge, sir," said a tanner to me, "and kept it rather more than two years. I was often teased by my mates to drink, but they got tired of that. I used to say, when I walked past Simon the Tanner, 'Simon, you'll get no more tanners out of me'; but I found, or fancied, though I don't think it was fancy, that I couldn't work so well without a reasonable allowance of beer, so I gave up teetotalling." I may explain that "Simon the Tanner" is the sign of a house of call, much frequented by the fraternity, and that a "tanner", in slang language is sixpence. One custom still prevails—but very partially, indeed to only one-tenth, if so much, of its former prevalence—which is now known in very few trades, viz. the payment of men in public-houses. These public-houses are called "garrison" houses. The foreman makes himself responsible to the inn-keeper for all the liquor drunk on the premises of the employer when the men are at work, and he deducts the amount from their wages on the Saturday night. The journeyman shrewdly suspect that there is an understanding between the foreman and the publican, and that the beer, which is fourpence a pot to the workmen, is but $3\frac{1}{2}$d. to the foreman. On inquiring of a man who gave me information on this subject, if the masters approved of such a mode of payment, I was told that the master was perhaps a rich man, having his country house at some distance, and that, provided his returns were satisfactory, he left all such matters entirely to his foreman. The system seems dying out, however, and is commended by no one, not even by those workmen who are addicted to drinking. . . .

. . . In one of the principal tanneries, the regular hours of labour—which are from six to seven in summer, and from daylight to dark in winter—have been extended for an hour, gas being now used. This increase of labour has not, however, been accompanied with any increase of remuneration, so that it is a virtual decrease of wages, to the extent of more than half a day's work in a week, or of six hours. The cause assigned is the cheapness of provisions enabling men to live at less cost; but the house in question, rather than reduce the actual amount of payment, has added to the hours of work. The men resisted at first, but gave way rather than lose their employment. Another large firm has just proposed a similar measure, but the matter is as yet unsettled.

From a shedman, a strong, fresh-coloured man, I had the following statement:

"I learned all parts of the tanning trade, and I was apprenticed to my father, who had the management of a business in the country. I've known the London trade for twenty years, or thereabouts. I work in the shed now, and have for a long time. I don't remember how long. I work by the piece at present, and have from one shilling to one shilling and ninepence a hide, according to size. My work's constant now, and I make about twenty-four shillings a week. I live as comfortably as a working man can, and support a wife and two children on that. I have a sort of double room, and pay two shillings and threepence a week for it, unfurnished. I could read a little once, but I've been out of practice so long that I've forgot it; but I'm very fond of hearing my wife read the paper on Sundays, as I smoke my pipe. It was capital reading about Manning and his wife, as they lived just by us, you see. My children both go to school. . . .

. . . The London tanners have a society with three branches—the Old Union with 172 members, the Tramp Union with fifty, and a branch of the Old Union, and consisting chiefly of elderly men, number also fifty; in all 272. There are, moreover, now in London between 600 and 700 working tanners not belonging to any society. . . .

Apprenticeship used to be the regular mode of acquiring a knowledge of the tanner's business, but it is now much less so—the reasons given to me being that so few would now pay any premium. The apprentices are now generally the sons of the operative tanners. . . .

. . . A currier who had worked about eight years in London, a man of about thirty-five, gave me an account of his earnings, which, as he had been fortunate in obtaining good work, ranged from thirty shillings to forty-two shillings a week. His earnings, however, are those of the very best, the readiest (the usual word in most trades for a quick workman), and the most skilful workmen; and his statement gave me no interesting facts beyond what he mentioned of the changes in the trade as he had heard them from his father and grandfather, both curriers. The principal employment of both these men, from thirty-five to sixty years ago, was on "saddle-bag hides" (the leather for saddlebags), which were formerly slung over the horse's back, being attached to the saddle and the saddle girths, containing the "patterns" of the commercial traveller, and the change of linen, etc., of the ordinary traveller, as he travelled on horseback. This department of the trade has now entirely, or almost entirely, disappeared. The great grievance of the superior workmen in currying is the employment, at inferior wages, of non-society men, who, in all branches of the leather trade, are called "blacks".

The curriers in society, and working for good shops, are the most intelligent of the operatives engaged in the trade I am treating of. One currier knew of none but what could read and write, and some of them were very well informed and took an interest in politics, there being as many Free-traders as Protectionists, or nearly as many among them. The abodes of the curriers are in different parts of the metropolis and of the suburbs, as the trade is not so exclusively confined to Bermondsey as that of the tanners, though Bermondsey is its head quarters. They are principally married men, occupying one or two comfortable rooms. The non-society men, on the other hand, are driven to the usual shifts of slop workmen.

The working dress of the curriers is generally very thick blue flannel trowsers and jacket, strong coarse shirts, and blue flannel aprons. As is common enough with working men of the better class whose trade necessitates the wearing of coarse and inexpensive clothing, and linen all day, the curriers are rather remarkable for being well dressed and with superior linen on Sundays, or when they "dress to go out on an evening". Their boots are often of the very best.

The wages of the operative curriers were settled by agreement with their masters in 1812, and have continued unchanged. . . .

. . . The instruction of the currier in his ancient art and mystery is by apprenticeship. In the "fair" or honourable" trade an employer has, if he chooses, two apprentices and one turnover, or two turnovers and one apprentice. Among the rules regarding the apprentices I find: "N.B. No foreigner can be admitted." . . .

MANUFACTURING DISTRICTS

MANCHESTER

Letter I

In the majority of mills labour begins at six o'clock a.m. throughout the year. In a certain number the engine during the dead winter months does not start until half an hour later. As a general thing, however, the Manchester operative is up and stirring before six. The streets in the neighbourhood of the mills are thronged with men, women and children flocking to their labour. They talk and laugh cheerily together. The girls generally keep in groups with their shawls twisted round their heads, and every few steps, in the immediate vicinity of the mill parties are formed around the peripatetic establishments of hot coffee and cocoa vendors. The factory bell rings from five minutes before six until the hour strikes. Then—to the moment—the engine starts, and the day's work begins. Those who are behind six, be it but a moment, are fined two pence; and in many mills, after the expiration of a very short time of grace, the doors are locked, and the laggard, besides the fine, loses his morning work.

Breakfast hour comes round at half after eight o'clock. The engine stops to the minute, and the streets are again crowded with those of the operatives who live close by the mills. A great many however take their breakfasts in the factory, which, as a general rule, supplies them with hot water. The practice of the people taking their meals in the mills, though I believe contrary to the letter of the law, is quite necessary, owing to the distance which many of the workpeople live from their place of labour, and to the short times—only half an hour—allowed for the meal. Its constituents are generally tea and coffee, with plenty of bread and butter and in many cases a slice or so of bacon. At five minutes to nine the factory bell sounds again, and at nine the engine starts again. The work goes on with the most perfect method and order. There is little of any talking, and little disposition to talk. Everybody sets steadily and tranquilly about his or her duties, in that calm methodical style which betokens perfect acquaintance with the work to be done, and perfect skill wherewith to do it. There is no hurrying or panting and toiling after the machinery. Everything appears—in ordinary phrase—to be "taken easy"; yet everything goes rapidly and continuously on. . . .

. . . In Manchester everybody, master and man, dines at one o'clock. As the chimes sound, all the engines pause together, and from every workshop, from every industrial establishment—be it cotton, silk, iron, print works or dye works—the hungry crowd swarms out, and streets and lanes, five minutes before lonely and deserted, are echoing the trampling of hundreds of busy feet. The Manchester operative in prosperous times need never want, and seldom does without a dinner of what he calls "flesh meat". This he sometimes partakes of at home, sometimes at a neighbouring cook-shop; occasionally he has it brought to him at the mill. A favourite dish with the operatives is what they call potato pie—a savoury pasty made of meat and potatoes, well seasoned with pepper and salt, and roofed in with a substantial paste. Many of the men, after despatching their dinner, which they do comfortably in half an hour, spend the other moiety of their leisure in smoking or lounging about, until the never-failing bell proclaims that time is up, and that the engine and its attendant mechanism are ready to resume their labours. The work then proceeds until half after five o'clock, at which hour all labour finally ceases; the periods of toil having been from six o'clock until half-past eight o'clock, from nine o'clock until one o'clock, and from two o'clock until half-past five o'clock, making an aggregate of ten hours. This arrangement, however, although very general, is by no means universal. Some of the mills do not open until seven o'clock, and half-past seven o'clock, while a few prefer commencing at eight o'clock, after their people have breakfasted, and making but one stoppage during the day. There seems, however, to be a general and I think a very well-founded opinion, that this division of ten hours is a bad one, inasmuch as it protracts the time of working until late in the evening, and casts the additional leisure, which it was the object of the Ten Hours Bill to secure to the workpeople, into the middle of the day, when they cannot well be expected to settle down to those domestic pursuits and means of self-improvement, which I am assured they are most eager to seize and avail themselves of, when they have a reasonable space to come and go upon between the closing of the mills and bedtime.

I stood to-day at the principal door of Messrs. Birley's establishment, watching the hands take their departure. It was curious to observe how each sex and age clung together. Boys kept with boys, men with men, and the girls went gossiping and laughing by, in exclusive parties of their own. I chanced to overhear a proposition confidentially made by one of these young ladies as she passed me to a comrade. There was not much in it, to be sure; but the proposal, at all events, showed that the fatigues of the day had by no means the effect of preventing a personal brushing-up for the evening. "I say, Jane," said the damsel in question, "I tell you what—you come home and braid my hair, and then I'll braid yours." The out-door dress of the men is comfortable and respectable. Velveteen jackets and shooting coats seem to be in great favour, with waistcoats and trowsers of dark fustian cloth. The people are uniformly well shod; and their general appearance is that of unostentatious comfort.

Letter III

The house of the Manchester operative, wherever it be—in the old district or in the new—in Ancoats or Cheetham or Hulme—is uniformly a two storey dwelling. Sometimes it is of fair dimensions, sometimes a line fourteen feet long would reach from the eaves to the ground. In the old localities there is, in all probability, a cellar beneath the house, sunk some four or five feet below the pavement, and occupied perhaps by a single old woman, or by a family, the heads of which are given to pretty regular alternation between their subterranean abode and the neighbouring wine vaults. In the modern and improved *quartiers*, the cellar retires modestly out of sight, and is put to a more legitimate use as a home for coals or lumber. Nothing struck me more, while visiting and comparing notes in the different operative districts of Manchester, than the regularity with which the better style of house and the better style of furniture went together; it being always kept in mind that, so far as wages are concerned, the inhabitants of one locality are almost, if not quite, on a par with those of another. But the superior class room seemed, by a sort of natural sequence, to attract the superior class furniture. A very fair proportion of what was deal in Ancoats was mahogany in Hulme. Yet the people in Hulme get no higher wages than the people of Ancoats. The secret is that they live in better built houses, and consequently take more pleasure and pride in their dwellings.

I visited several of the better class houses in Hulme, and shall sketch, in a few lines, the parlour of the first which I entered, and which may be taken as a fair specimen of the others. The room was about ten feet by eight, and hung with a paper of cheap quality and ordinary pattern. In at least two of the corners were cupboards of hard wood, painted mahogany fashion, and containing plates, teacups, saucers, etc. Upon the chimney-piece was ranged a set of old-fashioned glass and china ornaments. There was one framed print hanging upon the wall—a steel engraving of small size, reduced from the well known plate of the "Covenanter's Marriage". Beside this symbol of art was a token of allegiance to science, in the shape of one of the old-fashioned tube barometers, not apparently in the most perfect state of order. There were two tables in the apartment—a round centre one of ordinary material, and a rather handsome mahogany Pembroke. Opposite the fireplace was one of those nondescript pieces of furniture which play a double part in domestic economy —"a bed by night, a wardrobe all the day". The chairs were of the comfortable old-fashioned Windsor breed; and on the window-ledge were two or three flower-pots, feebly nourishing as many musty geraniums. The floor was carpet-less—a feature, by the way, anything but characteristic. In the passage, however, was laid a piece of faded and battered oil-cloth. The general aspect of the place, although by no means a miracle of neatness, was tolerably clean and comfortable.

. . . In the majority of the streets, inhabited by operatives the front room on the ground floor is used both as parlour and kitchen. Sometimes a second room, of small dimensions, opens back from it, and when such an apartment exists, it is generally seen littered with the coarser cooking and washing utensils. I have described the principal "public" room in a house of the first class in Hulme; let me sketch the generic features of the tenements in the older, worse built, and in all respects inferior quarter of Ancoats. Fancy, then a wide-lying labyrinth of small dingy streets, narrow, unsunned courts, terminating in gloomy cul-de-sacs, and adorned with a central sloppy gutter. Every score or so of yards you catch sight of one of the second and third class mills, with its cinder-paved courtyard and its steaming engine-house. Shabby looking chapels, here and there, rise with infinitesimal Gothic arches and ornaments, amid the grimy nakedness of the factories. Now a railroad, upon its understructure of arches, passes over the roofs; anon, you cross a canal, with wharfs and coal-yards, and clusters of unmoving barges. In most cases the doors of the houses stand hospitably open, and young children cluster over the thresholds and swarm out upon the pavement; you have thus an easy opportunity of noting the interiors as you pass along. They are, as you will perceive, a series of little rooms, about ten feet by eight, more or less, generally floored with brick or flagstones—materials which are, however, occasionally half concealed by strips of mats or faded carpeting. A substantial deal table stands in the centre of each apartment and a few chairs, stools and settles to match, are ranged around. Occasionally, a little table of mahogany is not wanting. Now and then you observe a curiously small sofa, hardly intended for a full-grown man or woman to stretch their limbs upon; and about as often one side of the fireplace is taken up with a cradle. Sometimes there is a large cupboard, the open door of which reveals a shining assortment of plates and dishes; sometimes the humble dinner service is ranged on shelves which stretch along the walls; while beneath them are suspended upon hooks a more or less elaborate series of skillets, stewpans and miscellaneous cooking and household matters. A conspicuous object is very frequently a glaringly painted and highly-glazed tea tray, upon which the firelight glints cheerily, and which, by its superior lustre and artistic boldness of design, commonly throws into the shade the couple or so of tiny prints, in narrow black frames, which are suspended above it. A favourite and no doubt useful article of furniture is a clock. No Manchester operative will be without one a moment longer than he can help. You see here and there, in the better class houses, one of the old-fashioned metallic-faced eight-day clocks; but by far the most common article is the little Dutch machine, with its busy pendulum swinging openly and candidly before all the world. Add to this catalogue of the more important items of '*meublement*' an assortment of the usual odds and ends of household matters, deposited in corners of window-ledges or shelves—here a box, there a meal or flour barrel—now and then a small mirror gleaming from the wall— now and then a row of smoke-browned little china and stone-ware ornaments on the narrow chimney-piece—in general a muslin window-screen, or perhaps dingy cotton curtains—and not infrequently a pot or two of geraniums or fuchsias, rubbing their dry twigs and brown stunted leaves against the dim and small-paned lattice. Picture all these little household appliances, and others of a similar order, giving the small room a tolerably crowded appearance, and you will have a fair notion of the vast majority of the homes of the factory operatives, such as they appear in the older and less improved localities of Manchester. The cellars are, as might be expected, seldom furnished so well. They appear to possess none of the minor comforts, none of the little articles of ornament or fancy furniture which more or less you observe in the parlours. The floors seem damp and unwholesome, you catch a glimpse of a rickety-looking bed in a dark airless corner, and the fire upon the hearth is often cheerlessly small, smouldering amongst the unswept ashes.

Decidedly, the worst feature of the house tenements is the (in some districts) invariable opening of the street-door into the parlour. One step takes you from the pavement to the shrine of the Penates. The occupant cannot open his door, or stand upon his threshold, without revealing the privacy of his room to all by-passers. This awkward mode of construction is objectionable in other respects, as tending, for example, to be a fruitful source of rheumatic and catarrh-bestowing draughts. But, as I have stated, the new houses are almost

POWER LOOMS

MANCHESTER

KNIGHTS CYCLOPÆDIA OF THE
Industry of all Nations

MULE

ROVING

Manchester Operatives   from Knights' *Cyclopaedia of the Industry of All Nations*

invariably furnished with a decent lobby, a characteristic which of itself places them 50 per cent above those built after the old fashion.

Saturday is generally the great weekly epoch of cleansing and setting things to rights in the homes of the Manchester workpeople. The last day of the week may, indeed, be generally set down as a half holiday amongst all the industrial population exclusive of artisans and tradespeople. At the ordinary dinner hour, there is a vast stir amongst the denizens of counting-houses and warehouses, many of whom have country establishments to visit upon the Saturday, and one o'clock sees a simultaneous starting of scores of heavily-laden omnibuses bound for every suburb and village of and round Manchester. The mills knock off work at about two or half after two o'clock, and if you visit the class of streets which I have been attempting to describe an hour or so thereafter, you will marvel and rejoice at the universality of the purification which is going forward. Children are staggering under pails and buckets of water, brought from the pump or the cock which probably supplies a small street. Glance in at the open portals, and you will witness a grand simultaneous system of scouring. The women, of course, are the principal operators—they are cleaning their windows, hearthstoning their lintels, scrubbing their furniture with might and main. The *pater familias*, however does not always shirk his portion of the toil. Only last Saturday I came upon two or three lords of the creation usefully employed in blackleading their stoves.

Every evening after mill hours these streets, deserted as they are, except at meal times, during the day, present a scene of very considerable quiet enjoyment. The people all appear to be on the best terms with each other, and laugh and gossip from window to window, and door to door. The women, in particular, are fond of sitting in groups upon their thresholds sewing and knitting; the children sprawl about beside them, and there is the amount of sweethearting going forward which is naturally to be looked for under such circumstances. Certainly the setting of the picture is ugly and grim enough. A black, mean-looking street, with a black unadorned mill rising over the houses, and a black chimney pouring out volumes of black smoke upon all— these do not form very picturesque accessories to the scene, but still you are glad to see that, amid all the grime and dinginess of the place, there is no lack of homely comforts, good health and good spirits. . . .

. . . Unhappily the bulk of Manchester arose during a period in which . . . master and man more commonly regarded each other as mutual enemies rather than as mutual dependants whose best interest it was to be mutual friends. A vast population suddenly sprang up round the mills. This population had to be housed, and they fell into the hands of unchecked speculators, who ran up mobs of filthy and inconvenient streets and courts, utterly unheeding, or perhaps profoundly ignorant of the sanitary and social guilt of their doings. In the cases of the country mills, I am told that the case is very different. There the cottages of the labourers are in many, if not in most, instances the property of the millowner, and the isolated and disciplined character of the population render it exceeding easy to exercise a wholesome social influence over them. I promise myself pleasure from a visit to one of these communities.

In Manchester, however, the constant flux and reflux of poor population, seeking successfully or unsuccessfully for work, and provided with wretched and demoralizing accommodation, renders the city hardly a fair test of the social condition created by the factory system. . . .

. . . "I have worked, sir," said an intelligent "cardroom hand" to me—"I have worked in that mill, sir, these nineteen years, and the master never spoke to me once. I think if he did I would be gratified like, and go on working with better heart." "The masters", said another man, from another mill, "are afraid that if they speak to us they will be losing their authority; and so they say the overlookers and the managers must see to everything; but we would often like to speak to the masters themselves. We could often tell them a many things." . . .

. . . I said before, however, and I repeat now, that matters in this respect are decidedly upon the mending tack. The tone of the masters and the men in their business relationship is, I am assured on all hands, incredibly improved. Unions, trade combinations, and strikes have gone greatly out of fashion. The men shake their heads doubtfully if you bring up the subject, and refer—many of them did, at least, in my communications with them—a long list of defaulting secretaries and treasurers who had levanted with the funds of too many of the combinations. Besides, a system of amicable conference upon the subject of wages is springing up. Some time ago, a deputation of four of the female weavers in a very large mill, the name of which I am not at liberty at this moment to give, waited upon the partners, and presented the following memorial very neatly lithographed:

> Respected Sirs—We, the workpeople in your employ, approach you with great respect, and beg most respectfully to solicit an advance of wages of 10 per cent. During the recent depression of trade, we patiently submitted to the reductions then made—reductions which we could ill afford to endure; and now that trade has revived, we trust that you will restore us to the full amount of reductions to which we were then subjected. In making this appplication we are not unmindful of the fact, that the interests of masters and men are so interwoven that one cannot suffer without the other. Notwithstanding our opinion upon this point, we believe the time has come when we are justified in making this application, and hope to find to it a ready response.

A long argument was the result. The Price Current in that day's *Manchester Guardian* was appealed to, and calculations gone into to show the impossibility of raising the rate of wages without paying the increase out of capital. The result was, that the deputation professed itself satisfied, and withdrew, acknowledging that the partners were in the right.

"Four years ago," said the manager of the mill in question, "it would have been a turn-out and a strike."

. . . I have personally conversed with at least two dozen young men and women who have learned to read and write since the passing of the Ten Hours Bill. Night schools for adults are now common; most of these have libraries attached to them. The men and boys learn reading, writing, and cyphering; the women and girls, in addition to these branches of education, are taught plain, and are in many instances teaching themselves fancy needlework.

I have seen, no later than yesterday, . . . a most gratifying exhibition, illustrative of the good use to which the young women put their evening time.

Upon a hint that samples of the industry of over hours would be acceptable, I was invited the next day to inspect a counter in a mill near the Oxford-road, which was actually heaped up with specimens of crochet work, netting, sampler sewing, and a whole series of copy-books.

Manchester is known as being of late years a decidedly musical place. Since the passing of the Ten Hours Bill, a great Monday night concert for the operative classes has been in successful operation. I visited it the other night. The musical attractions to be sure were rather mild—a small organ, a piano, an amateur chorus of some thirty voices, assisted by a few professors of only local celebrity. But the programme comprised selections from Handel, Meyerbeer, Rossini, and Bishop; and if these were at the best only respectably performed, they were listened to with the most reverent silence, and then applauded to the echo by an assemblage of between two or three thousand working men and women, who had respectively paid their threepence for admission, and who took up nearly the entire area of the Free-trade Hall.

Letter VI

The substance of the remark with which I open this communication must be kept steadily and keenly in sight by those who would acquire from my letters a true insight into the social condition of the great capital of the cotton cities. The Manchester which I am describing is the Manchester of prosperous times. True, there has not been any recent fever of production; there has been no sudden and imperious demand for calicoes, such as in the olden times, before Ten Hours Bills were heard of, would have kept the steam-engines throbbing, and the mechanism whirling for fifteen or eighteen hours out of the twenty-four; but there has been for some time a fair and steady trade; the workpeople have for some time earned fair and steady wages, and the butcher and baker have happily had the power of being reasonable in their demands. But good times in Manchester hang—so to speak—on a fibre of cotton. In Birmingham, where a hundred trades employ a hundred different guilds of handicraftsmen, the stagnation of any one branch of employment affects only one working family out of a hundred working families. Here, universal well-doing, or universal suffering, depend solely upon the one article of cotton— upon the supply of the raw material—upon the demand for the manufactured fabric. The whisper of a hostile tariff amid the markets of the East, the rumour of a worm or a blight in the plantations of Alabama or Louisiana, is sufficient, by checking the demand of the warehouseman on the one hand, or raising the prices charged by the cotton broker on the other, to produce, in a week, short time and short wages—to change, as by the waving of a wand, the industrial and consuming power of a vast community. In most towns, in periods of operative distress, the pressure is partial, and little, if any, of it is seen upon the surface. All trades cannot be bad at the same time. Here, speaking in general terms, the distress of one operative is the distress of all. Let there come a glut or a panic in that one grand item of cotton, and straightway the smoke ceases to pour from the tall chimney; the great halls, crowded with complex machinery, are silent and lone; and, lingering round the corners of courts and alleys, groups of wageless workmen curse the chance which keeps them idle and their children hungry. . . .

. . . I have already, in general terms, noticed the almost universal testimony borne by those who know the Manchester "mill hand" best, to the mild and inoffensive character and bearing of the cotton population. The colliers and metal workers throughout the north, indeed, profess to hold the men of the loom and the mule in great contempt, as a set of spiritless milksops—as soft and pliable as the woolly fibre which they twist. And truly there can be little doubt but that the men who habitually deal with bobbins and threads must form a very different race to the sturdier and more turbulent spirits whose lot is cast among sledge-hammers and pick-axes. A turn-out of the cotton-workers is a very different, and generally speaking, a far less riotous affair than a strike in the districts of iron and coal. Occasionally, no doubt, there have been deeds of crime and lawless violence, perpetrated by Manchester turn-outs. The persecution of the "knobsticks" as the workmen were called who, during a strike, were willing to labour at lower wages than those which the union sanctioned, and to obtain which the stand was made—the persecution which on one or two occasions these poor wretches underwent, was at once cowardly and cruel. They were set upon in lonely places, and beaten and ducked by mobs. Their feet were wounded by blows from iron-spiked sticks, and blinding vitriol was flung into their eyes. Still it must be recollected that these atrocities were committed by the most fanatical rabble of the mills, during a period of intense excitement—during a struggle between labour and capital which was as for life and death, while the attacks were made upon men who were esteemed by their persecutors as enemies to their order and traitors to their peers.

As a general rule, the men of cotton are essentially a peaceful and moral-force generation. They are greatly under the influence of leaders, whose mental powers they respect. There are not a few of the weavers and spinners whose capacity for thought is considerable; and these again have to deal with a population whose faith is one of their most distinguishing moral attributes. The cotton-mills of Manchester abound with hard-headed, studious, thoughtful men, who pass brooding, meditating lives, sometimes taken up in endeavours to sound those profound social problems which lie at the bottom of the relations between capital and labour; sometimes, again, occupied with the various phases of physical and mechanical science; and not infrequently sturdy theologians profoundly versed in the subtleties and casuistries of all the warring schools of Calvinism. . . .

. . . Such men often rise to be overlookers in their respective mills, and in many instances pass their evenings in teaching adult classes of their fellow labourers. As a general rule, they are nearly all either professed or virtual teetotallers, and as such are greatly given to that cant of temperance which denounces as a folly and a crime the most harmless degree of social indulgence. I had one long conversation with a man who was a good specimen of the class in question. He is now an overlooker in a mill in Hulme. He told me he had been a thoughtless scamp in his youth, and that he had led a vagrant sort of life, thinking of nothing but sensual pleasures until he became a man. Then he began to reflect upon the degrading life which he was leading, and to ask himself what was the use of his having a soul if he did not strive to elevate it; so, setting to work, he found—in his own words—that he was "endowed by God with a great capacity for study". He liked mechanical science the best, and now it was a great pleasure to him to strive to make his children fond of reading, and to educate and enlighten his fellow-workmen. He was at the head of a small library, principally scientific. "Did they admit novels?"—"Yes," with a melancholy shake of the head, "they found that they could not get on without something of that kind—the people liked stories". My friend, however, did not seem by any means "up" in the fiction department of his library, for he mentioned the "Pickwick Papers" and other works by Eugene Sue". He highly approved of the cheap summer trips which the railways were giving the people. He had thus been able to "take his good woman one hundred and twelve miles from Manchester", and explained the country to her as they went along. Sometimes, in the department of which he was overlooker, they worked so fast that they got ahead of the others and had half a holiday. They were lucky in this respect lately. It was a fine day and he had taken not only his own family, but all the workers in his department, out in a body to enjoy themselves in the fields, "a far better place than the public-house".

Another intelligent operative I encountered in his own house, just as he returned from work. The room was cheery and clean. Two little girls, with fat dimpled legs and arms, sat on a stool before the fire. The plates and pot-lids shone as brightly as old china or armour from the white-washed walls. The wife bustled with the tea-things, and the good man sat him down in his rocking-chair—that delicious piece of furniture of which the Yankees borrowed the idea from Lancashire, and now impudently take credit for having invented.

My friend was a Ten Hours Bill man: "The people had health, and time, and spirits now to clean their houses, and teach themselves something useful. The cotton folks were improving. Oh, yes, they were; the next generation would be better than the present. No one ever thought of schools for children when he was a child. No; he had wrought many and many a time for twelve hours a day when he was not eight years old. The children were lucky now to what they were in them old times. There were good evening classes too for the men and women, only he was afeard that a good many of them, particularly the boys and girls, were too fond of going to the magic saloons, where they did not hear no good, and did not do no good. He had gone to one himself lately." A look from the wife. "Oh, of course, only to hear what was going on —only that—and he was disgusted, he was. Nigger songs," and, with a significant wink, "other songs, and nonsensical recitations and trash—and girls dancing on the stage, with such short petticoats. Oh, places like them wasn't no good. But there was the Monday night concerts—there was music—there was the place for a working man to have a rational night's amusement.". . .
. . . Each spinner is obliged by the Factory Act to pay for the education of his piecers and scavengers. The fees are sometimes collected in the mills, but occasionally the boy is entrusted with the amount himself, the consequences of which piece of faith are not infrequently a day's truant-playing, and a terrific debauch on unripe apples, toffy, and gingerbread. Mr. Clay, the principal master of the Lyceum, informed me that he had great difficulty in instilling

anything like a moral sense into the children—particularly as respects lying. They saw no moral degradation in the idea of a falsehood, It was only inconvenient to be found out. The boys, too, were obstinately dirty, and he had often to send them home to wash themselves. In summer he told me they seldom wore shoes. Mr. Clay is confident that a vast deal is being effected for the factory population by the education now provided for them.

"Do you lose sight of the children when they leave school?" I asked. The answer was cheering—

"No—especially the girls—for they come back so often to the library for books."

Mr. Clay teaches a night adult class. He has grey-haired scholars, and sometimes mothers bring their children. This class had "decidedly increased" since the Ten Hours Bill. The worthy teacher was anxious to impress upon me that the young men and women attending the evening schools were kept very carefully apart. "I sometimes tell the young women that they only come to pick up sweethearts; but I take care that the one set has gone before I dismiss the other."

The Manchester Mechanics' Institution is supported by decidedly a better class than the average of mill operatives—that is to say, by workmen exercising a more skilled species of labour, and by shopmen. In the pianoforte class there are thirty-five pupils, generally tradespeople's daughters. The library is a good one. The books principally inquired for are, first, novels and romances; secondly, voyages, travels and biographies; thirdly philosophic works. Books in foreign languages are rarely demanded.

Every London publisher knows that Lancashire furnishes no unimportant part of the literary market of England. I was very desirous of ascertaining, therefore, the species of works most in demand amongst the labouring and poorer classes. The libraries in the better parts of the town are of course stocked in much the same way as the libraries in the better parts of London. I wished to ascertain the species of cheap literature most in vogue and accordingly applied to Mr. Abel Heywood, of Oldham-street, one of the most active and enterprising citizens of Manchester, who supplies not only the smaller booksellers of the town, but those throughout the county, with the cheap works most favoured by the poorer reading classes. The contents of Mr. Heywood's shop are significant. Masses of penny novels and comic song and recitation books are jumbled with sectarian pamphlets and democratic essays. Educational books abound in every variety. Loads of cheap reprints of American authors seldom or never heard of amid the upper reading classes here, are mingled with editions of the early Puritan divines. Double-columned translations from Sue, Dumas, Sand, Paul Feval and Frederick Soube jostel with dream-books, scriptural commentaries, Pinnock's Guides, and quantities of cheap music, Sacred Melodists, and Little Warblers. Altogether the literary chaos as very significant of the restless and all devouring literary appetite which it supplies. Infinitely chequered must be the morale of the population who devour with equal gusto dubious "Memoirs of Lady Hamilton", and authentic narratives of the "Third Appearance of John Wesley's Ghost", duly setting forth the opinions of that eminent shade upon the recent speeches of Dr. Bunting. . . . Of these publications the Lancashire Beacon and the Reasoner are avowedly infidel. I have not had an opportunity of seeing the latter, but in the number of the former which I perused, I found nothing more fatal to Christianity than abuse of the Bishop of Manchester. The Lancashire mind is indeed essentially a believing, perhaps an overbelieving one. Fanaticism rather than scepticism is the extreme into which it is most likely to hurry. In Ashton-under-Lyne Johanna Southcote's bearded followers still meet under the roof of the New Jerusalem. In remote districts astrologers still watch the influence of the planets; and all quackeries, moral and physical—the remedies of Professor Mesmer or of Professor Holloway—equally find a clear stage and very great favour. . . .

. . . Mr. Heywood informed me that the sale of cheap books has decidedly not increased in consequence of the Ten Hours Bill. The same assertion was made by another extensive though a much smaller bookseller in the vicinity of Garrett-lane. The department of the literary trade which alone seemed to have received any impetus from recent legislation was the sale of copy books, which improved. The only classification of the purchasers of cheap literature which I found it practicable to make was, that the comic or *soi-disant* comic publications were usually patronised by clerks and shopmen, while tales were inquired for by the working classes commonly so called. It is, indeed, by the links of a story that the operative taste seems to be most bound. For the encouragement of literary speculators, I may add, that every cheap book is sure of a sale in Lancashire—at first.

At the library of the Mechanics' Institute, and at that of the Ancoats Lyceum, I was informed that the Ten Hours Bill had decidedly made no change in the reading habits of the subscribers. . . .

Letter IX

. . . In this letter, then I shall detail what further information I have collected with reference to subjects already partially disposed of, and what particulars I have ascertained regarding ground still untrodden. Without any very strict view to a symmetrical order of arrangement, but rather having respect to the abstract value of the facts and information presented, I shall begin with some account of the Sunday-school system as it exists in Manchester, many of my observations being also applicable to the system as it exists in the manufacturing districts generally.

The Sunday schools of the industrial north form not only a vast moral and educational engine, but a curious and characteristic social fact. The system originated by Mr. Raikes, some seventy years ago, took deep root in Lancashire, and grew with the growth of manufacturing industry. The serious cast of the Lancashire mind, and its earnestness and zeal, acting upon the facilities afforded by the order and discipline which it is the very nature of the factory system to instill, formed a soil in which the Sunday-school system took very deep root, and bore very rich harvests. I rather understate than overstate the numbers, when I say that in the Sunday-schools of Manchester, may be found from 40,000 to 50,000 scholars, and from 4,000 to 5,000 teachers, inspectors and visitants. . . .

... The early patrons and early champions of Sunday-schools are now dying fast away. The great world has never heard of them, but yet amongst a large and influential class in the north they have left immortal memories. Often and often have I lately had occasion to see the walls, both of drawing-rooms and humble kitchen-parlours, hung with portraits of grave sober-clad men, whose names I had never heard of, and who were yet pointed out to me as among the greatest and most glorious of Englishmen. Local poets, too, have, hymned the departure of locally famous Sunday-school worthies. To those who know nothing of the excellent man commemorated, there is something which almost savours of the ludicrous in such a couplet as

"... Oh, was it not
The meek and earth-unblazoned name of Stott!"

Yet Mr. Stott was a hero in his way. He was for half a century the foremost champion of the Lancashire Sunday-schools. When he commenced his labours, he had to struggle against all the chimera terrors with which the first French Revolution peopled England. If he assembled a knot of children on a Sunday afternoon, he was accused of preaching Jacobinism to the rising generation. If he caused the children to walk in orderly procession from the school-room to the church, he was drilling them in military tactics, preparatory to the outbreak of an operative Jacquerie. Yet Mr. Stott worked steadily on. He began with two score pupils. In the school which he founded, I last Sunday saw 2,600. Sunday-schools in Manchester, as I have said, form not only a great educational engine, but a great social fact. Nearly every school has its library, and, besides the library, many have their sick and burial societies. At Whitsuntide, the yearly week of rest in Manchester, nearly every school enjoys its gala and its country trip. Many of the richest and most prosperous men in Manchester will tell you, that to the Sunday-school, which taught them to read and write, and inculcated honesty and sobriety, they now owe their villas and their mills. Sunday-schools, as they are worked in Lancashire, more than any set of institutions which I know, tend to bind different classes of society to each other. Men in the middle ranks of life very commonly act as teachers, or at all events take a practical interest in the proceedings; and acquaintance-ships first formed in the class-rooms, lead in very many cases, to subsequent and often life-long business connections. It often happens that families are for generations connected, as pupils or teachers, with the same Sunday-school. "A great number of the children before you", I have been repeatedly told, "are the children of old scholars, and a great many of our teachers were themselves scholars in the classes which they now instruct."

The education afforded in the Manchester Sunday-schools is, of course, of an elementary and religious character. The pupils are first taught to read; then scriptural extracts, or the Scriptures themselves, are put into their hands; and instructions in psalmody are diversified by familiar moral and doctrinal addresses and examinations into the contents of the chapter or passage last studied. This general description applies pretty well to all the Sunday-schools connected either with the Church or with Dissent. Most of the schools, however, meet upon week days and week evenings, when secular instruction is communicated, consisting principally of reading, writing, cyphering and a little geography. The Sunday education is purely gratuitous. For that which goes on upon working days a small fee, varying from twopence to sixpence a week, is commonly charged. Many Sunday-schools have adult classes for men and women. I have repeatedly seen grey-haired scholars. In general, the ages of the pupils vary from eight to twenty, the girls commonly remaining in connection with the school longer than the young men. . . .

. . . Before proceeding to give a more particular account of the schools which I visited, I would wish to state—as showing the extent to which the moral restraint exercised by these institutions goes—that when, on the famous 10th of April, a great Chartist meeting was being held, under circumstances of intense public excitement, within three minutes' walk of the largest establishment of the kind in Manchester, the number of pupils in attendance was only six beneath that of the previous day. This school is that of St. Paul, Bennett-street, the one founded by Mr. Stott, and that to which—taking it as a good example of the Church schools—I last Sunday paid a very lengthened visit.

The Bennett-street Sunday-school is a vast plain building, fully as large as an ordinary sized cotton-factory, and exhibiting four long ranges of lofty windows. The number of pupils at present on the books is 2,611 and the average attendance 2,152. The number of Sunday scholars who learn writing and arithmetic, two evenings a week, paying for their paper, pens and ink, etc. is 260. The number attending the daily schools, and paying twopence per week is 330. The members of the School Funeral Society amount to 1,804; and of the School Sick Society to 400. The total amount of relief afforded by these societies since their commencement is upwards of £7,285. I may add that, on one evening in each week, the female scholars are instructed in plain sewing and housewifery.

I have said that the building is composed of four stories; the girls occupy the two highest, the boys the two lowest. As to ages, the former ranged from little things of five and six, brought by their elder sisters, to well-grown young women. Many of them were the children of small shopkeepers and mechanics, the others were mill-hands. Every girl there was decently attired, and many of them were neatly and tastefully dressed. . . .

. . . Descending to the most crowded of the boys' rooms, I found . . . the class . . . was composed in the main of commonplace-looking boys, dressed, some of them, in fustian, others in coarse cloth, and generally sallow-faced, thin, and rather undersized, as Manchester urchins too often are. . . .

. . . The boys are commonly employed in branches of trade, many of them of a laborious nature, for several hours a day longer than the term during which they could be legally employed in factories; and that for a much smaller amount of wages than they could earn in the different processes of the cotton trade. In this one class were boys earning from six shillings to seven shillings in factories, whilst those employed as workers in iron did not make much more than half the money. It must be borne in mind, however, that the future prospects of the young mechanics are better than those of the young spinners and weavers. . . .

. . . In the afternoon I visited a very large Dissenting Sunday-school, connected with the Independent body—that attached to the Hope chapel, in Salford. In this school it is not uncommon to see assembled on one Sunday, three generations of the same family—children, their parents, and their grand-parents. There are three large school-rooms for the youthful scholars—from those who are mere children up to those of eighteen or twenty years of age; and separate rooms for the adult scholars of both sexes. The male adult class is managed by Mr. William Morris, the principal partner in a very large cotton-working establishment—some features of the internal economy of which I shall presently allude to. Mr. Morris, who is one of the most respected citizens of Manchester and who is justly proud of having worked himself up "from the ranks", takes the deepest practical interest in Sunday-school and temperance movements, and is a distinguished advocate of both causes. He passes many hours every Sunday, surrounded by his adult class, in the Hope chapel. The total number of pupils taught in those schools is about 1,200 and the average afternoon attendance is about 924. There are 160 in the infant class, and about 600 above fourteen years of age. More than 100 of the pupils are married persons. The absentee children are visited by the teachers. In the day school connected with the Hope chapel there are about 300 scholars. To the sick relief fund there are about 100 subscribers, and to a clothing charity about 530. This school raises annually about £50 for missionary purposes. The number of adult scholars taught separately is about 250. . . .

. . . In general intelligence and acquirements the children of both the St. Paul's and the Hope schools seemed pretty much upon a par. The children from ten to twelve years of age were able to read with tolerable fluency and correctness. . . .

. . . I have no reason to doubt the accuracy of the statements made by the Sunday scholars as to their giving their wages almost entirely to their parents; and the inference which one would naturally draw from the fact, knowing what we do of the general practice, is, that the Sunday-school system has, to some extent, the effect of discouraging the generally speedy rupture of the family tie. . . .

. . . I have already alluded to the practice, too common in the cotton districts, of dosing infants with narcotic medicine, to keep them quiet while their mothers are at their daily work in the factories. In my former communication, I stated that the druggists were exceedingly shy of giving any information upon the point; but it is one of such great interest and importance, that I resolved *coute que coute,* to obtain a body of evidence upon the subject. . . .

. . . The information given to me by medical men was general in its character, and may be summed up in the evidence elicited from Mr. John Greg Harrison, one of the factory medical inspectors, and a gentleman carrying on a very large practice amongst the operative classes: "The system of drugging children is exceedingly common, and one of the prevailing causes of infant mortality. Mothers and nurses both administer narcotics; the former, however, principally with the view of obtaining an undisturbed night's rest. . . ."

. . . Dr. Harrison added, that the practice of procuring abortion was sadly common, particularly among unmarried women, and among married women living separated from their husbands. A person in Stockport is notorious for the extent of his practice in this way, instruments, and not drugs, being the usual means employed. . . .

. . . An intelligent male operative in the Messrs. Morris's mill, in Salford, stated that he and his wife put out their first child to be nursed. The nurse gave the

baby "sleeping stuff", and it died in nine weeks. The neighbours told his wife
how the baby was dosed, but the nurse denied that the child had ever got
anything of the kind. They never sent a child out to be nursed again. For that
one they paid three shillings and sixpence a week, and the weeks that the nurse
washed for it, four shillings. The mother had to get up at four o'clock, and
carry it to the nurse's every morning; but the distance was too far for her to
suckle it at noon, so the child had no milk until the nurse brought it home at
night. The nurses are often old women, who take in washing, and sometimes
they have three or four children to take care of. The mother can often
smell laudanum in the child's breath when it comes home. As for mothers
themselves, they give the "sleeping stuff" principally at night, to secure their
own rest. . . .

. . . By a druggist carrying on an extensive business in a low neighbourhood in
Ancoats, inhabited almost exclusively by a mill population, I was informed
that personally he did not sell much narcotic medicine, but that it was tolerably
extensively vended in small "general shops", the owners of which bought the
drug by gallons from certain establishments which he named. . . .

. . . He expressed his belief that the drugging system was gradually going out,
and that the "old women" and midwives, who were its great patrons, were
losing their hold upon the mill population. . . .

. . . Children who had been drugged with "sleeping stuff" he could recognise
in a moment. They never seemed fairly awake. Their whole system appeared
to be sunk into a stagnant state. He believed that when such doses were administered, nurses were chiefly to blame; for mothers often came to him with
their ailing children, asking, in great trouble whether he thought that "sleeping
stuff" had anything to do with the child's illness. The proportion of illegitimate
children carried off through insufficient nursing was terrible. As to adults, he
knew that a good deal of opium and laudanum was taken by them. Women
were his chief customers in that way. He had seen a girl drink off an ounce
and a half of laudanum as it was handed to her over the counter. Most of
these people had begun by taking laudanum under medical advice and had
continued the practice until it became habitual." While we were talking,
another druggist entered the shop, and confirmed the main points of the above
statement. He added, that "when he was an apprentice, twenty years ago, in a
country place, principally inhabited by hand-loom weavers, his master used
to make Godfrey in a large boiler, by twenties and thirties of gallons at a
brewst. He believed that the people did not drug their children half so much
now-a-days. Coroners inquests were good checks. Almost all the laudanum he
sold was disposed of in pennyworths. A great number of old women took it
for rheumatism.

I beg, however, to direct particular attention to the following evidence, given
by a most intelligent druggist, carrying on a very large business in a poor neighbourhood, surrounded by mills, and a gentleman of whose perfect candour
and good faith I have certain knowledge: "Laudanum, in various forms, is
used to some extent by the adult population, male and female, and to a terrible
extent for very young children. I sell about two shillings worth a week of
laudanum, in pennorths, for adults. Some use raw opium instead. They either
chew it, or make it into pills and swallow it. The country people use laudanum

as a stimulant, as well as the town people. On market days they come in from Lymm and Warrington, and buy the pure drug for themselves, and "Godfrey", or "Quietness", for the children. Habitual drunkards often give up spirits and take to laudanum, as being cheaper and more intensely stimulating. Another class of customers are middle-aged prostitutes. They take it when they get low and melancholy. Three of them came together into my shop last night for opium to relieve pains in their limbs. These women swallow the drug in great quantities. As regards children, they are commonly dosed either with "Godfrey", or "Infants' Quietness". The first is an old-fashioned preparation, and has been more or less in vogue for near a century. It is made differently by different vendors, but, generally speaking it contains an ounce and a half of pure laudanum to the quart. The dose is from half a teaspoonful to two teaspoonfuls. Infants' Cordial, or Mixture, is stronger, containing on the average two ounces of laudanum to a quart. Occasionally paregoric, which is one-fourth part as strong as laudanum, is used. Mothers sometimes give narcotics to their children, but most commonly the nurses are in fault. The stuff is frequently administered by the latter without the mothers' knowledge, but is occasionally given by the mothers without the fathers' knowledge. I believe that women frequently drug their children through pure ignorance of the effect of the practice, and because, having been brought up in mills, they know nothing about the first duties of mothers. The nurses sometimes take children for one shilling and sixpence a week. They are very often laundresses. Half-a-crown a week may be the average charge of the nurse, and the "nursing" commonly consists of laying the infant in a cradle to doze all day in a stupified state, produced by a teaspoonful of "Godfrey" or "Quietness". Bad as the practice is, it would not be so fatal if the nurses and parents would obey the druggists' instructions in administering the medicine. But this is what often takes place. A woman comes and buys pennorths of "Godfrey". Well, all is right for five or six weeks. Then she begins to complain that we don't make the "Godfrey" so good as we used to do; then she has to give the child more than it needed at first; and so nothing will do but she must have "Infant's Quietness" instead, for, as she says, she has heard that this is better, i.e. stronger. But in process of time, as the child gets accustomed to the drug, the dose must be made stronger still. Then the nurses, and sometimes the mothers, take to making the stuff themselves. They buy pennorts of aniseed, and treacle and sugar, add the laudanum to it, and make the dose as strong as they like. The midwives teach them how to brew it; and if the quantity of laudanum comes expensive, they use crude opium instead. Of course, numberless children are carried off in this way. I know a child that has been so treated at once it looks like a little old man or woman. I can tell one in an instant. Often and often a mother comes here with a child that has been out to nurse, to know what can be the matter with it. I know, but frequently I dare hardly tell; for if I say what I am sure of, the mother will go to the nurse and charge her with sickening the child; the nurse will deny, point blank, that she did anything of the sort, and will come and make a disturbance here, daring me to prove what, of course I can't prove legally, and abusing me for taking away her character. The children also suffer from the period which elapses between the times of their being suckled. The mothers often live on vegetables and drink quantities of thin ale, and the consequence is that the children are terribly subject to weakening attacks of diarrhoea."

Hearing in several quarters of the "little shops" which retailed "Godfrey", I looked out for such an establishment, and in a back street in Chorlton, surrounded by mills, I hit upon what I wanted—a shop in the "general line", in the window of which, amongst eggs, candles, sugar, bread, soap, butter, starch, herrings, and cheese, I observed a placard marked "Children's Draughts, a penny each". There was a woman behind the counter, and on my making inquiries as to whether she sold "Godfrey", or any similar compound, she replied that she had not for six months. The draught announced in the window was purgative.

"Then you used to sell 'Godfrey'?"—"Oh yes, we used to make it and sell it for children, when they were cross; but the people did not think ours strong enough.". . .

. . . "But very strong stuff is generally used?"—"Indeed it is; you may know the children that get it at once—if you have any experience in them things—they're sickly, and puny, and ill-looking. It's a shocking thing that poor people should be obliged to give their children such stuff to keep them quiet.". . .

. . . In returning last Sunday night, by the Oldham-road, from one of my tours among the druggists, I was somewhat surprised to hear the loud sounds of music and jollity which floated out from the public-house windows. The street was swarming with drunken men and women; and with young mill-girls and boys, shouting, hallooing, and romping with each other. . . . The public-houses and gin-shops were roaring full. Rows, and fights, and scuffles, were every moment taking place within doors and in the streets. The whole street rung with shouting, screaming, and swearing mingled with the jarring music of half-a-dozen bands. A tolerably intimate acquaintance with most phases of London life enables me to state that in no part of the metropolis would the police have tolerated such a state of things for a single Sunday. I entered one of the musical taverns—one of the best of them. It was crowded to the door with men and women—many of them appearing to belong to a better station in life than mill-hands or mechanics. The music consisted of performances on the piano and seraphine. In the street I accosted a policeman, telling him of my surprise that music should be allowed in public-houses on Sunday evenings. Such a thing was never dreamt of in London. "Oh", quoth he, "there is an understanding that they don't play nothing but sacred music." "Sacred music," I said; "well, it is the first time I ever heard the 'Bay of Biscay', and the 'Drum Polka' invested with the title!". . .

ASHTON-UNDER-LYNE

Letter VII

In selecting the minor cotton towns round Manchester, which I think it my duty to visit, I try to fix upon those which present local peculiarities and distinct social characteristics. In general, indeed, these towns wear a monotonous sameness of aspect, physical and moral. The rates of wages paid are nearly on a par—the prices of the commodities for which they are spent are nearly on a par—the toil of the people at the mills, and their habits and arrangements at home, are all but identical. In fact, the social condition of the different town populations is almost as much alike as the material appearance of the tall chimneys under which they live. Here and there the height of the latter may differ by a few rounds of brick; but, in all essential respects, a description of one is a description of all.

In searching, however, for minor shades of social distinction, I find some two or three characteristics which separate Ashton-under-Lyne from its spinning neighbours, and which may excuse me for making it the main subject of a letter. Ashton is occupied by a "new" population, and, in some respects, it is as much a model cotton-working town as any we have. The nucleus of the place is indeed old, filthy, and dilapidated in the extreme; but nine-tenths of the town owes its existence immediately to the power-loom, and, in nearly all that large proportion, the houses are more comfortable, the streets more open and better drained, than in the great majority of industrial Lancashire towns.

Ashton lies about seven miles from Manchester, and directly "under" the "Lyne" of that long healthy ridge of hills called the "Backbone of England"— a chain which, under the local name of Blackstone Edge, separates Lancaster from York, and then runs northward through Westmorland and Northumberland, until it loses itself among the undulations of the Scottish Cheviots. Ashton is built upon the banks of the Tame, a stream rising in the Yorkshire moors. The country around is level and bleak, the soil marshy and cold. In 1811 the population of the town was 24,000; at present it is over 34,000. The mills about Ashton are very generally the property of large capitalists, who can afford, and often do afford, to employ their people at full hours, when a period of temporary slackness in trade obliges those masters whose command of capital is less at once to curtail their producing operations. In this respect Ashton is the reverse of Oldham. In the latter town small capitalists abound. It is not, indeed, uncommon there for several masters to unite to rent a mill, and sometimes to unite to rent even the floor of a mill. These employers conduct their operations in the hand-to-mouth style which naturally follows from such a state of things. They spin, moreover, generally speaking, the coarse and inferior kinds of thread, and the slightest check in the demand falls at once upon the workman. There is no shield of capital to stand between the humble producer and the immediate fluctuations of the market. From what reason I know not, but no returns of the pauperism of Oldham are given in the last tabular statistics presented by the Somerset House Board to Parliament; but I was informed by Mr. Tipping, the active and very intelligent relieving officer of Ashton, that an estimate had been constructed, showing the relative amount of pauperism at Oldham to be nearly double that at Ashton. The latter union contains a population of 101,000 and includes one or two small hamlets. The amount at present paid by the guardians is about £125 weekly for out-door relief, while there are in the workhouse about 200 inmates. I may add that the locality has been very slightly visited by cholera—only about thirty deaths having taken place throughout the union.

The population of Ashton have the reputation of being turbulent and fanatical. A policeman was killed in a disturbance here lately. The most ultra-political and theological opinions run riot amongst the population. The only manifest opposition which I have observed to the late day of humiliation was in Ashton, where the dead walls were covered with placards denouncing the "Humbug"; but adding—and Heaven knows with much truth—that the people want feasts quite as much as fasts. Ashton, too, is still the stronghold of the Southcote faith. A handsome row of grocers' shops with long-bearded men behind the counters, was pointed out to me as a sort of colony of the people who still hold the strange creed in question. There is a "New Jerusalem" too, in which the faithful still meet . . .

. . . In Ashton, too, there lingers on a handful of miserable old men, the remnants of the cotton hand-loom weavers. No young persons think of pursuing such an occupation; the few who practise it were too old and confirmed in old habits, when the power-loom was introduced, to be able to learn a new way of making their bread. The Ashton handloom weavers live, almost to a man, in the old filthy, and undrained parts of the town. . . .

. . . The system of the mill owners building and letting out comfortable cottages to their workpeople prevails as much, or even more, in Ashton than in any town in Lancashire. It is common, particularly in the outskirts, to see every mill surrounded with neat streets of perfectly uniform dwellings, clean and cheerful in appearance and occupied by the "hands". The first of these snug little colonies to which we went was that attached to the mills of Messrs. Buckley. Here are ranged in rows and squares, some of them with gardens attached, a little town of dwellings, regularly planned, and each house, let, according to the number of rooms which it contains, at three shillings, three shillings and sixpence, and four shillings and sixpence. If a garden is attached, a few shillings annually are charged in addition. The Messrs. Buckley, I am informed, live among their people, and are in the habit of familiar intercourse with them—facts which operate as very great checks upon drunkenness and all sorts of disorderly behaviour. "If a master," says Mr. Tipping, "never puts eyes on a man from Saturday till Monday, he may be drunk all that time with impunity; but here any conduct of the kind can't fail to be noticed; and so the man at once gets a hint that if he doesn't mend his manners he may look out for other employment." "Such a thing as an application for parish relief from the people hereabouts," Mr. Tipping added, "is scarcely ever heard of.". . .

. . . The last mill cottages which I visited were those built by the Messrs. Mason and Sons. The first thing which these gentlemen did, in laying out the ground, was to spend £1,000 on drainage, by which the refuse from every house is carried down into the river. The cottages were of two kinds—four and six roomed. For the former, three shillings per week is charged; for the latter, four shillings and threepence per week. The inhabitants of the better class of houses are, therefore, voters. I inspected one of the four-roomed class. There was a lobby, and the stairs leading to the bedrooms were nicely carpeted. The front room was furnished strictly as a parlour; but the back one, or kitchen, which opened into a flagged yard, was obviously the ordinary sitting room. . . .

. . . At the Messrs. Mason's I was furnished with a note of the wages weekly paid to the different classes of spinners in their employment, giving an average of more than £2 2s. to each spinner, and a general average for adults, in all the branches of employment, including skilled and unskilled labour, of £1 2s 3d. It must be distinctly observed, however, that piecers are not included in the calculations. . . .

. . . I have before alluded to the sporting propensities of the hand-loom weavers. I learn that in better times, the same spirit actuated the cotton, flax and woollen hand-loom weavers of Ashton. There is, or used to be, a capital pack of harriers kept in the vicinity, and the Ashton weavers, armed with huge leaping-sticks, by the help of which they could take hedges and ditches as well as the boldest rider of the hunt, were usual attendants on the pack. The mill system has, however, utterly extirpated every vestige of the ancient sporting spirit. The regularity of hours and discipline preserved seem, by rendering any such escapades out of the question, to have at length obliterated everything like a desire for, or idea of, them. The taste for botany, common to the district, seems, however. nearly as strong in Ashton as in Manchester. I observed a public-house, kept by an enthusiast in the science, called the "Botanical Tavern". . . .

BOLTON

Letter IV

There exists no means of ascertaining with statistical exactitude the average period in the lives of parents and children, throughout the cotton districts, when the home is broken up, and the members of the family dispersed. The results of the enquiries I have instituted in different quarters are contradictory and unsatisfactory. There are—if I may use the phrase—a great number of shades of family disruption. Sometimes the scattered members of a household remain in constant communication with each other. Sometimes only occasions of sickness or death bring them together. Sometimes they sicken and die without any mutual knowledge, and without much mutual regard, each isolated member of the family having become part and parcel of a new circle of social relationship. In fact, it would appear as if, in the manufacturing districts, everything moves quicker than in other parts of the world. The child toils sooner, has children in his turn sooner, and, in the present sanitary state of matters, dies sooner. But over and above this natural precocity—this crowding together, as it were, of the ordinary epochs of life—it may be observed that an existance of constant labour, and not unfrequent privation, has a universal tendency to diminish the time which the family tie subsists in all its cohesive powers. The members of a family living in comfortable ease, continue bound together far longer than those of a family struggling to live. This rule is natural as it is universal. In the latter case each, as it grows up, must necessarily labour for itself. The family income is not earned by a common head, nor does it flow from a common source. The circle becomes a sort of joint stock company; and as that great and universally prevailing law of self-preservation comes gradually into play, the force of habit and of affection weakens, while that of individual interest strengthens; and as surely as the different personages of the company begin to perceive that they are contributing, either in money or in comfort of situation, more to the family than the family contributes to them, so surely do they withdraw from the association to labour in isolation, or to form new or more profitable social combinations for themselves.

The age at which the administrators of the new poor-law calculate that they have to provide for individuals, as items in the population, and not considered as members of a family, is, in the manufacturing districts, sixteen. I am assured, on the very highest authority, that nothing in Manchester is more uncommon than a child after the age of sixteen systematically contributing to the support of his or her parents, or parents doing anything for the support of a child above that age. The family tie may therefore be considered—allowing three children to each family—as broken up about twenty years after the marriage from which the children spring. "Nothing," says my informant, a gentleman of high official standing" "nothing can be more warm and keen than the affections of parents throughout the cotton districts for children, so long as they continue children, and nothing more remarkable than the lukewarm carelessness of feeling which subsists between these parents and their children after the latter are grown up and doing for themselves.". . .

. . . As a general rule, it may be safely asserted that comparatively few family disruptions take place which do not lead to early marriages, or which are not occasioned by the system of early marriages. The one tendency, in fact, is closely and inevitably connected with the other; so much so, indeed, that they may be described as different phases in the operation of the same great system. . . .

. . . In the minds of how many are even the best features of the cotton-mill associated with the worst features of a squalid town. And yet, thickly sprinkled amid the oak-coppiced vales of Lancashire, with the white-washed cottages of the work-people gleaming through the branches and beside the rapid stream, or perched on the breezy forehead of the hill, are to be seen hundreds on hundreds of busily working cotton mills. In the vicinity of these there are no foetid alleys, no grimy courts, no dark area or underground cellars. Even the smoke from the tall chimneys passes tolerably innocuously away—sometimes, perhaps, when the air is calm and heavy, dotting the grass and the leaves with copious showers of "blacks", but never seriously smirching nor blighting the dewy freshness of the fields and hedge-rows, through which the spinner and the weaver pass to their daily toil.

I visited the other day the country factory of Egerton, belonging to the Messrs. Ashworth, and situated a few miles to the north of Bolton. The railway from Manchester to the latter town, spans ten miles of open breezy country, dotted here and there with mills and calico works snugly nestled in the valleys. . . . Every mile or so down in the valley beside the running stream lies a factory of some sort or other, often half-hidden by the sheltering trees; and further up the hill, upon the green slope, you mark the decent row of substantial stone-built cottages, where the "hands" live. Churches with neat spires, and the more unpretending tabernacles of dissent, plain, capacious buildings, with "Sion" or "Bethesda" deeply-carved over their simple lintels, bespeak the different shades of religious feeling of the district while the handsome garden-circled mansions which you frequently pass remind you that the proprietors of the wealth-producing establishments around are rarely, if ever, absentees. . .

The village of Egerton principally consists of a long street running along the highway. The Messrs. Ashworth's mills lie beneath it, at the bottom of a rather deep and wooded valley, and thither we will descend.

. . . The labour which was proceeding in this airy and well-arranged *etelier* was clearly of a nature which could have no prejudicial effect upon health; and the women looked very obviously better than those in the town mills. Their faces, in hardly a single instance, wore that thorough blanched hue which is an almost unvarying characteristic of the city cotton spinners; while many of the girls had very perceptible roses in their cheeks. Their working dresses were scrupulously neat, and upon the shoulder of each was embroidered the name of its proprietor.

The Messrs. Ashworth are in the constant and excellent habit of mingling familiarly and kindly with their work people, all of whom they are personally acquainted with. They do as much as they can to discourage the working of married women with young families in the mill—a practice which I confidently hope to be able to stigmatise as being, beyond cavil, infinitely the blackest plague spot on the whole of the manufacturing system. Not above four women of the class in question labour in the Messrs. Ashworth's Egerton mills. The average wages in the country mills are a trifle below those paid in towns; but rent and provisions being usually lower in the rural districts, there is little virtual difference. Seven-eights of Messrs. Ashworth's people live in cottages built upon their employers' land, but this is left to their free option. The rent of these cottages varies from one shilling and sixpence to three shillings and sixpence weekly. For the latter rent a labourer can possess a substantially built stone cottage, containing a good parlour and kitchen, two or three bedrooms, a cellar and a small garden. The latter advantage is not, however, much in request among the Egerton workpeople. The amount of rent quoted is the sum total payable for the occupation of the house. It is generally deducted from the wages; but the tenancy being, as I have said, purely optional, there is no objectionable approach to the truck system in the transaction. I wish, however, I could say that this practice prevails universally. The case of certain mills in Bolton has been brought under my notice, in which the charge of a complement of spinning mules—the best operative situation in a cotton-mill—is always clogged with the condition that the spinner shall live in a house belonging to the employer. In the workpeople's own phraseology, "a key goes to each set of mules". Now, although, I do not mean to say that the houses are not worth the rent charged, yet a spinner may be unmarried and have no occasion for four or five rooms. I heard it stated, indeed, that in one instance, in Bolton, a young man so situated sub-lets his house for sixpence a week to an individual who keeps pigs in it.

To return, however, to the Egerton mills. The cottages are not supplied with water in the interior, but there is plenty in the vicinity. The three-shilling houses have a bedroom less than the first-class cottages. There is a news-room attached to the mill, in which twelve papers, besides periodicals, are taken. For its support the operatives who frequent it pay a penny per week. There is also a library, numbering about 300 volumes. The children under thirteen years of age go as usual to school, and play one half of each day, and work the other half.

The village of Egerton, although inhabited solely by a factory population, is as sweet, wholesome, and smokeless as it could be were its denizens the most bucolic hinds of Devon. I wandered up and down its straggling streets. The houses are, furnished much in the same fashion as those of the middling Manchester class; but every article of household use looks better, because cleaner and fresher. Here is no grime nor squalor. The people are hard-working labourers, but they live decently and fare wholesomely. There is no ragged wretchedness to be seen, no ruinous and squalid hovels. There are two taverns in the village—quiet, decent places. One of them, called the Globe, boasts of a sign which, I trust, may not lead astray the geographical wits of the rising generation of Egerton seeing that the hydrographer has drawn the outline of Europe as encircling the South Pole. This by the way, however. There are no dram shops in Egerton, and no pawnbroker. None of the people in the mill belong to any trades' combination, and there has been on turn-out

since the village was a village. In the country around hares and rabbits are
plenty, but no poaching is heard of. The few agricultural labourers in the
vicinity get, on the average twelve shillings a week. For this they frequently
labour fifteen hours a day. They live in the farm-houses with their employers.
Altogether, the village of Egerton presents a gratifying spectacle of the manufacturing system working under favourable auspices. I was perfectly delighted
with the healthy and ruddy looks of the young children. While I was lounging
about, a caravan came toiling up hill, and the news of the arrival of the wonder-
laden vehicle having quickly spread, the youngsters came swarming out of
every cottage to wonder and admire—fine chubby red-faced, white-headed
urchins, the picture of health and good feeling. This very gratifying result I
attribute partly to the pure air, but mostly to the mothers seldom or never
labouring in the mill. It is, as I shall, afterwards prove, the neglect of very
young children at home, while their mothers toil in the factories, which causes
nineteen-twentieths of the infant deaths in Manchester. The people of Egerton
are described to me as being very healthy, and epidemics are rare amongst
them. The late Dr. Cooke Taylor, in one of his able and interesting works on the
factory system gives a gratifying account of the morality of the mill population
of the district, taking, as an index to the general feeling of respect for property,
the case of the garden of the Messrs. Ashworth, which, although it was full of
the finest fruit, perfectly unprotected, and passed every day by the mill hands,
young and old never suffered so much as the loss of a cherry or a flower. This
statement, from my own observations, I can readily believe. There are a
number of country mills excellently ordered in the valley of Egret. Conspicuous amongst those is the establishment of Mr. Bazley, the president of the
Manchester Chamber of Commerce. This gentleman has constructed ranges
of admirably built cottages, each of them supplied with water in the interior. A
lecture-room, capable of accommodating 400 to 500 people, is one of the
principal public buildings of this excellent operative colony.

Returning to Bolton, I proceeded to visit the mill and the cottages belonging to Messrs. Arrowsmith and Slater, upon the outskirts of the town. The
gentlemen in question have taken the lead in Bolton in providing good accommodation, at reasonable rates, for their workpeople, having built two comfortable ranges of cottages, respectively called after Mr. Cobden and Mr. Bright,
in which their spinners reside. Indeed, at present, Mr. Arrowsmith lives in one
of these cottages himself. The houses are of two classes; the better sort have
each a good front parlour, a light and spacious kitchen, a commodious pantry,
a back yard with proper out-house conveniences; and above, two bedrooms.
In the inferior class one room serves for parlour and kitchen, the second
apartment on the ground floor being a sort of scullery or laundry. There was
a small but handy range for cooking by each fireplace. The rent for a dwelling
of this sort is four shillings and onepence per week—a sum which includes gas
and water, both of which are laid on. In the cottage which I visited, dinner
was just being got ready, and a dish of more savoury smelling Irish Stew I
have seldom encountered. On a slope stretching away from "Cobden-terrace"
is about an acre and a half of ground, laid out in unfenced gardens, one of
which belongs to each cottage. This summer, Mr. Arrowsmith gave his people
prizes of engravings for the best shows of vegetables and flowers. The wane

of autumn is a bed time for inspecting a garden, but I saw enough to satisfy me that the ground had been very carefully tilled and good harvest of vegetables reaped from it. I may add that, upon the occasion of a recent strike in Bolton, the turn-outs, although they tried hard, only succeeded in stopping for about two hours Messrs. Arrowsmith and Slater's mill. . . .

. . . There are very various opinions afloat as to the extent of female immorality in the mills. It is the sincere conviction of a mill owner in a town about thirty miles to the north of Manchester—a gentleman who has devoted a great deal of attention to the study of the social state of the cotton operatives—that there is hardly such a thing as a chaste factory girl—at least in the large towns. But this is an assertion the correctness of which is generally, and I believe with truth, denied.

The fact is, as I am assured, that there exists among the mill girls a considerable degree of correct feeling—sometimes, indeed, carried to the extent of a species of saucy prudery—upon these subjects. They keep up a tolerably strict watch upon each other, and a case of frailty is a grand subject for scandal throughout the whole community. Dr. Cook Taylor narrates that, in a register of instances of seduction kept by a millowner, it was found that the guilty parties never belonged to the same factory. They met, not at work, but casually and in other ways. The number of bastardy warrants granted by the Manchester magistrates in 1848 was fifty-three. Under these, two persons were discharged, eight summarily convicted and thirty-nine cases "amicably settled". There appears, however, to be no doubt whatever that prostitution is rare among the mill girls. In the Manchester Penitentiary, in 1847, the number of female inmates who had worked in mills amounted to only one-third of the number who had been domestic servants.

Speaking generally, the exceedingly quiet and inoffensive character of the Manchester mill population cannot be too highly estimated. "After ten o'clock", says Sir Charles Shaw, the late head of the police, "the streets are as quiet as those of a country town." The statement may be a little, but not much, exaggerated. The mill operatives are in general a most inoffensive and long-enduring people. How admirable has been their conduct in recent times of stagnation and distress. "I have visited Manchester", says Dr. Cooke Taylor, "at seasons when trade was pre-eminently prosperous. I see it now (1842) suffering under severe and unprecedented distress, and I have been forcibly struck by observing the little change which the altered circumstances have producd in the moral aspect of the population. Agricultural distress soon makes itself known. 'Swing' on this side of the water and 'Rock' on the other, write the tales of their grievances in characters which no man can mistake, and seek redress by measures strongly marked with the insanity of despair. But suffering here has not loosened the bonds of confidence. Millions of property remain at the mercy of a rusty nail or the ashes of a tobacco-pipe, and yet no one feels alarmed for the safety of his stock or machinery though in case of an operative Jacquerie they could not be defended by all the military force of England."

Similar sentiments I have heard expressed on all sides by those whose mental powers admirably qualify them for judgement, and whose position, while it brings them closely and habitually in contact with the poor, preclude the possibility of partiality either on one side or the other. In truth the Manchester operative is amongst the most industrious and patient of citizens. He toils cheerfully, and is day by day learning to read more, and to think more. If he has a turn for study, he devotes himself, in a few cases, to mechanical science —in the great number to botany. The science of plants is indeed a passion with the Manchester weaver. It is as common here as pigeon-fancying in Spitalfields. Every holiday sees hundreds of peaceful wanderers in the fields and woods around, busily engaged in culling specimens of grasses and flowers; while, generally harmless and industrious as the present generation are, there is good hope for expecting yet better things at the hands of their successors. . . .

OLDHAM, AND THE LOW LODGING-HOUSES OF MANCHESTER

Letter VIII

In this letter I shall give an account of the operatives of Oldham, in so far as they seem to differ from the average cotton population of Manchester and the surrounding towns. In Oldham, as I have stated in a previous letter, there are a great number of small capitalists renting floors or small portions of factories. These employers have themselves generally risen from the mule or the loom, and maintain in a great degree their operative appearance, thoughts and habits. . . .

. . . The visitor to Oldham will find it essentially a mean-looking straggling town, built upon both sides and crowning the ridge of one of the outlying spurs which branch from the neighbouring "backbone of England". The whole place has a shabby underdone look. The general appearance of the operatives' houses is filthy and smouldering. Airless little back streets and close nasty courts are common; pieces of dismal waste ground—all covered with wreaths of mud and piles of blackened brick and rubbish—separate the mills, which are often of small dimensions and confined and crowded appearance. The shops cannot be complimented, the few hotels are no better than taverns, and altogether the place, to borrow a musical simile, seems far under concert pitch. I observed, as I walked up from the railway station, melancholy clusters of gaunt, dirty, unshorn men lounging on the pavement. These, I heard, were principally hatters, a vast number of whom are out of employment. Another feature of the place was the quantity of dogs of all kinds which abounded— dog-races and dog-fights being both common among the lower orders of the inhabitants. . . .

. . . One of my first cares was to ascertain, so far as I could, the difference in the tone of relationship subsisting between the class of operative capitalists in Oldham and the workpeople, as compared with that existing between the mill-hands and the larger and more assuming capitalists of greater towns. This is exactly one of those delicate social points with reference to which the passing visitor is compelled to seek for information at second-hand. The particulars which I received from the different sources to which I applied differed widely. By two or three intelligent persons, life-long residents in Oldham, I was assured that the class of operative-employers were by far the most popular with the mill-hands. "These masters", I was informed, "are just the same as if they were the fellow-workmen of those they employ. They dress much in the same way, they live much in the same way, their habits and language are almost identical, and when they 'get on the spree' they go and drink and sing in low taverns with their own working hands." I inquired in what sort of houses these masters lived? "In houses a little better and larger than the common dwellings, but managed inside very much in the same way." "Do they educate their sons as gentlemen?" "They seldom do. They may give them a better education than the sons of common men; but they wish them to supply their own places, and to be just like what they themselves are." My informants added, that although masters and men often caroused together yet, on occasions of difference arising between them, the masters would get dreadfully abusive and terribly bad blood would ensue. This latter piece of information, as well as a little experience of human nature, inclined me rather to credit the opposite view, urged, among others by Mr. Clegg, the courteous clerk in the union, that the larger capitalists, the men who had not themselves been operative in the memory of the existing generation, were the class of mill-owners most generally and most continuously popular:

"Their establishments are the larger and the better regulated. The work there is more regular, the rooms often better regulated and more pleasant, and all sorts of minor conveniences for washing, shifting clothes, etc., better ordered than in the smaller mills." . . .

. . . Under the guidance of two intelligent relieving officers, I set out to see some of the characteristic manufactures and some of the characteristic population of the place. It was about noon, and the people were pouring out from the mills on their way home to dinner. I observed that the women almost universally wore silk bandanna handkerchiefs fluttering round their heads. "It has always been so in Oldham," I was informed. "They would pinch hard rather than go with a plain cap instead of a silk handkerchief." Presently I overtook two little girls, the eldest not above eight years of age, each carrying a baby some three or four months old in a pick-a-back fashion, the infant being snugly enough wrapped up, and only its head protruding from beneath the cloak of its bearer. These girls, I was informed, were nurses, paid for taking charge of the children while their mothers laboured in the mills. I accosted them.

"So you have these children to nurse? What do the mothers pay you?"

"Oh, please sir, they pay us one shilling and sixpence a week for each baby."

"And where are you taking them now?"

"Oh, please sir, to their mothers. They come out of the mills now, and we carry the babies down to meet them, and the mothers give them suck when they're at dinner."

"And so you take the babies in the morning, and nurse them all day till dinner-time, and then take them to their mothers, and then fetch them back,

"Yes, sir, that's what we do; but sometimes, you know, the babies have little sisters as old as us, and then they are nursed at home. . . .

. . . From thence we went to visit two factories, in one of which are spun very coarse threads, intended for the Indian market, and in the other of which are manufactured candlewicks. The proprietors of both politely accompanied me in my rounds. They had been working men, and were, in language, manner, and dress, very much akin to the people they employed. In the coarse spinning mill—a small airless building—I found an apparently chronic system of dirt and neglect prevailing. The stairs were rickety and filth-encrusted, and the drawing and spinning rooms not only hot, but what is much worse, chokey, and stifling, and reeking with oil. The women employed exhibited in a palpably exaggerated degree the unwholesome characteristics of the appearance of the Manchester mill-workers. They were not so much sallow or pale as absolutely yellow, and their leanness amounted to something unpleasant to look at. The mill was of the old construction, and had no means of ventilation. The wages of the people ranged a shilling or two beneath the average of the medium Manchester rate. . . .

. . . I afterwards went over two small mills, compartments of which are rented by different individuals. Both were dirty, and constructed in the old-fashioned unventilated style. . . .

MACCLESFIELD AND THE SILK TRADE

Letter XI

... The manufacture of silk may be said to be the only one in Macclesfield. There is but a single cotton mill in the town. Silk has been the staple of the place for more than half a century. Before that time Macclesfield was but a paltry village. "We took the trade", said a manufacturer to me, "from Spital-fields, and now the country places about are taking it from us; and with every successive stage of the expansion of the manufacture the wages seem to come down." About one-half of the labouring population of Macclesfield work at home, and the other half in the mills. The home labourers are exclusively weavers, and include a large proportion of men; the mill labourers are prin-cipally engaged in throwing, doubling, and other processes analogous, in a certain degree, to the drawing and spinning of cotton mills—in preparing the threads which are intertwisted by the loom. By far the largest proportion of the mill population is female, the weavers who work looms in the mills being inconsiderable in number, compared with those who work at home. I may add, that the amount of silk thread spun at Macclesfield is much greater than the amount woven there. The warp and the shute, being prepared for the loom, are sent out all over the silk-weaving districts of Lancashire and Cheshire, for the process to be completed. The wages earned in and out of the mills in Macclesfield do not materially vary. The throwsters and the spinners in the mills have the most regular work. The weavers can earn higher wages when in employment, but their looms stand idle upon the average fully three months in the year. A weaver may, one season with another, make from ten shillings to twelve shillings a week; a female throwster or doubler in the mill, from eight shillings to nine shillings. ...

... I premise by stating that I took great pains, in traversing the silk districts, to ascertain whether the accounts of the distress in Spitalfields seemed to have reached or to have affected the country weavers. In general, I found that the people knew very little and cared very little about the matter. It was only the state of their own district in which they appeared to take any interest. There did not seem to be any general ideas prevalent upon the causes of the distress of the metropolitan silk-weavers. My details upon the subject were listened to with an apathetic "Aye, indeed; well, they do seem very poorly off, to be sure." I frequently put the question as to what my listeners thought could be the reason why a trade, which was comparatively good in one part of England, should be so bad in another; but heads were invariably shaken, and a stolid "Well, I dunna know, indeed, sir," formed the most frequent response. One man, indeed, said he supposed Government intended to root out the Spital-fields weavers altogether; and another was of opinion that much of the Spitalfields distress was caused by there being no throwing mills in London, and the weavers being thus rendered dependent for their supplies of thread upon Italy and France. Such answers were, however, the exceptions to the rule. Nine-tenths of the people knew nothing and cared nothing about Spitalfields or their brethren there; the apathy in that respect being very different from the mutual understanding and the constant mutual correspondence kept up between the unions and operative associations of the various cotton towns. . . .

. . . In the next house which I entered I found in the loom-garret only a young man of about eighteen, a smart intelligent lad. He was working at "greys", a coarse kind of silk stuff, which is printed and made into bandannas. "He could manufacture six cuts a week, and the price for each cut was 2s. 4½d. He did not, however, receive all he earned. He was an apprentice to the undertaker who rented the house. He had been bound for three years, and he now received two-thirds of what he made. For the first two years of his apprenticeship he had received only one-half. Many of the undertakers tried to get apprentices bound for seven years, but people didn't like that. The work was terribly irregular, or it would not be bad work; but when folk was busy, it behoved them to save up money against they had to go 'play'. He had been three months playing, and several times six, seven, and eight weeks. The trade was generally slackest towards midsummer." "What did the men do when they played?" "Why, they did not do no work." "How did they pass their time?" "Oh, different ways, according to fancy. They were a great deal in the streets. They took walks, and went to each other's houses, or anywhere. Some of them had dog-fights, but they were the lowest sort. Only the lowest sort had dog-fights in Macclesfield. There might be pigeon-matches, but he had never heard much tell of them. As for himself, he liked to read and play the fiddle." "What did he think was the cause of these stagnations in the trade?" "Well, he had heard say as they were caused by over-production. More goods was made, nor people wanted. Then the masters couldn't tell what they had on their shelves, and of course they didn't want for more; so the looms stood idle. It was a necessity. The weavers there about didn't eat very much flesh meat. Certainly, as a general thing, not every day. Some would have it though, whatever came of it. They would think the world couldn't go on if they hadn't flesh meat to dinner. But a great lot lived poor in that town. A great lot, too, were fond of fine clothes, particularly the young women, and they would have their backs gay although their bellies pinched for it."

The Macclesfield Mechanics' Institute is a flourishing establishment. The great majority of the members are silk-weavers. They have recently been making considerable additions to the building, and they have a library containing more than 2,000 volumes. The secretary spoke in high terms of the general standard of intelligence of the silk population. Of their marked superiority in appearance to their neighbours, the cotton-workers, there can be no doubt. The nature of their occupation is not only more conducive to personal cleanliness, but to the development of those minor symptoms of health which are to be found in the presence of clear skins, bright eyes, and good complexions. One is inclined to wonder at the co-existence of comparatively so low a rate of wages, with the outward evidences of comparatively so fair a state of social comfort; and wages, I am informed, are, unhappily, likely to sink even still farther. The weavers living in remote country districts are gradually absorbing much of the work which used to be exclusively performed in Macclesfield. As the silk towns of the North served Spitalfields, so, I am assured, the rural districts are serving the silk towns of the North.

MIDDLETON

The Silk Weavers

Letter XII

... The place has a stamp of its own. Some of the oldest and purest blood of the Lancashire yeoman keeps its current still unmixed by the hearths of this village. Needwood and Charnwood sent forth no tougher bows nor longer shafts than twanged along the banks of the Irk, and amid the coppices of Birtle and Ashworth. On the northern window of the church transept are emblazoned the effigies of the Middleton Archers, who, like Hubert's grandsire, drew good bows, not indeed at Hastings, but on Flodden Edge. There, upon the coloured glass, march, like the merry men of Robin Hood, the staunch Middleton Archers, all of a row, with their long light Saxon hair, and their retainers' liveries of blue. Each carries his unslung bow upon his shoulder; over each bow is painted, in antique letters, the name of its owner, and every one of these names is still borne by an inhabitant of Middleton. It was curious, indeed, after the multitude of brown bricken Sions, and Ebenezers, and Bethesdas, to which I have lately been accustomed, to find myself standing upon the brazen memorials of buried crusaders, amid mullions and quatrefeuilles, carved by Norman chisels, and beneath mouldering standards and rusty spears, which were probably shaken and couched in the wars of the Roses. And in moral as well as physical attributes is the stamp of the old age strong upon this Lancastrian hamlet. A great deal of what was generally believed in England under the Tudors is believed in Middleton and its neighbourhood to this day. Indeed, says the courteous and accomplished rector, "the people are to but too apt to disbelieve what they ought to believe, and to believe what they ought to disbelieve." The fortune-teller abounds, and his oracles are as gospel. The astrologer still casts nativities and projects schemes, and the culler of simples is careful to pluck his herbs only during the waxing of the moon. Upon a dead wall I saw a placard announcing that the "Sacred Drama of Joseph and his Brethren" would be performed by certain Sunday-school pupils. Most unfortunately the date of the representation was past, or I would have astonished you by a critique upon something in the nature of a mediaeval *mystery*, seriously enacted almost amid the smoke of modern Manchester.

From what I have stated, the reader will be prepared for a population pursuing some distinct and ungregarious species of occupation. He is in the right. The "folk o' Middleton", to use their own vernacular, are almost all silk handloom weavers, pursuing their craft in their own houses, preserving an independent and individual tone of character, intermarrying to the extent of breeding scrofulous disease—clannish and prejudiced and peculiar as all such septs are—keeping up even amid their looms a great degree of the rural and patriarchal tone of by-gone times—a few of them handling the plough and the hoe as well as the shuttle and the winding-wheel, and the entire community great favourers of the old English manly sports. "When the Hopwood hounds pass the village (says the Rev. Mr. Dunsford, the rector), there is always a goodly train of sportsmen on foot in attendance."

On my arrival in the village I inquired where I could best see the weavers at their work, and was directed to the "club-houses". Do not imagine, however, a satin-weaving Pall-mall. Turning from the high road, which is also the main street, I climbed a roughly paved lane, skirted by common-place mean houses, some of them little shops, and presently I heard on all sides the rattle of the shuttle. Still the aspect of the place was half rural. Trees here and there bowered the cottages, and the noise of the flail mingled with that of the loom. The "club-houses" were a double row of two-storey cottages, constructed by an old club or building society—whence the name—and not dissimilar in general arrangement to those I have so often described as forming the operative homes of Manchester. They were reared upon the face of a steep hill, and the surface of the street between them being level, the ground-floors on the lower side of the way are unavoidably underground floors. You descend to them by means of a roughly paved area, extending the whole length of the street. The general aspect of the place was certainly humble enough; and the day being a dismally wet one, everything looked cheerlessly sloppy. I entered a house at random; as usual, the street door was the parlour door, that is to say, the door of the parlour and kitchen, and hall. Two apartments opened from the principal one, the small one to the back being a sort of scullery and store-room, piled up with dirty dishes and household utensils, waiting to be washed; the other, a room nearly, if not quite, as large as the dwelling chamber, was the "loom shop", where business is conducted.

First, of the living room. It was a sort of country cousin to the same class of apartments in Manchester, furnished a good deal after the same fashion— in rather a rougher way, to be sure—but wanting the grime and smoke-dried air, and the close hot smell of the town operatives' lodging. In the corners were niched the invariable cupboards. From the wall ticked the invariable clock; beside it hung little miniature-sized engravings in black frames. On the high chimney-piece were tiny pieces of nick-nackery, china, and glittering ware, in the usual cottage style, and on each side of the fire-place hung the usual polished pot-lids. There was good substantial furniture in the place; strong useful deal tables, an old-fashioned chest of drawers, chairs of different patterns—some of them antique, high-backed affairs, the wood carved into innumerable lumps—others like the ordinary Windsor pattern; and by the fireside the never-to-be-too-highly-honoured rocking-chair. The floor was stone-flagged, sanded, and clean; and I must not omit to mention that on either side of the grate stood excellent cooking ranges—a feature almost universal in the Middleton weavers' cottages. Altogether the place was by no means uncomfortable, inspiring neither the idea of privation nor unwholesomeness. I was met on the threshold by a decently dressed middle-aged woman, who ushered me into the loom-shop where sat busy at his work her lord and master. The work-room boasted but an earthen floor, scratched and scraped by half a dozen cocks and hens, which were jerking their necks about beneath the mechanism of the four looms which the chamber contained. The loom arrangements were barbarously primitive. There was a hole scooped in the earth beneath the treadles, and the weaver sat, like the craftsman of Hindustan, half buried in the earth, which, however, seemed as dry as Sahara. The walls were fairly whitewashed; and the stretching oblong window, or rather range of windows, separated from each other by a two or three inch broad strip of wall, furnished the "long light", already so often alluded to. Of the four looms in the apartment, two were at work—one of them wrought by the husband, the other by the wife. Before the former, on the loom, was stretched a piece of blue satin, the rich texture of the stuff contrasting well with the rude woodwork in which extended that glossy mesh of purple threads. I had some difficulty in drawing this weaver into conversation. He was not sullen, but not intelligent. While I stood by his loom, his wife took her place at hers, and began to labour upon a piece of brown silk shot with blue.

The man lamented over the fall of wages. Twenty years ago he used to make twice as much as now. He didn't know how it was. He supposed it was the masters. They was hard on the poor man. They was very grievous in their 'batements. When the weaver carried his work home, the master or the agents wor very clever to see flaws in it. They wouldn't see none, not them, if they wor a-selling it to a customer; trust 'em for that. And wages was falling still. For a piece he would have got twenty shillings and sixpence for eighteen months ago, he could hardly get sixteen shillings now. It wasn't so bad with some sorts of silks. It all depended on the fashions and the run there was in the market. It would take a very clever weaver to make ten shillings a week as a general thing, but there wor some good pieces as paid well, if the weavers could get plenty of work at them. He wrought, himself, ten hours a day, or twelve, just as he was in the humour—some days more nor other days. If he wor lazy beginning in a morning, he made up for it at night. Sometimes, in course, he stopped the loom and went for a walk—why not? I inquired whether the house belonged to him? No, he wished it did. A vast heap in them parts lived in their own houses—more nor in any town in Lancashire. The children (by the way, they were feeding the poultry with crumbs of bread left from the dinner table)—the children were just brought up to their father's trade. There was "naought" else for 'em to do.

The woman told me that she was weaving silk for which she was paid 6½d. per yard, and she could make only two yards by a hard day's work.

In the next house I visited, the man—a stalwart well-looking fellow—had just taken a piece of silk off the loom and was folding it on the table. He had to carry it to Manchester to be paid for his work. I admired the beauty of the stuff. "Aye, aye, but there be always soom'mut to find fault wi' when I take it whoam, that they may bate me down." He worked long hours—just as long as any factory hours. If he didn't begin so soon in the morning he kept at it longer at night. He *was* independent in that way, however. Yes, that *wor* soom'mut. They often wove in these parts till ten o'clock in the long winter nights. A good weaver couldn't make more nor eight or nine shillings a week. There wor some sorts of odd work as paid far better—perhaps a dozen, or it might be fourteen shillings; but they had seldom such a price. Wages wor falling—that was over true. He thought it was the fault o' the machinery.

I said that they were not so ill off at Middleton as at Spitalfields.

"Aye, aye, but it's a poor sort of work, and I dinna doubt but they want to banish silk weavers from Spitalfields. It's too low and too poor a life for the fine folks o' Lunnon."

I crossed the street, and made my way into one of the lower situated houses. The general arrangements were nearly the same as those which I have already described in the first dwelling that I visited. In this house a stout, burly-looking fellow, with a decided Milesian look, was smoking at the ingle corner; and a gaunt, pale-looking, middle-aged woman was seated on a low stool, rocking her lean body backwards and forwards, and pulling away at a pipe with great gusto. In the work-room were four looms. A rather nice-looking girl of fourteen was working one—a sallow, unshorn, lean man another. The latter was producing beautiful figured silk. He was paid for it ninepence per yard, and could weave three yards a day. The price within his recollection would have been two shillings a yard. "Worn't that enough to make a man bitter at his work?" For other sorts of silk fourpence a yard was paid, and he well remembered when it was one shilling and threepence. What was the cause of this? "Lord! he didn't know; I ought to know better nor him." Were there more people weaving now than when he was a boy? "Aye, that ther wor—twice as many."

I had several times asked whether there was any weaver among them whom they thought especially a clever man, and one who knew the history of the trade. Public opinion pointing with many forefingers to a certain door, I tapped thereat, and the latch was raised by a venerable old lady, adorned with a pair of silver spectacles on her nose, and a pipe in her mouth; she looked somehow like a nice indulgent grandmamma—she had such a kind old-fashioned face; but I could not help staring at it, for never in my life had I seen an elderly lady's countenance embellished at once with a pair of silver spectacles and a clay pipe. The master of the family was a very intelligent chubby old man, with grey hair, a pair of twin spectacles, but no pipe. After ascertaining that I was "not in the trade", and that I knew as much about the secrets of "dents" and "shute" as about the mysteries of Eleusis, he made me extremely welcome, and we had a long gossip together. In his workroom stood four looms, one of them the invention of the celebrated weaver of Lyons. When I entered, the master of the house was instructing a girl in the management of the loom. He straightway left his pupil, and, having heard my errand, launched headforemost into a sea of silk-weaving reminiscences.

I shall not attempt to classify the topics which I found scribbled in my note-book. In conversations with working men it is almost impossible to keep them to the point, and perhaps a more vivid idea is given of the colloquy, and especially of the principal interlocutor, by putting on paper his chat, rambling and disjointed, as it was uttered.

"Remember better times? That do I well. Twenty-six years ago we had thirteen pence a yard for what we have 3½d. now. It's the machinery—the machinery as has done it; for see that Jacquard, and the silk in it (there are many hundred Jacquards hereabouts)—well, the weaving of that silk used to be three shillings a yard. What is it now? Why, one shilling and threepence. About thirty years ago we were mostly cotton weavers hereaway. But the power-looms flung us out of work, and we were nigh starved. Then, sir, there came gentlemen from Lunnon, from Spitalfields (of course, as you come from Lunnon, you know Spitalfields), and they took down silk here, and they set us to work on it. We was very glad to get the chance. But the masters was using us to bate down the Spitalfields weavers. Some of them, sir—the weavers I mean—came down here, but their old masters wouldn't employ, no, not never a man on them, because they would want their old wages and old rules. That was the way, sir, that silk weaving became so general hereaway. Well, but we was soon served just as we had served the Spitalfields folk. There's a place called Leigh, not far from here, where there was then a heap of hand-loom weavers as wrought cottons and such like. Well, after some time, our masters didn't give us our due, and so we combined and had a strike. What did the masters do but took the work to Leigh, from Middleton, just as they did from Spitalfields to Middleton, and the weavers at Leigh wrought at one ha'penny a yard less than we did. To be sure they was glad to get the work at almost any price. The wages are not very different now, but there are grievous and unjust abatements. The masters are some of them honourable good men—but some of them are very tyrannous. They were very tyrannous in this way at Leigh, and a committee of the weavers collected information to abatements, and printed it in a book. I have the pamphlet before me. Very often, sir, there was one-and-sixpence and two-and-sixpence unjustly 'bated out of a week's work. The poor people could not live under it; they couldn't."

At this point we adjourned to the parlour. Grandmamma, with the pipe, swept up the hearth. A nice tidy girl sat peeling apples, apparently for a pie. Another weaver, a sturdy, good-humoured looking fellow, flung himself into a cosy elbow chair, with his legs over the arms, and we resumed our talk somewhat in this fashion:

"What rent may you pay now for this house?" "Seven pounds a year, and a good many folks pay six."

The room was comfortable, and comfortably and substantially furnished. In an open corner cupboard sparkled two antique silver salt-cellars. I am always glad to see such things in a poor man's house. They were possibly heirlooms. The old weaver resumed:

"Some folks live in their own houses—but I don't. This better nor factory work? Aye, that it is. You see, you keep your children at home about you, and you don't lose control over them. We live very friendly like. There be all sorts here, but we're good folk the'gether. When the children are ten or twelve years old we put them to the loom, but we must attend them, you know, and teach them. It takes long to make them perfect in the trade."

"Perfect in the trade!" exclaimed he of the elbow chair; "there's naought on us perfect in the trade. We are aye learning."

The *pater familias* gravely coincided, and went on. "There's many drawbacks to a weaver's work. Sometimes it takes a week to get a loom" (prepare it for a web of particular fineness). "I heard say that in Spitalfields all that is done at the master's charge, but here we do it ourselves. How do we live? Well; there's not much flesh meat eaten. There would be a deal more if we could get it. But there's tay (the Lancaster peasant invariably pronounces the word *more Hibernico*)—there's tay, and bread and bootter—that's ready cooking."

"Tay!" interrupted the younger weaver; "hot water and a little sugar, ye mean. It's not tay."

"Well," resumed his elder, "in this family we only have an ounce of tay a week; but I'll just tell you how we live in homely Lancashire sort. Well, we have tay and bread and bootter, morning and afternoon. At dinner we have potatoes, and perhaps a little meat. Here's in this house a family of four or five, as it may be. Well, at the end of the week we buy two or three pounds of beef, and that's all the flesh meat we have till next week. So we make it into as many dinners as we can scheme. We cook, may be, half a pound at a time, to give the potatoes a flavour like. But what's that for eating? Why, my share at meal-times is not bigger nor my thumb. So I often throw it in, and take a fried ingan and two or three drops of vinegar to relish the potatoes. That's about our general way of living. To be sure, we may get a lift in spring time when the spring fashions come; but very often we've been getting into debt in the winter; and first, you know, we must keep our credit; and then there's clothes want renewing. Teetotallers here? Aye, there be a few on 'em; but we're all very moderate."

"We wouldn't be so very moderate if we could afford a little drink better," said the second weaver.

"I like my glass of ale myself," resumed the first; "and I like good company, and a good joke and soom'mut to laugh at, I do. I like to sing a song too." How the conversation turned round I do not remember; but the next entry I have upon my note-book is that the old gentleman was fond not only of a good song, but that he was especially fond of reading the "Skootchings" which Cobbett used to give to people he didn't like. Then we got back to convivial matters, and so gradually to the *morale* of the village.

"We've got a rural police here. But, Lord! we haven't no more use for them nor you have for water in your boots. There's three policemen and the devil a thing they have to do but walk about with their hands in their pockets, like gentlemen. Why, they haven't had a job this three months; except, may be, when a chap gets droonk like. The sergeant, as they call him, thinks it's quite ridiculous. He says he never saw such people. If he offends one he offends all. We like each other so well, and we turn out after dinner, and have a great talk about politics, and what they're doing in Lunnon, and smoke our pipes. We often have long discussions—we're great chaps for politics, and we just go into each other's houses and talk. I like to be idle myself sometimes. I dare say you do, too. Yes, of course you do. Well, then, when I feel idle, I go and walk about in the fields may be, and work harder to make up for it after."

I quite regretted being obliged to tear myself from my garrulous friend, who, I doubt not, would have talked till midnight with very great pleasure.

The next weaver I saw I was introduced to by the worthy rector. He was the patriarch of the village—a fine-looking old man of eighty-two, with the remains of a well-cut massive set of features and curling white hair. He was feeble, and at times wandered in his speech. His dame was still a stout hearty body, enjoying a green old age; and busily employed when we called in scouring the flagged floor with hearthstone, a bucket, and am op. She must have seen seventy winters, but she worked as vigorously and spoke as briskly as a damsel in her teens; her white hair all the while streaming from under a narrow-frilled calico nightcap, the ordinary head-dress of the Middleton matrons.

The patriarch sat before the fire and babbled of times present and past. "The first silk ever woven in Middleton was made into bandanna handker-chiefs. Sixty years ago and better he had woven such himself. Some folk farmed then—others wove cotton. After the bandannas came twills and sarsnets and satins. Wages were lower, much lower now, than in the old times."

"But did the people then live better than they do now?"

Somewhat to my surprise the old man said, "No, sir; no, they live better now. They have tay and coffee liken (observe the lingering Saxon idiom); tay and coffee *liken* the gentlefolk. I had coffee to my dinner this day, sir. They had porridge and milk then instead; and often, sir, they had to go three miles to fetch the milk. But still they didn't work in the old days as now. They ran after the hounds, or went a-shooting and a-sporting in the fields nigh three days a week, and many had farms and tilled them likewise."

"I suppose you drink a glass of beer sometimes," said the rector. "You can brew it yourselves in this capital range."

At this the buxom old dame took up the word.

"Well, sir, some on 'em does, but others drink it at the hush-house—that is sir, the places where they keep it *withouten* being licensed. But we have naought to say to such like. Oh, there's much drinkin'—too much: folk com round door by door, and ask, 'Will we buy a knife?' and if we say, 'Aye,' why then they out with a bottle of smuggled whiskey and sells it. That's the knife, sir."

Leaving the octogenarian and his dame, Mr. Dunsford said he would show me a house built by an industrious and intelligent weaver, entirely out of his own savings—a house which, in the phraseology of the district, "all came through the eye of the shuttle." We crossed the Irk by a slippery wooden bridge. "That," said my companion, "that is, for its size, about the hardest worked brook in England." There had been many hours of heavy rain, and the flood was rushing turbulent and strong. It looks as if it had been a likely trout stream long ago, but the gudeon is now the only tenant of its waters. Verily the gudgeon must be a long-enduring fish—patient of foul things—an ichthyologic Job! The house we went to see was a neat and substantial cottage, built on the summit of a steep garden-planted bank. The industrious family who dwelt in it were its architects, and snugger kitchen or a neater parlour, in a small way, might not easily be found. Over the dresser were arranged a fair collection of useful books.

To the Rev. Mr. Dunsford I am indebted for some interesting notices of the "Middleton folk", touching matters on which a stranger could not, during a hurried visit, well gain information for himself. The people are very generally careless and indifferent about the education of themselves or their children, taking the latter from school as soon as they can be useful at the loom. Writing is the attainment which they most prize, and most excel in. The art is a mechanical one, and Mr. Dunsford is convinced that the symmetrical order and due slope of the threads constantly stretching before their eyes exercise no little effect in producing good penmen from amongst the weavers. The young people marry early, and although long periods of betrothal are common, they almost invariably take each other for better or worse, without a stick of furniture or a shilling of saved money. The bride and bridegroom then go to live in the home of the parents of one of them; or frequently one takes his or her meals and remains during the day with his or her own friends; the other doing the same thing at another house; and the couple coming together again in the evening. During this time they pay for "loom room", or, in other words, hire a loom a piece, and pay also for their board. Sometimes the father thus becomes a sort of capitalist, letting out, in a large family of sons and daughters, as many as half a dozen looms. Generally, by the time the first child is born, the young couple have saved something towards furnishing a dwelling for themselves; and that the more often, inasmuch as their notions of setting up housekeeping are very modest. If they have a bed, a chest of drawers, and a corner cupboard, they think that in all the essentials of furniture they are set up. The bedrooms are very generally neat, clean, and tidy beyond what might be looked for. The hand-loom system here appears, so far as family is concerned, to exercise exactly the opposite effect of the factory system. The Middleton weaver keeps not only his sons and daughters, but often his sons and daughters in law, long about him; while the children who are too young, and sometimes the adults who are too old for the heavy labour of the loom, turn the winding wheel, and prepare the glistening silk for the frame. They are great politicians the good folks of Middleton, and occasionally given to lazy fits, during which smoking, sauntering, and chatting listlessly are the amusements most in vogue. The women very frequently smoke, but it is always with some pseudo-medical excuse. They feel a "rising" or a "sinking", or a headache, or a toothache, or any ache, or no ache at all. A curious indication of the prevailing shade of Radical politics in the village is afforded by the parish register, the people having a fancy for christening their children after the hero of the minute. Thus, a generation or so back, Henry Hunts were as common as blackberries; a crop of Feargus O'Connors replaced them; and latterly they have a few green sprouts labelled Ernest Jones. A very small proportion of the weavers only labour in the fields; but in many farmhouses around there are looms which the women work during the long winter evenings. The Spitalfields hobby of pigeon fancying is not uncommon, particularly among the young men; and pigeon marches, which give rise to a good deal of gambling, are frequent. The birds are taken some miles away, and then flown back to their homes. *Apropos* of the betting propensity, there was a bagatelle table in the quiet tavern where the omnibus from Manchester deposited me, above which was inscribed the following *naïve* and ingeniously worded proclamation: "No gaming allowed on this board. Any person having a wager or wagers on this board, the landlord shall seize it, and spend it on liquor."

I mentioned to Mr. Dunsford the complaints which I had heard of the masters being grievously tyrannical in abating the nominal wages given, on account of alleged imperfections in the work. Most of these stories, he said, like other stories, has two sides to them. He had known weavers work for years for a firm without any abatement being made, or at least any that was not admittedly just. Many of the abatements, so called, were fines for broken contracts for work not being finished at the stipulated time. Still he did not doubt but there were often cases of real hardship in the system—cases in which shabby and screwing agents sought, by extreme ingenuity in finding or fancying flaws, to bate down the fair price of the work. In the pamphlet published by the Leigh weavers' committee upon the subject, one fact most damning to the masters, if true, is broadly asserted—viz., that the weavers who are abated the most, and who, consequently, were the abatements justly made, must be the worst workmen, received by far the greatest share of labour from the employers. Many of the cases reported by the committee in question seem harsh and cruel to the last degree. As regards the amount of these abatements, I may mention, quoting at random from a great mass of tabular statistics, that out of £265 10s. 8d. of wages nominaly earned by 171 weavers, £45 12s. 3d. was abated on account of real or alleged imperfections in the fabric, being an average of five shillings and fourpence clipped from each man's pay.

By the time I had completed my tour of inspection, lights were gleaming from the "loom-shops", and in the wooden-roofed market-place gas jets flared amid the meat, and on the eager faces of chaffering customers. Two Manchester omnibuses, each with three horses, and an indefatigable horn-blowing conductor, stood at different inn doors, and I naturally selected the lightest laden. Although the rain was coming down in bucketfuls, and the interior of the vehicle I had chosen was all but empty, the other was thronged outside and in. I mentioned the matter to my only *compagnon de voyage*. "Oh," he said, "you don't know how queer they are, the weaver folk of Middleton. They have a line of omnibuses belonging to a man they like, and won't go in the other people's buses, not if you paid them: they'd walk through all this rain and dirt to Manchester first. Sometimes they hoot the people who ride in t'other bus, and if we were each of us Middleton tradesmen, and to be seen where we are, why, we'd never sell another ha'porth to a weaver of them all!"

THE RURAL CLOTH-WORKERS OF YORKSHIRE

Saddleworth

Letter XIII

The name of Saddleworth is applied to a range of wild and hilly country, about seven miles long and five broad, lying on the western confines of Yorkshire, and including one spot from which a walk of ten minutes will carry the visitor across the boundaries of four counties, into Lancashire, Cheshire, Derbyshire, and Yorkshire. To all intents and purposes, however, Saddleworth lies in the latter county, its heathery hills and deep valleys dividing the woollen from the cotton cities, and being themselves peopled by a hardy, industrious, and primitive race, engaged in the manufacture of flannel and cloth—sometimes in mills, sometimes by their own hearths; in which latter case the business of a dairy farmer is often added to that of a manufacturer, and the same hands ply the shuttle and milk the cows. Saddleworth is now intersected by the Leeds and Huddersfield Railway, and, as a consequence, is beginning to lose much of those primitive characteristics for which it was long renowned. Until recently there was no regular means of transit from many of its valleys to the more open parts of the country. Goods were conveyed by the Manchester and Huddersfield Canal; and many a small manufacturer and comfortable farmer grew grey amid the hills, without ever having journeyed further than Oldham and Staleybridge on the one hand, and perhaps Huddersfield, or at furthest Leeds, upon the other. The rail has, however, thrown open the wilds of Saddleworth to the world. Mills, driven by water and steam, are rising on every hand, and the old-fashioned domestic industry, carried on in the field and the loom shop, is gradually dying away. . . .

. . . The appearance of a cloth-weaving room is very different from that of a cotton "shed". The looms are larger, heavier, and clumsier in appearance, and the shuttle traverses the twelve or fourteen feet, which it has frequently to cover, with a far more deliberate motion than the glancing jerks of the cotton shuttle, flying through the fast growing webs of calico. The stuff having been woven, is subjected to the action of steaming hot water and the "fulling" hammers, which cause it to shrivel up almost to one half of its former dimensions. The wages earned by the artisans who labour in the steaming atmosphere of the fulling mill are from eighteen to twenty-one shillings. The next process is exclusively performed by women. It is called "birling", and consists of picking out of the cloth, with a sort of tweezers, all the little knots and inequalities which may be apparent upon the face of the fabric. In the country this operation is very generally performed at home. In towns it is executed in the mills, the cloth being spread upon a wooden frame placed at an obtuse angle to the window, and three or four women, closely jammed together, being seated on benches before each frame. This is almost the only department of the trade in which married women are extensively employed away from their homes. In the birling room of a Huddersfield mill, I heard more giggling, and saw more symptoms denoting a relaxed state of discipline, than I had previously observed in any department in any of the textile industries. It was clear, from the atmosphere, that some of the women had been smoking, but the pipes were, of course, instantly smuggled away on our entrance. . . .

. . . From the mill I proceeded to visit some of the cottages of the workpeople. Without a single exception, I found them neat, warm, comfortable, and clean. They consisted almost universally of a common room, serving as a parlour and kitchen, a scullery behind it, and two more bedrooms up-stairs. The main rooms were, I think, as a general rule, larger than those I have lately been accustomed to see. The floors were stone-flagged, nicely sanded. Samplers and pictures uniformly ornamented the walls, and the furniture was massive and old-fashioned; the chairs with rush bottoms and high, well-polished backs. One characteristic feature of these cottages was universal. It consisted of a sort of net stretched under the ceiling, and filled with crisp oat cakes. These formerly constituted almost the only bread consumed in the district, but home-baked wheaten loaves are now coming into general use. Indeed, almost every family in Saddleworth bakes its own bread and brews its own ale—a capital nutty-flavoured beverage it is. The composition of the oat cakes is, however, held to require a particular genius, and when a matron gets a reputation in that way, she frequently bakes for half a village. In the first cottage I entered I found a rosy-cheeked girl occupied in "birling". Her father worked in the mill; her mother had her household to attend to, and did a little "birling" besides. The matron, upon her appearance, informed me that the house had five rooms, and that the weekly rent which they paid for it was three shillings and fourpence. The girl could, by devoting the whole of her time to the work, make seven or eight shillings per week by "birling". It was common for married women to birl enough to pay the rent, which they could do, and get ample time to attend to their families. Very few married worked in the mills. They found no difficulty in getting as much work as they wanted at home. In the second house which I saw there were also five rooms, and the rent was three shillings and one penny per week. Besides this the occupants paid sixpence a week for gas, which they could keep alight until half-after ten, and on Saturdays and Sundays as long as they pleased. The woman of the house was a fine, fat, hearty-looking dame of sixty, the very picture of health and matronly enjoyment. There was a bed, with curtains, in a corner of the room. Who the occupant was I do not know—he did not think proper to show himself; but ever and anon a voice from amid the blankets joined vigorously in the conversation. The old lady corroborated the statement I had heard as to the small proportion of married women who preferred working in the mills to "birling" at home. The use of oat cake, she said, was gradually decreasing, and she produced a substantial home-made wheaten loaf as a specimen of the bread coming into favour. She could remember when the people ate nothing but oat cakes. These were then made four times as thick as now. The people used to eat a great deal of cheese. Indeed, they used to live on cheese, oat cake, porridge, and butter milk; but now-a-days nothing but tea and coffee would do for them. They took a good deal of porridge yet, however, for breakfast; but generally they had some meat for dinner, perhaps some bacon, perhaps some beef. At all events, they had plenty of porridge and bread and potatoes. The price of meat was a little dearer than when she was a girl. Good mutton could not be had now under sixpence a pound, but she thought, on the whole, that people lived just as well now as they did forty years ago. . . .

. . . From this place we proceeded by a steep path up the hill-side to a cluster of old-fashioned houses called Saddleworth-fold, and which were the first, or amongst the first, stone buildings erected in the district. They are occupied by several families, who are at once spinners, weavers, and farmers. The hamlet was a curious irregular clump of old-fashioned houses, looking as if they had been flung accidentally together up and down a little group of knolls. Over the small latticed windows were carved mullions of stone, and in a little garden grew a few box-wood trees, clipped into the quaint shapes which we associate with French and Dutch gardening. The man whose establishment we had come to see was a splendid specimen of humanity—tall, stalwart, with a grip like a vice, and a back as upright as a pump-bolt, although he was between seventy and eighty years of age. We entered the principal room of his house; it was a chamber which a novelist would love to paint—so thoroughly, yet comfortably, old-fashioned, with its nicely sanded floor, its great rough beams hung with goodly flitches of bacon, its quaint latticed windows, its high mantlepiece, reaching almost to the roof, over the roaring coal fire; its ancient, yet strong and substantial furniture, the chests of drawers and cupboards of polished oak, and the chairs so low-seated and so high-backed. An old woman, the wife of the proprietor, sat by the chimney-corner with a grandchild in her lap. Her daughter was engaged in some household work beside her. In this room the whole family, journeymen and all, took their meals together. Porridge and milk was the usual breakfast. For dinner they had potatoes and bacon, or sometimes beef, with plenty of oat bread; and for supper, "butter-cake", or porridge again. The old man had never travelled further than Derby. He had thought of going to London once, but his heart failed him, and he had given up the idea. He did not at all approve of the new-fangled mill system, and liked the old-fashioned way of joining weaving and farming much better. He could just remember the building of the newest house in Saddleworth-fold. He thought the seasons had somehow changed in Saddleworth, for snow never lay upon the ground as it used to do, and the scanty crops of oats here and there sown did not ripen so well. The daughter having in the meantime placed oat cake and milk before me, the patriarch observed that until he was twenty he had never tasted wheaten bread, except when his mother lay in. In the room above us were two or three looms, and as many spinning jennies. They produced flannel and doeskin. Weaving and spinning formed the chief occupation of his family; they attended to the cows, of which he had four, and to the dairy, in their leisure time. He paid his sons no regular wages, but gave them board, lodging, and clothing, and "anything reasonable", if they wanted to go to a hunt or a fair or "sooch-loike".

I may as well state here that the country weavers of Saddleworth are, like

Nimrod, mighty hunters. Every third or fourth man keeps his beagle or his brace of beagles, and the gentlemen who subscribe to the district hunt pay the taxes on the dogs. There are no foxes in Saddleworth—the country, indeed, is too bare for them to pick up a living; but hares abound, and occasionally the people have "trail" hunts—the quarry being a herring or a bit of rag dipped in oil, dragged across the country by an active runner, with an hour's law. A few, but only a very few, pursue the sport on horseback; the weavers, who form the great majority of the hunt, trusting to their own sound lungs and well-strung sinews to keep within sight of the dogs. Even the discipline of the mills is as yet in many instances insufficient to check this inherent passion for the chase. My informant, himself a millowner, told me that he had recently arranged a hunt to try the mettle of some dogs from another part of Yorkshire against the native breed. He had tried to keep the matter as quite as he could; but it somehow leaked out, and the result was, that several mills were left standing, and that more than 500 carders, slubbers, spinners, and weavers formed the field. The masters, however, are often too keen sportsmen themselves to grudge their hands an occasional holiday of the sort. The Saddleworth weavers must be excellent fellows to run. A year or two ago, a gentleman, resident there, purchased a fox at Huddersfield, and turned him loose at Upper Mill, a spot almost in the centre of the hills. There started on the trail upwards of 300 sportsmen on foot. Reynard led the chase nearly to Manchester, a distance of about twenty miles, and then doubled back almost to the place where he was unbagged, favouring his pursuers with an additional score of miles' amusement. Of the 300 starters, upwards of twenty-five were in at the death. My informant had reason to remember the chase, for it cost him the bursting of a blood-vessel. In passing through the little village of Dubcross I observed a quaint tavern sign, illustrative of the ruling passion. On the board was inscribed, "Hark to bounty—hark!"

From Upper Mill I proceeded to a village called Delph, where there are only a very few mills, and round which is scattered a thick population of small farmers and hand-loom weavers. The cottages of many of these people are perched far up among the hills, on the very edge of the moors. As a general rule, the houses are inferior, both in construction and cleanliness, to those nearer the mills; and I should say, although the accounts I received were often most puzzlingly contradictory, that the run of wages is decidedly lower. In several of these remote dwellings I found beds of no inviting appearance in the loom room; and broken windows were often patched with old hats and dirty clothes. The hand-jenny spinners, when in employment, earn, as a pretty general rule, about eight shillings a week. The weavers, as I have said, may, and often do, make fifteen and seventeen shillings per week; but, taking the year round, and the good webs with the bad ones, ten shillings in many parts of Yorkshire would be too high an average. . . .

. . . Another weaver, a very intelligent man—much more so, indeed, than most of his class, for he had travelled much, and had been twice in America—gave me some curious information. He confirmed what the old man at Saddleworth-fold had stated as to the non-ripening of the oats sown now-a-days, and spoke sensibly enough about machinery. "Machinery," he said, "had been a great advantage to the weaver as long as it was pretty simple and cheap, for then he could use it for his own behoof." His mother had told him that in her young days the distaff was the only drawing implement in Saddleworth. The carding was performed by the women with a rude instrument placed upon their knees, and the old-fashioned wheel, with its single spindle, was the only spinning apparatus known. "Look, sir," he continued, "at that yarn. It was stretched out by the road-side today. In those days it would have taken a dozen of people, with a dozen of wheels, more than a week to spin it. Now my mistress can make it with the hand-jenny in two days and a half, and a power mule could spin it in a forenoon." He feared that it was but natural that the power mule would supplant the hand mule, just as the hand mule had supplanted the spinning wheel. It was during the time that machinery was in the medium state, when any industrious man could obtain it, that the weavers of Saddleworth flourished most. At one time he had paid a journeyman £35 a year, besides his board, lodging, clothing, and washing, and they did not use in those times to work more than five or six hours a day. They were too often out following the hounds. Now his average wages were not above ten shillings a week, although the could sometimes make nearer twenty shillings. His wife worked the hand-jenny, and could make, when in full work, about fifteen pence a day. Thirty years ago she could have easily earned eighteen shillings a week. He kept a cow, and paid £7 10s of rent for the requisite land. His family consumed most of the dairy produce, selling very little. The ordinary price of buttermilk was about one penny for three quarts; of blue or skim-milk, one penny for three pints; and of new milk, about twopence a quart. Milk of all kinds was sent down during the summer time, in great quantities, by many of his neighbours, who kept donkeys to carry it to Staleybridge, Oldham, and other cotton towns, where the factory hands consumed it as fast as it could be sent in.

Adverting to the work and food question, I asked him whether the high prices a year and a half ago had exercised much influence in his trade. He answered nearly as follows:

"Did they not, indeed? Why, when corn is very dear, we have next to no trade at all. It stands to reason. The fabrics we make be mostly for the home market—the best and most nat'ral of all markets, sir; and if the poor people have to spend all they earn to pay for their food and to keep the roofs over them, why, they can't buy no good warm clothing. Two years ago flour was three shillings and sixpence a stone, and oatmeal was three shillings and twopence, and potatoes were selling as high as two shillings and sixpence a score. Then, sir, there was next to no work. I was better off than many, but even in our house it was hard living, I assure you; and a great lot of the weavers had to go work along with t'navvies on the railroad."

I am happy to say that this honest man appeared to be in better case when I saw him. His house was beautifully clean, and his wife was preparing a comfortable stew for dinner. One of his children was recovering from scarlet fever, and two plump fowls were being boiled down to make chicken broth for the invalid. They had had fifteen fowls, of which ten had been thus used up, and they expected every day to get a fresh supply of poultry.

Comfort such as this must, however, by no means be taken as the rule. The weavers in the upland districts who have no farms, and those in the lower grounds who, although they possess no land, have got advantages of a particular class from the vicinity of the country mills—these two classes are generally decently off, and live wholesome and tolerably agreeable lives. But there are districts, principally in the neighbourhood of the large towns, where competition keeps the wages miserably low, and where hard labour brings in but a hard and scanty substance.

THE "STUFF" DISTRICTS OF YORKSHIRE

Halifax and Bradford

Letter XV

. . . In an architectural point of view, the best features of Bradford consist of numerous ranges of handsome warehouses. The streets have none of the old-fashioned picturesqueness of those of Halifax. The best of them are muddy, and not too often swept. Mills abound in great plenty, and their number is daily increasing, while the town itself extends in like proportion. Bradford is, as I have said, essentially a new town. Half a century ago it was a mere cluster of huts; now the district of which it is the heart contains upwards of 132,000 inhabitants. The value of life is about one in forty. Fortunes have been made in Bradford with a rapidity almost unequalled even in the manufacturing districts. In half a dozen years men have risen from the loom to possess mills and villas. At present, stuff manufacturers are daily pouring into the town from Leeds; while a vast proportion of the wool-combing of the empire seems, as it were, to have concentrated itself in Bradford. I was struck by the accent in which many of the woolcombers addressed me; and, in answer to my inquiries, I had frequently a roomfull of workmen exclaiming, "I'm from Leicestershire!"—"I'm from Devonshire!"—"I'm from Cornwall!"—"I'm from Mount Mellick, in Queen's County!". . .

. . . During my investigations at Bradford I had more than one opportunity of seeing how the parochial authorities in agricultural districts pack their paupers off to the manufacturing regions. I select two cases. The first was that of a widow from a purely rural part of Yorkshire. She had a large young family. Her husband had been an agricultural labourer at fifteen shillings a week in summer, and in winter he broke stones on the road for fifteenpence a day on his death the family became chargeable. The parish immediately offered to pay the expense of removal, and gave the family £1 1s. if they would go to Bradford. They consented, and several of the children being sickly and subject to fits, so as to be unable to work in the mills, they have been mainly supported by Bradford ever since. The woman who told me these particulars said that she knew many families who had been sent to Bradford from the same locality in the same way.

The other case is that of a poor Irishwoman, one of the cleanest, tidiest, and best specimens of her country people, in that walk of life, I have ever seen. Having heard of her case, she came out of the mill to speak to me, and conducted me to her chamber. A poorer one, and yet a cleaner one I never saw; the deal table had been scoured until it shone again; there was a faded bit of carpeting on the floor, and not a speck of dust from wall to wall. I had never witnessed a more striking instance of cleanliness taking away all the squalor of poverty. In the room were three children. The eldest, a girl of seven, was rocking the cradle of the youngest, and attending to the proceedings of her other little sister.

"This is my housekeeper," said the mother, "and I can trust her, and feel easy about the younger ones when I am at my work." The story of the family I shall relate nearly in the mother's words:

"My husband and me lived at Minstun (an agricultural district of Yorkshire). He was a hand-loom weaver. Wages were very low, and times were very hard with us. We were at Minstun ten months, and in that time we tasted flesh twice. My poor husband had a consumption on him, and little by little he was forced to give up work. The farmers and the neighbours were very hard-hearted to us. They never sent as much as a ha'p'orth of milk, even to the dying man. When he was gone, the parish offered me and my four children one shilling to pay the rent every week, and one shilling to live on. If we didn't like that, they said we might go to Bradford and they would give us thirty shillings, but they gave us twenty-nine shillings, and we came here. If they had only given us three shillings a week I would have stayed. I have a little boy, and I brought him to the mill, and told them all about us. The people at the mill were very kind much kinder than the farmers. They took the little boy, and set him to easy work, and gave him two shillings a week. Then the manager said I might come to the mill and see him, and try if I couldn't learn to do something myself. So I got to know how to pick lumps out of the slubbings, and first I got five shillings and sixpence, and last week I was raised to six shillings; so we have now eight shillings a week. Well, first I lived in a room belonging to the mill, with an outside stair, and I paid one shilling rent. But I was afraid of the children breaking their necks there. The only other place I could get near the mill was this. There are two rooms here, and the rent is two shillings. I know it's too much for the like of me to pay; but think of the children. Well, sir, the parish are very good to me, and give me three shillings a week—two shillings for the rent and one shilling for coals—and we live and clothe ourselves on the other eight shillings. We live chiefly on bread. I get a stone and a half of flour every week, and I bake it on Sundays. Then we have a little tea and coffee, and sometimes we have a little offal meat, because it's cheap. A good gentleman gave me the furniture I have, and the bed in the other room. It cost altogether fifteen shillings. Everybody has been very kind to me, and the neighbours come in often to look after the children when I'm at work. I was born in Shandon parish, in Cork; and oh! I wish there were mills there for the poor to work in. It would be a blessing to them indeed."

Leeds

Letter XVII

. . . The east and north-east districts of Leeds are, perhaps, the worst. A short walk from the Brig-gate, in the direction in which Deansgate branches off from the main entry, will conduct the visitor into a perfect wilderness of foulness.

Conceive acre on acre of little streets, run up without attention to plan or health—acre on acre of closely-built and thickly-peopled ground, without a paving-stone upon the surface, or an inch of sewer beneath, deep trodden-churned sloughs of mud forming the only thoroughfares—here and there an open space, used not exactly as the common cess-pool, but as the common cess-yard of the vicinity—in its centre, ash-pits employed for dirtier purposes than containing ashes—privies often ruinous, almost horribly foul—pig-sties very commonly left *pro tempore* untenanted, because their usual inmates have been turned out to prey upon the garbage of the neighbourhood. Conceive streets, and courts, and yards which a scavenger never appears to have entered since King John incorporated Leeds, and which, in fact, gives the idea of a town built in a slimy bog. Conceive such a surface drenched with the liquid slops which each family flings out daily and nightly before their own threshold, and further fouled by the malpractices of children, for which the parents and not the children deserve shame and punishment. Conceive, in short, a whole district to which the above description rigidly and truthfully applies; and you will, I am sorry to say, have a fair idea of what at present constitutes a large proportion of the operative part of Leeds. I have seen here and there in Bradford spots very nearly, and in Halifax spots quite, as bad; but here it is no spot —the foulness over large sections of the town, particularly towards the suburbs, constitutes the very face and essence of things. I have plodded by the half-hour through streets in which the undisturbed mud lay in wreaths from wall to wall; and across open spaces, overlooked by houses all around, in which the pigs, wandering from this central oasis, seemed to be roaming through what was only a large sty. Indeed, pigs seem to be the natural inhabitants of such places. I thing they are more common in some parts of Leeds than dogs and cats are in others; and wherever they abound, wherever the population is filthiest, there are the houses the smallest, the rooms the closest, and the most overcrowded. One characteristic of such localities is a curious and significant one. Before almost every house-door there lies, of course until the pig comes upon the deposit, a little heap of boiled-out tea-leaves. Although all the domestic refuse is flung out, you hardly ever see bones; but the tea-pot is evidently in operation at every meal. Here and there, I ought to add, the visitor will, even in the midst of such scenes as I have tried to sketch, come upon a cluster or a row of houses better than ordinary, and through the almost invariably open doors of which he will see some indications of domestic comfort; but such buildings are the exceptions—and, exceptions as they are, they rise out of the same slough of mud and filth, and command the same ugly sights as their neighbours. There is, I believe, a Nuisance Committee in Leeds. I inquired whether they were aware of even the most flagrant of all these sanitary enormities. Had their attention, for instance, been ever drawn to the practice of keeping pigs, or rather of letting the pigs keep themselves, in crowded neighbourhoods? "Yes," I was answered, by a gentleman much interested in the subject; "yes, I have reported these things over and over again, until I was sick and tired of reporting; but, you see, nothing has been done."...

NORTHUMBERLAND AND DURHAM

The Coalfield

Letter XVIII

... As a general rule, the mines in the coal district of Northumberland and Durham are worked by lessees, either companies or individuals, who rent the royalty, including everything beneath the surface, from the proprietors. The lessees have generally power to vacate the colliery by giving a year's notice. They are bound to leave the pit in an open and tenable state, and they are liable for all damage done to the surface in the course of working. The principal coal-pits worked by and for behoof of their owners are those belonging to the Marquess of Londonderry and the Earl of Durham. The engagements made with the pit hands are always by the month, with an occasional stipulation for a certain number of days' work, greater or less, according to the season and the state of the market. The Miners' Union in the Newcastle district was almost totally overthrown by the great strike of 1844, which exercised a very important influence upon the trade. . . .

... The beginning of the present century witnessed some of the greatest fluctuations which have occurred in the trade, with reference to both masters and workmen. In 1804 there was a mania for coal-digging, and a literal scramble for workmen. Previously to that time, it had been usual to bind pitmen for the twelve month, and to give them two or three guineas as binding or bounty money, at the season at which the annual engagement took place. In 1804 the binding money rose to twelve or fourteen guineas per man on the Tyne, and to eighteen guineas on the Wear. Drink flowed abundantly on all sides, and the pit districts were the scene of one vast orgie—the regular wages being raised at the same time upwards of forty per cent. The consequence was a speedy overflow of labour. Workmen of all kinds flocked to obtain employment in the pits, and gradually the wages settled down to their former level. No binding money whatever is now paid. . . .

... In 1832 occurred one of the great pitmen's strikes, the consequence of which was the introduction of a vast quantity of hitherto rural labour into the trade. To this era a number of good authorities look back as the point subsequent to which the amount of labour in the trade became permanently too great for the demand, and the quantity of coal raised too great to allow of the profits formerly made by the traffic. In 1844 a second great and ineffectual turn-out took place, the yet existing effects of which are principally displayed in the still dissolved colliers' union. . . .

... Women were occasionally, but not commonly, employed under ground; but they laboured in great numbers at the pit heaps, and at the staiths, emptying the waggons into the keels. . . .

... I have repeatedly mentioned the great strike of 1844. It commenced on April 5 of that year, on which day nearly the whole of the underground workers in Northumberland and Durham ceased to labour. It was the fourth great industrial disturbance which took place in the district since 1826. The strike had been long debated, and was deliberately resolved on. At first it was believed that the turn-out would be general over the kingdom, but a meeting of delegates was held in March, at Glasgow, at which it was decided that no such movement should take place. Delegates representing 23,357 miners voted for the general strike, but delegates representing 28,042 miners were of a contrary opinion. As, however, it was represented that the organisation of the Durham and Northumberland pitmen was complete, it was resolved that in that section of the kingdom, underground labours should be suspended on April 5; but that the other districts should not be called upon to contribute to the expenses of the turn-out. The demands of the colliers were principally as follows: They sought for payments every week; for six-monthly engagements sure; to be guaranteed five days per week at three shillings a day; to be paid by weight; hewers not to be called on to *put*; day's work to be limited to eight hours, at three shillings. In cases of accident, they required to be paid ten shillings a week, with medical attendance. In cases of death, five shillings per week to widow or children for twelve months, and £5 for burial. The terms of the owners were chiefly as follows: They would give no guarantee for work or wages; term of engagement to be for twelve months, terminable on either side at a month's notice; pay once a fortnight; and hewers to *put*, or do any work required. On the commencement of the strike great bodies of special constables were sworn in; but the conduct of the people, except in a few exceptional instances, was perfectly peaceable. Little or no injury was done to person or property. Every day great meetings were held, and exciting speeches delivered. Many conferences with the masters failed to bring about any amicable result. A religious feeling came to be strangely mixed up with the movement. The Ranters' chapels were crowded, and the success of the strike was prayed for from the pulpit. The people went to chapel and held prayer-meetings, as they said, to "get their faith strengthened". The local preachers were frequently their fellow-workmen. These were often persons gifted with a rude energy and picturesque fluency of language, and their influence was almost unbounded. The men sustained themselves during the strike by various expedients. There were some who had saved money, in anticipation of it, and all began with a fortnight's wages in hand. When these were spent, and the short credit which the small shops could afford to give was exhausted, the pawnbrokers for a time supplied the funds, and in many cases the wedding-rings of the wives were the last valuables to be parted with. The next resource was found in the funds of the benefit clubs, which were broken up. But contributions from the other coal districts came in sparingly and slowly, and the conditions of the colliers at length became desperate. Meantime the coalowners were moving heaven and earth to obtain labour. Men were sent for from Staffordshire, Derbyshire, and Wales, and great numbers were taken from other species of work and sent into the pits. Hardly one colliery was entirely stopped even for a short time. The number of hewers generally employed in the districts of Tyne, Wear, and Tees is 6,000. On June 1, the third month of the strike, 1,386 hewers were at work;

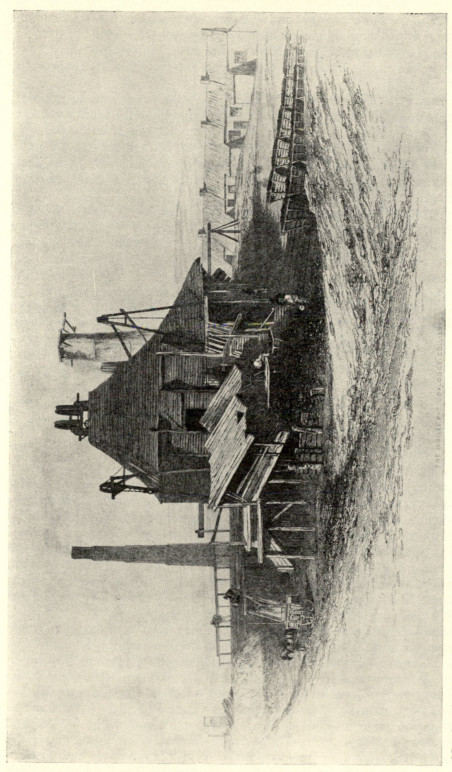

Northumberland - The Jubilee Pit, Coxlodge Colliery

from Sketches of the Coal Mines in Northumberland and Durham
by T. H. Hair, 1839

on the 16th, 2,656 were at work; and on July 6, 3,975 were in the pits. From the beginning of June the combination melted rapidly away. The influx of strangers intimidated even the most resolute, and towards the end of July there was a rush for employment—the strike was at an end, and the union utterly prostrate and overthrown.

The principal move of the union, previous to the strike, was to impose a restriction upon labour, by which each hewer bound himself to earn as little as possible above three shillings a day. The average amount of earnings before the restriction was 3s. 9½d. per day, so that the men submitted to a voluntary loss of about 9½d. a day. Although the union, as I have said, is shattered, there are pits in which the men still restrict their labour. These cases may now, however, be said to be exceptional.

The consequence of the strike was disastrous to coalowners and coalworkers. The former lost upwards of £200,000 by the four months of partial cessation from labour. The number of the latter was greatly increased by the immigration from other coal districts. Before the strike it was calculated that there were 30 per cent. more labourers in the market than the number requisite to perform the work; and since the resumption of labour, strangers in many cases occupy the places in the cottages and the pit of old hewers, who have been forced to seek employment in the new iron-works springing up upon the moors of Durham, Northumberland, and Yorkshire.

What a Coal-Pit Is

Letter XIX

. . . The spot for digging having been fixed upon, the operations are commenced by gangs of "sinkers", who are to regular pitmen what navvies are to regular railway servants. A sinker will sometimes take employment as a hewer, but only when no sinking work is to be got. As soon as he hears of a new mine he is off with his pickaxe and shovel at once. The work of sinking never ceases after it is begun, until the necessary depth is reached. The sinkers work in three gangs, and relieve each other every four hours, day and night. Their turns are so arranged as to give every man alternate spells of four hours' work and eight hours' rest. Their wages may average about three shillings and eightpence per day—the daily work-hours numbering, of course, eight. . . .

. . . The toil of the hewer depends greatly upon the thickness of the seam, which prescribes the attitudes in which he is obliged chiefly to labour. Sometimes he stands; sometimes he works on his knees; sometimes he flings himself down on his side, to get at the lower part of the bed. The skill and endurance of the hewer are mostly shown by the facility with which he can accommodate his postures to the nature of the seam, and the vigour and effect with which he can labour in them all. The coal is always pretty compactly lodged, and requires a smart blow to bring down even any ordinary shovel-full; and this is the more he felt from the cramping position, often among props and posts, in which the limbs have to be exerted. The men work in flannel shirts and short drawers, with the perspiration washing every now and then a white streak in their besmirched faces. Close behind the hewer stand one or more empty tubs, which he has to fill. He then attaches to the staple fixed in the corner of each one of the little cords and wooden labels already described, and the putter wheels it out, by main force, through the narrow passages. The hewers of course take down with them as many labels as they expect to fill tubs. Their hours of work are, at present, eight or nine per day. Here and there a very hard-working man will work somewhat longer. In some pits there are relays of hewers so as to carry the work on until late at night, but the following plan is more generally adopted: The hewers enter the pit at two or three in the morning, and set to work; the putters come to their aid two hours from the time they have commenced, so as to find coals hewn and ready to be carried out. In some pits another set of hewers enter at eight or nine o'clock; but this, I repeat, is not general practice. As the putters arrive two hours later than the hewers, so they remain behind them to accomplish their task. There is one putter to every three or four hewers, and the like proportion of drivers and other labourers employed about the waggons and inclines to every three or four putters. These last are, as has been mentioned, lads generally under twenty. Their work requires constant stooping, and constant and severe muscular exertion. They have generally begun as trappers—then they have been team-drivers—after which they have been promoted to putting, and of course look forward to becoming hewers. It is not easy for people who never saw the employment to realise to themselves what putting is. Let them, however, just try to fancy a pitch dark, oblong hole, just about big enough to contain an ordinary sofa. Then let them fancy the shoving and dragging of waggons holding about 7 cwt. of coal from one end of this hole to the other—the labourer always of course stooping almost double, and the thermometer seldom below 75 degrees. This is what is called "putting coals". Although mere lads are engaged in it, I fancied the muscular exertion to be even more than that requisite in the hewer's labour. Both hewers and putters are paid by the quantity of coals extracted, and the latter make nearly as much as the former, their wages averaging from three shillings to three shillings and sixpence per day. Of course, the amount must depend on the quantity of coal picked by the hewers. The latter will earn, if they do not restrict themselves, something like three shillings and tenpence or four shillings per day; and besides this, they have certain advantages in the way of house accommodation, which I shall afterwards allude to. The pitmen take what provisions they need during their working hours down with them. They have canteens and bags for the solids, called "bait pokes". No beer or spirits is allowed in any mine whatever, and the men all agree in the reasonableness of the regulation. In the canteens they have coffee, which they drink cold, milk, and water. The putters consume an immensity of water, notwithstanding the heat and perspiration in which they are continually bathed. In many pits casks of the pure fluid are provided for these poor thirsty fellows. I have peeped into several "bait pokes", and generally found their contents to be great hunches of bread, with smaller portions either of meat or of cheese. These small haver-sacks are hung to nails upon props, until their proprietors feel sufficiently appetised to attack them. The hewers generally labour by threes or fours in the same board. They are, I was told by some good authorities, although the statement was denied by others, by no means fond of working alone, from superstitious considerations. Many of the old-fashioned ideas in this respect are dying away, but the mining population, particularly the hewers, are still very attentive to signs and omens before they commence their day's work. They account it specially unlucky to cross a woman on their way to the pit. Considering the hour at which they leave home, the conjunction does not probably often take place; but many a miner, if he catches a glimpse, or fancies he does so, of the flutter of a female dress, will turn on his heel, and go back to bed again. A gentleman informed me that he had once unwittingly stopped the day's working of a pit by passing the "row", when the men were going to their labour, wrapped up in a light-coloured plaid. He afterwards learned that there was a grand consultation held on the bank, and that it was unanimously resolved that nothing could be more rash than going into the pit after several of the party had distinctly seen a ghost. The superstitions of the pitmen, however, form a subject on which I shall afterwards have occasion to touch.

The labour of the putter is at present being considerably infringed upon by the introduction of Shetland ponies, small enough to traverse the head-ways, and strong enough speedily to hurry out the tubs. The horses used in mines, after they are once brought down, seldom see the light again. They are generally in capital condition, the warm air making their coats sleek, and their docility is very striking. Indeed, unruly horses would never do for pit labour. The stables are usually situated close to the down-cast shaft, and, except being a trifle darker, are very like stables situated above ground. The horses are attended to by stablemen, who do not interfere in any other work of the pit. . . .

The Mining Districts

Letter XX

. . . Until 1844, pitmen, and indeed everybody connected with pits were always hired by the year. The "binding" as it was called, took place at the end of March. The men then assembled at the colliery, and met the proprietor or his agents, who read the bond, detailing the terms to be paid, and the discipline and regulations of the mine. To this the labourers affixed their names or marks. Earnest money called "arles", was then given. Up to 1804 the arles frequently amounted to two or three guineas. At that date the sum was reduced to half-a-crown, and since the strike in 1844 the custom has been totally abolished. The bond, as it is at present drawn out, invariably stipulates that the engagement on either side is terminable at a month's notice. The pitmen, I must say, are a class of people not always to be easily pleased. When the bond held them for a year, they urged that it placed them under an unduly lengthened thraldom. At present, complaints are not wanting that the monthly system enables masters to dismiss their hands without giving sufficient warning. The bond usually commences by binding all the persons hired to hew, work, fill, drive, and put coals, or to do such other work as they may be directed, and as shall appear necessary to the owners for carrying on with advantage the operations of the mine. Thus, at a pinch, any man is bound to perform any sort of work. The bond next sets forth that the wages are to be paid fortnightly, and it recounts the rates to be adopted for the working of different seams—the coals to be in all cases sent to bank in a clean and mercantile state, and free from all refuse. The method of working to be pursued is then stipulated, and the allowance, if any, of gunpowder to the hewers set forth. Since the abolition, however, of the yearly-binding, powder, is very rarely furnished by the owners. The rate of wages payable to the putters is next stated—that rate differing according to the distance which they will have to push the tubs. Next, the wages of the day labourers are set forth, and parents of trap-boys are cautioned against deceiving the managers of the pits as to their children's ages. Stipulations are also commonly made for the weighing of the coals sent to bank. The allowance for deficient weight (if any) and the quantity of refuse permitted in each tub, are then stated, with the penalties to be incurred if either condition be violated. Articles are then inserted, binding the workpeople to continue the servants of the proprietors, in the case of the working of the mine being temporarily discontinued, and binding the proprietors to pay a certain amount of wages for all such times of abeyance; the men, meantime, obliging themselves, in consideration of these wages, to set themselves to any work which the proprietors direct.

Such then, is a general statement of the stipulated terms on which the pitmen descend to their work. I proceed to detail their habits of daily toil and life. The hewer only requires tools. There are drills for boring into the seam when gunpowder is to be used, picks for separating the masses of coal, iron wedges and mells for loosening the mineral, when blasting is not permitted, and shovels for filling the tubs. The picks and drills are usually the property of the hewer; the mells, wedges, and sometimes the shovels, are found him. A hewer possesses at least half a dozen picks. They may cost about one shilling and eightpence each. He generally fits the hafts to them himself, and a blacksmith, partially paid by the colliery, keeps the iron part in order. The picks have to be sharpened every day, so each hewer when he ascends goes straight with his implement to the blacksmith's shop, and next morning, finds it laid out in readiness for him. The hewer pays twopence per fortnight to the blacksmith. Gunpowder for blasting is, as I have said, in the great majority of cases, found by the men themselves. Sometimes they are compelled to buy both it and their candles of the overmen, who occasionally supply the articles. The powder, which is very coarse stuff, costs sixpence per pound and hewers will often use from three to four pounds in a fortnight. They make the cartridges in which it is fired at their leisure. . . . Davy lamps are always found and partly kept in order by the colliery. . . . Drivers are supplied with lanterns—called, I believe, "mistresses", by the pit. The poor little trap-boys have no such advantage, and light is too expensive a luxury for them to buy. If their parents are indulgent they will give them a couple of candles per day to light them in and out of the pit. These poor little fellows often complain grievously of sitting for twelve hours at a stretch in the dark. After the first few hours, the pitmen have told me that the constant cry of the trappers to all who pass their solitary stations is "What o'clock is it?" or "Will it soon be time to call kenner?"—the latter phrase signifying an expression shouted down the shaft by the banksman, and repeated throughout the workings, when the hour has arrived for knocking off and ascending to the surface. As might be expected, the trap-boys are not by any means devoid of superstitious terrors. After an accident they are especially sensitive, and have a great aversion to going near places where the dead bodies have been laid previously to being brought to bank. For all this, however, it rarely happens that the parents have to use any compulsion to force a boy to work. The hewers are in the practice of taking their children very early down into the pit, and habituating them to its repulsive features; while, if a boy has been at school, he is generally delighted to exchange the discipline of the class even for work underground. The number of trap-door boys required at present is, however, far less than it used to be; the doors being now commonly constructed with springs so as to swing-to every time they are opened. As a general rule, a trap-boy is placed as near his father or brothers as is practicable. The putters who pass by the doors are notoriously careless as to whether the trapper does his duty or not. Indeed, this recklessness appears common to almost every workman in coal pits. . . .

. . . Both overmen and deputies are ordinarily selected from the hewers. Their wages range from eighteen shillings to twenty-five shillings per week, and to them are usually assigned the best houses in the pit village. The overmen in a mine hold analogous positions to boatswains' mates on shipboard, or corporals in a regiment. They are the lowest persons in authority. The deputies are employed in fixing props and brattices, and generally in taking charge of the wood-work of a mine, a department on the efficient discharge of the duties of which the ventilation of the pit entirely depends. When gunpowder is used in safety-lamp works, the deputy always fires the charge. Both classes of officials are nominally, and, no doubt often really, selected from the most experienced and most intelligent of the hewers; but an unpopular appointment of the kind is sure to result in a charge against the masters of partiality and favouritism. A number of the deputies, I have been informed by the pit hands, are "blacklegs" —that is, men who have kept aloof from the Union, and generally declined to join in strikes. It is the duty of the overmen and deputies to descend into the pit by midnight, or before it, and to traverse the whole of the workings, in order to see that there is no appearance of dangerous gases or of symptoms of fall from the roof. When anything wrong is apprehended, the inspecting party leave a rude caution, in the shape of a prop or a shovel flung across the path, as a token for the hewers, when they arrive, to go no further. Sometimes they chalk a word of warning upon the blade of a shovel, and stick it upright in the castle; but so profound is the ignorance of many of the pitmen, that an intelligent hewer informs me that shovels have been frequently kept until he made his appearance, when they were presented to him, with a request that he would decipher the mystic hieroglyphics.

There is, generally speaking, a watch kept all night upon the pit-heap; and at the proper hours, the sentinel, who is termed from one part of his duties the "callsman", proceeds round the colliery village to rouse the hewers—rapping at every door and proclaiming that it is time to turn out. A great number of the pits are worked by two shifts or sets of hewers—called respectively the fore-shift and the back-shift. In these cases the callsman proceeds on his first round about one'clock in the morning. The hewers composing the fore-shift thereupon turn out and array themselves in their working dresses, which are generally left roasting before the fire. They let themselves out, falling-to latches being attached to the door, for the purpose of securing them thereafter, and proceed to the shaft, which they descend in parties of half-a-dozen or more. About two hours after the hewers have been at work, the callsman makes a second round, and summons the drivers, putters, and trap-boys. By this time the hewers have field a sufficient number of tubs to set their coadjutors to work, and as soon as the engine begins to heave up its first load of coals to the bank, the day's work, so far as regards those who work by the day, is held to have commenced. The back-shift of hewers "go in" about eight or nine o'clock in the morning. The fore-shift come out about ten or eleven a.m., and the back-shift about four or five p.m. The men of each shift change hours every week, the fore-shift of one week being the back-shift of the next.

About eleven o'clock in the forenoon, then, the first party knock off work. They place their picks in the waggons, take them out again at the bottom of the shaft, and, having ascended, proceed with them to the blacksmith's shop. By the time they get home, their well-earned breakfast is waiting them. But instead of sketching in general terms a fore-shift man's method of passing his day, I will transcribe, almost verbatim, the statement of one pitman—a statement which, upon very extensive inquiry, I find may be taken as giving a fair specimen of the habits of the body.

"Well, sir, when I get to bank I'm very ready for my breakfast. We're all that. Pitmen have the best of appetites. No one can beat the hewers in that way, except, perhaps, the putters. They've a wonderful swallow, certainly. My mistress knows better nor to keep me waiting when I come to bank. If I expect to ride (ascend the shaft) at ten o'clock, she has the coffee hot by nine o'clock, in case I should be sooner nor I thought. I don't wash until I have my breakfast. I'm too sharp-set for that. Aye, aye, I must have my coffee and bread before I do aught else. 'Refreshment in the pit?' No, sir, I only take in a bit of bread in my bail-poke, or may-be, wrapped in a bit o' clout, and a drop of water in the canteen. The drivers and trappers take down more, because they stay longer than us. Well, when I've had my coffee—it used to be porridge, but we've got more genteel now—I warrant you I've a good wash—a wash all over. There's always warm water ready, and soap. Cold won't bring the muck off, and besides warm's comfortabler like—I get to bed. 'Too tired to wash, and go to bed without it?' Bless you, sir, ask the mistress if she would let me do that. No, no. She has over-much respect for the sheets. Pretty sheets they would be if colliers got into them without washing. Well, sir, I have a sleep of two or three hours, till the afternoon; then I get up, and feel quite ready for dinner. We don't get so much flesh-meat as we could eat, I assure you. What a man has in that way depends on circumstances. If he has a large young family, it's little enough, you may take your oath of it. Still, a man who works like a hewer must have nourishing meat. That's a necessity. He couldn't handle the pick without. A single man gets two or three pound of meat in a week, but we make it go as far as we can. We have often suet pudding and dumplings. They're great things with the pitmen, are suet dumplings. We never have any beer or ale at dinner—only water; but we generally manage to have some ale on

Saturday nights, particularly on pay-weeks. Well, after dinner I've generally a lot of little things to do, perhaps about my tools, perhaps about my garden. Maybe I may sit down and make cartridges for the shots, or put new hafts to the picks, or I may dander in and speak to a neighbour, or have a game at quoits, or a walk to breathe the fresh air. Some of us that have a turn that way read books, or make small things in the furniture way, especially bird cages and little chests of drawers for ornament, or we smoke our pipes before the door. Then we have some tea, and go to bed, perhaps about seven o'clock or eight o'clock. Those who go in late in the mornings have dinner when they come to bank, and then go to bed. They have tea when they rise again, and can do what they like till night, when they turn in in time enough to get up very well by seven o'clock or six o'clock; and that, sir, is a very fair account of a pitman's day."

The clothes used for the mine are, as I have said, made entirely of coarse flannel. Sometimes the wives are competent to shape and sew them. Sometimes they are purchased at slop-shops at Newcastle. A hewer's dress consists of a long jacket with large pockets, a waistcoat, a flannel shirt, a pair of short drawers reaching to the middle of the thigh, a pair of stout flannel trowsers worn over them, with worsted stockings or "hoggers"—that is, stockings with the feet cut away. Many of the hewers who wear hoggers envelop their feet in rags to prevent the coal dust getting between the toes. They all wear stout shoes. While at their work, the heat is commonly found so oppressive that the hewers often fling off every stitch save the short drawers. They generally, however, come to the pit mouth fully dressed. The putters, on the contrary, make their appearance, as I have already described, in the short drawers with or without "hoggers". A pit suit of good material and fair workmanship will cost about a pound. In spite of their grimy avocation, there are probably no members of the labouring classes more clean than the pitmen of Northumberland and Durham when above ground. They have a thorough, scrubbing with soap and hot water every day of their lives, and they generally dress in far better style than the ordinary run of labouring men. Indeed, it is difficult to believe than the clean, respectably-attired person who accosts you is the same begrimmed, three-parts naked being, whose white gleaming eyes and teeth you remember as he turned round from the wall of coal, and held up his Davy-lamp for your convenience. I was remarking one day how exceedingly black a putter looked, when, half-an-hour after, I beheld him emerge from his home, his complexion almost as light as that of an Albino, and a profusion of "lint-white locks" streaming in dandified curls down his cheeks.

A pit-row is like nothing whatever in the shape of a collocation of dwelling places that I know of in England. It is neither like a country village, nor a section of the meaner part of a manufacturing town; but it appears to me to possess more than the inconveniences of the one, and more than the ugliness of the other. The shops, if anything worthy of the name exist at all, are of the meanest and most miserable description. From end to end there is not a single large house, a tree, or a church spire to break the shabby uniformity of the pitmen's cottages. The general run of chapels, principally belonging to Methodist bodies, which abound, may be distinguished from barns only by being far smaller and more paltry looking. . . .

... Opposite the doors, on either side of every row, will be observed small detached buildings with the roof sloping in one way only, and here and there will be scattered little houses like miniature dwellings, but adorned with chimneys from which smoke occasionally issues. The first erections are pantries and larders, one of which is attached to every house; the second are ovens, at which the bread of a dozen families can be baked at once.

Let us now proceed along the streets of the colliery village. Almost without exception they will be found in a miserably filthy condition. Sometimes ash-pits have been formed with singular judgment close to the larders, but most commonly the ashes and all sorts of domestic refuse are flung into the centre of the street. All the way along the dismal thoroughfare runs a sierra of "middens", with here and there a filthy pig-sty. In a few colliery villages there is a feeble attempt at surface-drainage, the liquid refuse in these channels, being very frequently stagnant; but in not one pit-row out of the scores I have seen, and in not one pit-row, I am told, in Northumberland and Durham, is there a single foot of underground drainage, calculated, by means of sinks, to carry away domestic slops. And these rows, be it observed, were not built piecemeal by poor men, ignorant of the importance of drainage to health and life; they were, one and all, constructed wholesale by the owners of the neighbouring pits, for the accommodation of their workpeople, and they are the only houses in which these workpeople can possible live. But I have a more serious charge to bring against the owners of colliery villages even than that involved in lack of drainage. There may be exceptions to the general rule (if there be, I have not seen them); but the general, almost the universal rule in Durham and Northumberland is the construction of little towns—for many pit villages may be so called—without the erection of one single privy or cesspool, either public or private. The few privies which, in rare instances, do exist, are rude construc-tions of boards, built by the occupants of the houses themselves, and generally located in corners of gardens. ... I have dwelt upon the point, because I have been over and over again most earnestly entreated by the pitmen to bring the circumstance before the public, as one in which not only the convenience and the health, but the feelings, and the morals of the mining population are deeply concerned.

The houses of the pit villages, may, as I have stated, be divided into three classes. Those of the lowest grade usually contain only one room; those of the second class contain a large room and an attic. The best houses consist of two rooms on the ground floor, with generally an attic over one of them. In all cases, the sitting-room door is the street-door. It will be obvious that tenements so arranged furnish miserably deficient accommodation. The largest families have only two habitable rooms, the others being wretched lofts, with the tiles left bare, and so low that even beneath the ridge of the roof a man cannot stand upright. But two-roomed houses fall to the lot of perhaps only one-third of the mining population. The dwellings, as I have stated, are accounted part of the wages, and they are apportioned by the proprietor or his agents, not so much according to the family of each pitman as according to the family he has working, or likely to work, in the mine. A young married couple go, after their union, into one of the back or lean-to houses. Here they remain until they have a young family around them. Then they are probably transferred to one of the second-class dwellings, of one room, with an attic, and by the time that the boys begin to work in the pit the father can claim a first-class or double house. If the family consist wholly or principally of girls, they must make shift in the second-rate house. Parents with growing boys have always the preference in obtaining work in a coal-pit, and houses in a pit-village: indeed, married men without families are sometimes turned out of their own into inferior houses to make room for the more useful circle of juvenile labourers. Practically, and for all the purposes of living, the attic seems, from all I can gather, to be of small use; and the deplorable consequence is, that more than one half of the pit population virtually live—each family— in a single room. Here is bedroom and kitchen—here the men and boys, on their return from the pit wash their almost naked bodies; too often in the presence of growing up daughters and sisters—and here, too, the women dress and undress, unless the presence of an absolute stranger compels them to run across the street, in order, as I have over and over again witnessed, to change their attire in the pantry. The men say that they cannot wash up-stairs, as the water would splash through the frequently warped flooring down upon the furniture, and perhaps the bed below; and in the infrequent cases of two-storied pit houses, complaints are frequently made of the spillage caused by the occupants of the higher room. The best sort of houses in a pit village are always occupied by the deputies, the overmen, and the principal waggon-drivers, and the range is commonly nicknamed "Quality-row". As a general rule, a garden goes with every house, the ground being sometimes attached to it; but by far the most frequent plan is to subdivide a field into patches, wherein each pitman may grow a few pecks of potatoes or cabbages. The miners sometimes take pains with their gardens, but they are more commonly neglected. Besides his house, each miner receives fuel, not quite for nothing, but for threepence per week, the trifling amount in question being nominally paid, not for the coal, but for the "leading", or carting it to the door. Let us imagine, then, if we would form an idea of a colliery village, some half dozen rows of perfectly uniform one-storied cottages, the intersecting lanes dotted with ash-heaps and "middens", with, in rainy weather, perfect sloughs of mud formed round the hills of refuse. On the outskirts rise one or two modest-looking dissenting chapels, as unadorned as though the line of beauty typified the path to destruction, and about as big as ordinary sized parlours. At one end probably rises the pit heap, at the other extends the garden field, and all around stretches a labyrinth of deep rutted, miry cross roads, through which, in this wintry weather, the wayfarer, as I have had woeful experience, wades rather than walks.

We will now enter one of the ordinary class of houses. In one respect, particularly in the cold season, the pitman's dwelling is especially comfortable; it is sure to have a blazing fire, the bright red reflection of which dances cheer-fully on everything around. As a general rule, the furniture is decidedly good; some articles are even costly. The visitor's attention will be especially drawn to the bed and the chest of drawers. In a great proportion of cases neither of these would be out of place in a house of some pretensions. The bedstead is very frequently of carved and turned mahogany, and the bed, clean, soft, and comfortable, with white furniture and a quilted coverlid. The chest of drawers is an article which frequently costs from £8 to £10. It commonly rises almost to the ceiling, only leaving room for a few old-fashioned china or stoneware ornaments to be placed upon the top. The chairs are sometimes deal, and sometimes mahogany. The mantelpiece is generally crowded with little ornaments of china and glass; the plates, cups, and saucers, are usually kept in cupboards; but highly polished brass candlesticks, placed on shelves, or hung upon nails, glitter from the wall. Birds and birdcages abound. The songsters are generally fine canaries, or carefully bred mules, and the cages have often been manufactured by the occupant of the cottage. The stock of books is generally very small, but there is almost always a large folio Bible to be found, often accompanied by a few Methodist tracts, and—strange literary jumble—assortments of dream-books, "Oracles of Fate, as consulted by the Emperor Napoleon", and "Little Warblers".

The women are the great agents in getting the houses so well furnished as they are. They strive to outdo each other in the matters of beds and chests of drawers, the two great features of their rooms. When a young couple get married, they generally go to a furniture broker in Newcastle or Sunderland, with perhaps £10 of ready money, obtaining a considerable part of their "plenishing" upon credit, and paying for it by instalments. Like the Manchester mill-hands, the colliery folks have a great notion of clocks; but, unlike the cotton workers, a great proportion of the pitmen's timepieces are regular eight-day clocks with metallic dials. The floors of the houses are seldom or never boarded. Sometimes they are formed of a hard composite, but they are more often paved with red brick—here and there, perhaps, covered with strips of carpeting. Complaints of dampness are very rife, and the chimneys frequently smoke abominably. The attic is invariably gained by a perpendicular flight of steps and a trap-door. The pitmen represent that it is so bare and cold as to render sleeping in it in the cold season a matter of real suffering to people accustomed to the hot air of the mine while at work, or to blazing fires in their living rooms at home. I may add, that I have seen houses of a decidedly superior class to those just sketched, but I have good reason to believe that most industrious pitmen can attain to the state of comparative domestic comfort above described. . . .

I have now to turn for a brief space to the sad subject of accidents in coal mines. . . .

. . . the fearful scourge of the coal mine is the distillation from the mineral of carburetted hydrogen or fire-damp. The pure gas is unexplosive; but when mixed with eight times its volume of air, the fluid acquires powers more terrible than even those of gunpowder. A mine explosion is a thing unhappily often heard of; but its terrible features are not in general correctly realised. A light is brought in contact with the aerial agent immediately it bursts, with a smothered roar into a vast sea of scathing flame, flying from passage to passage, and corridor to corridor, wherever the explosive compound exists, and dashing planking, brattices, and doors before it, as though they had been shattered by cannon-balls. In a pit near Newcastle three men were employed close to the bottom of a shaft, coaling up the entrance to an old deserted working. Behind them, at a few paces distance, was a brattice, or partition, extending down and across the shaft, and formed of seasoned three-inch planking. A candle was fetched, the better to survey the masonry. Gas was present—it fired—and the three men were blown right through the three-inch planking, and smashed into pulp on the opposite side of the shaft. In other cases, men have been shot up out of the shaft like bullets out of a gun-barrel, and their blackened limbs picked up scattered in the adjacent fields. But generally, the loss of life from actual flame, or from being dashed against the sides of the mine is comparatively small. The worst comes after the explosion. No sooner has the sheet of flame spent itself than volumes of carbonic acid— the fatal choke-damp or stythe, one breath of which, in its pure state, is death —come rolling in suffocating fumes along the neighbouring passages. The explosion has frequently blown down the brattices and trap-doors; the ventilation of the mine is, therefore, in a moment suspended, and the stythe works its deadly will. It frequently happens that ten men are killed by stythe for one burnt by the fire-damp. The poor fellows are found unscathed in face and limb, but choked by the suffocating vapour. Several men have given me descriptions of what they witnessed of the effects of explosions taking place in quite a different part of the mine from that in which they were working.

"I remember, sir," said one, "an explosion happening in our pit. It was far from us, and we heard no noise; but all at once the air was chopped off from our mouths. Then we knew what had happened. Not one of us spoke a word to the other, but we cast down our picks, and we ran to the shaft for life! I did not think of death to myself, but I thought of Jane (his wife) and the five little ones. Thank God, we got safe to the bottom of the shaft; but if the stythe had chanced to come across we should have fallen down and died where we lay."

The miners know when they are in foul air by the appearance of the flame in the Davy-lamp. It becomes elongated, and presently if the gas continues to pour forth, the ordinary flame is, as it were, lipped and haloed by a second bluish-hued fire, formed by the burning of the carburetted-hydrogen within the gauze-screen. It used to be not an uncommon practice for miners to continue working in the full consciousness of the atmosphere with which they were thus surrounded, and perfectly aware that their lamps were, as it is called "afire". Recklessness of this kind is now, however, by no means so common as it was. In such cases as I have mentioned, an accident to the lamp from a fall, or the chance blow of a pick, would have produced an instantaneous explosion. Still, however, men do not scruple to carry the Davy into at atmosphere which they know to be highly inflammable. . . .

. . . What the miners are almost to a man in favour of is, regular Government inspection of the collieries—the inspector to have the power of enforcing his recommendations. Petitions to this effect have been in former sessions presented to Parliament and the question will be again agitated next year. Tracts are at present being published upon the subject, under the auspices of the delegate-council of the Pitmen's Union. The men urge that of all classes of labour none has a greater claim upon the paternal vigilance of a Government than a dangerous and little understood toil, surrounded with special causes of peril, and carried on apart from the general eye, in the dark recesses of the earth. They argue that while the factory labourer and the emigrant are officially cared for and protected, and while not a train is allowed to be run upon a new railway until a scientific agent of the Government has minutely inspected and testified to its safety, that vast numbers of people are daily obliged to hazard their lives in an occupation which, for its safe conduct, imperatively demands constant, vigilant, and scientific superintendence—a species of superintendence, moreover, carried on in a different spirit to that now exercised on the part of the owners themselves; and who, the men allege, in the management of coal mines, are very often apt to make the safety of the pit a secondary consideration as compared with its profitable working. For these reasons, amongst others, the miners are anxious for the appointment of Government inspectors, men of scientific knowledge and practical skill, able not only to recommend, but empowered to put their recommendations into practice. . . .

Letter XXI

I have stated in a previous communication that the great strike of 1844 paralysed, if it did not temporarily break up, the miners' combination in Durham and Northumberland. . . .

. . . Whatever may be its future operations, however, the Miners' Union is now again making head. The association in the north is local being confined to the counties of Durham and Northumberland. It numbers at present upwards of 7,000 members, of whom a few, and only a few, are boys. It employs six paid labourers to disseminate and enforce its views—comprehends upwards of sixty collieries, many of them among the largest and most important in the district —and holds regular fortnightly meetings, at which a delegate from each pit attends to consult and report progress. . . .

. . . In those portions of Mr. Tremenheere's Reports, devoted to the educational facilities afforded to the colliery districts, the phrase continually occurs when describing a pit seminary—"Until within a late period the only means of instruction for the people were dance schools." Many of the old class of schools, taught by masters were also wretchedly inefficient—the teachers being frequently disabled workmen, and the number of their scholars forming but a miserable per centage of the work people of the colliery. The consequence has been that the mining population are exceedingly low in point of education and intelligence; and yet they contradict the theories generally entertained upon the connection of ignorance with crime, by presenting the least criminal section of the population of England. Indeed, the disproportion between the mining districts of Northumberland, Durham, and the average of England, particularly as regards the more trifling class of offences against property, is very remarkable; and great as this disproportion is, that of female crime in the mining districts, as contrasted with the general average, is still greater. In 1847, the number of persons offending against property in England was twenty-eight out of every 10,000 of the population. In the mining districts, including Northumberland, Durham, Cumberland, and Cornwall, the proportion was only seven in every 10,000. Again, for the three years ending 1847, there were, in the mining districts, only 9.33 female thieves out of every 10,000 women. The proportion in Middlesex was 34.69; while, throughout England and Wales generally the proportion was 17.67. The author of "Tactics for the Times", in adducing these results, attempts to account for them on the supposition that the uncertainty of human life caused by the frequency and terrible nature of accidents in mines, produces a deep and salutary effect on the minds of the people. But the explanation seems very fanciful. A sailor undergoes at least as much risk as a miner; and sailors are not reckoned a particularly thoughtful race. Besides, taking one of the most exclusively coal-mining districts I can find—that of Auckland, Teesdale, and Weardale—the Registrar-General's last Report makes the general value of life within it as one in forty-nine—a higher proportion than that of London, and more than twenty per cent. higher than that of Manchester. The fact, to some extent, appears to be, that that naturally sombre and earnest mental temperament which distinguishes the people of the north of England in general, has, in the case of the miners, been fostered and wrought out into strong religious convictions through the agency of the Methodist bodies, who have obtained almost the entire spiritual control of the people; the efforts of the thousands of local and itinerant preachers being greatly aided by the comparatively isolated condition in which the mining population live—seldom or never coming in contact with the members of any industrial class except their own, and little exposed to the influences and excitements of great towns. Let the cause be, however, what it may, the miners are the reverse of a criminal population, and they are also the reverse of an intelligent one. An educational census of the people employed in the collieries of the Earl of Durham was lately instituted; and the results may, I believe, be taken as giving a tolerably fair view of the general state of education and intelligence throughout the coal districts. The number of people directly or indirectly connected with the Earl of Durham's collieries was about 4,500. This estimate includes persons engaged in a variety of occupations having more or less reference to pit labour, embracing waggon-way wrights, waggon fillers, blacksmiths, engineers, banksmen, etc. From the total number, more than 700 was deducted for children below five years of age; of the remainder, numbering 3,706, there were 1,461 who could read and write; 1,339 who could read only; and 916 above the age of five who could neither read nor write. This is the general result, applying to all the workpeople above and under ground; but the details of the inquiry proved that while upwards of one-half of the families—the males of which were not, strictly speaking, pitmen —could read and write, only one-third of the pit families were so far educated. But a pitman's notions of reading and writing, I was informed by an intelligent member of their own body, are very modest. "Many a hewer and a putter", said this individual, "will tell you that they can write; but you would be sorely puzzled to read the specimens they would give you." In a colliery in another part of the district, where an educational investigation was set on foot, the results were, that of 331 persons capable of being educated, only 165 could read the Bible. A school-master with whom I conversed and who has had a lengthened experience amongst a pit population, estimated that only about twenty-five per cent. of the children were kept at school so long as to be really benefited. He said that their parents commonly professed to be very anxious about the education of their children, but that they sadly grudged the fees, and the boys were sent down to the pit as soon as they could earn a shilling.

At many collieries, the pitmen have been found to prefer sending their children to schools taught by inefficient masters of their own class, rather than to seminaries managed by properly trained instructors. As in the cloth and cotton districts, Sunday-schools have played a principal part in affording to the present generation of pit-labourers what degree of education they do possess. In every pit village there are one or more Wesleyan or Primitive Methodist Chapels, and attached to every one of these there is a Sunday-school. With the exception of what is done in these institutions, the education of a pitman may be said to terminate with the day when he first descends the mine to labour. He begins, perhaps, as a trapper, and sits twelve hours of the day in the dark. Indeed, during a considerable portion of the year, the trappers, drivers, and putters never see daylight except on Sundays. They descend the mine before dawn, and ascend it after nightfall. The work of boys, both in driving and trapping, is, therefore, so drearily monotonous and sombre that they are very unwilling to undergo anything like additional restraint above ground—while the labours of putters and hewers is physically so severe and exhausting, that by the time they ascend to day, there seems to be but little left of that energy and vigour which, in so many instances, prompt the manufacturing operative to visit the lecture or the concert-room. The pitmen, as a body, know little, and care little, about politics. Their ideas are limited to the mine in a far greater degree than the spinner's or the weaver's are confined to the factory. If they have no particular technical grievances to complain of, they seldom disturb themselves about abstract political claims, or abstract political wrongs. I have been in scores of pitmen's houses, and I do not think that I saw a newspaper in one of them. Where there were books, they generally consisted of Methodist religious publications. The Bible is, however, to be found in almost every house, and the religious feelings of the community, if unenlightened, are strong and practically binding. The Church of England is, I believe, from what I have seen, regarded by a large proportion of the mining community with feelings of positive and active enmity. They almost invariably class it with the aristocratic institutions and influences which they believe to be hostile to them. The church clergymen, they say, take part with the masters, but the Ranters take part with the men; in fact, most of the local preachers are themselves working men, addressing their comrades in their own patois, and treating every scriptural subject in the peculiarly technical tone of mind which is common to the whole community.

In the mining districts the family tie remains almost invariably unbroken until the marriage of the children. Trappers invariably give their wages to their parents. When a boy comes to be a driver he is allowed a small weekly amount of pocket-money; and when he attains to the dignity of "putting", he either pays his father for his board and lodging, and clothes himself, or hands over the entire amount of his wages, requiring to be found in board, lodging, and clothes, and demanding a certain sum, usually about two shillings and sixence per fortnight, for his *menus plaisirs*. The pitmen do not generally marry until they become hewers, and their wives are almost invariably chosen out of their own community. Whole villages are thus often related by marriage. Occasionally, but not often, a pitman's child will go out to service; but in the vast proportion of cases a hewer's daughter becomes a hewer's wife. Should she be left a widow she still remains in the pit row, sometimes opening a small huckstering shop, and taking in clothes to wash and mangle. A disabled man also occasionally takes to dealing in small wares; and in some cases super-annuated hewers will, in addition to what light jobs they can pick up about the pit, occupy themselves in collecting the clay used for the workmen's candles. A hewer is past his prime at forty. Pains and stiffness in the back and loins begin to come on, and he finds, particularly in difficult seams, that he can no longer send to bank the same quantity of coals as he managed ten years before. Old pitmen are very generally supported in whole or in part by their grown-up families—a filial duty, the performance of which is far more common in the mining than in the manufacturing districts.

The amusements of the pit population are, as might be expected, somewhat limited. Dog and cock fighting used to be prevalent, but both of these cruel sports are now dying out. The cocks, when pitted against each other, are always armed *secundum artem* with steel spurs, and a few men still rear bull-dogs for fighting purposes. The fights generally took place in slack times, or upon the Saturday following the fortnightly pay Friday. At present the sports most in use are quoit-playing, foot-racing, and bowling. The latter game, as it is understood in Northumberland, and Durham, means simply trundling a ball of stone, iron, or heavy earthenware, along a certain distance, either upon a road or across a moor—the victor being the player whose bowl traverses the space propelled by the fewest number of throws. Foot races are often got up at public-houses, for such stakes as pints of ale. Putters are the usual performers; hewers soon get too stiff in the joints to do much in the running way. A piece of Christmas mummery, now dying out, was formerly much in fashion, and it appears from the descriptions I got of it, to have very much resembled the chimney-sweeps' antics on May-day. The exhibition is called the sword dance, from five of the performers going through evolutions armed with weapons of the kind. The whole party consisted, generally, of about ten persons; of these five were dancers. One was called the "gunner", another the "clothes carrier". The two principal personages were termed "Tommy" and "Bessy", and a performer on the fiddle usually made up the troupe. All were more or less fantastically dressed. "Tommy" and "Bessy" especially, wore masses of fluttering ribbons of the gayest colours. The part of the lady, be it remarked, was always enacted by a man. The functions of the "clothes carrier" are explained by his title—the party proceeding across the country from colliery to colliery, at each of which they donned their masquerading attire, and were made very welcome. After due obeisances had been paid to Tommy and Bessy, the dancers drew their weapons, and proceeded, in peaceful fashion to use them. They capered about, clashing the cold steel, and as it was necessary in some of the evolutions that every man should grasp the end of his partner's blade with one hand while he held his own with the other, the sharp edges were carefully concealed beneath a lashing of rosined cord. Meantime Tommy and Bessy carried round the hat, and at every fresh largesse the report of the gunner's musket saluted the liberality of the donor.

The pitmen are, generally speaking, a decidedly temperate race. Dram-drinking, for instance, is unknown amongst them. Ale is their usual festive beverage; but, except on Saturday nights, they very seldom exceed in it, and often do not touch it. Once a fortnight, however, there is a general *gaudeamus* at the public-houses in or near the colliery village. The men assemble in great sociality at the sign of the "Pit Lad", or the "Davy". Pipes are lit; songs, in the curious patois of the district—which sounds like broad Scotch, ill spoken— are roared in chorus; the strong ale does its duty; and the wives who have come to coax their good men home find themselves on a bootless errand. Unhappily, however, a very frequent termination of the festivities is, or rather was—for the pitman is improving in that respect as in many others—a quarrel, a scuffle, and a battle royal, fought by the whole of the *dramatis personae*. Sometimes the apple of discord appears in the shape of money transactions. At others, squabbles and little jealousies between the women are broached and discussed—the husbands, brothers, and sweethearts taking different sides; and occasionally, says my informant (himself a pitman), they begin to boast of each other's personal prowess. "I'se a better mon than thee'st," one self-satis- fied gentleman will remark to his competitor. A depreciating rejoinder of course follows. "Debate arising", as the journals of the House of Commons say, a general row is in the issue. "Pitmen", remarked my informant, "will fight fair, and mainly with their fists, if they are one to one; but in a general scuffle each will catch up and lay about him with anything handy. I have seen candlesticks, pots, and even chairs flung about; and in one public-house in particular the landlord was obliged to keep the poker chained to the hearth."

It is, however, to be distinctly understood that these descriptions refer to a state of society in rapid process of change for the better. The same remark applies to the superstitions of the mining population. I have had some diffi- culty in getting at even the traditions of fancies which were once generally and devoutly believed by the coal-workers of the North. The old men, I have been frequently told, have still a lingering faith in the legends of the mine; but the young men only laugh at them. The class of superstitions which still maintains some hold is that involved in the belief in omens, token, dreams, and lucky or unlucky occurrences. I have already mentioned that a pitman dislikes meeting a woman when he is going to his work. The walk from home to the pit mouth, often performed in the dead of night, is the period most rife in warnings of some fatal result which the day's labour is to bring forth. A supernatural appearance, of a warning character, was often supposed to cross the miner's path in the shape of a little white animal like a rabbit. In fact, anything moving and white was held to be an omen of impending disaster. Mental as well as visual warnings abounded. The miners had frequent presentiments that some- thing was about to go wrong, and the teachings of the inward monitor were very carefully attended to. The pitmen of the Midland counties have (or had) a belief, unknown in the North, in aerial whistlings ringing through the night air, and warning them not to descend the shaft. Who or what the invisible musicians were, nobody pretended to know. One therefore feels somewhat surprised at their having been enumerated and found to consist of seven, thenceforth designated the "Seven Whistlers". I have only heard of two actual goblins known to haunt the mine. The one is a mischievous elf, whose presence is only indicated by the damaged which he perpetrates. He is called "Cutty Soams", and appears to employ rope-traces or soams by which an assistant putter, honoured by the title of the "foal" is yoked to the tub. The strands of hemp are left all sound in the board at night; in the morning they are found severed in twain. "Cutty Soams has been at work," says the putter dolefully, knotting the injured rope. The second goblin was altogether a more sensible, and, indeed, an honest and hard-working bogle—much akin to the Scotch brownie, or the hairy fiend whom Milton rather scurvily apostrophises as a "lubber". The supernatural personage in question was, in fact, a sort of ghostly putter, and his name was Blue Cap. Sometimes the scared miners would behold a light blue flame, or "low" flicker through the air, and settle down on a full coal tub, which immediately moved towards the rolley-way as though impelled by a stalwart putter. Industrious Blue Cap was at work. But he required, and rightly, to be paid for his services, which he modestly rated as those of an ordinary average putter. Therefore once a fortnight Blue Cap's wages were left for him in a solitary corner of the mine. If they were a farthing below his due, indignant Blue Cap would not pocket a stiver. If they were a farthing over his due, conscientious Blue Cap left the surplus revenue where he found it. I asked my informant whether, if Blue Cap's wages were left out for him nowadays he thought they would be appropriated. He sensibly replied that he had no doubt that they would be pocketed by Blue Cap—or somebody else.

Letter XXII

I have already alluded to a combination among the coal-owners for restricting the amount of coals brought to market, and thereby keeping up the prices. The combination, or, as it was called, "Limitations of the Vend", after having existed at intervals for many years, is now extinct. A practical "Limitation of the Vend" still, however, exists as regards a considerable proportion—more than one-third—of the Durham and Northumberland pits. This restriction, or, as its participators prefer calling it. "Regulation", is the work of the men themselves; and although they will not admit that it is an offshoot of the union, and although it may not exist in all pits connected with the union, it never exists save in such pits. This "Regulation" is a rule among the men themselves not to send up to bank more than a given quantity of coals per day per man. The amount is fixed by each colliery for itself, and the arrangement is always spoken of as perfectly voluntary, and one which any hewer may take part in or not as he pleases. The practical consequences, however, is that the regulation, wherever it is introduced into a pit, speedily becomes all but universal. The proprietors do not sanction the arrangement, but I cannot find that they are very violently opposed to it. The fact is, that it stands them in some respect instead of the old "Limitation of the Vend,'. I have not neglected to make inquiries into the working results of the "Regulation", as well as into the policy of its champions.

The first practical effect of the "Regulation" is of course to curtail, and in some degree equalise, the rate of pitmen's wages. These wages I have generally reckoned as from three shillings and sixpence to four shillings a day, with a free house and garden, and coals at almost a nominal rate. The drawbacks, as I have stated them, may amount to about one shilling and sixpence per week. . . . "Many and many a man", said the hewer to me, and I believe with perfect truth, "is not touched by the restriction at all. He can't come up to it." It would follow that the best men lose by this restriction at the very least ninepence and many of the less skilful more than 4½d. a day. The reasons why they subject themselves to this very serious deduction from wages which they are admittedly capable of earning, were detailed to me by an individual, who, I have good grounds for knowing, possesses the full confidence of the restricting hewers. These reasons were much of the following import: "The restriction is fixed at the limit of what we consider a fair day's work for a man of ordinary powers and endurance, engaged in the toilsome and exhausting labour of hewing. We believe that working men in this country work too long and too hard, and we would like to see the time and the fatigue both abridged. Besides, we think it fair to stand by each other as a body, and not to go on competing the one with the other. We feel assured that if we worked to the utmost that we are capable of, we should suffer severely in health, and perhaps ultimately in wages. We know that there are more men in the trade than are requisite to raise the amount of coals required for the average vend; but by restricting each individual's work, we compel the masters to employ all, or nearly all of us, and thus to bring into operation what, under the competing system, would be the surplus labour. We conceive that this arrangement while it benefits the body of hewers, does not injure the masters, because they are only asked to divide the same amount of wages amongst a greater number of men; the only hardship upon them, and we think it a very slight one is, that there may be the loss of part of the interest of the money laid out upon the machinery, because that machinery does not work every day so long as it was calculated for. But we have also this reason—we think, and so did the masters when they had their limitation of the vend, that this restriction limits the quantity of coals brought to market; and in our opinion, if the quantity be limited, prices will rise, and our wages will—or, at all events, ought to—rise with them. It may be very well to say that if the price of coals rises, so much will not be bought. But we know what we are about; we know that coals must be had. This country could no more go on without coals than without meat. That is our vantage ground. Every steam-engine—in every factory—on every railway—on board every boat and ship—depends upon us, and if we chose to be united we could stop them all. We therefore are of opinion, that, were the restriction universal—and we are trying to make it so—we could not only shorten the hours of our labour, but cause the hours in which we do work to be paid for at a higher rate."

This I believe to be a fair and perfectly uncoloured view of the opinions of an overwhelming proportion of the pitmen—of those of them, at least, who have opinions at all; and this section always leads the remainder, who follow the advice of those of their own class whose abilities they feel to be superior to their own, with the blindest confidence and the most unerring exactitude. . . .
. . . I now pass to a part of the coal system from which springs much bad blood between employers and employed. It is not, as has been already explained, the tendency of the coal-raising trade to create inland towns. Every pit has its village, exclusively inhabited by the people employed in the mine; and almost as a matter of course the dwellings in which they live are erected

by the owner of the works, nobody else having any interest to speculate in the building of cottage-villages. These cottages, as I have also stated, are held not as tenements, but as wages. It follows, that on occasions of strikes the payment of wages and the right to the occupancy of houses cease together. Hence frequently arises a system of evictions which I believe not only to be productive of the worst moral consequences to the people, but to be continually sowing seeds of bitter grudges between them and their employers. The mere act of ceasing to pay wages when men cease to work, has in it something so perfectly and obviously natural, that it involves no idea of hardship; but the turning a man out of his house, particularly when, as must happen in the very nature of things in the coal districts, he has much difficulty in finding another roof to get under—such a proceeding is regarded, by those who suffer from it, and by those who sympathise with them, as harsh, if not tyrannical. They do not readily realise an abstract idea of right—and not only of right but even of necessity, on the coal-owners' part—particularly when all their household goods are overturned by its exercise. A strike followed by an eviction has very recently occurred at a colliery called Kepier Grange, a mile or two to the south of Durham. Hearing that the turnout workpeople were huddled together, principally in the public-houses in the neighbourhood, I proceeded to the spot, and was conducted by several of the hewers to see what they termed the "tender mercies" of the coal-owners. . . .

. . . A great number of the body seemed to be lounging all day in and about the public-houses, smoking and discussing the chances of the strike. The publicans gave them lodging for nothing, charging only for provisions; and those of their poor neighbours who could, appeared very ready to make room for as many as possible. Whilst I was standing at the door of one of the taverns in question, a man went by, escorted by one of the rural police. The hewers told me that he was a tailor, who had taken employment in the pit, and they laughed at the notion of his pseudo-guardian. "If we wished to injure the man," they said, "it wouldn't be a single policeman who could prevent us." . . .

. . . The cases are frequent in which evictions give rise to tumult, and even to bloodshed. On the very day on which I visited Kepier Grange an eviction took place at Charlaw, a colliery, not very far distant. In this case there was also a strike, and the men had had repeated warnings that they would be forced to give up possession of their houses. On the Friday they were told that all those who did not begin work on the Monday following must find other homes. A few complied; the rest remained firm; and a body of police were despatched to carry out the ejectment. Before, however, any steps were actually taken, and while the policemen were in the act of descending from the vehicle in which they arrived, a rush was made at them by the miners, prefaced by a shower of stones—and in the scuffle which followed, a policeman was severely hurt about the head, and one of the attacking party had his skull fractured. This seems to have put an end to active opposition. The people left their houses without resistance, but at night I understand that a good many of them broke through the windows and took possession again. They were to be proceeded against for trespass. . . .

... As I am now approaching the termination of my account of the Durham and Northumberland Coalfield, I may as well devote a paragraph to those miscellaneous facts and morsels of information connected with the subject which from time to time I became acquainted with—frequently after the letters in which they would severally have been most in place had been already despatched.

Hewers are apportioned to different seams, and different parts of seams, by lot; or, as it is technically called, "cavil". The cavil takes place once a quarter. The men's names, written on scraps of paper, are placed in a hat, and the first name drawn settles the place of its owner, and through him the places of his comrades, according to a pre-determined arrangement. It not unfrequently happens, under the present system of monthly hiring, particularly if the demand for hewers is brisk, that a workman who has had a "bad cavil"—that is, a place in a hard or difficult seam—gives his month's warning and betakes himself to another colliery, in the hope of meeting with better luck. That the proceeding is obviously unfair does not prevent it from frequently taking place. In cases of removal, the old plan was for the new master to pay the expenses of the "flitting", but this has been discontinued, and the colliers must now transport their goods and chattels from place to place at their own cost. In a great number of collieries within a reasonable distance of Newcastle, the proprietors send in one or more carts every Saturday, to carry out the marketings of the women, who proceed to town to lay in their stock of groceries, etc. for the ensuing week. The carts put up at some central point in the town. Thither the tradesmen send the purchased goods, which are thence conveyed to the doors of their owners without any expense, other than the pence paid by each family to the driver of the vehicle. In cases of fatal accidents in coal-pits, the widows of the men killed are almost invariably allowed to retain houses rent free in the Pit-row—although if they occupy double tenements, they must often remove to smaller ones. Women placed under these circumstances seldom or never quit the colliery. They set up little huckstering shops, and take in washing. The owners always pay the funeral expenses of men killed in their employment, and make a money present to the surviving relations. One or more benefit societies are in connection with each pit. They grant allowances on their largest scale in cases of accident; on a smaller scale in cases of sickness; and they commonly also afford small superannuation pensions. Generally speaking, some light sort of work about the pit is found for hewers who have grown grey in the service. The fines from "laid out" and "set out" are sometimes set apart by the owners for charitable purposes. But there are cases—the Haswell Coal Pit afforded a recent one—in which the men have absolutely refused the offer of the proprietors to apportion the fines in this way. "If you take them," said the workmen, "you take them unjustly, and you may keep them." The tone occasionally adopted by the pitmen may be judged of by this reply. The small chapels which abound in colliery villages are "served" three Sundays out of every four by "local preachers", themselves working men. These persons proceed from mine to mine agreeably to a regular printed arrangement, a copy of which may be frequently found suspended from the walls of a hewer's cottage. They officiate gratis, generally dining at the table of any zealous member of the congregation. These local preachers exercise the deepest influence over a very large proportion of the coal-mining population. Their sermons are usual couched in the homeliest patois and are very often full of technical allusions and illustrations.

STAFFORDSHIRE

The Collieries

Letter XXIII

. . . The change from the collieries of Northumberland and Durham to those of Staffordshire seems like going back at least a century in the art of mine engineering. On the banks of the Tyne and the Wear, science the most profound, and practical skill the most trained and enlightened, are brought to bear upon the excavation of coal. The pits are worked under the constant superintendence of regularly educated viewers, each of whom has a staff of assistants, of more or less scientific and practical skill, to carry his directions into execution. In the Staffordshire coal district, on the contrary, everything seems to be done by the roughest rule of thumb. The pits, as regards depth, are mere scratches, compared with those in the North; and, except in the case of a few of the thick-seam mines, they are ventilated solely by the agency of the vast number of shafts with which the whole coal-field is honey-combed—and anything like artificial means for creating a current of air being seldom or never thought of. The workings in such excavations are, of course, very limited. The labourers could not breathe at any considerable distance from one of the shafts; and the consequence of the whole system is, that the coal is worked in the slowest, most dangerous, and least economical fashion. . . .

. . . There are scores of coal-pits scattered through the Wolverhampton district, worked without any steam-engine at all, simply by the aid of a rude gin and a blind old horse. This gin is a species of capstan—the cylinder, on which the rope winds, being usually about six feet in diameter. It is strengthened by a rude but massive scaffolding, and the horse is harnessed to a strong circulating bar. A gin is seldom employed to work more than two shafts. The ropes used are common round hempen ones, and each winds in a different direction upon the cylinder. In these small pits there are usually about ten men under ground, and a couple of men and as many women at bank. In no case which I have seen is the shaft furnished with those wooden partitions and guiding spears down which the cages glide so smoothly in the North. The hole has the appearance of a huge well, and the skip has ample room to oscillate as it swings up or down along the greenish slimy brickwork. . . .

. . . The Staffordshire coal miners are almost universally worked upon the "buttie" system. The buttie is a sort of middleman or contractor. Generally speaking, he has been a working man himself, and still preserves the appearance, dress, and style of living of his original condition. The buttie is, in most cases, an entirely uneducated man. He may be, and usually is, a person of practical experience, and often of much natural sagacity; but it frequently happens that he cannot write, and can hardly read—and to this individual the whole working and management of the mine is entrusted. The engine and the machinery belong, in the majority of cases, to the proprietor of the royalty. He pays the buttie a certain sum for every ton of coal extracted, and leaves the mode of working entirely to his agent. The engineman and some few of the people employed above ground are sometimes paid by the proprietor, but all the underground workmen are hired and remunerated by the buttie, who, in fact, is at once a commercial agent and a managing engineer. The buttie has always a foreman called a "doggie", who passes the whole day in the pit, super-intending and aiding in the proceedings of the workpeople. The doggie is paid regular wages, generally either four shillings or four shillings and sixpence per day. The great mass of the workpeople are either "holers" or "bandsmen". The holer answers in some respects to the northern hewer, but the manner of working the seam is different. . . .

. . . The holer is paid by the stint—this stint being the undermining of a certain breadth of coal, differing, of course, with the hardness and difficulty of the seam. The present remuneration for a "stint" is 2s 3d. Many holers are able to work at least a stint and a half a day, and are paid accordingly. The greater number, however, I am assured, do not earn, at the present prices of coal, more than two shillings and sixpence per day. The holer may ascend as soon as he has completed his stint, or he may remain until the termination of the twelve hours, or twelve hours and a half, of daily toil. The holers who can and do earn their two stints a day are, I am informed, exceptions to the general rule. A few years ago, when the coal and iron trades were in a more prosperous condition than they are now, there were great complaints of the self-restrictive system upon which the pitmen worked. In 1847 Mr. Parker, of the Chillington Iron Works, near Wolverhampton, stated that the colliers were then restricting themselves to eight and nine hours daily work for only five days in the week, their wages being, upon the average, 4s. 4½d. per day. He added, that if the men would work twelve hours more per week, the differ-ence would suffice to make up the quantity of coal and iron-stone required, and that three pits out of every twenty might be then closed up. I have said enough, however, in a former letter, to show that this is one of the questions on which the men conceive that their interests, and those of their employers, lie in quite opposite directions. At present, however, the trade is too slack for any-thing like restriction to exist. The men are only overglad to get what labour their employers can afford them. I have made enquiries in many quarters among the working men, and they all tell me that the coal union is extinct in Stafford-shire. "They may get it up again," said one of them, "in the North—but we're people from a great many counties here, and we don't trust each other."

Next in position to the holer comes the bandsman or bondsman. This func-tionary completes the work which his comrade began—breaks down with mallets and hammers, and sometimes blows down with gunpowder, the masses of coal already undermined by the holer—and then piles them upon the skip. In the majority of coal-seams no putter is required. The horse which draws the skips comes close up to the workpeople, and from thence tugs his burden to the bottom of the shaft. In very many pits there is only a single horse below ground. It is in the iron-stone mines, were the seams are often very thin, that putters are necessary. They are always mere boys, and the tubs which they "put" or "pitch" are the small skips called "dans". The bandsman is paid by fixed wages, varying in different pits from four shillings to four shillings and threepence per day. For this he remains underground for twelve hours, descending at six a.m. The holer generally keeps beforehand with his work, so as always to leave the bandsman plenty to do. The boy who drives the horse and attends to him is paid from two shillings to 2s 3d per day; and about the same amount of wages is earned by the hooker-on, a functionary who attaches the skips to the chain at the bottom of the shaft and gives the signal for hoisting.

Upon the bank at the mouth of each shaft there are two or more women, superintended in their operations by a man. It is difficult to conceive anything more utterly or coarsely unfeminine than the aspect of these persons. They are lean, haggard, and grisly creatures—their skins engrained with dirt, which is very often never washed off from Saturday to Saturday—while, as for their ages, the great proportion actually seem to be of any age between 20 and 50. They generally wear men's coats buttoned over their dresses, and squab flattened bonnets, often crowned with a wisp of straw done up in a clout, on which to lay the basketfuls of coals which they often choose to carry upon their heads. These women seldom use spades or shovels in emptying the skips into the waggons. They work amongst the lumps of mineral with their bare hands, and they are altogether, in their persons and their minds, melancholy examples of the effect of rude coarse toil in absolutely unsexing the women who are employed in it. The lowness of the wages paid to these individuals is the chief reason why the butties employ them, since frequent shaft accidents occur through their heedlessness. Their pay is sometimes a shilling, but more frequently they have only 10d or 11d per day, and many of them assured me that sometimes they do not make more than 3s per week. As tolerably long intervals take place between the arrival of the different skips, the banksmen and women are unoccupied for a considerable portion of their time. They then retreat into the "hovel" a wretched hut built of loosely piled stones, furnished with a coarse bench, and in the winter time with a brazier of blazing coals. One of those "hovels" stands by the mouth of very shaft. The boys employed in the Staffordshire coal-pits are not numerous. There are few or no traps for them to attend to, and their principal work consists of waiting upon the men, carrying their picks to be sharpened and put in order, and holding and trimming their candles. The provisions of Lord Ashley's act, so far as regards the ages of boys working in coal-pits, are, I have reason to know, habitually set at defiance in South Staffordshire. In none of Mr. Tremenheere's reports which I have by me is the subject alluded to; but when I have inquired of the people themselves, I have almost uniformly been answered by a laugh at the absurdity of the question. "Not till they're ten years old! Ah, sir, they're in the pits long, long before that." The women have never been in the habit of working underground in this district. . . .
. . . The Staffordshire coal workers, behind their northern brethren in most respects, are especially so in point of cleanliness. The aspect of the beds in the cottages is alone sufficient to prove this. I should be loath to suppose that the statement is true generally—but it was asserted to me by a Northumberland pitman, who had passed many years in Staffordshire and Lancashire, that "he

STAFFORDSHIRE COLLIERS.

Staffordshire Colliers   from *Illustrated London News*, Volume 1, 1842

knew many a holer and bandsman whose legs were never washed since their
mothers washed them". If such things can be, one ceases to wonder at the
terrible ravages of cholera in Wednesbury and Bilston—especially when we
remember the general intemperance of the working-people hereabouts. The
Staffordshire colliers take all their meals, except supper, in the pit. The general
dinner time is one o'clock, and an hour is allowed for the meal. The whole
"pit's company" then assemble at the bottom of the shaft while their wives,
sisters, and daughters, make their way to the bank with the respective dinners.
Each portion is placed in a bowl, tied over with a handkerchief or rag, very
often none of the cleanest, and marked by some peculiar token which guides
each man to his own mess. "Some people," said a woman to me, "will sew a
button on the rag in a particular way; others will pin on a bit of the skirt of a
dress which their husband knowns the pattern on." The men fetch home the
bowls at the end of their day's work. The dinner almost always consists of a
portion of meat, with plenty of bread and potatoes. "My husband's dinner,"
said the wife of a bandsman near Bilston, "is usually half a pound of bread,
half a quartern of potatoes, and a piece of meat—bacon very often—more or
less of that according to how the money is, and sometimes none at all." "Well—
yes—I do generally have meat to dinner," a miner answerd to my inquiries,
"but it's darned seldom I have so much as I could eat on it. Only on Sundays
we does manage a little bit extra." This man showed me his basin, which certainly did contain a rather overwhelming proportion of potatoes. When times
are better than they have recently been, the colliers of Staffordshire live well.
Their pleasures are essentially animal, and it was said to me by a gentleman
who knows the population intimately, that if every man had £5 a week he would
spend it in eating and drinking. In Bilston, says Mr. Mosely, the Government
inspector of schools, the improvidence of the pople may be studies with
advantage in the market-pace. "No other market is supplied with finer poultry,
or, comparatively to the population, in greater abundance; and this is chiefly,
if not entirely, for the consumption of the labouring classes—for the resident
inhabitants not of those classes are few in number. There, sordid and ill-
favoured men may be seen buying on Saturday chickens and ducks and geese,
which they eat for supper, and in some instancs of which I was informed they
drink bottled porter and wine. Yet so little have they beforehand in the world,
that if the works were to stop, they would begin within a fortnight to pawn
the little furniture of their cottages for subsistence or for drink." This extract
applies, perhaps, rather to the iron-workers than to the miners; but to a great
degree I believe it at certain times to be true of both. The supply of poultry in
Bilston market is a fact which I can corroborate, both from inquiry and from
personal observation.

When the dinners of the workpeople are all collected at the mouth of the
shaft, they are placed upon a skip and let down en masse. The women then
fill a basket full of coal, to which each who has a male relation in the pit is
entitled, and they walk off very often with more than twenty pounds weight
a piece upon their heads. Soon after noon the Willenhall, the Bilston, and the
Dudley roads are lined with these women marching uprightly and steadily
under their well-poised burdens. In the northern coal pits the most rigid teetotalism is enforced under ground; but in Staffordshire the butties themselves

find their workpeople in beer. I am bound, however, to say, that, from what I hear of the quality of the liquid, not much danger can be apprehended as likely to accrue from it to the sobriety of the consumers. The beer which the work-people can "command" is, by the custom of the country, that sold at twopence per quart; but they tell me that the buttie very often sends them down stuff which would make them sick to drink. Adults claim an allowance of a quart, and boys of a pint. The liquor is sent down into the pit in huge wooden bottles, each containing several gallons. . . .

. . . And indeed, the vast number of beer-shops which abound throughout the district amply corroborate what I heard as to the immense trade driven by the publicans. In Bilston, there are eleven churches and chapels—several of them very small—and 142 public-houses. In this parish, I may also add, that although there are hundreds of pit-shafts, and although the whole country is hollowed out, there is not a single resident engineer. The butties and the doggies dig and blast away, each after his own fashion.

A more miserable class even than the bankswomen are the poor creatures who come out to pick coal from the rubbish heaps at the pit mouth. Sometimes they are suffered to make their black gleaning in peace—but at other times, perhaps, if the buttie or the doggie happen to be not in the best of humours, they are given in charge, and hurried off to goal for stealing coals. "I go to pick at the pit-heaps," said one poor woman to me. "It's the only way I can get fuel to keep me from starving these cold nights; but I must be very careful, and not go too near the shaft. There were two poor creatures committed to Stafford goal last week for stealing coal, and they were only just picking out a few bits from what the pit people throw away for rubbish." Children are often sent out from Wolverhampton to pick.

There does not seem to be any regular grievance, such as the "laid-out and set-out", rankling in the minds of the Staffordshire coal-workers. Occasionally they summon the butties before the magistrates for stopping part of their wages on account of alleged insufficient work; but the only special hardship which seems to be of a chronic nature is "builtass work". The derivation of the term is curious. Builtass is, or was, an abbey or religious house in Shropshire, which as tradition states, was constructed by the forced labour or *corvee* of the peasantry. The name has been imported into Staffordshire, and "builtass work" there signifies forced labour. Applied to the coal pits, the phrase implies a day or half a day's work periodically imposed by the butties, and for which no wages are paid. The toil consists in clearing the mine of those accumulated masses of rubbish which, were they not periodically got rid of, would seriously impede the working of the pit. This gratis labour, whether or not it be objectionable in principle, hardly appears, however, to be very oppressive in practice.

The Staffordshire miner seems to have little superstitious feeling about him. His strongly-developed animal propensities appear to keep him often in a state of actual mental stagnation. If he dreads anything as ominous, it is the appearance, as he goes to his labour, of that unlucky creature—a black cat. But the only strong and general feeling which approaches to superstition is the uniform abandonment of a mine in which a fatal accident has taken place, until the victim shall have been buried. So long as the corpse is above ground, I am assured that nothing will tempt the survivors to resume their labour. The notion that it is unlucky to meet a woman before descending the shaft has no place here. Indeed, the employment of so many women upon the bank effectually neutralizes any idea of the kind. . . .

The Collieries and the Truck System

Letter XXIV

Defective as are the dwellings occupied by the pitmen in the North, they are 100 per cent superior to the tenements of their brethren in Staffordshire. The coal population in the latter county live, sometimes in poor detached cottages, sometimes in detached rows or clusters of houses, sprinkled here and there amidst the rubbish waste, or along the roads—sometimes in overgrown villages, of each portion of quartier of which a smelting or a forging work forms the nucleus. These villages or small towns are, like the northern pit-rows, only to be paralleled by themselves. The Rev. Mr. Owen, the excellent vicar of Bilston, has felicitously sketched one of three joined, yet still disjointed— crowded, yet scattered—collection of dwellings, describing it as "broken up into thick parenthetical tufts of population in three or four separate faubourgs, baffling the visitor, as he emerges from suburb after suburb, to discover which of them is "the town", till he finds that there is no town in particular, and no suburb above another, but that the suburbs are like their inhabitants all of a class—all of a piece; street after street, and man after man—continual duplicates of each other . . . black red bricks and black red men, equally indebted to the everlasting coal and smoke for their hue and complexions." The majority of the houses belong to small proprietors, and fetch, considering their accommodation and construction, high rents. . . . I have already learned by ample experience never to expect good furniture in ill-constructed and inconvenient houses. The dwellings of the South Staffordshire collier confirm the rule. They exhibit neither the well-stocked cupboards, the well-arranged crockery racks and shelves, and the gaily-painted clocks of the Manchester operatives—nor handsome beds, ample and polished chests of drawers, and burnished teapots and candlesticks of the Northumberland and Durham pitmen. In the dwellings of the poor, the degree of comfort of their occupants may be very fairly gauged by the bed and bed linen. In the South Staffordshire cottages, both are very commonly mean, uncomfortable, dirty, and neglected—of course there are exceptions, but I state my general impressions after having visited scores of pitmen's dwellings. The furniture is of a piece—paltry and huddled. There is seldom or ever a carpet, and the accommodations for cooking are very deficient. In many living-rooms I found washing going on, the place reeking with the peculiar fumes of soap and hot water applied to dirty linen and everything splashed and uncomfortable. I was struck by the almost total absence of newspapers and books—a few dirty tracts, or paltry collections of songs, lying enwreathed with dust on the window sills being the only things literary to be seen. In many of the houses the evidence of slatternliness was just as visible as that of poverty. Dishes lay about unwashed, unswept grates were littered with the grey ashes, and beds were very frequently left unmade, their whity-brown sheets presenting anything but a pleasant spectacle. The ornaments in the South Staffordshire colliers' houses are few and paltry, consisting almost entirely of little earthenware figures, rudely painted, and the meanest description of plates. In the north, there is hardly a pitman's room but is enlivened by the song of canaries and goldfinches. Cage birds are few in South Staffordshire, and when they do exist, their shabby rushed prisons are quite a contrast to the large and elaborately woven wire receptacles which the northern pitmen themselves delight to fashion for their song birds.

Gardens are quite unknown in the coal and iron districts of Staffordshire. Indeed, for mile after mile, nothing green will grow. Here and there an individual has attempted to form a sort of artificial garden, by bringing soil from a distance and lying it upon the coal refuse, but the constant smoke kills every bud and sprout. I have already alluded in general terms to the cracked and dilapidated state of immense numbers of the houses, owing to the continued sinking and shifting of the earth. This is one of the worst features of the district. It makes great numbers of the houses uncomfortable—almost uninhabitable—and not a few absolutely dangerous. A visitor to the western outskirts of Bilston, in the direction of the village of Ettingshall, might well imagine that he gazed upon a tract which had been recently convulsed by an earthquake....

... The mortality in the latter place from cholera considerably exceeded the proportion of deaths at Paris. Out of a population of about 24,000 more than 700 people died in seven weeks. In the neighbouring district of Cosely the mortality was also great. There had been repeated strikes for wages in the collieries around, and the dietary of the people had consequently been so poor as to render them especially liable to the disease. Bilston is almost exclusively inhabited by colliers and iron-workers. Its population is, as I have stated, about 24,000. Out of these I was informed that about 5,000 persons attend the different churches and chapels, while 11,000 never go near them. There are about 4,000 children connected with the various Sunday and day school, and upwards of 400 Sunday-school teachers. Out of 5,000 miners in the neighbourhood, it is calculated that 4,000 never attend any place of worship whatever. The prevalent ignorance is, of course, deplorably gross. "Many butties," says the Rev. Mr. Owen, "come to me to prove wills, often to the extent of thousands of pounds, and in nine cases out of ten they affix their marks." Complaints are very rife in the district of the unwillingness of the colliers to make any sacrifice whatever for the education of their children, or even to send them to school gratis. Mr. Parker, the proprietor of very large iron works in the neighbourhood, once offered to pay twopence a week for any of the children of his workpeople whom their parents would send to school. Out of 1,500 workmen whom he employed, only thirty embraced the offer.... Through Mr. Owen's exertions a series of familiar lectures, suitable to the capacities of the audience, have from time to time, been given, principally by clergymen of the church.... These lectures are attended on the average by about 500 persons; and here, I found, for the first time in the mining districts, the dissenters in a great minority as compared with the church. The clergy of all persuasions, however, work harmoniously together; and, indeed, the field seems amply wide for the labourers. Mr. Owen informed me of the somewhat curious fact, that not one single regular member of the Methodist body at Bilston had died of cholera. This he attributed to the general sober habits of the persons in close communion with and strictly under the discipline of the persuasion in question. The great proportion of deaths at Bilston were amongst the dirtiest and most intemperate of the population. The vast proportion of the town is however, pitiably behind-hand as to sanitary matters. Only about one-third of it is drained, and the sewage of that third flows into an open and filthy brook, which runs through the lower part of Bilston, and on the banks of which more than 100 persons were swept away by the epidemic. Lining this open sewer, for such it is, are groups of small unventilated houses, without back doors, and surrounded by masses of mud and filth. . . .

. . . I have now to direct attention to the great and flagrant social and industrial evil of the truck system. In many portions of the iron and coal district of South Staffordshire the law upon this subject is so habitually and grossly violated as to be all but a dead letter. Employers of all classes and of all the staple trades are, in this respect, equal sinners. I found that the very worst "Tommy shops" in this district are kept, not by the ignorant butties, but by great iron-masters—vast capitalists, who employ men by the hundred—and regularly *mulet* them out of five, six, ten or even more, per cent of their wages by paying these wages in goods—the latter, sometimes, but not always, of inferior quality, and in the case of many articles charged at least 5 per cent above the market price of the country. I have not, indeed, been more startled by any phenomenon in the course of my researches than the constant and daring violation of the Truck Act in Staffordshire and the utter helplessness of the people under the oppression of the Tommy masters. I am told that not a few magistrates are themselves notorious truck store-keepers. Of course their names are not openly displayed over the Tommy-shop door, but the fact is just as well known as if they served behind the counter.

. . . The local press is overawed by the iron-masters. The people fret and chafe under the exaction, but are compelled to submit to it; and thus, by notorious, flagrant, and habitual violation of the law, workpeople, tradespeople, and "honourable" masters are alike made subservient, and alike suffer through the cupidity of men who ignore every consideration save that of profit.

The Potteries

Letter XXIX

. . . The Pottery district is about ten miles long, and two or three broad, running north and south in the valley of the Trent, and consisting mainly of a chain of large villages, or small towns, or perhaps, to speak more correctly, neither villages nor towns in the ordinary acceptation of the terms, but straggling districts more or less built over—the streets here clustering thickly together—there spreading out in long arms, which just extend far enough to connect the main groups of buildings; the intervening patches of country sometimes consisting of pleasant fields and undulating pastures, sometimes chequered with isolated manufactories and detached rows of smoky houses, surrounded by plots of waste ground, heaped with cinders, scoriae, and fragments of broken pots which have not stood the fire—the whole being diversified here and there by those black mounds and grimy buildings which denote that a coal shaft is sunk beneath them.... As for the Pottery towns, there is hardly more distinctive individuality between them than between the plates and saucers of the well-known willow pattern, which they produce in such abundance. In Hanley alone, there is a market-place distinguished by some new and handsome ranges of buildings. But you may wander from township to township, and parish to parish, and still imagine, from the aspect of things around, that you have not moved an hundred yards from your starting point. Everywhere there stretch out labyrinths of small, undistinguished, unpaved streets, the houses generally of two stories in height, and built of smoke-grimed brick. Here you will find a new row of cottages, the uniformity of the walls slightly broken by stone facings; hard by may be a cluster of old-fashioned houses, with lead-latticed windows, and perhaps some attempt to cause ivy to train up the wall. Every few steps bring you in sight of a plain brown-brick chapel—Sion, or Ebenezer, or Bethesda—and, numerous as are the Methodist places of worship, I regret to say that the public-houses are more numerous still. I thought that Bilston and Willenhall, in the southern part of the country, were unsurpassable in this respect; but I have repeatedly seen localities in the Potteries where every fourth or fifth house was a tavern....

... In sketching the outward and obvious peculiarities of the Potteries district, I must not forget the significant number of Old Testament names to be seen on every sign-board. Moseses, Jacobs, Seths, Joshuas, Daniels, and Enochs, meet you at every turn. The same peculiarity of nomenclature will be recognised by any one acquainted with the well-known names of many of the principal Pottery firms, Wesley himself planted his church in the district; and at Shelton, near Handley, is one of the very largest Methodist chapels in the kingdom.

As a whole, the appearance of considerable portions of the Pottery towns, is not very unlike that of the better parts of the iron and coal districts which I have described in the south of the county. The population, however, from the nature of their occupation, look clean and respectable. At meal times, or in the evening, they pour out from the manufactories—men, women, and children— with aprons and sleeves plentifully besprinkled with dashes as of liquid white clay. Here and there, however, you see a symptom of the neighbouring coal-mines, in the appearance of men and boys in coarse besmirched flannel clothing and wooden clogs, with faces and hands like sweeps....

... There is little difference between the species of ware manufactured by the different pottery towns. In all of them all the branches of the art are more or less carried on. Longton, locally called Lane-end was, until lately, to some degree an exception to this rule; the coarser sorts of earthen and stone ware, manufactured in a great degree for the use of hawkers, and sold to them for ready money, having long been almost exclusively produced there; but of late years the finer branches of the trade have been carried on there, as well as the coarser departments. The tone of the population of Lane-end is somewhat behind that of the other pottery towns. The wages of the people are not materially lower, but the strongest local patois, the coarsest and roughest manners, and the lowest and most brutalising amusements, such as dog and cock fighting, still linger in Lane-end to a greater degree, and with a firmer hold, than in the other districts. The locality is also more tinged with colliery population than any other in the Potteries, a circumstance amply sufficient, considering what Staffordshire coal mining and Staffordshire coal-miners are, to account for the phenomenon in question.

Letter XXX

... The possession of house property is much coveted by the better-class of operatives in the Pottery districts. There are several flourishing building societies, and I was gratified to learn that instances were very common of working men living in their own houses. Rows of newly-erected cottages, upon a plan infinitely superior to the old class of houses, are very common in many districts. In some of these the stone facings, well-kept door steps, and smart window blinds, give the streets quite a jaunty appearance. The old and widespread fault of making the entrance door the living-room door is, however, still generally persevered in. Public bakeries are common throughout the Potteries, and are mostly open at fixed hours every day. A great proportion of the bread consumed is home made, and baked at these ovens. The charge for baking is generally one penny a lot—the lot to consist of not more than four quartern loaves. I was told that it was only the most improvident among the working classes who purchased their bread at the baker's. Home-making insures a cheaper and a more unadulterated article.

The water supply of Hanley and the surrounding districts is partly derived from wells, partly from the North Staffordshire Water-works Company, which conducts the water in its pipes from springs welling out in the high moorland ranges near Leck. Stand taps are common in the poorer localities, the charge to each cottage benefiting by them being generally twopence a week. I presume that the inhabitants are not very punctual with their rates; for in several instances, in the course of my wanderings through back courts and unpaved alleys, I found the supply "cut off". In many cases, however, the ingenious defaulters, fertile in expedients, had managed to perforate the leaden pipe, or partially to wrench open the metal lips at the place where the sides of the tube had been crushed together, and so to ensure a small but continuous dribble. In one instance the pipe had either burst or been broken below ground, and so furnished the supply of a small well which came bubbling up, not in the clearest condition, in the centre of a muddy unpaved court. The regular wells seemed to me for the most part forbidding receptacles for mere surface water. Those sunk deeper and provided with pumps yielded a somewhat purer supply. Before leaving the subject of house and street architecture I may be permitted to observe upon the constant recurrence of a phenomenon which I have remarked in many industrial districts of England. In the houses of the worst class—in those the inhabitants of which are obviously at once slatternly and poor—the seldom failing pictorial decoration upon the walls is derived, with significant frequency, from the illustrations of some highwayman novel. In more comfortable dwellings although occupied, perhaps, by individuals of the same nominal rank in the social scale, you may find a stiff family portrait or two—probably a crown or half-crown's worth—from some vagrant artist; or, perchance, there are engravings of some Chartist or Radical leader belonging to the political school of the *pater familias*. But enter the dirty untidy dwelling, where the hearth is unswept, the bed unmade, and everything betokens want and squalor—and almost to a certainty you find, stuck by pins or wafers to the wall, a coarse woodcut showing Claude du Val with his face masked, prancing in a laced coat beneath a gallows, or Dick Turpin, on Black Bess, with a cocked pistol in either hand, clearing the turnpike-gate, on his famous ride to York. . . .

. . . The accusations of improvidence and of a tendency to waste an over proportion of their money upon eating and drinking, which I heard so often urged against the working men in the south of Staffordshire, I find re-echoed and applied to the potters of the north. Upon a point of this sort, all I say must rest on the authority of informants who, living in the district and intimately acquainted with the habits of the people, can base their statements upon far-extended and long-continued observation. A gentleman connected with the Poor-law administration of Stoke observed that in many cases there was "nothing but roasting, and broiling, and frizzling in the houses on the Saturday nights, the Mondays, and the Tuesdays, after which time the families had too often to pinch for it until pay-day came round again". The favourite beverage is ale—the newer and sweeter the better. With the exception of a little cricketing the people are not much in the habit of engaging in manly games. "The public-house is in general," I was told, "the greatest attraction when the day's work is over." The principle supporters of Mechanics' Institutes among the pottery population are the painters and the figure moulders, who may be supposed to belong to a higher class than the ordinary run of workmen; but in North Staffordshire, as almost everywhere else, the institutions in question are practically for the benefit of shopmen and clerks. Dog fighting and cock fighting are both dying out. You see, however, a great number of ferocious-looking bull-terriers still lurking about. In many instances, I was informed, that when a dog or a cock fight is got up, its patrons and supporters are not working men, but individuals moving in a better rank of life. The vigilance of the police, however, has all but suppressed these miserable exhibitions. Very little out-door relief is granted by the Poor-law administrators in the district, except in cases of widows and old and disabled men. Almost all relief to able-bodied persons, given out of doors, is in the form of food, or necessaries. The workhouse test is sometimes put in force, by requiring able-bodied paupers to pick oakum, or break stones within doors all day, and then permitting them to return to their homes with food, or perhaps a trifle of money, at night.

SOUTH WALES—MERTHYR TYDFIL

Letter I

... The approach to the mineral district of South Wales lies on all sides except the north, over richly cultivated flats and fertile slopes; but when you reach the point where the limestone appears, upon which the iron and coal repose as above stated, suddenly the face of the landscape changes—and there rise before you lofty barriers of rocky mountains, nearly destitute of cultivation, whose storm-balanced summits and heather-clad declivities afford sustenance only to the heathcote and a few sheep—all is dreariness and sterility. But the value of every acre of this land is immense. Mr. Moses states, in the book I have referred to, that he "is acquainted with landed property in the mineral basin of South Wales which at the present time is considered to be worth upwards of £100,000, and which could have been purchased fifty years since for less than £1,000". I was myself shown, by Mr. Joseph, of Plymouth works, on the side of the mountain facing the new forge at Duffryn, a small farm of fifty acres, which, as the deeds of conveyance show, was sold in the reign of Charles II for £27; at present the lease of the minerals only, the surface being let separately, brings in upwards of £1,000 a year to the fortunate proprietor. This is but one of several striking instances of the increased value of property which have been pointed out to me....

... It is a happy coincidence, and worthy of remark, that the iron ore, the limestone, and the coal, each being a necessary element in the manufacture of iron, are found together, being raised from the same pits. With these may be enumerated the red sand-stone and peculiar clay from which the fire-bricks are made, for lining the furnaces, no other materials being capable of enduring the intense heat employed without fracture or fusion. It might have been that the ore, like that of copper, was to be found nowhere but at a distance from the fuel necessary for smelting it: in which case, as all our manufacturers repose on our iron and coal, the expense of smelting being greater by the cost of transport than it now is, our productive industry would have been proportionally obstructed, and the national wealth would have been far less than it is at present....

... The town of Merthyr Tydfil is situated amidst lofty mountains at the upper end of a narrow valley where the Morlais unites its waters with the Taff. Extending from Plymouth Works, on the main river, it follows the course of the Taff on the left up to Cyfarthfa; branching off at an intermediate point on the right, it skirts the precipitous valley of the Morlais up to Dowlais. It is a town of modern date; for, though a village known in Welsh history as the scene of the murder of a Christian Princess, Tydfiil, by a party of Saxon pagans about the eighth century, it was not until some eighty years ago, when the attention of an enterprising man named Bacon was directed to the coal and iron mines in this neighbourhood, that it began to enlarge. So light was the value at that time set upon property in this district, that Mr. Bacon obtained a ninety-nine years' lease of a tract eight miles in length and four in breadth, for a reserved rent of £200 per annum. In 1783, after having acquired immense wealth, he disposed of the remainder of his interest in leases, the greatest portion to Mr. Crawshay, the grandfather of the present owner of Cyfartha works, and the remainder to Mr. Hill, whose descendant how holds the Plymouth works. At different periods the works at Dowlais and Pen-y-carran were established, and the town, from time to time, was enlarged, co-extensively with the advance and prosperity of the iron-trade. In 1796, there were in Merthyr, including Dowlais, nine furnaces; at present, there are forty-four. The length of the town, from the turnpike near Plymouth works to the extremity of Dowlais is two miles and a half. The population, at the census at 1841, was 34,977, but is now above 40,000. . . .

. . . Carefully examining every quarter of the town, I found but three pumps and one shallow draw-well, which, being without apparatus for raising water, I conclude was of no service. In Dowlais and Pen-y-darran there are a few "spouts" fed by landsprings, from the mountain above, which afford streams insufficient in quantity and of uncertain supply. To these the women and children resort in crowds, often waiting hours before their turn comes round. In summer, when the drought cuts off the water, the sufferings of the people are very severe; women then wait the night through, in order to get in their turn a pailful of this indispensable element. This, though strange, is literally the fact. This evil is felt the more acutely because the occupation of the colliers and miners is of so filthy a nature that they are compelled to wash themselves all over at their return from their day's work, for which purpose a large quantity of water is, in this large town, daily required. Everywhere great complaints were made to me of the privations and inconvenience this circumstance occasions. One woman said, "My husband earns eleven shillings a week, and I would give one out of it for plenty of water." In the lower town, the supply is scarcely better. A woman in a wretched court informed me that they had to fetch water for domestic purposes from the other side of the Taff, which was done by wading the river, but when there was flood, they had to go round for it by the iron bridge, a distance of a mile. Almost directly afterwards, having wandered to the side of the Taff, I saw girls of from ten to fourteen years of age, wading the river, which reached above their knees, bearing on their heads small barrels, or in their hands large tin jugs, some going to, and others returning from the well which my informant alluded to. This scarcity of water was pointed out to me by the Rev. Mr. Campbell as the most crying grievance the people have to endure; and I am convinced it is. Yet water is abundant in the mountains above, and the traveller who, on his way to the town, passes fine reservoirs kept up apparently regardless of expense, and with extreme care, might suppose that at least the houses, if not the streets, would be well supplied. But the water in these reservoirs, and the copious streams of the rivers Taff and Morlais, are absorbed entirely in the works. The ironmasters have a long-vested and absolute right in them, and the only question affecting them in this particular is whether, knowing the condition of the town, they ought not to have assisted the inhabitants in procuring a supply from a quarter which would not affect their own interests. There is a point in the mountains not far from the town where water might be obtained from a rivulet called Taff Vachan; the ravines below it, which are nevertheless much higher than the town, might at small expense be dammed up so as to form natural reservoirs, from which a supply of pure and good water might be had at a comparatively trifling expense. But in this place the working classes and the poor are almost entirely unrepresented; they are from their circumstances and position utterly helpless as regards the improvement of the town, and although they have the sympathy of the clergy, professional men, and trades-men, amongst whom exists a great degree of public spirit, hitherto nothing has been done. The rest of this evil is to be found in the want of a central authority—a corporation, or at least commissioners under a local act, by whom the administration of the affairs of the town may be conducted. Though coal is to be had for almost nothing, there is not a single public lamp in Merthyr; the consequences as regards crime and public decency in a manufacturing town of forty thousand inhabitants may be well imagined. There exists, indeed, a gas company which supplies the tradesman, and such persons as care to consume gas. Formerly, the town was lit by the Commissioners of Roads from the turnpike funds, but the reduction of the number of toll-gates, which took place at the period of the "Rebecca Riots", so narrowed their income as to necessitate the giving up of the public lights. Since then the town has remained unlit as it is at present.

Letter III

. . . It is a fact well known by the local gentry and tradesmen of Merthyr that domestic servants are eagerly sought as wives by the workmen and miners in this neighbourhood. The reason is obvious. The poor man knows that such women are well trained in the economy of the house; and that, having domestic habits, they will make his home comfortable and happy; whereas, if he marries "a working girl", he takes a wife entirely uninformed in the home duties. Without reasoning upon it, and, perhaps, unable to assign a motive for his choice, he intuitively prefers a domestic servant. But the greater number must, per force, marry females engaged in the works; and the results are too often traceable in the drunkenness and profligacy of the husband, the apathy or wretchedness of the wife, and the premature deaths of neglected children.

Letter V

With a population of 13,000 souls, there is in Aberdare, strange to say, church accommodation provided for no more than 200 persons, and there is not a single free sitting in the parish church. I was struck with the circum-stance that the church, which should form the centre of the town, was at one end of it, and had few houses near it. On inquiring the cause, I was informed that the owners of the glebe land would not grant building leases; by which means the town, which is rapidly enlarging, has extended down the valley instead of surrounding the church, as it otherwise would. The impropriators of the great tithes, and owners of the glebe land, are the Dean and Chapter of Gloucester. The living is a vicarage, the clergyman recieving £10 a year of the vicarial tithes. The clergyman's income is made up of small tithes, Parliamentary grant, and Queen Anne's Bounty, amounting to £180 gross: and the surplice-fees make about £20 more. It has been calculated that the glebe land, if properly turned to account, would bring in £2,500 a year. Three years ago, when the present clergyman, the Rev. John Griffith, was inducted to the living, there was school accommodation for 120 children. Since then, by untiring and highly praiseworthy exertions, he has raised the means for educating 1,000 children. More than once he applied to the Dean and Chapter of Gloucester, as owners of the glebe land and impropriators of the great tithes in this very large and populous parish, for assistance in this behalf; but he never received from them one farthing. His success in other quarters has been remarkable. The parishioners, according to the clergyman's statement, have seconded his exertions in the most cordial spirit.

I visited and inspected the schools. The girls' school is held in a spacious, well-lighted, and airy room. There are 163 girls on the books, varying in age from five to fourteen years. They are taught—in addition to the usual feminine accomplishments of sewing and knitting—reading, writing, arithmetic, and singing. For some time there was no school for the daughters of the middle classes in the town, and the tradesmen's children then attended this school. But that want has since been supplied, and the scholars I saw were the children of the working classes. They were strikingly clean, and neatly dressed and well-behaved. The governess, a very intelligent and superior woman, is from the training-school at Westminster. She is unassisted, though the attendance sometimes amounts to ninety-six scholars. The average, however, is eighty. Two of the girls have passed the "Government Examination" for apprenticeship—and that very creditably; they will be indentured in February. Some of the children are taught singing on Wilhelm's system. The entire school sang for me a little song—the multiplication and addition of money tables in verse—and acquitted themselves extremely well.

From the girls' school I went to that of the boys. The house accommodation of both is temporary; proper school-rooms will soon be ready. There are 124 boys on the books; the average daily attendance being ninety. The boys all belong to the working classes. I found them healthy and strong, comfortably clothed, and looking like true schoolboys, with their slates slung around their necks, and their books in their hands before them. They pay at different rates, from one penny to threepence a week—very few pay the largest sum. They learn reading, writing and arithmetic. The regular course here followed is that recommended by the Committee of the Privy Council for Education, called "Baker's Circle of Knowledge", comprising natural history, and some other of the useful sciences. The boys are drilled daily; they went through their exercises for me with great spirit and exactness. They learn singing—a few of them on Willhelm's method. One master, who has his classes in excellent order, and three monitors, have the management of the school. At present it is inconveniently crowded; but there will be accommodation for 400 boys, in the course of a few months. There will be an equal, if not a greater, extension of the girls' school. It is proper here to add, that in neither of these educational establishments is it compulsory on the children to learn the Church of England Catechism, if the parents object. . . .

Mines and Collieries
A Welsh Coal Pit

Letter IV

There exists in the mines and collieries a system of "middle-men", which requires mention in this place. A man called a "gaffer" undertakes a certain quantity of work at a given price, in the performance of which he employs a number of hands, whom he pays, having generally a profit upon their labour. Sometimes there is a friendly understanding between the gaffer and the men that the former shall contract for the work, dividing the money equally—or at most keeping only a small sum from each, in repayment for the time and trouble experienced in negotiating the undertaking and paying the men. This is an arrangement for mutual convenience, and is therefore unobjectionable. Neither can exception be taken where the work is of such a nature that the masters find it more advantageous to let it by contract—such as sinking pits, driving horse-ways, and the like, where a fixed sum per yard is paid, instead of so much a ton for the material removed. There is something speculative in this kind of work, which ought, therefore, to have a broad margin of profit to compensate for its uncertainty—whilst the men are secured the pay agreed upon almost as safely as if they worked for the principals themselves. But it is in cases where "the gaffer" employs a number of hands in cutting the minerals, that the system is to be deprecated; here there is no occasion whatever for a middleman between the master and the men. Until lately, many "gaffers" were the keepers of public-houses or beer-shops, where they paid their men, and, as a matter of course, the latter there spent much of their earnings in drink. The iron-masters have very properly ordered that in future no "gaffer" shall keep a house of entertainment of such a kind. But the system of payment in public-houses continues, and there still exists, it is to be feared, in too many instances, an understanding between the gaffer and the beer-shop keeper which virtually defeats the good intentions of the iron-masters and owners of collieries, whose desire is to abolish this temptation altogether. The best conducted and most provident of the men complain of this state of things, and wish to see it remedied. They were utterly unaware that by law all such payments are of no effect—that, having once been paid in a public-house, they could compel the repayment of such amount, and that there is a penalty (not exceeding £10 nor under £3) attached to "the payment of any sum in respect of wages for work or labour" which shall be made contrary to the provisions of the statute (5th and 6th Vic., c. 99, secs. 10, 11, and 12). The gaffers deduct threepence from each man for what is termed "getting change" a matter often of some difficulty where a great number of men are to be paid. The offences committed under this act are cognisable by magistrates; and if the law were put into operation, it is quite equal to the suppression of this baneful practice....

MERTHYR AND DOWLAIS

Letter VI

The town of Merthyr is seen to the greatest advantage by night.... Entering the outskirts of the town by the Brecon-road, the extensive works of Cyfarthfa are upon your right hand; on the left, seated in a park backed by plantations, stands Cyfarthfa Castle, the residence of Mr. Crawshay, who is the sole proprietor of these works....*

Wisely endeavouring to improve the intellectual character of his workmen by means of a refined amusement, Mr. Robert Crawshay has established amongst them a brass band, which practises once a week throughout the year. It is entirely composed of workmen. They have the good fortune to be led by a man (one of the roll-turners) who must have had somewhere a superior musical education. I had the pleasure of hearing them play, and was astonished at their proficiency. They number sixteen instruments. I heard them perform the Overtures to Zampa, the Caliph of Bagdad, and Fra Diarolo, Vivi tu, some concerted music from Roberto, Don Giovanni, and Lucia, with a quantity of Waltzes, Polkas, and dance music. The bandmaster had them under excellent control; he everywhere took the time well, and the instruments preserved it, each taking up his lead with spirit and accuracy; in short, I have seldom heard a regimental band more perfect than this handful of workmen, located (far from any place where they might command the benefit of hearing other bands) in the mountains of Wales. When I was informed of the existence of this band, I knew how to account for a circumstance that had puzzled me hearing the boys in Cyfarthfa works whistle the best airs from the most popular operas. The great body of men at these works are extremely proud of their musical performances, and like to boast of them. I have been told it cost Mr. Crawshay great pains and expense to bring this band to its present excellent condition. If so, he now has his reward. Besides, this he has shown what the intellectual capacity of the workman is equal to, and, above all, he has provided a rational and refined amusement for classes whose leisure time would otherwise probably have been less creditably spent than in learning or listening to music. I greatly wish his example were followed at other works. Give a man an instrument to learn or play, and his spare time is employed in a manner equally entertaining and improving, whilst his family benefits by an occupation which, in a great degree, keeps him out of temptation.

Whilst they are respectful to their superiors, and even regard with something like veneration their masters, when the latter come amongst them, the workmen, as a body, have a high spirit, and resent anything which they consider in the light of a meanness. In proof of this I will relate an illustrative story. It appears to have been a long-established practice in Merthyr for the tradesmen to present each regular customer at Christmas with a sufficient quantity of

* This paragraph has been inserted from Letter II.

rice, sago, or groats, with currants and lemon-peel, to make the Christmas pudding. Last year they determined on abandoning the rule, and issued a notice headed "Christmas Boxes", wherein they stated that, whereas the said practice usually occasioned dissatisfaction equally to the party who gave and the party who received the present, and whereas such a custom was "totally opposed to a sound system of doing business", they, the undersigned, (there were two long columns of names) had determined on discontinuing it. Almost immediately on the appearance of this placard, the workmen issued the following remarkable handbill, one of which I obtained.

"OH, DEAR! OH DEAR!! WHAT CAN THE MATTER BE?

"We, the workmen of Merthyr, having our attention drawn to a placard posted in our town, headed "Christmas Boxes", informing the public the intention of our shopkeepers not to give Christmas boxes this year, as usual; we, the workmen, knowing there must be a reason for the same, and, judging from appearance, our shopkeepers must be desperately impoverished, and in many cases poverty leads to crime; therefore, as a preventative is better than a cure, we, the workmen, judge it unsafe to deal with such suspicious characters, and deem it expedient to form a fund, in order to procure our provisions from the cheapest markets, or deal with those whom we can rely on.

"THE WORKMEN".

This was succeeded by a doggerel poem, in seven stanzas, of which also I obtained a copy. This gives me an opportunity of remarking that there is a great disposition for versification amongst the working classes in Wales. Here, in the iron-works, they have an abundance of what I may call "native songs", many of which, in Welsh and English, are in praises of the works and their employers. The poem above referred to commenced and concluded as follows:

"THE POOR'S LAMENT, FOR THEIR CHRISTMAS PUDDING.

"Alas! alas! bad news, indeed,
To all who want their rice and seed,
The news is shocking bad to read
　　About the Christmas Pudding:

For by going down the street one day,
Large bills we saw of great display,
Which appeared unto us for to say,
　　You'll get no Christmas Pudding.

CHORUS
Oh dear! Oh dear! what times are these,
The shopkeepers do as they please,
The poor they're trying for to tease,
　　About a Christmas Pudding.

"Now all good folks advised be,
And mind where you do buy your tea,
And get a Christmas box do you see,
　　Where at the shop you're dealing;

They'll soon come round to beg and pray
Saying, t'was all a joke, do of us buy,
Them don't believe when so they say,
  But mind what you are after".

I have said that the workmen regard their masters, when the latter come amongst them, with something like veneration; I may add, that where the habit of the master is to pass much of his time in the works, this feeling ripens into affection. And it has always been so in the Welsh iron-works. The rejoicings upon every marriage or other festive occasion in the families of such masters are as sincere as they are universal. I cannot forbear relating, as I had it from a gentleman on the spot, the following incident, which perhaps changed the destiny of one of the most influential and important houses in the manufacturing interest of this kingdom. Many years ago, when the Cyfarthfa Works were not the sole property of the Crawshay family, there was a difference amongst the partners, which disgusted Mr. Crawshay, and he proposed retiring from the firm. As this vast concern had been established by the enterprise of a Crawshay, and had ripened to perfection under the superintendence of that family, the men heard this piece of news with great regret. In the meantime, negotiations for the dissolution of the partnership went forward, and Mr. Crawshay, accompanied by his son, the present proprietor of the works, who was then a boy, went down to Cyfarthfa, from which place he had for some time been absent, for the purpose of completing the act by which he was to take his share and retire. The deed was at the counting-house of the works, but not quite ready, the testature clause or something having to be added. Whilst this was being done, Mr. Crawshay entered the works for "a last look at them". He was received everywhere with the accustomed respect, and with a cordiality which seemed increased by the prospect of a severance of the relations that had existed between himself, his family, and the workmen. At length, after eager running to and fro and hasty consultations by the men, a grim old puddler, who had grown grey in the service, left his glowing furnace, approached, and wiping his sweaty face, addressed Mr. Crawshay:

"We have heard, sir," said he, "you are going to leave us."

"I am so, Daniel," said Mr. Crawshay, for well he knew the old man, "but what of that? You'll have others who will be as kind to you, and whom you'll like as well.

"That may be so, sir," rejoined the furnace-man; "but the men can't endure it. A Crawshay came here, and made the works; he did great good here abouts. The people have always been used to a Crawshay, and they can't bear the change. There have been more talk about this amongst the men than you know of."

Many voices assented to this; those who were out of hearing, aware of the prevailing sentiment, divined what was going forward and came flocking round. They begged Mr. Crawshay not to leave them. For a few minutes he was absorbed in thought, then turning to his son he exclaimed:

"By jove, Will, we'll not sign, there is no harm done to any one. All parties are in the same position as before the negotiations. I cannot leave the men."

The news spread instantly through the works, causing great satisfaction; and

Mr. Crawshay, with his son, posted straight to London, where, expecting a suit in equity for a specific performance of the agreement, they at once retained Sir Samuel Romilly. Whether such a suit was instituted I cannot say, but shortly afterwards Mr. Crawshay bought out the other two partners, and became sole proprietor of the works. Such is the story as it was related to me.

The influence of Chartism, which once was great over the population of these hills, as witnessed by the sanguinary conflict at Newport, has not only lessened, but nearly died away in these districts. This statement is supported by the paucity of Chartist works taken by the people. From the account above given of periodicals sold by Mr. Wilkins, emphatically "the workmen's bookseller", the reader will find that, though Mr. Wilkins attends the markets all through the iron-works, and supplies the wants of a population of some 80,000, his sale of the Northern Star is but one dozen copies a week. Itinerant orators and delegates sometimes come amongst them. Even at the period of my visit, when wages were at a low ebb, and they subsisted with difficulty, yet in the iron works all was peaceable, and quiet, and orderly, and there were no indications whatever, of disturbance, though some dissatisfaction existed, as I have heretofore shown, with the cause of the reduction.

Public Health, The Irish, Religion in the Iron-Works

Letter VII

A memorable event in the annals of Merthyr was the visit of the cholera to the town last summer. It was a four months' reign of terror and desolation. Go where you will—but especially amongst the labouring classes and the poor—the people still speak of it as of a heavy trial, and a frightful calamity. Remembering the virulence with which the disease raged at its former visit in 1834, and aware that no substantial improvement had since been effected in the sanitary condition of the place—that the houses and streets were still undrained—that the supply of water was precarious and insufficient—that the roads were one mass of decomposing rubbish—and, in short, that the town, in various other ways, presented a favourable field for pestilence—the parish authorities exerted themselves most strenuously in anticipation of its coming. They built temporary refuges on the surrounding hills; they removed vast heaps of house refuse, which had been accumulating and decaying for years around the dwellings; and they limed, and washed, and purified every stagnant hole and corner, as diligently as activity, backed by competent means, could perform those duties. Nor were the great iron-masters backward or parsimonious in their arrangements to meet the exigencies of the time. They strengthened their medical staffs by the addition of competent assistants, and furthered the endeavours of the parish authorities in removing the augean nuisances which abounded everywhere throughout the town. Scarcely had these preparations been completed ere the cholera came. It broke out on May 25, attained its height in August, and ceased on the last day of September. During those four months it swept away nearly 1,500 out of a population of 40,000 souls. The number of houses in Merthyr and Dowlais is 7,500, while the total of persons attacked was 3,260; so that, assuming that only one person in a house had been smitten by the disease (and the instances were not numerous where there were more, because immediately on a death the medical officers removed the inmates to the temporary refuges on the neighbouring hills)—and excluding the residences of the tradesmen and professional men, whose inmates passed comparatively unscathed—the disease must have visited nearly every other house. The streets were black with funerals, and resounded all day with the hymns sung, according to immemorial usage amongst the Welsh, at the burial of friends and relatives. . . .

. . . At a distance of a mile and a half below Merthyr, and near the New Forge at Dyffryn, Mr. Hill has built 300 cottages, which, with the exception of Mr. Crawshay's new houses at Cyfarthfa-row, are the loftiest, roomiest and best arranged of the workmen's dwellings that I examined in this neighbourhood. They have pumps which supply water, ovens for baking, and covered privies. At the approach of the cholera, ventilators were put in the ceilings, and proper arrangements made for the daily removal of house refuse. Not less than 1,100 of the workmen were living in these houses, of whom only twenty-five died of cholera; whilst of 1,700 workmen, who resided in the ill-ventilated and water-less town of Merthyr, 150 died of that disease. Can anything be more conclu-sive in favour of pure air, abundance of water, and wholesome streets, than the contrasted statement I have here given?

Desirous of learning what attention the great iron-masters paid to the com-forts and interests of the working classes, when the cholera actually prevailed (I have already stated their preparations for it), I inquired of a gentleman, wholly independent and of some standing in the town, with respect to their conduct. His answer in writing is now before me. I give the following in his words:

"Mr. Crawshay organised and kept a staff of house visitors, gave away soup to workmen and the poor, carted away filth, and gave much lime away.

"Mr. Hill was active, and through his principal agent, Mr. Wolridge did much service. His men were visited daily and provided with little necessary comforts. He limed the bottom of the town, where his men chiefly live, free of expense to the parish.

"The Dowlais Company did all that could be done, but the previous condi-tion of Merthyr was too bad to admit of great benefit. They charged the parish for lime and cleansing to the extent of nearly two hundred pence, although one-third of the houses in Dowlais are their own.

"Thompson and Co., Pen-y-darran, evinced much apathy. Though the disease was awfully fatal at Mount Pleasant, Pen-y-darran, there was here no organisation of visitors or scavengers. They did sprinkle a small quantity of lime, but, in fact, beyond this they did nothing. The men died like rotten sheep. It is true they made advances to the men who were debilitated after cholera, by way of loan, which of course is paid back. They charged the parish for all lime had by the authorities."

The antipathy which the Welsh entertain against the Irish was notably in-creased at this time, from a belief that the latter, whose habits are as filthy as those of the Welsh are cleanly, imported the disease to Merthyr. A Welsh maid-servant in the house of Mr. David James, the chairman of the board of guardians, who was most indefatigable and fearless in attending the sick Welsh, carrying them every comfort which Mrs. James thought needful, could not be prevailed upon to enter the house of an Irishman. The conduct of the people of these two nations, as remarked to me by the clergyman, was equally at variance and remarkable. The Welsh showed strong sympathy for their fellows, and the difficulty was to keep them out of the sick-room; whereas the Irish fled, leaving their relatives to the care of the men-nurses and others engaged by the authorities to give assistance. There were instances where the inmates of an Irish house, on a death occurring, fled, carrying with them the key of the front door; and it was necessary, in order to save breaking in the door, to get out the corpse for interment through the front window.

Ireland is now prostrate, and it seems hard to strike her. But Truth has neither predilections nor antipathies, and recognises no distinction of nations. My duty is to describe the labouring classes and the poor; and the Irish must not be overlooked. What, then, can I say of them? They are laborious, patient, and lighthearted. On the other hand, I have found them here filthy, sensual, crafty, quarrelsome, and brutish in their habits. Their houses are unfurnished, foul, and stinking; their children uncared for—barefoot, ragged, unwashed, and uneducated. And this not from necessity, but from natural habits. They are compelled to segregate in their dwellings for the Welsh will not reside amongst them. They inhabit the lowest and worst quarters of the town. There is in Pen-y-darran, on the high road, an "Irish colony" in which the passer-by may see, through the open doors and in the street, the striking difference that exists between the same class of labourers in the Irish and the Welsh; the houses and children of the former being such as I have just described, whereas the dwellings of the adjoining Welsh are neatly and comfortably furnished and the children clean and warmly clothed. In this quarter of the town I have seen Irish children of six or seven years of age rush to the doors of the houses when the omnibus was passing, stark naked; though the frost was severe, they seemed happy in their nudity, and equally to disregard decency and the sharp-ness of the cold. . . .

. . . . But before quitting the subject I must caution the reader against supposing that because the Irish are naked or in rags, with their houses unfurnished, their children uneducated, and themselves professing poverty, they are necessarily poor, improvident, or intemperate. Many instances of drunkenness and im-providence no doubt are to be found amongst them; but these vices are not so general as to produce the universally low state of domestic life in which I found them. They are content to live in this abject and loathsome condition from two causes, of which the first and most powerful is habit—they have been unaccustomed to a better state, and are content to live as they have always lived before; the second is, that they do not look upon themselves as permanent denizens of the country, but hope to save enough to return in comfort to "Ould Ireland", and settle where their inclination leads them. Often they save and sew up money in their clothes. They resort to various and numer-ous devices to obtain assistance from the parish for their wives and families, whilst they are themselves in full work—in which sometimes they succeed, but more frequently are foiled. Mr. Edward Davies gave me two instances of this kind; and Mr. Roger Williams, the relieving-officer, can probably furnish abundance of others. Only a few days before I visited Merthyr, an Irishman was killed by falling into a coal-pit; he was always thought a poor man, but on stripping the body about sixty sovereigns were found sewn up in his waistcoat. . . .

. . . I now come to the important subject of religion in this densely-populated and interesting district; and, first, of the Established Church. There were, until within the past three years, only two churches, one in Merthyr and another at Dowlais, for the accommodation of 40,000 inhabitants. Here I feel bound, for the sake of the English church, and in order to show the reason, in part, why the Established religion has not kept pace with Dissent in Merthyr, to make some allusion to the dead. The rule du mortuis nil nisi bonum should apply only to private life. A man's public character, be he living or dead, is open to remark. Society may profit as well by bad as by good example; therefore I shall not scruple to state the facts which have retarded the progress of the Church in Merthyr. The late incumbent, Mr. Maber, for the last thirty-two years of his life was non-resident in his parish. During that time he derived an income from it of about £1,000 a year; but he never paid a visit to the parish once only excepted, when he came in a post-chaise (almost as great a curiosity at that time to the townspeople as the sight of their rector), to vote for a church-rate. The consequence, was, that the charge of the parish being confined to curates who were continually changing and had no permanent interest in the place, the congregation fell away almost to the clerk and sexton, and dissent gained what the Church lost. In the meantime the parsonage was allowed to become dilapidated; one half of it had fallen to the ground; the other half, though unsafe was, on Mr. Campbell's appointment to the living, inhabited by a policeman. Having been so grossly neglected, and the population having largely increased, especially in the up-lying district of Dowlais, the parish, on the death of the late incumbent, was divided into two—Merthyr Proper and Dowlais—the latter being endowed with one-fifth of the tithe and glebe. When the present incumbent of Merthyr, Mr. Campbell, took possession of the living in 1844, the whole accommodation in the church was for 860 persons. A subscription had been opened some years before for the erection of an additional church, and considerable sums promised, but difficulties had arisen respecting the plan and other details, and it was not until the March 24, 1846, that the foundation stone was laid. This church, which is an exceedingly handsome Norman structure, built of bluestone faced with free-stone, was consecrated in September, 1847; it contains 1,200 sittings, of which one-half are free and unappropriated for ever. Before the opening of the new church there were four services every Sunday in the parish church; two in the English and two in the Welsh language; the English services being at 11 a.m. and 2 p.m.; those in Welsh at 9 a.m. and at 5 p.m. This distribution of hours was obviously unfair to the Welsh portion of the population, which consists almost entirely of the labouring classes; "The consequence was," says Mr. Campbell, in a communication he addressed to me, "that at my first coming here the Welsh congregation varied from 70 to 100 in the afternoon, and was even less in the morning. My wish then was to devote the parish church entirely to the

Welsh, and the new church to the English congregation; but this was disagreeable to some of the latter, who occupied in the old church large pews, secured to them by faculty—so I consented to meet their wishes so far as to have an English service in the parish church at three o'clock in the afternoon. This service, indeed, was badly attended, but not worse than I had anticipated. On the other hand, the new distribution of services has been attended with the happiest results. Instead of an average congregation of about eighty, there are now nearly 400 communicants, while the evening congregation is only limited to the size of the building. I must, however, add that the zealous labours of two successive curates, Mr. Griffiths and Mr. Rowland, have contributed largely to this result."

About three years ago a district was formed out of this parish, and endowed by the Ecclesiastical Commissioners, under Sir Robert Peel's Act. It is called "the Cyfarthfa District." The number of souls it contained in 1841 was about 6,000, but it has since shared in the general increase of the population of this town. To meet the spiritual wants of this district, a large "school-room", capable of containing some 250 persons, was licensed by the late Bishop of Llandaff, and service is there performed twice on Sunday and once in the course of the week, in Welsh. The populous district of Pen-y-darran, lying between Merthyr and Dowlais, whose inhabitants cannot amount to less than 4,000, is without either church or school, except some insignificant private schools. There is also a rapidly increasing population springing up near Dyffryn, about two miles down the valley (as I have already remarked), which, numbering at present about 1,200, is unprovided with efficient means for the ministrations of the Church. There was, indeed, service performed, by the permission of the proprietor of the works, Mr. Hill, in a small cottage-room, but this is obviously insufficient for the spiritual wants of so thickly peopled a locality. Such is the provision made for the accommodation of a vast and rapidly-increasing population, by the Church of England, in this important district. It well deserves the consideration of all who believe that the moral improvement of the people depends upon the extent of spiritual accommodation provided by the Established Church. I need hardly point out how utterly inadequate are the means at the disposal of the Church to meet the wants of this district. Even now the new church remains unprotected by railing—the committee being incumbered with debts for gas-fittings, and therefore wholly unable to fence in the churchyard. The present net value of the living of Merthyr is about £500 a year, out of which £54 is paid to the treasurer of Queen Anne's Bounty, in repayment of money borrowed for rebuilding the parsonage-house.

The up-lying district of Dowlais next claims attention. With a population of 16,000 souls there is only one church, which affords accommodation for only 400 persons. There are here four services every Sunday; three in English, and one in Welsh. One service is devoted exclusively for the benefit of the soldiers, whose barracks are in Dowlais; this was necessary because there was no room for them at other services. The Rev. J. Jenkins is the present incumbent, and he has one curate to assist him. There is one Welsh service by the bishop's license on Sunday evening, at the girls' school-room, which is, however, not large enough to contain the congregation. The clergyman contemplates arrangements by which there will be service at 11 a.m., at 2 (for the soldiers), at 3 (in Welsh), at 5 (in English), and at 7 (in Welsh). This distribution of service has been rendered necessary by the insufficiency of the school-room to accommodate the Welsh congregation. The Dowlais Iron Company have promised another church. In the course of the week there is an English service on Tuesday evening; and one in Welsh every Wednesday throughout the year. There is, further on Wednesday, a Welsh service at one of the schools. It will be seen by the above that there are eight services every week, and these performed by two clergymen. Besides this, there is not a single evening of the week in which there are not cottage lectures, meetings for prayer, and readings of the Scriptures. I give the following in the words of the Rev. J. Jenkins, the incumbent: "There is not a single locality in South Wales, where church accommodation is more wanted than in this neighbourhood. The feeling of the great mass of the population towards the Church has been, of late, rapidly improving. In proof of this there is the fact of a great increase of communicants. In my church, which accommodates 480 persons, the communicants, English and Welsh, average 350. There was an increase of 200 at the visitation of the cholera, and I am happy to say they all remain steadfast to their faith."

After disgressing to educational matters, we returned to the Church, and discussed the subject of dissent; when he said—"The Church in these mountains, so long as the people have two separate languages, will never prosper unless there are distinct places of worship for each nation. The Welsh are fond of their own language. There is but one spot, Merthyr Old Church, where the Welsh can be said to have a church of their own; but see the result—it is crowded to an overflow."

The promise of the Dowlais Iron Company to build a church where one is urgently needed, will, I hope, not be forgotten. The obligations of the company to their workmen are so heavy, that they can hardly be too liberal in making provision for the spiritual necessities of the town of Dowlais, a full third of which belongs to them.

The labouring classes and the poor amongst the Welsh are decidedly religious; if not actually communicants, they nearly all attend with great regularity some place of worship. They are mostly Dissenters; the cause of this has partly been explained above; at present, I forbear going further into the question, which will more properly arise and be treated when I come to describe the people, their habits and customs, in the counties of the Principality; it is enough here to state the fact that Dissent greatly preponderates. But Merthyr, even whilst a mere village, and before the establishment of the iron-works, was always the abode of Dissent. Here it was that the first dissenting congregation in Wales was formed and established. It was founded by Vavasor Powell, a man of unquenchable zeal, sincere convictions, and great natural eloquence, in the year 1620. This man, famous in the annals of Nonconformity, was not, as his name might lead one to suppose, of purely Welsh extraction—his mother being of the Vavasors of Yorkshire, who settled in Wales. About sixty-four years ago there was, however, only one chapel in this place, which belonged to the Welsh Independents; but the Welsh Baptists preached occasionally about that time at Gwenllwyn, a farm-house in Dowlais. At present there are thirty-three. Some of these structures are of very large dimensions, and are capable of accommodating 1,500 persons. Though they have no pretensions to architectural beauty, their immense roofs form a prominent feature in the view of Merthyr, as seen from the surrounding hills.

I wished to obtain an accurate account of the religious accommodation afforded by the churches and chapels, as well as the educational provision made by them, for the 40,000 inhabitants of this town. I obtained these particulars from the church, and I called on the leading ministers of the three principal sects here, and asked their co-operation which was promised me, but from one minister only—Mr. Fletcher of the English Wesleyans—did I obtain what I required. I have seen a statement which showed that in 1845 there were 6,000 dissenters in Merthyr and Dowlais, and that the places of worship would contain 18,000 persons. Obviously, from the number of chapels and the church accommodation here, both particulars are understated. I give the names of some of the chapels as I find them in a list before me; they are characteristic: Bethel, Zion, Tabernackle, Ebenezer (two), Zoar, Adulham, Bethesda, Siloh (two), Elim, Pennsylvania, Car Salem, Hebron, Bethania, Hermon, Carmel, Tabor; the others bear the name of their locality. The English Wesleyans have two chapels, and the Welsh Wesleyans two; the congregations of the English Wesleyans Society in Merthyr and Dowlais are returned to me at 310—the number of communicants, 270. Beyond this I can give no exact particulars of the numbers of the congregations in these chapels. The English Baptists have one chapel, whilst the Welsh Baptists have not less than eight. The English Independents have one chapel only; the Welsh Independents have ten. The Welsh Calvinistic Methodists have five chapels. The unitarians have two chapels. Besides these there is a Catholic chapel, supported mainly by the Irish; and the Jews have also a place of meeting. Strange as it may appear, after the exposure of the frauds of Joe Smith, there are in and around Merthyr many Mormonites; they call themselves "Latter-day Saints". There has been some emigration of this sect to Nauvoo, their Holy City in America. Regarding the number of chapels as a criterion for judging of the relative extent of each sect in Merthyr and Dowlais, they will take numerical precedence as follows:

1. English and Welsh Independents.
2. English and Welsh Baptists.
3. Welsh Calvinistic Methodists.
4. English and Welsh Wesleyans.
5. Primitive Methodists.
6. Unitarians (The number of Primitive Methodist chapels and of Unitarian chapels is the same, but the congregations of Primitive Methodists being the largest, I have given them precedence).
7. Roman Catholics.
8. Mormonites, or Latter-day Saints.
9. Jews.

I could not learn that the "Plymouth Brethren" have any followers here, a circumstance that, considering the proselytising zeal of that body, somewhat surprised me. There are no Quakers here.

It is impossible to advert to these particulars of the number and variety of dissenting chapels in Merthyr and Dowlais without being struck with the preponderance of Welsh over English services. Taking the instance of the four most popular sects, as stated above, it will be found that twenty-five out of twenty-nine of their meeting-houses the Welsh language alone is used. This is the best and most conclusive argument that can be urged in favour of the adoption of Welsh services, in the Church of England. The general intelligence of the people and their knowledge of the English language are not ripe enough to enable them to appreciate the English service. The practical sagacity of the elders and authorities in the dissenting congregations perceived this; they recognised the predilection of the people for their own vernacular tongue; and saw that, to be efficacious, their system must be accommodated to that circumstance. Many of the preachers are wholly uneducated men—that is to say, their learning extends no further than to simple reading and writing. Some of them—indeed I may say many of them—were, at the outset of life, daily labourers, like the classes whom they now lead. I was told that there are more miners in the dissenting ministry than any other class of workmen. But zeal, earnestness, and energy of character supply the place of educational acquirements with the rude, untutored masses who are here to be worked upon. The preacher who has himself been a labourer knows best the labourer's nature, and adopts the most likely means of affecting and ruling it. There is a world of native eloquence in their sermons; they are, in consonance with the genius of the Welsh language, abundantly figurative; and the preacher himself, unaccustomed to close reasoning, which would indeed be ill adapted for his audience, appeals more to the feelings than the understanding. He affects the heart, which he can touch—and not the head, which is above him, and beyond his reach. The sight of one of these huge meeting-houses during service is memorable. Next to the violent and rude gesticulation of the preacher, as in a sonorous and guttural language he denounces, expostulates, persuades, and comforts, one is struck first with the vast throng of cleanly and well-dressed people that literally fills the chapel, and in the next place with the circumstance that they express sympathy with the sentiments of the discourse or prayer by ejaculations, and sometimes groans. The effect upon a stranger, accustomed to the well-trained congregations of England, where there are no such audible expressions of emotion, is peculiar.

The singing in these chapels is generally very good; in some of them great pains are taken to keep up an educated staff of singers. As I was walking one evening, I saw two girls of about twelve years of age, their arms twined round each other's necks, and singing as they advanced, a Welsh duet to the old-fashioned tune of "In my cottage near a wood". Their voices were clear and equal; the second preserved an interval of a sixth below the first voice, and whenever the laws of harmony (of which, no doubt, they were blissfully ignorant) required a change, it was made with unerring accuracy. I stepped up and asked them where they learnt singing? Unfolding their arms, and ceasing their song, they answered, preserving the Welsh allocation of words, "It was in Chapel Bethesda."

At the time when the cholera raged here, one effect it had was to increase three-fold the number of communicants in the churches and chapels. This had the effect of settling, to one or other of the denominations of Dissenters, many who previously had wandered from sect to sect without any definite or fixed notions on religion. The increase of church communicants in Merthyr during the cholera was 230—that in Dowlais 200—as stated to me by the clergymen.

"Truck" in the Iron-Works and Collieries

Letter X

... A conviction under the Truck Act is very rarely heard of in South Wales. In the absence of any power to examine the parties, the law, as it as present stands, is wholly inoperative. By a colourable and transparent device the intention of the Legislature is effectually defeated, and the evils attendant upon payment of wages in goods are now as rife, as enormous, and pernicious as if the Truck Act had never been passed. It may be well to specify a few instances, which have been communicated to me by the sufferers, of the mischief resulting from the intervention of contractors between the proprietor and the workman. Wherever the truck system prevails there is what is called a "monthly pay"; but this is merely nominal—the men (owing to inability on the part of the contractor to meet his engagements, and the interest he has to make his payments entirely through the shop) frequently going as much as thirteen weeks without the settlement called "a pay". Not unfrequently during this period they receive no more than five shillings in money, and they are compelled—when they want a shilling to pay for the repair of shoes, their "sick club" money, or for anything that cannot be supplied at the shop—to get goods and sell them for half their value amongst their agricultural neighbours, in order to possess themselves of the required amount in cash. The difference in the quality of the provisions furnished at the "tommy shops" and those obtainable at the same price in the neighbouring towns, is from 1d. to $2\frac{1}{2}$d. per pound; and in the same proportion for articles of drapery and the like. Strong in their monopoly and conscious of the utter helplessness of the men, the keepers of the tommy shops treat them haughtily, and sometimes rudely; they must take the goods delivered to them or go without....

... It may reasonably be asked, why do the men endure this state of dependence and slavery? The answer is, they do so under the pressure of necessity. The competition in the labour-market, amongst the iron-works and collieries, is so great and urgent, that men are constrained, by the dread of being out of employment, to put up with these hardships and inconveniences—they have to choose between two evils, and they prefer the least. Some, no doubt, bred in the neighbourhood, and accustomed to the system from their childhood, are less impatient under it than others who elsewhere have experienced the happiness of a sounder state of things. Again, not a few have associations of relationship which they are averse to sever by leaving the neighbourhood where they are located. One man, in reply to my question why he did not push his fortune in another quarter, informed me that, of himself, he should long ago have done so, but his wife, in whose native place they lived, was unwilling to quit her relations. The general effort, however, is to get employment in respectable collieries, or in iron-works where the wages are paid in cash; and, in several of such places, I heard men who had once lived under the truck system, on its being alluded to, speak loudly in condemnation of it, and congratulate themselves on their emancipation from its hardships. . . .

LIVERPOOL

The Liverpool Docks
Their Management and Mismanagement, and Their Influence upon the Social and Moral Condition of the Poor

Letter II

... The docks of Liverpool may be divided into three classes—first, those which are not enclosed with walls; second, those which are enclosed; and third, those which are enclosed with walls and warehouses. ... There is but one dock in the town which is thoroughly enclosed and protected, and in which the cargoes can be at once lifted from the ship's hold into proper warehouses without the expense of cartage to distant parts of the town, and without the risk of fire. That is the Albert Dock, erected on the earnest remonstrances of the merchants, as an experimental one to test the principle, and which was opened by Prince Albert with the usual solemnities of such occasions on March 15, 1845. The Northern Docks are all walled in, but they have no warehouses within the enclosure. Their gates are open all day, and any one may walk in—with business or without business—man, woman, or child. It is true that the police are stationed inside and at the gates to protect property, but, as will hereafter appear, they are not able to prevent frequent if not daily robberies to an enormous amount. The Southern Docks have not even the protection of walls. They are as open as the streets to all comers, although the quays are absolutely incumbered with valuable property, as if to tempt the superabundant and starving population to help themselves. Cotton bales lie in immense heaps upon the quays, where, in defiance of the utmost vigilance of the police, swarms of children prowl about during the day, and the night to abstract it by handfuls, and conceal it amid their rags until they can transfer it to a depraved mother or father, who watches in a dark alley or in the shade of a large warehouse to receive it from them. Sacks of meal, corn, beans, rice and coffee—all equally tempting to dishonest poverty—invite young thieves to learn their unhappy trade at the expense of the merchants of Liverpool and Manchester. The Southern Graving Docks belonging to the corporation are equally open. When ships have been placed upon the stocks to be re-coppered, the young thieves drive a profitable business in picking up the copper nails and the old copper sheathings that are scattered about with no protection but the eyes of a policeman. Cotton picking is, however, the principal source of plunder for the juvenile criminals of Liverpool, and this, together with copper nails and sheathing, old ropes, and other ship-stores, supplies the marine-store dealers with a great amount of property. The evils of this state of things, are well-known to, and keenly felt by, the merchants of Liverpool—not simply as regards the losses sustained by robbery, but as regards the charges imposed upon commerce under a deficient and erroneous warehousing system. . . . With reference to the general question of the burdens upon the commerce of the country, caused not only by these constant robberies, committed by the starving poor, and by warehousemen in situations of trust, but by the expense of cartage to distant parts of the town, the additional rent demanded by private warehousemen, who are uncontrolled in their charges by the trustees of the docks—and also by the additional premium of fire insurance. . . .

. . . The warehouse owners and the carters form a numerous body in the town; the carters alone are supposed to amount to 3,000. All the warehouse owners have votes in the election of the town council, as have also a number of the carters. The whole of their influence is used to prevent the erection of ware-houses connected with the docks. The question has been mooted, in the town council and dock committee, at various times from 1807 to 1837—when, and in subsequent years, the then Dock Committee brought forward plans for dock warehouses, which the town council, under the paramount influence of the warehouse-owners, rejected—until 1841, when the Albert Dock Act was passed. In this Act, which provided for a new dock, to be surrounded with warehouses, the warehouse-owners succeeded in imposing restrictions against building the north and east sections of the Albert Warehouses until two years from the opening of the warehouses on the west and south side of that dock; and clause 58 enacted that "it should not be lawful for said trustees to erect or build, or to adopt any proceedings for enabling them to erect or build, any warehouses (other than those authorised by this act) on any of the present dock quays belonging to them, until the expiration of four years from the comple-tion of the warehouses by this act authorised to be erected or built."

The Prohibition of Fire and Light in the Liverpool Docks

Letter III

. . . The vessels that arrive in this or any other British port may be divided into three classes—foreign vessels, British ships in the foreign and colonial trade and coasters. Foreign vessels maintain their crews all the time they are in port; coasters do so likewise; British ships in the foreign and colonial trade discharge their men on arrival. . . .

. . . In the year 1802 a fire took place in the Goree warehouses, a large and valuable pile of buildings, filled with an immense quantity of property, the whole of which was destroyed. The damage was estimated at £330,000. The fire created very great alarm in Liverpool, and the smouldering ruins emitted smoke and occasional flame for a period of nearly three months. The value of the warehouses destroyed was £44,500; and of the articles consumed, the grain was estimated at £120,000; the sugar at £60,000; the coffee at £8,500; the

cotton at £30,000; and sundries at £60,000. Before the alarm caused by this
conflagration had died away, a flat or lighter from Northwich, in Cheshire,
took fire in the docks. The fire was speedily extinguished, but, although it did
no mischief, it acted upon the minds of the Liverpool people, upon the merchants, upon the fire-insurance offices, and upon the warehouse owners in such
a manner, combined with the still prevalent fear created by the Goree conflagration, as to make all parties yield their assent to a provision introduced into
a subsequent Dock Act, that neither fire nor light should be allowed on board
of any vessel in the docks of Liverpool. This law has now been in operation
for nearly half a century, and most necessarily have affected for good or for
evil a very large number of men. Whatever may be the daily number of sailors
in the port, it may be presumed that it is wholly or partially changed, from
time to time. Perhaps it would not be far wide of the mark if it were admitted
that the maritime population is changed fifteen times in a year, which would
allow a period of three weeks and a half for every vessel to arrive, discharge
her cargo, transact her business, take in a fresh cargo, and depart. This would
make 135,000 as the total amount of the maritime population periodically
entering and leaving Liverpool in the course of a twelve-month. As many of
these appear in the town several times in a year, no possible estimate can be
formed of the exact number of individuals. We may safely infer, however, that
the number, whatever it may be, is very considerable, and that about one-half
are engaged in the coasting trade, or belong to foreign ships frequenting the
port. It was in the interest of this large body of men, who cannot cook on
board of their ships for want of fire, nor remain in them in the evening for
want of light, and who will not sleep on board without fire and light, while
they have money to pay for a lodging, reputable or disreputable, on shore,
that, in consequence of representations made to me by aggrieved parties, I
instituted an inquiry into the practical operation of the law prohibiting fire and
light. The regulation is, it seems, peculiar to Liverpool. Fires and lights are
permitted on board of vessels in the docks in London, up to a certain hour of
the evening, when it is time for the men to go to their berths. Fire and light
are also permitted on board in every other British, and in every European and
American port, as far as I could learn. It is only at Liverpool, that the sailor
is driven on shore to save himself from the discomfort and hardship of cold
and darkness. The society into which he is led will appear from the evidence
collected. . . .

. . . Among those who made statements were several American captains engaged in the American trade; the captains and mariners of coasting vessels;
and many flatmen or lightermen from Wales, Cheshire, and the inland counties
who frequent the port.

The first, an American captain, sailing with American and partially with
British crews, gave the results of his experience, as an apprentice, a mate, and
a commander, in the following terms:

"I have been in the trade between Liverpool and Philadelphia for twenty-
two years; for nearly twenty of which I have commanded a vessel. I have
regularly made six passages per annum across the Atlantic, ever since the year
1828. I have only missed one voyage during all that time. Previous to coming
as a master, I came as a boy and mate for two years. As a boy, I was compelled

to live on board in Liverpool, and sleep in the forecastle without fire or light, exposed to damp and wet. In the winter time, about six o'clock in the evening, myself and the other apprentices left the ship to get our tea or supper at a boarding-house. After tea, as we had no place to stay at, and as we did not choose to return on board to the dark and cold forecastle, we sallied out in search of adventures, and often found ourselves in very disreputable places, that I do not at present care to think of. They were as bad as bad could be. If I had been addicted to liquor, which fortunately I was not, I should have been ruined as a seaman before I became a mate. As it was, I did myself no good; and whatever harm I then imbibed, I can attribute to nothing else than to the denial by the Liverpool dock authorities of those absolutely essential articles to the comfort both of boy and man—I mean fire and light. On my return to Philadelphia I was enabled to sleep on board ship if I pleased, or go home. I had no inducement to go into any kind of bad company. As a mate, I frequented Liverpool for about eighteen months. My experience was of the same kind as when a boy—or, if anything, worse; for, having a little money to spend, I was led to spend it in public-houses, and still more improper places. I don't think I would have done so if I could have had light and warmth on board ship. I have often preferred to remain on shore till two or half-past two in the morning, even when the ship had to sail the next day, such a dread had I of going into a cold, damp berth without a light. Out of all the mates that I knew at that time—and they were a good many—only two ever became captains of ships in the Liverpool trade. They were all spoiled by the temptations and dissipations into which they were led on shore. They were positively ruined in health, character, and prospects. . . . Liverpool is notorious for the depravity of the population, male and female, that make it their business to prey upon the sailor. . . . It used to be, and I believe is still, the practice in Liverpool, to 'skin' the sailors—that is for prostitutes to rob them of their clothes, and send them out into the streets in a state of nudity. The sailors often come on board in the morning, after having been out all night, with nothing on but their drawers and shirts. I have known cases where they have been left without even their drawers, having been robbed of all their money and every article of clothing but their shirts. In one instance, I saw a man who was robbed of everything—shirt and all—and who on finding out his deplorable plight in the morning, seized hold of a sheet, tied the ends round his neck, wrapped it round his limbs in the fashion as I should suppose, of an ancient Roman toga, and in this trim ran through the streets to the docks. A mob followed at his heels, shouting and hooting, and pelting him with mud and filth all the way to his ship. As he ran the gauntlet down the street, the sheet was of very little use to cover him—he might almost as well have been without it. There were hundreds of people after him, men and women, boys and girls, shouting and yelling in the most fearful manner. . . ."

The next evidence is that of a captain of a New York liner, delivered in presence of five other captains, four of them American and one English, who severally agreed in the general truth of his statements, and confirmed it in all essential particulars by the result of their own experience. This gentleman, I should add, has taken an active part in urging upon the dock committee the justice as well as expediency of a change. He said: "I am the captain of a ship trading between New York and Liverpool, and have been in the trade, more or less, for twenty years, and regularly for the last three years. All the captains that I know dread coming to Liverpool, and would never come if they could help it. I commanded a packet from New York to London for four years. In London there is no law forbidding the use of fire and lights on board ships in the docks. The consequence is, that the captains and crews of foreign ships live on board, with all the comforts about them to which they are accustomed at sea, and which they can procure at almost every port in the world except Liverpool. In London, by this system, the captain has the complete control of his crew: they pass the night on board, and are not led away into drinking shops, and low lodging houses, and dancing shops, with prostitutes and other bad characters. The captain of a New York packet, on arriving with a crew in London, can keep the whole of his men till he sails again, and can save from £10 to £15 a week by the difference of price between feeding and lodging them on board and feeding and lodging them on shore. . . . On arriving at Liverpool we generally lose two-thirds of our crew before we have been three days in port. I find it utterly impossible to attempt to keep the men on board at night without either fire or light. It is also an evil to be compelled to send them to and fro between the ship and their boarding-houses, two or three times a day. To get to the boarding-houses they are obliged to pass through the most profligate and disreputable parts of the town. Both in going and coming to their vessels they are waylaid by gangs of prostitutes and other bad characters; and sailors are not very well able to resist such temptation. . . . In many instances they have not only spent all their money in ginshops and brothels, or been robbed, but they have pawned the last article of clothing they possessed to provide funds. Every captain knows that a sailor at sea without proper clothes, is of very little use. Indeed I can't say that he is of any use at all. He goes about the decks half dead, and is fit for nothing. Not unfrequently there is but one pea-packet and a pair of mittens among a watch of fifteen or twenty men, which passes from one to the other as the wheel is relieved. . . ."

. . . An English captain, who had formerly commanded a ship in the coasting trade, and who is now engaged in connection with the Bethel Union, a society established for the spiritual instruction of seamen, made the following statement as the result of his experience, both as boy and man:

"About seventeen years ago, when I was an apprentice on board a ship coming to the port of Liverpool, we generally arrived in the depth of winter. It was so uncomfortable in the ship's forecastle, that we generally made up our minds to have lights, although we well knew that we should get into trouble if we were found out. None of the crew slept on board, except the apprentices. The lights were of very little use without fires, but they were better than total darkness. If we heard anyone on deck we put our candles into buckets of water. Frequently on account of the cold and the dampness of our beds, we determined to go ashore, although by the captain's orders we were forbidden to do so. It was a treat to set sight of a fire, at a dancing shop or public-house. Then the lads would go from the public-house to worse places, where they were frequently robbed of all they possessed by prostitutes. I have known cases where they have returned not only without a farthing of money, but without their coat, waistcoat, trowsers, shoes, or hat—with nothing, in fact, but their shirt and drawers. On two occasions the mate of our ship came on board in this state. The first time he lost, besides his money and a great portion of his clothes, a valuable watch, and the second time he had literally nothing whatever left him but his shirt. . . . I have discharged and loaded in the St. Katherine's Dock, London, and in the London Dock, and have remained there for a month at a time, without ever having been out of my ship to sleep, nor the sailors and apprentices either. We were allowed to have lights and fires on board till eight or nine in the evening, which made us very comfortable. The boys could then read and improve themselves in the study of navigation. One boy would read aloud while the others mended their clothes. Nothing of this kind can take place at Liverpool; but instead of that is the grog-shop and the brothel. It was in the port of London, when a boy, that I studied mathematics and obtained a knowledge of navigation, and I am quite certain that if I had always traded to Liverpool I should have had no such opportunity, and should not have become a captain, or what I am now. My education in London fitted me for my business; my education in Liverpool would have ruined me body and soul. I have known several captains of coasting vessels, who before they frequented the port of Liverpool were considered sober moral characters and good seamen; but who as soon as they arrived in Liverpool and were driven out of their ships in the cold winter nights, by the denial of fire and light, took to the public-house, and ruined themselves. . . ."

The Tailors, the Slop Trade, and the Sweating System

Letter VII

. . . The tailors of Liverpool allege that the trade is even in a worse condition in their town than it is in the metropolis. However this may be, I am convinced, from the inquiries I have made among both employers and employed, and from the visits I have paid to the slop-workers at their own homes, that nothing can well be more deplorable than the condition to which these hard-working men and their families have been reduced in Liverpool. Before giving the detailed results of my inquiries amongst them, it will facilitate the reader's comprehension of the subject if I present a short history of the trade as it existed when the men were generally in the receipt of earnings sufficient for the support of their families, and when the work was carried on exclusivly in the workshops of their employers. The object of the operatives who have stirred in the matter at the present time is to restore the trade to this condition.

The following information relative to this subject extends as far back as the year 1792, and was derived from an aged tailor, who was for nearly fifty years in the trade, but who has been for six or seven years engaged in the business of a furniture broker. Prior to the year 1792 the trade was solely carried on by respectable master tailors, who had regularly served their apprenticeship. The business of the woollen drapers was entirely distinct. All the journeymen worked on the premises of their employers, and no journeyman was allowed to work in any shop who had not served his full time. This was a rule of the trade, observed both by masters and by men. The wages at that period were sixteen shillings a week, and the hours of work were from six in the morning till seven in the evening, allowing an hour for dinner. All kinds of work were then done on the premises, including sailors' work, and such work as now goes under the name of slop-work. No women were employed in any portion of the business. The number of journeymen in the town was computed at between 200 and 280. In the year 1792 a man commenced business both as a tailor and as a draper; others, followed the example who had not served their apprenticeship. The old master tailors felt aggrieved at this innovation, and insisted that the trades of the tailor and the draper should be kept separate. After this display of some angry feeling, they combined with some of the journeymen to prevent the operatives from working for any man who had not regularly served his time to the business. The drapers suffered so much inconvenience in consequence that a few of them, on behalf of the rest, commenced proceedings against certain master tailors for a conspiracy to injure them. The case came on for trial at the Lancaster assizes, and excited much interest in the trade. The drapers gained the victory, and the business of tailoring was thus thrown open. Shortly afterwards, from 1797 to 1798, the journeymen tailors struck for an advance of wages, and claimed three shillings a day as a fair reward for their labour, alleging as their principal justification that the rise in the prices of provisions was so great that they could not live upon their former wages. The contest did not last long. The drapers, of whom there were by this time a considerable number in the town, consented to the advance demanded by the men. The regular master tailors speedily followed their example. As provisions advanced in price, the men continued to demand more wages. In 1801 the price of flour was sixpence per pound, and gradually wages rose from thirteen shillings to twenty-one shillings a week. About this time, slop-shops for the supply of seamen's clothes began to be established, but the slop-shops had all their work done upon the premises, and the system was introduced of working by the piece, instead of by the day. There existed at this time a society of tailors, for the protection of the trade, and for the purposes of a sick and burial club. This society gave its sanction to the new arrangement as regarded piece work, because a number of old and infirm journeymen were likely to become burthensome to its funds, unless this permission were accorded. The Society of Tailors, therefore, made the first great step towards breaking up the old system, for they not only sanctioned piece-work in the slop-shops, but they allowed the old members of the trade to take the work home and to employ the female members of their families. Slop-work at this time was wholly confined to the clothing of sailors. The ultimate result of this change was to bring a number of women into competition with men, especially in waistcoat making.

In 1805 there was another strike for an advance of wages, from twenty-one shillings to twenty-four shillings a week; and as the drapers, notwithstanding the result of the trial in their favour, still dreaded the effects of another combination against them, they were generally well disposed to buy off such opposition, by agreeing to the terms of the journeymen. In all the strikes at this time the drapers invariably gave in first, and the old master tailors were compelled to follow. This contest was no exception, and the men obtained the twenty-four shillings. In the year 1806 a society, called the "Blue Last", after the name of the tavern at which its members assembled, was formed for the purpose of more generally establishing the "piece-work" system. The men appear to have been dissatisfied with their weekly wages, and to have imagined that the more industrious and more rapid workers could earn more money if paid by the piece. Some of them also took work home from the shops, and thus made another innovation upon the ancient system, that all work should be done on the premises of the employer, except the work allowed to be taken home as a special privilege by aged members of the trade. The number of men in this society was between sixty and eighty. They were looked upon with much ill-will by the rest of the trade, avoided as much as possible both in public and private, and called "Dungs". From this time up to the year 1808, the slop system in sailors' clothes were extensively carried on, and the women who had been engaged in making sailors' waistcoats applied to the drapers, and obtained waistcoats to make in the general trade. This gave much offence to the regular journeymen, and in that year a general strike took place against all drapers and master tailors who employed in the business any women except the wives and daughters of regular journeymen, who had served their apprenticeship. The contest was not a long or severe one, as the principal masters alleged that there was too much reason in the demand to justify them in resisting it. The next strike took place in April, 1810, when the number of journeymen in connection with the Tailors' Society, or Union, was upwards of 400. Their demand was for twenty-seven shillings a week wages, and the prohibition of all out-door work whatsoever. The strike did not last above three or four days, when the masters gave in. In November of the same year, in consequence of the death of one of the Royal Family, the operative tailors claimed a privilege peculiar to their trade, which was, that they should have double wages during the whole time of public mourning. The masters resisted, and the men struck. After they had been out a fortnight, a proposition for a compromise was made by the masters, that the operatives should have their double wages, but only when engaged upon black clothes, and not when making coloured garments. The journeymen agreed without demure to these terms, and returned to their work. The price of flour at this time was threepence per pound, and of butcher's meat from eightpence to ninepence per pound. In 1812 another contest took place between the old master tailors and the drapers, in consequence of a second combination by the former. The operatives only supported the master tailors to a limited extent, as the drapers were generally, if not always, the first to agree to any advance of wages, and had consequently made themselves popular. Another trial for conspiracy or combination was the result, and, as in the former case, the old master tailors were defeated. At this time the London system of "three books" was introduced. The object of this system was to classify the workmen according to their standing and abilities. The qualification for a "first-book" operative was a two-year residence in the town, without fault having been found with his work by his employer; for the "second book" one year's residence, without fault found with his work. Town apprentices were admitted to this book. The "third book" included all strangers, and every other description of tailor, good, bad, and indifferent. The men in the first book had the first chance of work, those in the second were only employed when those on the first book were provided for, and the third came last. The wages of all these operatives were the same—namely, twenty-seven shillings a week. Things, went on smoothly enough in the trade until April, 1813, during the American war, when the men once more struck for three shillings a day wages, or thirty shillings a week, in consequence, as they stated, of the high price of provisions—flour of an inferior quality selling at one shilling for two pounds, or two pounds eight ounces, and butcher's meat ranging from ninepence to tenpence per pound. The men remained out for nine weeks—but the masters were enabled to resist them, by the aid of the "Dungs" and others who took work home, and by sending their work to other towns to be made. The men at last gave in—the masters not having yielded in the slightest degree. In May 1814, the men once more demanded an increase of wages to thirty shillings a week, and obtained their request without a strike. In consequence of the great stagnation of trade, and the general distress that prevailed in 1818, large numbers of tailors were glad to accept work in constructing the "Princes Dock". The distress continuing, the unemployed tailors formed themselves into a society to offer their services to the trade at the reduced wages of twenty-four shillings a week. The masters, however, did not approve of this movement. They seem to have imagined that if so large a reduction of wages was made, their customers would expect a corresponding reduction in the price of their goods. Ultimately, an arrangement was entered into, fixing the rate of wages of twenty-seven shillings a week, and leaving the price to the consumer unaltered by the change. The members in connection with the Tailors' Society amounted at this time to nearly 600. The price of provisions was high, inferior flour being sold at sixpence per pound and butcher's meat at tenpence.

In the year 1823 there was much ill-feeling and agitation among the tailors in the town—arising out of the following circumstance. A large establishment in the trade took a number of out-door workers, not belonging to the Trade Society, to work upon their premises. They placed them in a separate workshop, apart from their regular journeymen. The Society men were indignant at what they considered an infringement of their rules, and sought every occasion to annoy and insult the "Dungs". Breaches of the peace occurred, and ultimately several of the ringleaders were arrested, tried at the Liverpool Quarter Sessions, and sentenced to three and six months' imprisonment in Kirkdale Gaol. The cost of defending these men was £335, which fell upon the Tailors' Society.

In 1824 wages rose to thirty shillings without a strike; but in 1826 the masters reduced them to twenty-seven shillings. The men struck in January, and held out till April 20, when they gave in, and accepted the twenty-seven shillings per week. The number of men on this strike was 750. It cost the Society £235, independently of the loss of wages. The number of out-door workmen was upwards of 200, amounting with their wives and families, to probably 800. This was the last general strike of the Liverpool tailors; and the out-door system has continued gradually to increase from that time to the present. The regular operative tailors trace the growth of the out-door work, as well as the slop and sweating system, to this strike. It greatly exasperated the employers, who, even after it was concluded continued to give preference of their work to men who had not been engaged in it. The regular operatives have been unorganised and quite powerless since this time. The "Society" gradually fell off in numbers, and finally expired about four years ago. There are still two "benefit" societies for tailors for sickness and burials, but their numbers are very small.

The following statement was made to me by a master tailor and draper, now in business in the town:

"In the year 1818, I first entered a tailor's establishment in Liverpool. I served seven years' apprenticeship, worked a few years as a journeyman, seven years as a master tailor, and about fifteen as a master tailor and draper. From 1818 to about 1827, the trade of the tailor was divided into master tailors and journeymen. Of the master tailors there were three classes. 1. Those who had served an apprenticeship of seven years, who sold cloth and everything appertaining to their business, took the part of foremen-cutters themselves, and inspected their journeymen's work. 2. Those who had served an apprenticeship, acted as their own foremen, and occasionally sat down to assist the journeymen in the making up of the garments. The cloth was generally purchased from the drapers, either by themselves or their clients. 3. Those who had not served an apprenticeship, but had capital sufficient to purchase cloth, and to employ a tailor as foreman-cutter, and others to inspect the work done for them. There has been a great number of this class of masters from time to time, who have had not the least knowledge of the trade, being decayed merchants, pawnbrokers, drapers' assistants, etc. etc.

"Previously to the year 1826 the journeymen tailors were also divided into three classes:

"1. Those who could do a full day's work of the best description, and in the best manner, in twelve hours.

"2. Those who could do a day's work in twelve hours, but inferior in its execution.

"3. Those who could not do twelve hours' work in that time.

"The journeymen had a trade society among themselves, and laws and regulations by which they were governed. The most important of these was the 'house of call', where all who were out of employment assembled three times a day, to answer to their names, and to receive information as to what masters were in want of workmen. If there were any of the first-class men out of employment, they had their option, according to their priority on the roll, of taking the work offered, or of refusing it. Should none of the first-class men be out of employment, the work was given to those of the second class, and so on until it came to the third class. Thus the work was distributed to all our of employment according to their abilities as workmen. And, for the better distribution of the work amongst the unemployment, no man in employment was allowed to work more than twelve hours a day, as long as there was a man upon the roll unemployed. No man, under any pretence was allowed to take a stitch of work home. Should he do so, he was branded as a 'Dung' and fined one guinea. If this sum was not paid, he was expelled from the society. No man was allowed to work under the prices agreed upon between the master and the journeymen, under a similar penalty; nor for any shop which did not employ men from the house of call. Every man worked on the master's premises. The men had a sick club, and made subscriptions among themselves for charitable purposes. The men and masters of every shop had one day of their own, when they dined together in harmony, thus keeping up a kindly feeling between each other, called 'The Tailors' Bean Feast'.

"In the year 1826, a panic took place, which caused a great depression in trade; and, in order to retrench, the master tailors reduced the journeymen's wages from thirty shillings to twenty-seven shillings per week. This caused a strike, which lasted from January 1827, to April of the same year. The combination of the workmen was so strong, that it was impossible for the masters to get their work done without sending for men from other places. A number of runaway apprentices and unskilful workmen who could get employment under no other circumstances were introduced into the town from Ireland and elsewhere. They were placed under the superintendence of some skilful workmen, who were employed at good wages, to examine their work. As it was not considered safe to employ these men at the workshop of the master, on account of the insults and assaults to which they might be subjected, they were taken to some private dwelling-house, where they could not be found out and enticed away by the workmen belonging to the strike. As many of them received good wages during this time, they were willing to be huddled together like pigs, and to work night and day to complete their work. When the strike ended, unskilful tailors could find no employment, and those who had superintended them during the strike lost their occupation. In order to get employment the best way they could, many offered the masters a still further reduction of wages if the work should be given to them out of doors. Many masters were tempted by this, and those men employed unskilful tailors at still lower rates than were paid to themselves, and worked them longer hours per day. It was thus they acquired the name of 'Sweaters'.

"The Sweaters may be arranged in three or four classes:

"1. Sweaters for the public. These are men who cut and make up clothes and find the sewing materials, charging only journeymen's wages. To enable them to do this, they employ women and boys to assist them at less than one-half the general wages.

"2. Sweaters for drapers, who are men the drapers keep as customer-hunters, giving them ten shillings, twenty shillings, or thirty shillings, upon all custom they may bring, together with a chance of being recommended to those who may inquire of the draper for a tailor to make up their clothes. These men employ under them persons similar to the first class.

"3. Sweaters for master tailors and drapers, who have the work ready cut and the trimimngs found. They make up the clothes at a less rate than the journeymen's wages, but employ less unskilful hands than the two first classes, though they work them longer.

"4. Sweaters for the ready made and slop shops. These are men who have a small sum of money sufficient to deposit as a guarantee for the work given out to them, and who take the work at about two-thirds less than the standard rate of wages. They employ the surplus labour, working them an average sixteen hours, Sundays included, and that at a rate at which the poor workmen can barely keep body and soul together.

"It is a fact that the ready-made clothes sellers and slop sellers have enough and more money than will pay the wages of all the work given out to these sweaters placed in their hands without interest, as a guarantee for the safe return, etc. of all the goods. Thus the men who are employed by them have to provide money for their own wages. This, as well as the fact of the public paying cash on delivery, enables the ready-made tailors to go into the best market with cash in their hands, and buy at the lowest prices. Thus, and by making an inferior article appear well by an unnecessary quantity of work in the making-up, they are able to display articles by which apparently they get little or no profit, whereas in reality they gain sometimes four times the amount of profit a respectable master tailor gets, whose prices appear higher. If the public would pay cash to all the respectable master tailors who have their work done on the premises, instead of taking twelve months or two years' credit, tailors would be enabled to make a very great reduction in prices, and to give a much superior article for less profit than is taken at any of the ready-made shops. This would tend in a great measure to put an end to the demoralising system of sweating."

The Amusements and Literature of the People

Letter XVI

The attention of the stranger who walks through the streets of Liverpool can scarcely fail to be directed to the great number of placards which invite the public to cheap or free concert-rooms. Of all shapes, sizes, and colours to attract the eye, they cover the walls of the town, and compete with one another in the inducements which they offer to the public to favour with its patronage the houses which they advertise. In some of these establishments a threepenny ticket of admission entitles the visitor to enjoy a musical entertainment, consisting of comic and sentimental songs by male and female singers, and to a glass of ale or porter besides. At other houses no charge is made for admission, the proprietors depending solely upon the sale of their liquors for the payment of their performers. One establishment, which is among the largest of the kind in Liverpool, depends upon the attractions of its tableaux vivans or poses plastiques for carrying away the greater portion of the public patronage. Another relies upon the vocal and mimetic powers of some popular favourite, whom the placards designate as "the laughter-creating son of Momus". A third holds out the superior inducement of "real Ethiopians", and "unrivalled Bones"; a fourth vaunts possession of the services of the "world-renowned Swiss melodist and sentimental vocalist"; while a fifth proclaims that the establishment which issued it is alone enabled to offer, by "an unparalleled expenditure of capital, an unprecedented combination of the highest talent in Europe". These huge placards set forth in large and many-coloured letters the prices of the various liquors supplied, from a twopenny glass of ale or porter to a fourpenny or sixpenny glass of spirits and water. The rooms are situated in all parts of the town, but the greater portion are to be found along the line of the docks and the adjoining streets, and in the densely-peopled district around Williamson-square. This last-mentioned place in full of them. As a preliminary to a decription of the entertainment they provide, the following authentic statement of their numbers will be found interesting. The number of public-houses in the town is no less than 1,480, and of beer-shops 700, or in all 2,180. Taking the population at 350,000, this would be one public-house or beer-shop to every 160 inhaibitants—men, women and children. Taking each family to amount to four persons—there would be one public-house or beer-shop to every forty adult males in Liverpool. But it is chiefly to the concerts held in public-houses that I wish at present to draw the reader's attention. A document which was drawn up by the police, in August 1849, and bearing the signature of the High Constable has been obligingly communicated to me by the authorities of the town. It is entitled "A return of the number of public-houses and beer-houses within the borough of Liverpool in which there are musical entertainments either vocal or instrumental, and of the number of persons employed therein, distinguishing males from females, and of the salaries respectively received by the performers." The number of public-houses devoted to these purposes at that time was thirty-two, and of beer-shops five. The total number of performers employed nightly was 218, of whom 145, including about forty pianoforte players and violinists, were males, and 73 females. The lowest salary was six shillings a week, and the highest £2. Among the salaries were several at nine shillings, twelve shillings, fifteen shillings, eighteen shillings, and £1 per week. The total amount paid was £218 2s. per week, making the average as nearly as possible £1 for each performer. . . .

. . . These concerts are generally well attended by sailors, to whom every night in the week is the same, but on Saturday nights the attendance is more numerous. The mechanics in receipt of their week's wages then make their appearance in the streets, and swarm into the free concerts in all parts of the town. On two consecutive evenings, a Friday and a Saturday, I made a tour of inspection among them. The first I visited is one of the largest concert-rooms in Liverpool. The advertised charge for admission was threepence, but on my tendering that sum to the money-taker at the door, he refused it, and informed me that the charge was sixpence. An explanation was asked and given, from which it appeared that the money-taker decided from the dress of the visitor whether he should pay the greater or the smaller sum. Threepence, he said, was the price to sailors and the working classes only; and sixpence was always charged to gentlemen. "But then," he added, "it comes to the same thing, as the full value of the ticket is returned in drink; and the 'gent' who pays his sixpence has a glass of spirits and water, or a bottle of porter for it; while the working man has no more than a glass of beer for his threepence." The room was large and handsomely decorated. It was also fitted up with a stage at the further end and with moveable scenery as at a theatre. There were about 400 people present. The audience were arranged on benches, in front of small tables, or rather ledges, with just sufficient room before each person to place a bottle and a glass. Men, women, and children were mingled together. A dense cloud of tobacco-smoke filled the room. The greater portion of the auditors were evidently mechanics and labourers, with their families; but there was a considerable number of sailors, British, American and foreign. There was also a large number of young boys, of from fourteen to sixteen years of age, of whom there was scarcely one without a pipe or a cigar in his mouth. The presence of these boys was the most melancholy part of the whole exhibition. Their applause rang loudest throughout the room—their commands to the waiters for drink were more frequent, obstreperous, and rude, than those of other persons—and their whole behaviour was unbecoming and offensive. The performer in possession of the stage was a man dressed from chin to heel in flesh-coloured cotton, fitting tight to the form, to represent nudity. He played the part of Lady Godiva riding through Coventry. In front of him projected the pasteboard figure of a pony's head and behind were seen the posterior quarters of the animal. A long drapery concealed his legs as he skipped about the stage, whilst a pair of stuffed legs to represent the nude limbs of Lady Godiva dangled over the saddle. He sang a comic song—a mixture of the old legend with modern allusions. The whole composition was not only vulgar and stupid, but indecent. He was greeted with loud applause and called upon for an encore. To him succeeded a genteel-looking young woman, who sang a sentimental song with considerable taste and feeling. . . . At the conclusion of the song, I left the place and visited another concert-room of the same kind. This establishment is divided into two separate rooms; the one entitled the "House of Commons" and the other the "House of Lords". The "House of Commons" is open to all comers, male and female; the "House of Lords" where the liquors are sold at a price somewhat in advance is reserved exclusively for the male sex. The Hall of the "House of Commons" was a large room, in which about three hundred persons, sailors and their wives and children, and a number of young lads and girls were assembled. The place was filled with tobacco smoke. The walls were adorned with gigantic full-length portraits of celebrated prize fighters all in boxing attitude, and painted apparently in fresco. As at the previously visited establishment, there was a stage and moveable scenery at the extremity. A man in the traditional stage garb of a sailor sang a nautical song and danced a hornpipe. He was followed by a female performer in the sentimental line, who was twice encored. She was succeeded by a couple, representing a cobbler and his termagant wife. They performed a comic duet, abounding in *double entendres*, which elicited roars of laughter. The performances in the "House of Lords" were of a similar character, the principal difference being the exclusion of women and the superior attire of the guests, who seemed to be composed of clerks, shopmen, and tradesmen.

Shipbuilding and Repairing

Letter XVII

The Mersey, unlike the Tyne, the Clyde, and the Thames, is not noted for ship-building. Liverpool was never a great port for the construction of vessels, although during the last twenty or thirty years it has been one of the greatest ports in the world for their repair. . . .

. . . A small building at the side of the Canning Dock is set apart as a "Regulating-office". At this place the harbourmaster of the port attends every morning at nine o'clock to receive applications for ships that require to go into the docks for repair. The length of the ship and her draught of water are given to the harbourmaster, who then decides when and in what dock she can be accommodated, and what other ships can go in with her. The operative ship-wrights usually gather about this place in large numbers to learn the name of the ship to be repaired, and of the master shipwright who has got the job, in order that they may apply to him or to his foreman for work. As the master shipwright has the use of a public dock for the repairs which he undertakes it is not necessary that he should have a yard of his own, and thus it follows that many men of little or no capital call themselves master shipwrights. They have perhaps a small workshop or forge, where the petty iron-work is done, and a place for the preparation of their pitch. They are commonly called by the men the "pitch-pot masters". It is customary in Liverpool for the merchant or owner of the ship to pay every Saturday to the master shipwright the wages of the men employed in repairing his vessel, so that a very small capital indeed will enable a man to set up in this business. This is the first evil of the system. The men have no respect for, nor confidence in such masters, and, finding that the tendency of the system was to reduce their wages, and that the pitch-pot masters endeavoured to introduce cheap and inefficient labour, and to employ apprentices almost exclusively, they entered into a union, which is the most powerful associated body of working men in the town of Liverpool. They hold their meetings not in a public-house as too many trade unions and friendly societies do, but in rooms of their own, at the north-western end of the town. The "Carpenters" Rooms, as they are called, or "Carpenters Buildings" are well known to all the working classes. At one time the shipwrights of Liverpool, being freemen of the borough, were a political body of some importance, and before the Reform Act had increased the number of voters in the town, they traded upon the franchise to a very considerable extent. Their importance in this respect has almost entirely ceased, and rich merchants are not now ob-served at election times walking down the fashionable streets, arm in arm with the leaders of the operatives, as in the years prior to 1830. The shipwrights form at present a mere Trade union, whose objects are to prevent the employ-ment of strangers; to keep up wages to the present standard of five shillings a day; to maintain a sick and burial club for the benefit of the trade; and to pension superannuated members. . . . They have regulated the employment of apprentices so as not to interfere injuriously with the work and wages of full-grown men, and they have maintained, though not without difficulty the rate of wages at five shillings a day—which is about two shillings a day more than is paid for the services of competent shipwrights in the Clyde, and in the ship-building ports of Wales, Cumberland, and the Channel Islands. The following statement, which was made to me by a member of the union, throws a further light upon the subject:

"The union or society of the shipwrights of Liverpool was formed for the purpose of protecting the labourer. We do not interfere with the apprentices of those who have ship-building yards of their own. The ship-builders keep as many apprentices as they like. Most of the ships built in Liverpool are built by apprentices. We reckon that there are about 600 apprentices in the town. There are also a few strangers, not members of our union. But while the trade allows a master to employ as many apprentices as he chooses in the building of vessels, it will not allow him in the graving docks to employ more than one apprentice to three men. In the graving docks the apprentices receive a man's wages, five shillings a day. That is the rule of the trade. The masters have agreed to it. There has been no strike for twenty-three years. Some of the smaller masters require to be sharply looked after to prevent them from infringing the rules. They often try to put lads on to caulking, to save the expense of employing men. They pay the lads seven to eight shillings a week, and charge the merchant or captain five shillings a day, putting the difference in their own pockets. They will not give the men a chance if they can help it. The union has not been able to regulate the number of apprentices in the yards. In some of the yards there are as many as twelve apprentices to one man. The masters will not give in on this point; and it is not now contested. The shipwrights, as a body, although their wages are considered high, do not earn upon an average eighteen shillings or £1 a week. Very few men can say that they have four days' work in a week the year round. He is considered pretty fortunate who has three-and-a-half days' work in the week....

probable that very few thousands of adults, in the most industrious of our towns, employ in any capacity some .... and obtain the aid of intoxicating liquor. It may further be stated, that .... shops for the .... sale and glass-works as those of the sale of bread, including bread shops .... short by no less than 277.... the .... of butter and bacon ...

BIRMINGHAM

Parochial and Moral Statistics

Letter I

... The present population of the town is not accurately known, but it is estimated on sufficient authority to be about 190,000 for the town, and 230,000 for the borough. Of these numbers at least 30,000 are supposed to be of the poorest class, inhabiting about 2,000 close, ill-built, ill-drained and unwholesome courts, for which Birmingham is as notorious even as Liverpool. ...

... Irish paupers, that are so constant a source of expense and annoyance elsewhere, do not trouble Birmingham, to any great extent. There is no demand within its boundaries as there is in the Liverpool Docks, and in the agricultural districts, for unskilled labour, and for the services of men who only require health and a pair of hands to become useful. In Birmingham a labourer must be skilled to have the slightest chance of obtaining a livelihood. Accordingly it is the mechanic, not the mere labouring man, that is in request, and the horde of Irish vagrants keep aloof. The few Irish who reside in the town are chiefly "navvies", bricklayers' labourers, and dealers in cat and rabbit skins. ...

... The statistics of drunkenness in Birmingham appear to be very high—and in this respect figures do not belie, but confirm the character which large classes of its working mechanics have unfortunately acquired. The workers in metal are proverbially thirsty; and many of the trades which consider their employment unwholesome—such as the gun-barrel grinders, the pearl button turners, and others—are said to drink with the idea that it is necessary to their health and strength. For their supply there are in Birmingham 364 public-houses and houses of entertainment, including hotels, inns, and taverns, in which wine, beer, and spirits are sold. Of these not above fifty or sixty are bona fide places for the accommodation of travellers. There are known to be 661 retail beer-shops, fifty-four wine and spirit merchants, fourteen ale and porter stores; or in all, 1,293 establishments, large and small, for the supply of intoxicating liquors. The total number of houses in the borough is about 43,000; so that in every thirty-three houses one is a wine, beer, or spirit shop, of a higher or lower degree.

If we suppose that each of these 1,293 establishments maintains four persons, either as part of their families or as servants—and the supposition is moderate rather than extravagant—it will follow that 5,172 persons live in this industrious town by the sale of intoxicating drinks—or one in every forty-five of the whole population. This is a larger number than is employed in some of the staple trades of the town. According to the census of 1841 there were but 3,000 button-makers. 1,000 pearl-workers, and 2,400 gun-makers in Birmingham; and as many, if not all of these, included women and children, it is but too probable that very few branches of industry, in the most industrious town in Europe, employ so many persons, young and old, as the sale of intoxicating liquors. It may furthermore be mentioned that the number of shops for the sale of beer and spirits exceeds those for the sale of bread, including hucksters and chandlers' shops, by no less than 422—the number of bakers and hucksters being 871 only.

One principal cause of the intemperance which appears to prevail to so great an extent in Birmingham is said by some employers to be the number of beer shops in the town, which are frequented by young boys. The apprenticeship system is gradually dropping into disuse throughout England. In no part of the country are so many children and young lads employed in manufactures as in Birmingham. The great majority of these boys, from eleven to twelve years of age upwards, work for their own wages, and own no allegiance to their masters or employers after they have left the workshop. The old licensed victuallers or public-house keepers would not allow young lads to frequent their houses. Their customers objected if youths under twenty-one were permitted to smoke and drink in their tap-rooms or parlours, but the beer-shop keepers have no such scruples, and it is no unusual sight to see precocious men of fifteen or sixteen years of age, drinking and smoking, and playing at games of chance in these places, utterly uncontrolled by parental or any other authority, and taking liberties of behaviour in which full-grown men would be ashamed to indulge. It is impossible to walk the streets of Birmingham after seven or eight o'clock at night without being painfully impressed with the fact that the youthful workpeople of the male sex are prematurely depraved; and have all the vices, without the common sense of adults. Perhaps, too, the elder workmen of no town in England more obstinately observe "Saint Monday" than the working men of Birmingham: and it is a common complaint among employers that when trade is good and wages high, they not only keep "Saint Monday", or "shackling day", as some call it, for drinking and pleasure making, but add a Tuesday, and even a Wednesday to the idle days of the week. "From various causes," says the Rev. T. Bowring, in the annual address to the subscribers to the Domestic Mission, "Birmingham is a very drinking town. Some drink because the work is hard, and others because they have no work to do; some because they are flush of money, and some to keep up their spirits when the purse is low. There are some who lose no work, and yet find time for tippling, and others who sot all the day long." The great number of clubs among the working classes of Birmingham are a cause, though by no means a necessary one, of the enormous evil of intemperance. In walking through the streets, and looking at the bills in the public-houses and beer-shop windows, it will be found that scarcely a beer or spirit shop in twenty is without one or more clubs, which meet periodically within it. Many of them are provident and friendly societies, and sick and burial clubs, both of men and women; and those who know any thing of the habits of the working classes of England, may be sure that the members of no club are allowed to meet in such places without being obliged to spend money in drink. . . . Guinea clubs and five-pound clubs are among the most common and the most mischievous of these associations. They are chiefly got up by the landlords of beer-shops. The following is a copy of a printed bill, of which any one who will take the trouble may count scores in a walk of half an hour through the streets of Birmingham:

"A guinea club is held here every Monday evening. Whoever joins the same, or brings a member, will confer a favour on his obedient servant"—(Signed by the landlord).

Each member of these clubs puts in threepence, sixpence, or a shilling, according to numbers or previous arrangement, and the guinea produced is put up for public competition, and purchased by the highest bidder, who not unfrequently pays as much as five shillings out of the twenty-one for the "accommodation". The loan is repaid by weekly instalments, and in three cases out of four is only sought for drinking purposes. The public-house interest in Birmingham is very strong, and boasts of being able, not only to influence parochial and borough affairs, but to return one of the two members to Parliament. But notwithstanding the intemperance which may be alleged against the working classes, it appears from the police returns that the state of crime in Birmingham is not formidable, and that the town bears a worse character for drunkenness than for any other more serious breach of the laws. The principal cause of this absence of gross offences against property is doubtless to be found in the generally prosperous condition of the town, and in the fact, for which Birmingham is noted, of the great numbers of its small master manufacturers—men holding a middle rank between the great manufacturers of other towns and the journeymen operatives who work for wages. It has been said of Birmingham, that its manufacturers leave off business with an amount of capital which the Manchester manufacturer considers barely sufficient to begin the world with. It is generally estimated that there are from 1,900 to 2,000 of these small masters in the town, who live generally in a state of comparative comfort, who husband their originally small resources, live within their means, run no commercial risks, and increase by slow but sure degrees. The journeymen they employ are for the most part in the receipt of good wages. The poorest of these masters are sometimes called "garrett" masters, and either have their little workshops attached to their own dwellings, or hire steam power in the numerous mills that partition off corners of their premises for this purpose. These form a singular and peculiar class in Birmingham, and will be described in connection with the various trades in the future letters of this series.

Sanitary Condition

Letter II

... The courts of Birmingham are chiefly situated in the main streets in the old town and the outlying hamlets. They are built on the model of those at Liverpool, and are generally so narrow at the entrance that two persons cannot enter or issue from them abreast. They are not so greatly overcrowded as at Liverpool, except in one or two districts inhabited by the Irish; but are estimated to contain a population of not less than 50,000 persons. Cellar occupation is almost, if not entirely, unknown. The new courts that have been constructed within the last ten or twelve years, for the occupation of the labouring classes, are so far an improvement upon those of the old model, as to have about double or treble the width of entrance from the street, and to be in all respects more spacious; but even the best of them are narrow and confined. Many of the old courts are unpaved, and in addition to the puddles of rain water and other worse moisture that stagnate in the holes of the soft and broken surface, they are encumbered with ashes, decaying vegetables, and nameless filth. There is often but one privy to a dozen of houses, and very few of the courts are supplied with water, except from a pump in the middle. In one place, called the Club-buildings, and so named, it appears more than a century ago, from its having been erected by a club of working men for their own accommodation, the discomfort, filth and squalor were extreme. The houses or cottages are built on the sides of an open space of sixty or seventy feet square. The under part of each house contains as ashpit, a privy, and a brew-house, the latter being the name given in Birmingham to a washhouse. Above this, entered by a ladder from the outside, is the dwelling, consisting of one room. On passing up the ladder the inhabitant not only smells, but sees the contents of the ashpit and the privy. Some of these cottages are used as workshops during the day.... There was one pump in the middle of this court, and all the water used by the inhabitants, either for domestic or culinary purposes, had to be carried up the outer ladders in pitchers or other utensils. It was painful to witness little girls of eight or nine years of age struggling along the court, and up ladders, with loads of water far too heavy for them to bear. In another place, called Myrtle-row, Green's Village, containing houses or cottages of three rooms, built back to back, there was but one pump for fifty-three dwellings. The pump was at one extremity of the row. There had been a second pump at the other end, but it had rotted away, and the property of these fifty-three dwellings being divided between three owners, who could not agree among themselves, the pump had not been repaired. Two of the owners were willing to contribute to the expense; but the third was obstinate in refusing—and so nothing was done. I could not ascertain the number of people in these fifty-three houses; but the inspector estimated that it could not have been less than from three to four hundred. There were eight women round the pump at the time, waiting for their turn to get water. One of them asked me to smell the water, for "she was sure", she said "that I would not taste it". I looked into her pitcher, and found the water of a greenish colour, and smelling as strongly of gas is if a gas-pipe had burst, and were emitting a stream through it. My hand, after immersion in it, smelt strongly of gas. The woman said that there was not enough even of that "filthy stuff" to wash the house with; and that she was obliged to buy water at a halfpenny a can for drinking purposes. More than a score of women soon gathered round the inspector and myself—all vociferous in their complaints of the "gas water".... In some of the narrow lanes, even more wretched than the courts, known by the name of the "Gullets", and of which there are several in the town, the deficiency of water is even more deplorable, and the deficiency of privies still more disgusting. To one house which we entered a small yard was attached; a ragged and very dirty counterpane was nailed across the corner of it—which being lifted displayed a sort of ash-heap—the only place for the men, women and children of this wretched hovel to retire to for the purpose of nature. When and how, if ever it was cleaned, I could not ascertain, but made my escape from the place as fast as I could. In another house in the same "gullet" a venerable old man and his wife were at work; the man was engaged in planing a deal board, and the wife, at the other side of the room, was making boys' caps of the cheapest kind, at sixpence a dozen. The man complained that often he could not stand to his work, on account of the smells from the neighbouring tenements, and showed the inspector where the foetid moisture from an adjoining cesspool percolated into the room. He said they had no water but such as they bought from the street carriers at a halfpenny a canful. The rent of the place was two shillings and sixpence a week. In a similar place in Digbeth, in a congeries of courts swarming with pigs, children, hens, and lean dogs, where the water from the pump was not impregnated with gas, the supply was quite inadequate even for the culinary wants of the inhabitants, and was too precious to be "wasted" for house-washing, or the necessities of personal cleanliness. The many evil consequences of the impurity of the water supply are too obvious to need recapitulation; but among the equally numerous ill effects of a deficiency, which are not quite so obvious, though very deplorable, are the quarrels and fights that arise among the women while waiting for their turns at the pump. It is trying to the temper of the hard-working poor to be obliged to undergo the extra labour of carrying their supplies of water into their houses, and quarrels that begin under these circumstances are sometimes of the bitterest. These quarrels give the magistrates of Birmingham considerable trouble, and occupy no mean portion of their time to adjudicate upon; and many of the cases of riot and breaches of the peace that swell the annual figures in the elaborate returns of the superintendent of police are traceable to this cause.

The Pearl and Fancy Button and Stud Manufacture

Letter IV

The pearl button manufacture gives employment to about 2,000 people in Birmingham. Of these 1,150 are male adults, and members of the Pearl Button Makers' Union, or Friendly Society. The remainder is estimated to be composed of fifty or sixty men who have not joined the union, and of the boys, women, and girls, who are employed in the operations of filing, polishing, drilling, sorting, and carding the buttons. . . .
. . . The pearl button trade is in a prosperous state at the present time—so prosperous that there is a general complaint of a want of hands to execute the orders that pour into the town. I am informed that there are only three pearl button manufacturers in Great Britain besides those in Birmingham; they have their establishment at Sheffield, and do not employ more than from twelve to twenty men. I am not certain of the correctness of the statement, but it is made on the authority of persons who ought to have the means of knowing. There is also one small pearl button manufacturer in Dublin. Some of the pearl

button manufactories in Birmingham are on a large scale, and employ from 100 to 130 people. One establishment employs upwards of twenty girls in the single operation of carding and sorting. In one establishment of the kind, the men, without solicitation from any parties, but solely from reading the news-papers what was doing elsewhere, organised a committee of their own mem-bers, and procured subscriptions for the proposed monument in Birmingham to the memory of Sir Robert Peel. The sum subscribed was £11. This circum-stance, while it corroborates the statement that trade is good among them at the present time, is highly creditable to their intelligence and public spirit as a body. There are besides these large manufacturers, many small masters who work at their own houses, either by contract for some of the general and Florentine button manufacturers who execute orders for pearl work, or on their own account, buying the shell and selling the buttons at the end of every week to the factors or dealers. These independent operatives are called "garret masters" a name given to the small masters in various other trades in the town. The larger manufacturers and the operatives combine in accusing that portion of them who do not work by contract at the prices of the trade-list, but on chance sale among the factors, of having severely injured the trade by forcing sales at unremunerative rates. I subjoin a statement made upon the subject by a manufacturer, and another statement made by a deputation of operatives—both tending to show the evils which the working classes sometimes bring upon themselves and upon their trade by attempting to carry on business without sufficient capital to enable them to wait for the sale of the article which they produce. The manufacturer said—"There is at present a union of the pearl-workers, which has been established by the mutual consent of masters and men, and which appears to give satisfaction to both. The number of small masters in the trade, men without either capital or credit, was formerly very considerable. There is no great mystery in pearl button making, and a man if he chooses can set up in the business for a few shillings. If a man were of irregular and dissipated habits, and did not like to conform to the rules of a shop, or if he had any dispute with his employer, he would occasionally become 'saucy', and set up for himself. He could hire the necessary tools for four shillings a week, and could purchase from the shell dealers as small a quantity as fourteen pounds of shell, for a few shillings more. Of course, in the shell trade, as in every other, the poor man pays the highest price, and a 'garret master', buying fourteen pounds or twenty-eight pounds of shell, would pay at a rate almost, if not quite, double that which would be paid by the large manu-facturer, who bought several tons at a time, and had his choice of the market, and his discount for ready money. Provided with this shell, the garret master sets to work, and, by the aid perhaps of his wife and children, produces by the end of the week a certain quantity of buttons. Saturday night brings its wants and liabilities, and it becomes imperative for these masters or for nine out of ten of them, to convert the buttons into money. They cannot wait until an order comes for them, and the quantity thus produced is to small in most cases to be worth an order, and consequently they are obliged to make the round of the factors or dealers, and offer them for sale. If it is early in the day they will not sell under a fair price; but the factor, not probably wanting the article at all—or, if he does want it, knowing full well that he can get it at a greatly reduced

BUTTON MAKING, STAMPING, PRESSING AND PUNCHING.

THE BULL RING BIRMINGHAM.

KNIGHTS' CYCLOPÆDIA
OF THE
Industry of all Nations

Button Makers in Birmingham   from Knights' Cyclopaedia of the Industry of all Nations

rate as the hour for closing business draws nigh—refuses to purchase at the fair market price. The garret master has no other resource, and is pretty sure to return before night, and sell his goods for any sum that the factor is pleased to give him. These factors are designated "Slaughtermen". They are generally dealers in shell, so that they manage to make a double profit out of the garret master; in the first place by charging enormously for the shell, and in the second by underpaying him for the buttons produced out of it. The small masters at the present time are for the most part men, who are not 'in society', and one inducement for some of them to set up for themselves in this way is the liberty it enables them to take of playing cards in beer-shops, and drinking and smoking away the Monday and Tuesday, which they cannot have in a regular shop. A good many men have tried this system for a while, but few have been able to carry on above a month or two. The practice, however, at one time, brought down the price of buttons, and was productive of great injury to the trade. The manufacturer not uncommonly endeavoured to protect himself against such a ruinous competition by reducing, wherever he could do so, the rate of wages. There has been considerable agitation in the town upon the subject, and a general strike of the trade took place in 1849. The trade, however, has lately been placed on a better footing, and the union seems to be firmly established. The scale of prices which has been agreed upon gives satisfaction both to masters and men.". . .

. . . Upon the whole the condition of the adults employed in the button manufacture of Birmingham may be considered to be favourable. They receive a fair rate of wages for work that is not exhaustive, nor, with a few exceptions already noticed, unwholesome. The hours of labour are nominally twelve hours a day, but out of these two are allowed for meals—thus reducing the actual day's work to ten hours. Though liable to the distress caused by sudden changes of fashion, which throw out of work the hands that may have been engaged for a lifetime in one particular branch of a manufacture—and of which the ease of the plated and gilt button manufacturers ruined by the invention of the Florentine button was the most striking—it must be remembered that such cases are rare, and that only one has occurred within the memory of a generation. In this respect, therefore, the button makers have not had much to complain of. With regard to the employment of such large numbers of children in the manufacture of the Folorentine, the horn, the glass, and the pearl button—a very serious and important question suggests itself, which is, whether society does not pay too dearly for the cheapness which renders necessary the employment of these infants? The master manufacturers themselves, as will have been observed from the statements made in this and the preceding letter, do not directly employ many young children under thirteen years of age. Infants from seven upwards are employed by the adults to assist them, and the manufacturers have little or no control over them, and neither know their names, their age, nor the amount of remuneration which they receive for their labour. The "cobbers", who are mostly boys of seven or eight years of age, are employed by the metal button stampers to arrange the buttons in a row, in readiness for the stamp, and must work as long as the adults whom they assist. If the adult has been keeping holiday, or Saint Monday, and is desirous of making up for lost time by working over-hours towards the end of the week, the child must be over-worked, and towards night it is no rare occurrence to see children nodding over their labour. A witness examined by the Government Commissioner, in 1840, stated that when there was extra work of this kind, the boys got sleepy and tired, and had to be shaken, or otherwise intimidated, to be kept awake. The boys sometimes object to the overwork, and would not, if left to their own free-will, submit to it—especially in those cases where the extra amount they earn is not given to them but to their parents. Many parents in Birmingham not only partially live upon the labour of their infants, but are known to borrow money to be repaid for the future labour of their offspring. Another witness, examined on the same inquiry, stated "that he had often seen boys of seven, eight, or nine years old severely beaten and knocked about for not being able to work fast enough for the men when the latter were anxious to make up for lost time." Parents often employ their own children to assist them as "cobbers", or "cobs". The "putters-in", or young girls who assist in the Florentine business, are, in the same way as the "cobbers" or "cobs", removed from the control and superintendence of the manufacturer, being hired and paid by older girls working on their own account. It is the opinion of many that if all these children, both male and female, were employed directly, by the manufacturer they would be better treated than they are at present; but it is argued on the other side, that the ordinary stimulus of self-interest is not sufficient in the case of such infants to keep them to their work, and that the necessary amount of labour could not be extracted from them by any other than the present system, when they work under the eye of the individual whose own earnings depend to a large extent upon the effective assistance which they render. It is quite clear, whether the system be or be not remediable, that, so far as the future interests of their children are concerned, it is highly injurious. Confined as they are for ten hours every day at the very least—and often, in cases of extra hours being taken by the adult whom they serve, confined for two or three hours in addition—they are too weary and sleepy, and in every way unfit, to attend an evening school with advantage. They are not only trained to one particular branch of a manufacture, such as cobbing, or putting-in, by which they learn nothing likely to be of service to them in their future life, but they are completely shut out from the chance of education on week days. On the Sunday their physical health requires fresh air and exercise; and they must forego this advantage to a great extent, if their parents send them to a Sunday-school. It may be questioned whether the education they receive at a Sunday-school is calculated to be of much service to them. Doubtless, it is better than no education at all; but, as the greater portion of the Sunday-schools object to teach writing, arithmetic, modern geography, physiology, or any of those branches which fit the young mind for the active life of the world, it is clear, however good in itself such education may be, that it is not sufficient. But, as this point is of great importance, and as the evil of the employment of such infants in the various sub-divisions of manufacture is not confined to the button trade, but extends to the pin, the nail and screw, the pin and many other branches of industry, I propose to make it the subject of a separate investigation, without reference to the particular manufacture in which the children may happen to be engaged. I shall merely say, in addition to the statement with regard to the button trade, that although the adults and young women of fifteen or sixteen upwards appeared, as far as I have seen, to be generally well paid and well clad, the young children were almost without exception ragged and dirty in the extreme. Many of the cobbers stood to their work without a sufficiency of clothes to cover them;—their knees peering through holes in their trowsers, and their shoulders through their shirts or jackets. They had for the most part a sickly and unwholesome look. The female children or "putters-in", were equally squalid and pale, and prematurely serious, if not melancholy, in the expression of their countenance. The women employed in the manufacture —even in that hardest, most disagreeable, and most inferior branch of it, the grinding and polishing of steel—expressed their satisfaction with their earnings, as being far superior to what a woman could earn at any description of needle-work. Eighteen-pence or two shillings a day were the common wages of a woman who chose to work with regularity and many were able to earn as much as fourteen shillings or fifteen shillings a week. Very few complained of the hardness or unwholesomeness of their work.

The Manufacture of Fire-arms

Letter VI

... In Birmingham, as well as in the neighbouring towns, large numbers of boys are employed in the two great branches of the gun-lock. These boys are not employed directly by the master manufacturers, but they work on their own account for the foreman of the shop, or other workman, who requires assistance. They are rarely, if ever, apprenticed, and their employers, persons of their own class, have no control over them after working hours. They are their own masters, except when they live under the parental roof; but, like the rest of the juvenile population in the receipt of wages for piece work, they are said to assume very early the bad habits of manhood, without having the sense or judgment to acquire the good ones. ...

... On inquiring into the general condition of the men, women, and children engaged in all the various departments of the gun trade, I found that they suffer from fluctuations in demand, with the exception of the lock forgers and filers, who are in this respect in a somewhat better state than the barrel-forgers, stockers, finishers, or others engaged generally in the production of the complete gun. The foreign demand for locks provides them with pretty regular employment; whereas the members of the other branches of the trade are dependent principally upon the demand for sporting guns, the African exports, and the irregular orders of the British and foreign Governments. "Wars and rumours of wars" are good for this trade, and the near approach of the sporting season always produces an increased demand, and a consequent improvement in trade.

An extensive manufacturer represented to me that generally speaking, of the whole of the workmen employed by him, in the various branches of the gun trade, those who were engaged in the gun-barrel forging, grinding, and boring, who all worked by the aid of steam power, were far more regular at their work than the lock forgers and filers, and others who worked at vices and presses. The men seemed, he said, to acquire regular habits from the regularity of the machine on which they were dependent, and to feel aggrieved at any waste of the power occasioned by neglect. The lock forgers and filers, not being dependent on steam, frequently idled away the Monday and Tuesday of every week. The same manufacturer kept for a twelve month an account against all his men of their hours of attendance, and stated that he did not find that they wasted the Monday and Tuesday more frequently when trade was good than when it was bad. I was particular in my inquiries upon this point, as some manufacturers complained greatly of their workmen, that, when orders poured in upon them and the men could earn as much in three days as they formerly earned in six, they were contented with the three days' work, and passed the other three in drinking and card playing. I could find no reason for the belief that such a waste of time and opportunity was general, although in some instances it did undoubtedly occur, and caused a serious loss to the manufacturer as well as to his workmen.

The Condition of Factory Women and their Families

Letter VII

... The first statement which I shall present was made by a gentleman who has raised himself by his good conduct and industry to a highly respectable position in the town:

"I was an operative button maker for fifty years of my life. I was born and bred among the working classes, and know their virtues and their vices. My own history and experience will throw some light upon the condition of women who work in factories. The early association of the sexes, and the control exercised over women by tool makers and others who have the management of workshops, and give out work to them, very often leads to improper intercourse, or to early marriage to hide or atone for past evil. Young men and women think that by clubbing their earnings, they will be in a condition to keep house and support a family, and they contract marriages long before they are justified in doing so. The case of my father and mother is but one of thousands which are still more common at the present day than when I was a child. My father was a metal button turner. My mother was in the same business in the same shop. My father was of age when he married, and that was all. He had no money to buy furniture. His wages were about a pound a week, and my mother's about eight shillings or nine shillings at the very utmost. They procured furniture on credit, and never got rid of their furniture debt as long as they lived. That debt hung like a millstone around their necks, and may have been one of many causes which drove my father to the gin-shop. My mother had eleven children, of whom I was the eldest. She was employed in the button manufacture all that time. My father had no comfortable home. He could not have, while my mother was obliged to work in a shop all the day. My mother worked at her trade till the last. Often till the day before her confinement she was at the lathe, and often returned to her work within three weeks. It was my business, as the eldest child, to nurse the younger ones. I was a nurse at five years old, and had sometimes to mind the children at home that they did not set their pinafores on fire, and sometimes I had to go to the factory to attend to the infant. My mother was allowed to take it with her, and it used to lie in a tub of sawdust, and sleep or roll about till it wanted the breast. I was obliged to watch over it and amuse it. I was put to work at the buttons at seven years of age, and I thought myself very fortunate in being relieved from the disagreeable labour of nursing the baby. We had a wretched place to live in. My mother ran home daily at one o'clock to get a hasty dinner for my father. She had no time for cooking anything. Bread and treacle, or bread and butter, was our usual fare, except on Sundays, when we got a joint of meat, and had it cooked at the public oven. My mother was a perfect slave. She could not read or write. She was naturally a clever woman. My father could read and write but he took no pains to let his children have the same advantages. He never sent any of us to school, but sent us all to work as soon as it was possible, that we could earn even as little as sixpence a week. He was always in debt, and fond of drink, and became latterly quite reckless. He spent his earnings in liquor, and trusted to my mother to feed the children somehow or other—he did not care how. Often and often, when only seven or eight years old, I have been sent to the huckster's to beg and pray for a loaf on credit to save us from starvation. I earned my food at that time, but did not always get it. The price of bread and other articles always went up when we were in debt; and our landlord, not being able to get his rent, allowed our house to fall into a miserable condition. He would not whitewash or repair it; and we were in constant dread of being turned out into the streets. My mother did double work —in the shop and at home. I have known her to sit up till three or four o'clock in the morning, after a hard day's work, washing and mending our wretched clothes. When four of her children were ill at one time of the small pox, she had to go to the shop to work, or we should have starved. She paid a neighbour one shilling and sixpence a week to look after them. During her long years of misery she several times tried to do without the shop, and make the labour of her husband and children support us all. My father's earnings were so small, and his drinking habits so inveterate, that very little found its way into my mother's possession. Her attempts to stay at home were in vain. She had always to go back to the shop. We have often been without fire and food in the winter, and exposed to distress and suffering of the most deplorable kind. When I was apprenticed I could not write my name. My sister, who was also sent to the button trade as soon as she could earn a penny a day, was never taught to read, nor to write, nor to use the needle, nor to cook, nor to wash. The whole of us were equally ignorant. It would be of no use to detail my own experience at that time, were it not, unhappily, the experience of thousands of people at the present day. The same causes are still at work. I constantly hear of, and see, cases quite as bad as mine was. Young girls prefer the work of shops to that of domestic servants. Though confined during the day, they are their own mistresses at night, or have every evening and the whole of every Sunday to themselves, which they could not have in service. Such work as "lacquering" is a favourite with them. It is tolerably well paid, and easily acquired, and it gives them freedom instead of thraldom. When they marry, they are quite unfit to be the companions and helpmates of intelligent and thrifty men. They make but miserable homes, and miserable homes send men to the alehouse and the ginshop. I believe that the employment of women in factories is one great cause of the intemperance of the working classes. When a man knows, if he returns to his home as soon as his labour is over, on a winter night, that his wife has no fire alight for him, and no comfortable place even to sit down in, he strolls into the warm ginshop, and soon learns to like the place and the society. He goes from bad to worse, and his wife speedily learns to imitate his example. A drunken husband makes a drunken wife, and then the whole family goes to ruin. The children receive no education, and are sent to work as soon as they can stand. The more the children earn, the more is left to the parents for the ginshop. Such was the case in our family, except that my mother did not drink, and such is the case with scores and scores of families in the town at the present day. My father worked at the lathe till within a week of his death. He had been drinking every day for a week previously. He died of a complication of diseases, brought on by intemperance. When I went to see him, being then married and having a family of my own, I found him in a wretched room, without a bit of bread in the house and not a farthing of money. I had to bury him. My mother died in childbed of her eleventh child, a few years before my father. Sorrow, privation, and hard work ruined her constitution. If she had had a sober husband, his wages might have supported us all. I could name many such men as my father, now at work in the town, some as bad, and a good many worse—drunken and lazy fellows who never work at all, but depend entirely on their wives and infants to support them. In justice to my father I must say that he never did this. He always was willing to work when he was sober, and during his life he worked very hard. But many men that I know will not work at all. Others, who do work think that the whole amount gained by their wives is so much drinking money gained for themselves."

The Manufacture of Steel-pens

Letter IX

. . . The first steel pens were made in garrets—the manufacturer and his family being the only workpeople. But now they are produced in factories of palatial appearance and extent. That of Mr. Gillott accommodates from 500 to 600 people. That of Messrs. Hinckes and Wells is equally large. Both establishments continue to extend, first to one side, and then to another, of their original location; and that of Messrs. Hinckes and Wells has spread to both sides of the street in which it is situated. Mr. Gillott's factory is considered a model of its kind. . . .
. . . The workpeople are all paid according to the amount of work performed. The younger girls earn from five shillings to six shillings per week, and some of the more expert and attentive women earn as much as twelve shillings or

fourteen shillings a week. The average wages are ten shillings to eleven shillings. There is no sub-employing. Every person is directly hired and paid by the manufacturer. The tool makers receive high wages, often as much as £3 or £4 a week. The wages of the men in the steam and fire departments are from twenty shillings to twenty-five shillings or thirty shillings and those of the boys who assist them from four shillings to seven shillings.

As regards the moral government of the factories, the following particulars were communicated by Mr. Gillott and by other persons. He takes as much care as possible to prevent the introduction of improper characters, whether male or female. He will not employ children under the age of thirteen or fourteen, and he advises all applicants under thirteen to go to school. He selects in preference those girls who have been to a day as well as a Sunday school, and who can both read and write. It is not possible, however, to insist too rigidly upon the qualification of writing, as so few girls can write as well as read, that he would be short of hands to work his factory if he excluded them on this account. He requires that they should be recommended for good moral conduct, for steadiness, and for cleanliness, by a Sunday-school teacher, a clergyman or other respectable person, before he will admit them into his employ. He find, if by any chance a girl of improper character is engaged, that the other girls immediately bring her conduct under his notice, and call for an investigation. If the charge of immoral life is proved against her, she is discharged. Among so many young women cases of the kind will sometimes occur, but they are exceedingly rare, and as a general rule the young women are modest and well-behaved. They marry much too early. On Sundays and holidays the unmarried girls, like most of this class in Birmingham, dress very smartly, but their finery too often is all outside show—and the silk dress very commonly covers ragged dirt and inferior under-clothes. Mr. Gilliott will not allow Saint Monday, but finds a general inclination among the girls to indulge in a holiday on that day. In the fine summer weather he occasionally yields, so far to their wishes as to close at five o'clock on Monday afternoon, instead of at seven, the usual hour. The whole of the persons in the factory, men and boys, girls and women, belong to the sick club established by Mr. Gillott. The club is encouraged by him, but it is not imperatively required that the workpeople shall belong to it. He and all his family, and all the clerks in his employ, pay regularly towards it, and the workpeople, when sick, receive an allowance. The subscription is threepence a week. The girls have other clubs among themselves, and put by from a penny to twopence and threepence a week, to purchase articles of clothing. There are shoe and boot clubs, shawl clubs, and dress clubs. The favourite club is for the annual "gipsy party", or excursion into the country. The gipsy parties are now very common in Birmingham, and form quite a feature in the social history of the working classes. Almost every class of workpeople in the town have them. They were scarcely known at all about five years ago; but owing to the cheapness of locomotion, and the trips advertised by the railway companies, a taste for excursions has sprung up, and "gipsy parties" occur almost every day, in the summer season. The favourite resorts are Kenilworth, to visit the magnificent ruins of the Castle, and the Clent Hills, from which there is a magnificent panoramic view, extending over an area of sixty square miles, and exhibiting glimpses of the Malvern Hills, the

Wrekin, and the Peak of Derbyshire. Mr. Gillott's gipsy party this year was spoiled by the bad weather. That of Messrs. Hinckes and Wells was more fortunate. The girls and women paid a penny a week for a twelve month towards it, and the men twopence a week, their employers contributing a handsome sum. The party mustered no less than 350 people. About 130 stayed away, some because they could not afford the money, and others because they stated that they had no clothes to go in. The party started from Birmingham at seven o'clock on a fine summer morning to Hagley and the Clent Hills to pass the day. They filled forty-five cars, which were gaily ornamented with banners and devices, and they were accompanied by a band of music. The whole of the party breakfasted in the open air, in tents, at the Hagley Arms. They walked in procession up to the Clent Hills and enjoyed the beautiful view into Wales. Quadrilles and country dances were got up and these and other amusements continued until dinner time. The whole party dined under tents in the open air, the band of music played all the time. It was not a tee-total festival, but the party were very temperate. A copy of the following regulations, neatly printed, was given to each individual before starting:

"REGULATIONS TO BE OBSERVED ON THE OCCASION OF MESSRS. HINCKES, WELLS, AND CO.'S PLEASURE TRIP, JULY 13, 1850

"Car No. . . .

"The holder of this ticket must ride there and back in this conveyance.

"Time of Starting.—Half-past six o'clock precisely; any one being later, will be left behind, and their money forfeited.

"The Road.—In getting out of the cars, to walk up the hills (on the road); you are requested not to mix with other parties, but to keep pace with your own conveyance.

"The Park.—In passing through the park the same order to be observed as in riding; to walk four abreast, and under no pretence to move out of the line; any one seen injuring or destroying trees, hedges, or plants, will be discharged.

"Clent Hills.—On the hills, dancing and other amusements. You are requested not to roam in small or detached parties, otherwise you will incur the severe displeasure of your employers; at the sounding of the trumpet, the whole to return to dinner in the same order as in first passing through the park.

"Time of returning Home.—Eight o'clock precisely. The same order must be observed in returning as in going. You are requested not to sing, or otherwise make a noise in passing through the streets; and it is hoped that the greatest order and propriety will be observed throughout the day.

"Any one requiring any information, must apply to either of the members of the committee.

"Programme for Dancing.—Triumph, Paine's 1st set, gallepade, Schottische, Circassian circle, Lancers, polka, Spanish dance, circular waltz."

These regulations were drawn up by a committee of the employed and the employers, and were so strictly and cheerfully adhered to, that neither in going nor returning, nor during the stay of the party on the hills, did there occur a single instance of disobedience to orders, of misbehaviour of any kind, or of drunkenness—a fact as highly creditable to the employers as to the workpeople.

Workers in Brass

Letter XII

. . . The number of persons employed in cabinet brass foundry alone has been estimated at about 1,300; but in this, as in other departments, there is a difficulty in procuring an accurate statement, from the fact that a considerable portion of the work is done by jobbing workmen or "garrett masters", in their own houses, or whom no accurate account can be made, and also from the circumstance that a very large number of lads and boys are employed by the journeymen, nearly all of them quite unknown and irresponsible to the managers and proprietors. The staple articles of production in the cabinet brass department are castors for chairs, sofas, and tables; hinges of all sorts; door-handles and knobs, bolts, escutcheons, etc.; window fastenings; bell levers, pulls, and cranks; stair-case eyes and rods; brass-headed nails; hat and coat pins; curtain rings; drawer-handles, sconces, table-fasteners, etc. The introduction of portions of ornamental china into cabinet brass goods, such as bell-pulls, and curtain bands, about ten years ago, opened up a new branch of industry, and has given a great impetus to the trade. Glass has still more recently been employed for similar purposes, and has tended to introduce into cabinet brass foundry a more expensive and superior style of workmanship. The character given of the workers in this branch of the brass trade, both by the employers and the operatives themselves, is highly favourable as compared with some other branches of trade. The habits of intemperance, carelessness, and irregularity, which are stated to have formerly prevailed amongst them, only linger among the elder race of workmen, and are fast disappearing among the younger men. The observance of "St. Monday" and all such holidays, is stated to be almost entirely confined to the older hands; "and it not unfrequently happens", said an intelligent journeyman, "that if one of the workmen absents himself from work for drunkenness, he returns to the manufactory amidst the ridicule and hootings of his comrades. The number of teetotallers in our establishment is considerable. In one shop, or department, out of ten men there are six teetotallers. They are not ridiculed and jeered at as they used to be, but on the contrary, there is a degree of shyness observed in bringing ale to the shop, particularly at eleven o'clock. No drinking fee, such as "foot-money" is insisted upon: Nevertheless, it is often voluntarily given, and then the men club together till they get enough to have a supper. On the occasion of a marriage the bridegroom generally gives five shillings or ten shillings towards a supper. The men are also inclined to enforce the payment of the 'shifting shilling', when a man moves from one lathe to another. These shillings are hoarded up till there be enough in hand to afford a 'jollification'; but these things are becoming rarer and rarer every year.". . .

. . . In the important department of the brass manufacture including "general" goods, or builders, carpenters, and unholsterers, and cabinet brass, there are general complaints, not alone among the better class of manufacturers, but among the public, of the inferiority of a large proportion of the goods which

are poured into the market. "Slop" brass seems to be as extensively manufactured in Birmingham as slop clothes are in London, Liverpool, and
Glasgow; and brass goods for builders' purposes, or for furniture, gradually
become lighter, thinner, and less serviceable, in consequence of the ruinous
competition of numerous small, and some large manufacturers, and of the
effect upon the market of the dealings of men who cannot afford to keep their
goods over the Saturday night without forcing a sale among the factors or
merchants. The very name of Birmingham threatens to fall into discredit in
the markets of the world for the wretched articles which, under the name of
"cabinet brass" find their way to the retail dealers, both at home and abroad,
and of which it is difficult to say whether the dishonest competition of men
who have capital, or the ruinous trading of men who have none, is the most
active cause.

Heavy Steel Toys

Letter XIV

"The manufacture of iron in Birmingham," says Hutton, "is ancient beyond
research, that of steel is of modern date." The historian, having given this information, follows it up with a disquisition upon pride, and ends his article
by stating that "from this warm, but dismal, climate (Birmingham) issues the
button which shines on the breast, and the bayonets intended to pierce it; the
lancet which bleeds the man, and the rowel which bleeds the horse; the lock
which preserves the beloved bottle, and the screw to uncork it; the needle,
equally obedient to the thimble and the pole". This with a statement that a
person of the name of Kettle, introduced the steel trade into Birmingham in
the seventeenth century, is the whole of the information derivable from his
pages on the ancient state of this important manufacture in the town. In this
department of the inquiry it will thus be seen that little did of any value is to
be derived from the labours of Mr. Hutton.

The trade at the present day may be divided into the two great branches of
Heavy and Light Steel Toys. In the first is generally included the manufacture
of edge tools. The word "toy" is a sad misnomer as applied to nearly the
whole of the articles in the heavy department of the business. Birmingham was
called by Edmund Burke "the toy-shop of the world"; but whether he knew
the kind of articles that were included under the designation by the people of
the town, or whether he meant by toys such articles of jewellery and nicknack-
ery as go by that name elsewhere, it is not easy to say, nor is it perhaps of
importance to ascertain. . . .

. . . The names of thirty-two makers of heavy steel toys and tools appear in
the "Directory"; but Sheffield and Wolverhampton, as well as Birmingham
carry on an extensive manufacture of these articles. Birmingham, however,
enjoys by far the largest share of the trade, except in the manufacture of edge
tools, which is principally seated at Sheffield. . . .

. . . The absence of costly machinery—for £4 or £5 is money enough to start a maker of common articles in business—has had the effect of inducing a considerable number of workmen to commence manufacturing on their own account, but they are confined to such articles as gimlets, corkscrews, bradawls, etc. The number of these small makers, and those whom they employ, is said to be greater than that employed in the larger manufactories, but their influence upon the makers of superior goods seems to be very insignificant, as both manufacturers and their workmen describe themselves as being in as good a position as ever they were.... The following statement, made by one who had worked at the heavy steel toy trade for nearly forty years, may be considered as affording a fair general view of the whole trade, although made with especial reference to one of the oldest establishments in the town—that of Messrs. R. Timmins and Sons—in whose service the narrator has been for upwards of thirty years:

"So far as I know of the trade, I believe that the workmen are in a better condition now than they were thirty-six years ago, which is nearly as far back as I remember. They are more provident for themselves and families than they used to be, and are in all respects better members of society. Their habits are more cleanly, and their tastes and feelings more refined; there is also less hard drinking than formerly. Gipsy parties are got up frequently among the men of this manufacturing district during the summer season. They have, I think, been the means of creating among the men a love of out-door exercises and sports. The favourite games are cricket and archery, and the men possess bats, wickets and balls, bows, arrows and targets in common. In summer the men turn out to play two or three times a week, and often sacrifice a Monday afternoon to the exercise of these sports, which, at all events, is better than drinking away the Monday, as thousands do in Birmingham. There are about 120 men and boys in this establishment, and nearly all of them participate in these sports. At present the men are consulting whether they shall have a gipsy party in summer as usual, or whether they shall make a trip to London to see the Great Exhibition. The feeling is in favour of London and the Exhibition, and I have no doubt but the men will make considerable sacrifices in order to gratify their wish. These gipsy parties I think have the effect of spreading a feeling of good-will and cordiality among the men, and they become better acquainted with each other. Within seven or eight years a Friendly Fund has been established among the men working in this manufactory, into which each man pays two pence a week; from the fund thus collected a workman receives five shillings a week when confined by sickness; at the death of a child he receives ten shillings; at the death of his wife he receives £1; at his own death his widow receives £2 for funeral expenses....

... The Edge Tool Manufacture, which is often combined in the same factory with that of the heavy steel toys, and is classed by some as part of the same trade, includes such articles as axes, adzes, bills, bill-hooks; Carolina, Demerara, and West Indian hoes; Columbia, Boston, Mamottee, Spanish, and Portuguese hoes; Spanish and Biscay shovels, grubbing hoes, pick-axes, wedges, ploughs, spades of all kinds; the heavier gardening tools, draining tools, and generally such agricultural implements as are not complicated enough to come under the head of machinery. The pattern books of an extensive firm contain the descriptions and prices of forty-five different kinds of axes, including fourteen different varieties manufactured expressly for the American market, orna-mented with the American eagle, and designated by such names as the Kentucky wedge axe, the Yankee axe, the American slinging hatchet, the New Orleans axe, etc. There are about twelve varieties of adzes; twenty-six of bills and bill-hooks; upwards of seventy of hoes for all climates and soils; and spades and shovels innumerable. The names of twelve master manufacturers appear in the Directory, and the trade is estimated to afford employment to between three and four hundred men. Birmingham, as already stated, is not the only seat of this manufacture, but its trade appears to be greatly on the increase, at the expense of that of Sheffield.

The following account of the past and present state of the manufacture was given by a small manufacturer: "Between thirty and forty years ago there were not more than four makers in Birmingham, and I think there were only three. They made the same sort of tools that are made now, and perhaps as good for practical purposes, though not so neat or so well finished. About thirty years ago the number of men and boys employed in the trade was under a hundred. A union has existed among the men for about ten years. Within thirty years prices have been reduced by about 20 per cent on nearly all goods, and about 30 per cent on plantation hoes. Readier methods of working have been intro-duced so that, although a reduction of 50 per cent has been made in the price of hoes, a man can make a good many more in the same time. The reduction in the receipts of a man working at hoes is about 25 per cent. The men are, however, as well off now in point of fact as ever they were, for living is cheaper, and they can find the same amount of comfort for less money. Prices have been further lowered in fact by the improvement that has been made in the quality of work. People are better judges of a good article now than they used to be, at least in our trade, and they will only purchase good things. The German competition five or six years ago had the effect of lowering prices and of improving the workmanship in our manufactures, for it was by making better articles that we drove them out of the market. The Germans cannot make such good work as the English; and we have not suffered any loss in the trade from their competition. Prices did not return to their old scale when we regained the market, but have had, as I think, a tendency to fall ever since. Within my recollection there has been a great change in the character of the Birmingham workmen, and in that of workmen generally in every part of the country. The improvement within thirty years is wonderful, and teetotalism has done a great deal of it. Even the amusements of the men have changed for the better. When I was a young working man, nothing was thought of by the workmen but cock-fighting, bull-baiting, rat-worrying, and such like; but these things are not popular now, and thereby, I say, the country is improved. The young men of the present day are better educated than they were when I was a youth. They go to the Town Hall on a Monday night to hear music for three-pence. Nothing of that sort was known thirty years ago, but the men spent their nights in the ale-house. When I was a young man I never saw games of cricket played by the workmen, or anything of the sort, except football and that was not common. Within the last twelve years these manly and healthy sports have become quite popular, and I hear of clubs being formed among the men for the purpose. Education is a great thing for the working classes. I wish they had more of it. A little is better than none. The more book-learning a young man has, the better workman he becomes. I am sure of that. I was a pretty tidy workman in my youth, but the young men of the present day beat me out and out. I think the general condition of Birmingham and of England is likely to become more prosperous than ever it was. Australia is already a large market for our edge tools and for manufacturers of all sorts, and it will soon require as much from us as America used to take."

Turning from the opinions of this hopeful old gentleman to those of a workman, on the condition of his craft, the reader may compare their statements. The question as regards the condition of the workmen and manufacturers at Sheffield, to which he alludes, is one of much importance to both towns:

"I left Sheffield to come to Birmingham about thirteen years ago, because work was slack there at the time. The strikes among the workmen are very numerous at Sheffield. In times of good trade a grinder will make three times as much at Sheffield as at Birmingham. They can make £3 a week there. A good deal of the heavy edge-tool trade has come to Birmingham and Wolverhampton. I should think that the reason of this is, that iron and coal are cheaper here than at Sheffield, and also that the Sheffield unions are opposed to the introduction of machinery in the trade. Light edge-tools are better made at Sheffield than, at Birmingham, and the greater part of the light garden hoes used in this country are made in the former place. Machinery is much more extensively employed at Birmingham than at Sheffield, and the prejudice against it is so strong at Sheffield that I have known an instance of a man being obliged to leave that town because he substituted a bellows for the ordinary blow-pipe used for soldering. He could do the work much quicker by means of the bellows. The tilt hammer, which is moved by steam or water power, does away with the necessity for employing a striker, and workmen at some sorts of work will make as much money in the course of the week by employing the tilt hammer as with the aid of an assistant, while he is enabled to produce a larger number of articles at a lower rate. Heavy work is paid about one-third less at Birmingham than at Sheffield, but in consequence of the use of machinery it is less exhausting. In those departments of the trade in which manual labour is employed, the Sheffield workmen are much better paid than those of Birmingham. Ever since I have known Sheffield there has been strife between masters and workmen, and as soon as orders come in briskly the men strike for the prices they had in 1810, when a list of prices had been formally agreed to by men and masters. But when trade slackens, the masters "put on the screw" and reduce wages as much as they can. The men come and offer themselves at lower wages rather than suffer themselves to be brought to the workhouse. Unions are much more general there than at Birmingham. I was once obliged to leave a place in consequence of not belonging to the union of the trade in which I worked at the time; but it was not the trade to which I had been brought up, and the men took care to inform me that I was looked upon as an interloper. I had been out of work for some time before entering that business, but was obliged to leave it. I have seen nothing of that sort in Birmingham. There have been several attempts made to form a trade union among the edge-tool makers in Birmingham and the neighbourhood since I have come here, but they have never succeeded. The men do not understand

unions here so well as in the north, and the trade lies in a very large circle, so that the men cannot be often and readily collected together. In Sheffield I have known the children hoot a workman in the streets who did not belong to the union of his trade. I dare say the trade unions of Sheffield, by keeping up the high price of labour, have helped in some degree to drive the trade from the town; but iron and coal are cheaper here, and I believe that to be the principal reason why the Birmingham trade has increased so much of late. Prices have been steadily decreasing in this trade. Some articles—as, for instance, the Brazil hoe—are now sold for the same money as was paid for making them twenty years ago. The men are obliged to work harder, and more hours, than formerly, and such relaxation as they have is in the ale-house or in sleep. As far as I know they have no games such as cricket, ball-playing, jumping and foot-racing, which are comparatively common at Sheffield, where, on a Monday afternoon, when little or no work is done, the men of one establishment challenge those of another to a game of cricket, or something of the sort, and spend the evening pleasantly in this manner. At Sheffield the workmen turn out two or three times a week to indulge in these sports. This may be the case in Birmingham also, but I never heard of it. As to the effect of unions, I am at a loss to balance their advantages and disadvantages in my own mind. The workmen are better paid wherever they exist, for in bad seasons they do not get less than elsewhere, and in good seasons they get more. But there are evils connected with them, the worst of which is 'rattening'—that is, destroying the property and tools of their opponents—an evil which I believe is always to be traced more or less to the unions; but if they could be carried on without violence, I believe trades' unions would be a blessing both to masters and to men."

The abominable practice of "rattening", to which this working-man alludes, does not appear to be much known in Birmingham. It is deplorably common in some towns, and instances are known in which injury has been done to the heavy grindstones to cause them to "fly", and to maim and kill the workman.

Light Steel Toys

Letter XV

. . . The following details, more minute than the information given by Hutton, or by any other person who ever wrote upon the buckle, as far as I have been able to ascertain, were communicated to me by a respectable old gentleman, upwards of eighty years of age, who worked at the trade in his youth, and who, to a memory remarkably clear, united a great interest in all that related to the profession of his early days. He was represented as a "storehouse of anecdote" in connection with the manufactures of the town, and he was certainly a fine specimen of the intelligent English workman. He had been not only a buckle maker, but a gun-lock maker; he had worked at the Soho Works for the firm of Boulton and Smith, at the time that Watt was a partner—had been engaged in various other mechanical trades, according as fashion varied—had also kept

a public-house—and, till within the last six years, had regularly worked as a journeyman, when he had retired to pass the remainder of his days in decent competence. He appeared quite delighted at the idea that any one in these times should take an interest in the ancient shoe buckle, and he communicated his information with much perspicuity. The following details were derived from his conversation and in answer to questions put to him at various times. "The shoe buckle" he said, "is believed to be a Dutch invention, and it had a 'run' for upwards of a hundred years. Bilston was the first place in England where it was manufactured, and it was afterwards introduced into Birmingham. Many fortunes were made out of it at Bilston before the Birmingham people took it up; and one named Jukes, originally a butcher, was especially noted when I was a boy, seventy years ago, for the large fortune he made by buckles in a very short space of time. I had an uncle at Bilston who made his fortune at it about the year 1775, and when he retired he sold his business to Messrs. Wilmer and Alstone, of Birmingham, who to the best of my recollection and belief, were the first people who ever made buckles in this town. It soon became a 'roaring' business; and Birmingham may be said to have lived by shoe and knee buckles from 1780 to 1790. Many thousands of people were employed and I have heard that 8,000 or even 10,000 hands, were at one time, engaged in the various factories, large and small, that abounded in Birmingham, Walsall, Bilston, and Wolverhampton. We supplied the whole world with the shoe buckles—Holland, Germany, France, Italy, Spain, America, and England, Scotland and Ireland. Both men and women wore them, and even the little children had buckles to their shoes—I mean the children of the rich. The children of the poor wore clasps. Mechanics worked with buckles in their shoes, and indeed all kinds of labourers, except those who followed the plough, wore them. Trowsers were not known in those days, nor for a long time after-wards, and boots were not invented; indeed, I don't think I ever saw either boots or trowsers, and I certainly never wore either, until long after the battle of Waterloo. The prices of buckles ranged from five to ten guineas down to a shilling a pair. The best were made of steel and silver; some were even set with diamonds; and it was very common for people to wear paste or Bristol stone buckles on Sundays. Great numbers were made of plated ware. . . .
They were made of iron, first tinned and then silvered, and were stamped or pierced out. There was but little workmanship in them, but they were tolerably well. Buckles soon grew monstrously large, especially for men, and reached right across the foot from sole to sole. They almost covered the foot, in fact, and were much too large for comfort in walking; but fashion reconciled people to them, as it will to anything however ridiculous. The silver buckles used to be sold by weight, and the chape, whether of iron or steel, used to be weighed in with them. The French war interfered a good deal with the foreign trade in buckles. The Spaniards used to take immense numbers of very large and very expensive buckles from us, but that demand fell off, after the French revolution, and the French demand came to nothing. I never heard of a deputation to the Prince of Wales on the subject of buckles, but I heard of the button-makers, when they went to London to induce the Prince to wear gilt buttons, and that he remarked to a member of the deputation that it was odd he should

ask him (the Prince) to wear gilt buttons, when he (the manufacturer) wore covered ones."

It may be observed, however, although the narrator did not remember the circumstance, that a deputation waited upon the Prince of Wales, in 1791—when there was great stagnation in the buckle manufacture on account of the loss of the foreign trade, and also of a partial change of fashion consequent upon the introduction of the shoe-string—to induce his Royal Highness to appear in public with buckles. The Prince, having heard that many thousand individuals were in distress in consequence of the change, informed the deputation that he would not only wear buckles himself, but order all the members of his household to do the same. The royal example was not altogether nugatory, and the trade revived to a considerable extent. A similar story to that of the button maker and the Prince is related of a member of this deputation, who is said to have appeared with shoe-strings when urging upon the royal attention the superior claims of the buckle. Which of the two stories is the original one it is difficult to determine. "The fashion", continued my informant, "began to change about the beginning of this century, but even then many fortunes were made out of the business. At the Soho works, Mr. Mathew Boulton introduced the patent buckle or latchet, which interfered a great deal with the old-fashioned buckle. Boulton and Smith employed some hundreds of hands in making latchets, and built very large workshops for this branch of the trade. These workshops were afterwards converted into the famous Soho Mint, where nearly all the British money was coined for many years. I worked at the buckle trade in the year 1810, when the Princess Amelia died. It was a very considerable trade at that time; and I remember that much distress was caused in some branches of the trade by the general mourning that was ordered for the Princess. Everybody, male and female, wore black buckles; and a great business in black buckles was consequently created at the expense of the general buckle trade. The wages of the workmen were good. A chaser got from thirty shillings to forty shillings a week single-handed; and if he had the assistance of two or three boys, he might make a £1 a week. The *bottomers*, who filed the bottoms of the buckles, got from twenty shillings to thirty shillings a week single-handed. No women were employed in the trade. A buckle went through a great number of processes in all, and was not begun and completed in Birmingham. The forging was principally done at Darlaston, and the chapes were almost exclusively manufactured at Bilston. The filing, chasing, and putting together were the work of Birmingham. A workman was a workman in those days. Hands were scarce, on account of the war, and the men were very independent in their whole behaviour. They would not work unless they pleased; and a good hand could always obtain employment at a good price. I cannot precisely remember when buckles went out of fashion, but it was after the death of the Princess Amelia. So many slop buckles—regular trash—were made, that people got tired of them. The plating wore off—and a spatter of mud was sometimes sufficient to ruin a fine-looking buckle that had been put on new a day or two previously. Shoe-strings, being more economical began to be worn; and long before buckles went quite out of fashion, the waiters at inns, and servants generally, used to be known by their shoe-strings. The shoe-makers did a good deal to drive the buckle out. When the fashion began to change, they did their best to encourage it, for the straps to fasten the buckle took a good deal of leather as well as workmanship—both of which were saved by the introduction of shoe-strings, while the price of shoes remained the same —the whole difference in the expense going into the pocket of the shoemaker. I remember that great indignation was aroused in Birmingham when it was made known that the Prince Regent had finally discarded the buckle, and had been seen in public with shoe-strings. The buckle never recovered itself. If I may so say, it never held up its head in the world again—it was quite ruined and done for. The working men in the buckle trade hissed whenever the name of the Prince was mentioned. Hundreds, if not thousands, of men were thrown out of work. I remember that a party of them having nothing else to do, hired a donkey and led the animal about the streets, with shoe-strings tied about its hoofs, and ribbons about its legs, to ridicule the new fashion, and to implore charity at the same time. Whenever a man or woman appeared with shoe-strings in the streets of Birmingham, he or she was hooted by the children, and by grown-up people too. The cry was 'Lick-dish! lick-dish!' or 'Dog-robber! dog-robber!'—meaning that a person who wore shoe-strings could only be a waiter at an inn, or a 'flunkey'. By 'dog-robber' was meant a man who picked bones after other people had done with them—in fact, a waiter. There used to be constant rows and disturbances in the streets, got up by the unemployed buckle-makers. But it was all of no use. The buckle trade was done for. Fashion had changed, and boots and trowsers were coming into vogue, to deprive it of all chance of revival. The men gradually went into other trades—some of them went into the saddlery buckle-making—but that was poor work in comparison with that they had been accustomed to. Some became carters and porters— some went to the workhouse—and many, being skilled in metal work, went into the brass trade—or to other branches of the heavy or light steel toys. I went into the gun-lock business, but I never afterwards found a trade that I liked so well as buckle making."

In corroboration of the statements of this venerable and intelligent working man, the following, from a still more ancient member of the light steel toy and buckle trade—the oldest man in Birmingham—will be found of interest. The narrator is upwards of ninety-two years of age, and is still able to move about his little house in the suburbs of the town. He always wears a pair of large and handsome buckles in his shoes, which he manufactured for himself in the days when the buckle "was the only wear". He remembers almost all the principal fluctuations which have taken place in his trade for the last seventy or eighty years. His ideas are strongly impregnated with a love of the "olden time", especially of buckles, and with a hearty hatred of steamboats and railways, which he declares have brought the country to the verge of ruin. "Before the first French revolution," said he, "the light steel toy trade was the best in Birmingham, and one-half the town was dependent upon it. By the revolution it was nearly annihilated, for the principal part of the trade was with France, Spain, and Portugal, and all orders were suspended, for the two latter countries were supplied through France. When Napoleon came to power he prohibited all English steel toys from being imported into France, and from that time the French began to manufacture steel toys, and to supply their own markets. The workmen in Birmingham were obliged to give up the work, and to turn to other trades. I myself took to gardening for awhile, and then, when the war was going on, I worked at military ornaments. I made sword-hilts among other things, and I have known sword-hilts to be made which were valued at £30 each, without either blade or scabbard. The steel toys made when I was an apprentice were much the same as those made subsequently, such as watch-chains, 'middle-pieces', for hanging seals and keys for watches upon, scissor-hooks, steel scent-bottles, ladies' hooks for the work-table, etc., and of course the shoe-buckle and steel latchet, which were the staple articles of manufacture. These and all other articles made were infinitely superior to anything made at present—indeed, there is nothing but rubbish made now—stuff that I would not pick out of the dirt, and should be ashamed to work at. There were few watch-chains made in my day which did not bring in from five shillings to ten shillings each, but now they sell them for less than half the money. For three years I remember working at nothing else but scissor-hooks for ladies. Wages were not so high sixty or seventy years ago as now, but provisions and house-rent were not so dear. For the best butchers' meat in Birmingham we paid only twopence or $2\frac{1}{2}$d. a pound, and we had fourteen pounds of bread for a shilling; coals and other fuel were also much cheaper, and for five shillings I could have a better pair of shoes than I can now have for ten shillings. I began working as a journeyman for twelve shillings a week, but I could live pretty well for seven shillings, or eight shillings a week. A good tool-maker for steel toy work at that time could make from fifteen shillings to twenty shillings a week, and a good cutter and filer could make nearly thirty shillings a week, but to do this they must have been able workmen and must have worked over time. Generally speaking I should think that the workmen seventy years ago made about twelve shillings or thirteen shillings a week regularly, and no more. At that time the usual hours for work were from six a.m. till seven p.m. in summer, and from seven a.m. till eight p.m. in the winter. But now-a-days, the men are such lie-a-beds that they cannot get to work, even in summer, till nearly eight o'clock. Our sports used to be cock-fighting, bull-baiting, skittle-playing, quoits, football, leapfrog, etc. But nearly all these manly amusements have passed away, and we see nothing of them among the young men. We used to have a 'wake' (a fair) in every parish of the town once a year, and with these and the neighbouring wakes there used to be one nearly every month, which the working men of Birmingham could attend. There was generally a bull to be baited at these wakes, and a great deal of drinking and fighting. There is less fighting now than in my day, for the young men now-a-days have not courage to fight as they used to do; but I think there is more drinking now-a-days, and the people are obliged to take to fourpenny ale instead of sixpenny, in order to keep within compass. The usual way of spending a jolly evening among the workmen some seventy years ago, was to go in parties to a public house, two or three miles out of town, where they played at skittles and drank ale, while cabbage and bacon were being cooked for their dinner. This was done very frequently. I used never to have anything to do with bull-baiting, or rat-worrying, or anything of the sort, and never 'backed' a cock but once, and then only for sixpence. But I know that these sports were very common among the workmen, and were more talked about and thought of than such games as foot-ball, 'foot and horse shoe' (leap frog) or prison bars, which were more popular among the boys and young lads. These games have also disappeared here, for Birmingham has grown so big now that 'the fellows have no ground to 'kick upon'. I was once laid up for a short time when a youth, from having sprained my shoulder while playing. There was no sick or relief fund among the men at that time, so I had to 'fight it out' for myself as best I could." "The buckle trade," continued this venerable buckle-maker, "was a great blessing to Birmingham, and if it were to be revived it would give employment to thousands of workmen. The use of the buckle was first done away with in the army, as it was found among cavalry soldiers that the buckles on their shoes caught the stirrup when they were mounting or dismounting, and frequently occasioned mischief. This was the commencement of its disuse, and in a very short time the buckle trade became confined to supplying country orders and America, and then sunk altogether. But the buckle is the only efficient shoe tie, and preserves the shoe much longer than tape or ribbon. The first great revival of the steel toy trade was when Queen Charlotte appeared in Court with steel latchets on her shoes, and having her dress adorned with steel buttons and slides. This set the trade in motion, and steel toys of all sorts became highly fashionable; but the demand did not extend beyond this country, and sunk again in about five years in consequence of the wretchedly inferior quality of the articles made. The buckle, I firmly believe, would have been worn to this day, if it had not been for the quantity of cheap trash that was made to disgust the people with this noble article of trade. I am convinced that nothing is so handsome for the leg and foot as knee-breeches, a sound shoe, and a good buckle. They beat all your boots and trowsers for beauty—yes, and for convenience too."

Die-sinkers, Medallists, Coiners, etc.

Letter XVII

. . . A few of the old workmen employed by Messrs. Boulton and Watt, in the days when the Soho Works were in full activity and renowned throughout Europe, are still in existence. The following statement was made by one of them: "Coining was first commenced at the Soho Works in 1787. They had then eight cutting out presses and eight coining presses, by which about sixty pence, seventy halfpence or about eighty pieces of Indian coin, called 'cock money' could be produced in a minute. Great quantities of Indian coins were made. Some are still made at Birmingham, but the Soho Company fitted up a mint for Calcutta, by which a large portion of the manufacture was transferred to India. This mint consisted of nineteen cutting presses and thirteen coining presses. The money made was principally copper, and generally very thin and small. The number of persons employed in this department of the Soho Works was not great. There were about fourteen or fifteen women engaged in 'cutting out' the copper; two men in attending to the machiner; sixteen boys and two men in the coining; seven or eight-women in 'lapping up' the coins; four or five women in milling; two men in turning the machines; and six men in *annealing* and shaking—in all twelve or thirteen men, about twenty-seven women and sixteen boys. The presses used at the Soho Works were exactly the same as those used at the Royal Mint at London, and just as effective. There was always a risk attending an overworking of the presses, so that no more than sixty pence a minute could be produced with safety. About twenty-four tons of pence a week were the usual quantity produced when the presses were in full operation, which was in the beginning of the present century, for about twelve months at a time. The coins were examined and weighed by agents from London. James Watt did not trouble himself much in the business, except with the engineering department. The dies for the coins were sunk principally by Messrs. Kuchler, Droz and Wyon, the inventor of the present Royal Mint die-sinker. Mr. Watt was very busy generally at the manufactory, and he came very regularly. Mr. Boulton used to take a great interest in the manufactory, and in those engaged in it. He had a series of rules drawn up for keeping the boys in order, and he supplied each of them regularly with duck trowsers and blue jackets, and all their dress, so that they were exceedingly tidy. The trowsers were changed and washed twice a week. They had all slippers to put on at the Mint. He gave the men and boys an allowance of beer every day at five o'clock. The Mint was kept in perfect order, and every kind of care was taken of the health and morals of the people."

"Birmingham," said another aged and intelligent mechanic, the same, whose account of the shoe buckle, and all the changes of fashion which it underwent, was detailed in a previous letter, "had a bad character for false money, when I was a young man. There were many coiners of false copper, silver, and gold money. Wolverhampton was, perhaps, still worse than Birmingham; but Bilston was the worst place of all, and actually swarmed with coiners of bad money. Almost any kind of rubbish used to pass as copper money, fifty or sixty years ago, button-tops, tokens, or any round bit of metal. And all this made the trade of the false coiner more easy. The trade was carried on so openly, that I often wondered at people's hardihood, considering the severity of the punishment on detection. They imitated the old copper halfpence of George II, and fried them in brimstone to give them an antique appearance. If anybody was detected in imitating gold or silver coinage, it was called a 'spiritual' business, because it touched his life; but if it were for copper money only, it was called 'temporal', because he was in no danger of the gallows for that. Those were the slang expressions of the town. Executions for coining were very frequent in the neighbourhood. I have known as many as three and four people strung up together at one time for that offence. The makers of false copper money used to be burnt in the hand and imprisoned, and I believe they were sometimes transported. A great deal of what was called 'workhouse' money used also to be coined in Birmingham. There were workhouse pence, sixpence, and shillings; or they might be called 'tokens' or 'promises to pay', for those amounts. The coiners forged these as well as the coin of the realm. The large manufactories in all parts of the country used to issue tokens to pay their workmen with, most of which were made in Birmingham, Bilston, and Wolverhampton, and the forgers would not even let these alone. A good deal of coining of false silver money is still carried on hereabouts, I have no doubt. It is a much easier business than it was, and can be done with less risk of detection than formerly. I worked at Boulton and Watt's and though not in the coining department, knew a good deal of what went on there. Mr. Boulton coined many hundreds of tons of copper money for the British Government, and silver money also. I remember once that the firm had a large order to melt down some tons of Spanish dollars and re-coin them into English five-shilling pieces. It was during the Spanish war, when the British cruisers used to lie in wait twice a year to capture the galleons bearing the tribute from Mexico to Spain. The dollars came to the Soho Works in waggon-loads, and a guard of soldiers was regularly stationed at the Mint for the whole time during which the order was in progress. Mr. Matthew Boulton was a great friend of the sober, and clever workman in every department of his business. He always rewarded merit, and would 'buy any man's brains'. The next Mr. Boulton did not push the business as his father did; his fortune was made; he had more money than he could spend, and was seldom or never seen about the place."

The establishment of the Royal Mint on Tower-hill, by which the Soho establishment lost a valuable portion of its trade—the constant changes in the fashion of other articles produced—the total cessation of the demand for others which formerly employed hundreds of men, such as the shoe-buckle and the latchet, added no doubt to the circumstance that the proprietors had made their fortunes, and were less careful than they might otherwise have been to extend their trade into new channels when the old ones ran dry—all conspired to deprive the "Soho" of its ancient renown in miscellaneous goods, and to confine the business to the one great department of engine-making, for which, in its new locality at Smethwick, it still preserves all its reputation. The final breaking up of the Soho establishment in the spring of 1850, consequent upon the death in June 1848, of James Watt, Esq., of Aston Hall, the son of the illustrious man to whom we owe the improvement of the steam-engine, scarcely received any notice at the time from the metropolitan press.

Gilders, Platers, and Electro-platers

Letter XVIII

... The introduction of the electro process, which may well rank among the most useful and beautiful inventions of our age and country, has already effected a revolution in the plating trade, and, brought within the reach of persons of moderate fortune articles of a style and excellence formerly only attainable by the most wealthy. ...

... The workmen employed in this beautiful manufacture are, as might be expected, of a superior class. It was remarked by an intelligent manufacturer in another branch of trade, that he always found men who worked by mere manual labour, and with ordinary tools, inferior to those who made use of steam power. The complicated machinery and the regularity of steam power tended, he thought, to make the men regular as well as intelligent. The electro process seems to have exercised a similar, if not a higher, influence upon the character of the workpeople. From an examination of the time-book of Messrs. Elkington, it appears that out of the 500 persons in their employ, not two, on the average, were absent on any Monday, or on any part of a Monday, during the year—a fact very remarkable in Birmingham, where the working classes make it a constant practice to neglect their work on that day, and where it is a common complaint among employers, especially when trade is brisk, that men sacrifice not only the Monday, but too often a portion of the Tuesday, to drinking and idleness. Ten years ago the platers are represented as having been "a rough set", but those employed in the superior branches necessary for the finer beauty of the electro process, bear the highest character, not only for regularity and sobriety, but for their provident economy. Great numbers of them save money. They have no union of the trade, but they have founded a sick and burial club, and have it in contemplation, in conjunction with their employer, to establish a school for their children and for the boys engaged in the manufacture, and a library and reading room for themselves.

Amusements of the People

Letter XX

The working men of Birmingham and the manufacturing districts of Staffordshire were notorious during the first twenty-five years of the present century—and, indeed, to a much later period—for the brutality of their sports. On Saturday afternoons in the open air, during the whole of Sunday in public-house tap-rooms, and again on the Monday at their usual haunts in the outskirts of the town, dog-fights, cock-fights, bull-baitings, badger-baitings, bear-baitings, and pugilistic encounters were the favourite amusements of the operative classes, and of some portion of their employers. Much of the ancient love for these and other demoralising exhibitions still exists among the uneducated portion of the workmen and small manufacturers; but the law has prohibited cruelty to animals, and rendered it difficult as well as dangerous for those who crave such coarse indulgences to indulge in them; and the growth of a taste for music and for reading has aided the efforts of the law, in rendering such exhibitions comparatively rare. Before describing the more rational amusements of the working classes in the present day, or noting the vast improvement which has been effected in the tastes and manners of the people, an account of the rougher sports of thirty or forty years ago—derived from the recollections of two gentlemen holding official situations in the town, and whose duties brought, and still bring them into contact with assemblages of the people, and with offenders against the laws—will no doubt be perused with interest by public of Birmingham and its neighbourhood, as well as by that larger public who delight to trace the progress of civilisation in the refinement of manners. "The popular sports in Birmingham," said one of these gentlemen, a man of much experience, and of excellent memory for local facts, "were, till within about twenty-five years ago, bull-baiting, cock-fighting, badger-baiting, and bear-baiting. These were the great favourites of the working men. A sort of arena was fitted up for these and other sports, which consisted of an inclosure, containing about 2,500 square yards of ground. The workmen and other young men of the town used very frequently to assemble here for playing at football, leap-frog, and other games of the sort; but cock-fighting, and more brutal amusements were more popular than healthy games. The cock-fights often lasted for two or three days, and were attended by thousands of people. Contests were got up between two counties as for instance between Warwickshire and Worcestershire, each side being presided over by some gentleman or nobleman of the respective counties. There was a covered part of the inclosure set aside for cock-fighting, in which a pit was dug for the cocks, and seats were ranged round, so that the fight could be seen by all around. There were generally two or three grant 'bouts' in the course of a year, and parties came from London, and greater distances, to witness the contest. The number of cocks brought forward on these occasions to support the credit of the respective counties or towns in which they were reared varied considerably, but generally, on grand occasions, about ten pairs of cocks were pitted against each other before dinner, and ten pairs in the afternoon, with a little badger-baiting or other sports by way of varying the entertainment. On a smaller scale, there used to be some cock-fighting carried on almost every Monday afternoon in public-houses in and around the town, and in winter still more frequently. The 'main' or prize contended for, varied according to the circumstance of the principals or the number of cocks produced. Many noblemen indulged in the sport, and made money by it, and the workmen thoroughly understood the rules of the game, and betted on the result of a fight according to their means, or even beyond them, if we take the authority of the ballad of "Wednesbury Cocking", an old song which is still popular among the country folks around Birmingham, and often sung by the older workmen of the town. Badger-baiting was almost as common as cock-fighting, and was carried on principally in an open space of ground in Smallbrook-street, on which a church is now being erected. A hole was dug in the ground, in which the badger was placed. There were generally a good many dogs ready to attack it in the hole, and one by one they were allowed to try to dislodge the badger, the owner of each dog paying a stipulated sum for the privilege of running his dog at the animal. Bull-baiting was a more costly, and consequently a rarer source of amusement. One bull was often baited on three or four successive Mondays. There was generally a baiting match at the three great 'wakes' or local fairs, held annually at Birmingham. Chapel wake was the best of sports of all kinds, and an unusual amount of bull-baiting, cock-fighting, badger-baiting, dancing, singing and sight-seeing was there indulged in. A good wake often lasted for three or four days, commencing on Sunday and terminating on the following Wednesday. Monday was, however, the principal holiday, and those who came from the country to participate in the wake generally selected that day. In almost every public-house music and dancing were carried on in the evening, and towards noon the whole town swarmed out in the streets to witness the sports. The Birmingham wakes are still held. They follow each other with only an interval of about a week. The three great wakes are those of Deritend, Bell, and Chapel, and there are two others, namely Ashted and Edgbaston. They are all held during the months of July and August. The difference between 'wakes' and fairs is, that the former are not attended by vendors of wares from the country, but are wholly confined to the people of the town, who erect stalls and tents much in the same way as country dealers do at a fair. For about twenty years, the wakes have been gradually falling off in importance, and are likely to become almost extinct in a few years. The gipsy parties got up by the workmen of most of the principal manufactories of the town have, I think, tended as much as anything to diminish their importance, as the men save up their spare cash to be spent then, rather than spend it as they used to do in bull-baiting and cock-fighting, or in dancing at the wakes. Both bull-baits and cock-fights, however, are still indulged in on the sly, by workmen of the old school; but their number is fast diminishing.". . .

. . . The following particulars relative to cock-fighting and bear-baiting, and the cruel and disgusting sport of bull-baiting, for which Birmingham used many years ago to be the most notorious place in England, were derived from the second of the two gentlemen already alluded to. It may be first of all mentioned, for the information of strangers to Birmingham, that one of the principal open squares of the town is still called the "Bull-ring", and that it derived its name from having been the spot where bulls were legally baited for the amusement of the populace. Hutton in his history states that one John Cooper, who had lived about two hundred and fifty years prior to the time at which he wrote, obtained three privileges from the lord of the manor of Birmingham— "that of regulating the goodness and price of beer, that he should, whenever he pleased, bait a bull in the Bull-ring, and that he should be allowed interment in the south porch of St. Martin's Church". "His memory", adds Hutton, "ought to be transmitted with honour to posterity for promoting the harmony of his neighbourhood (in the matter of beer), but he ought to have been buried on a dung-hill for punishing an innocent animal."

"The last time that a bull was baited," said my informant, "was in 1811, during the Chapel wake, which commenced upon the Sunday after St. Bartholomew's day. Upon this occasion the bull broke loose from the stake to which it was tied, and endeavouring to escape, the animal ran down a lane, which was crowded with people to see the baiting. In the rush of the people to escape from the bull, a child was crushed to death, and an old woman very seriously hurt. This precipitated the abolition of bull-baiting in Birmingham considerably before the general Act, by which this and other cruel sports were prohibited, was passed by the Legislature. The great times of bull-baiting and other sports were Easter, Whitsuntide, and during the wakes, when the workmen had holidays. Bulls were baited every Monday or Tuesday during these festivities, and sometimes the sport was indulged in every day for a week or more at a time. At the country wakes it was quite common to have three or four bulls to bait, and on one occasion, in the year 1793, I saw no less than seven bulls placed in a row to be baited on a level piece of ground close to a church in the neighbourhood of the town. The ground was about 150 yards long by about 40 yards wide. Generally, when a bull was baited at a country wake near the town on a Monday or Tuesday, it was brought into Birmingham on the Wednesday afternoon and baited again. These were chance baitings however. The regular matches were got up during the holidays or wakes in town; and to procure a bull it was customary for the workmen to club together a sufficient sum to purchase one. The animal was brought forward early on the Monday of the wake, and whoever had a dog paid sixpence or one shilling to let it have a fly at the bull. The proceeds went to pay for the bull, which was sold after the baiting. The dog, when let loose, flew directly at the bull, and was either tossed in the air or it succeeded in fastening itself upon him, either by the nose or ear, or some other part. If tossed, the owner immediately ran forward to catch the dog, and if uninjured it was encouraged to have another fly at him. Sometimes the dog seized the bull by the nose and 'pinned' him to the earth, so that the beast roared and bellowed again, and was brought down upon its knees; the people then shouted out 'Wind, wind!' that is, to let the bull have breath, and the parties rushed forward to take off the dog. This was no easy matter, and beating, pulling, the application of cold water, and other remedies were often for a long time ineffectual. The best way of loosening the dog was attended with a little danger; its owner went forward, accompanied by another person, and lifted the dog by its tail, while the other put its paw in his mouth and bit it as severely as he could. The dog, feeling the bite, let the bull go, and turned to attack its new enemy, but the moment the hold was loosened the master swung his dog round, and carried him off in triumph, while the bull breathed a little before the next encounter. The first baiting took place early in the morning, and lasted for about an hour; after breakfast the bull was again brought out, and baited for about the same time, and in the afternoon and evening the scene was repeated, so that the bull was generally baited for about four hours a day. The intervals were filled up with cock-fighting, badger-baiting, or bear-baiting. By practice some of the bulls became so conversant with baiting, that when in the fields or passing through a town, the boys had only to cry out, 'a lane! a lane!' to make them immediately assume a posture of defence and paw the ground impatient for the attack. These were well known in the neighbourhood, and I remember at least five noted 'game' bulls. They became so expert in defending themselves that even two dogs at once had no chance of success with them. I have seen such a bull toss a couple of dogs as lightly as a man might play with a couple of balls. A premium was frequently offered to the man who could produce a dog able to touch one of these game bulls. In this there was real sport, and it was much less cruel than hunting a fox with a pack of hounds, or spurring horses almost to death at a race.

"There was a large black bear called 'Old Nell' which stood the brunt of war for several years in Birmingham. Scarcely a Monday passed by on which Old Nell was not brought into the yard in Coleshill-street, to be baited. Her mouth and nose were protected against the dogs, or rather, she was muzzled to prevent her from biting them; the dogs flew at the ears, neck, or breast of the bear, which, on the other hand, tried to grasp them within her paws and crush them to death, or blow down their throats till they were almost suffocated. During wakes or festival times Old Nell was baited for two or three successive days, and did not appear to be much the worse for it.

"Cock-fighting and badger-baiting were the most common of the by-gone sports. They were indulged in almost every day in some part of the town, and much time was spent in training cocks to fight. On Monday there were almost invariably several pairs of cocks brought into the yard usually appropriated to such sports. The workmen of the town who were fond of 'cocking' bred 'fowl' themselves, and two workmen were always ready to bring their cocks to fight for a 'main' which was just whatever money they could spare more than was necessary to pay the owner of the pit. Noblemen and gentlemen frequently fought for a 'main' with their cocks, and the amount of it varied according to the number of cocks brought forward. It was frequently forty or fifty guineas and on a grand occasion as much as 100 guineas, were staked upon the result of the fight. Considerable care was required to arrange the preliminaries to a cock-fight. The birds had to be 'trimmed' that is, to have their wings clipped and dressed, and to have the spurs well adjusted for service; and it required an experienced hand to 'set' the birds properly on to fight, and to manage them while the combat was going on. Spurring a cock was a very important duty. The spurs were sometimes made of steel, but silver was preferred, as the blow from silver was considered to be less likely to be fatal. Both had disadvantages, however, as the steel frequently broke and the silver was liable to bend and double up, if the blow were not dexterously struck. The spurs were from two inches and a half to four inches in length. If badly put on, the cock ran a chance of choking itself with the spurs in the course of the fight. Out of fifty lovers of cock-fighting, there was scarcely one who knew how to spur a bird, or to set or handle them at a fight. A good deal of gambling used to be carried on at cock-fighting, as the issue was generally very uncertain. I have known several instances in which a cock had apparently killed or utterly subdued its antagonist, and stood crowing over it, when the vanquished one suddenly started up and struck the other such a blow as proved fatal.

"Cock fighting decreased a good deal before the passing of Martin's Bill for the prevention of cruelty to animals, but it is still carried on pretty freely within doors and in secret. About ten years ago there was a cock-fight in Birmingham, but the police interrupted it, and apprehended about 100 persons. They were all brought before the magistrates and bound over not to offend again either as spectators or principals. So long as fox-hunting, coursing and horse-racing are allowed by law, I do not see why cock-fighting should be forbidden. It was intended by nature that cocks should fight. Look at two cocks brought up in one brood; they will not fight so long as they belong to that brood, but separate them for some time, and then bring them together, and they will fly at each other's eyes the moment they meet. Now, in hunting, it is not enough that the horse strains itself to the utmost, with a good will, but the rider must keep digging his spurs into the poor beast's side to make him go faster, till at last he falls down quite brokenhearted. But two game cocks will by themselves fight till one or the other is killed, and nature has given them 'pluck', strength and activity for fighting. I dare say you will not agree with me about cock-fighting, but these are my opinions. Prize-fighting among men was always rare at Birmingham, though there was plenty of unprofessional boxing at a wake or fair in the town. Mondays and Tuesdays were the favourite days in the week for settling quarrels, or for making them, and the yard in Coleshill-street always saw plenty of fighting going on. There is very little fighting now compared with what there used to be in former times.

"Badger-baiting was almost as popular and as common as cock-fighting. The badger was put into a hole dug in the ground, or into a box, and as many dogs as were brought forward were allowed, one by one, to 'have a worry' at it. The badger was a serious enemy to encounter, and frequently bit and lacerated the dogs very severely. I remember once an impudent fellow taking a badger that had been two or three weeks dead, putting it into a box, and collecting around him several persons with dogs. One by one the dogs had a 'worry' at the dead badger, and the fellow stuck pins and small nails in its head, so that the dogs came from the encounter torn and bleeding, as if they had been bitten. The trick was, however, discovered, and the impostor soundly beaten."

The following particulars, referring to a period which the younger race of mechanics remember, were communicated by an intelligent workman in the chandelier and gas-fitting trade:

"The ancient sports of the Birmingham working men are not yet forgotten, and have not fallen into total disuse. About fifteen years ago or less, dog-fights used to be got up every Monday, and there are a few still in the summer time, when the men do not think much of walking a few miles out of this overgrown town to some quiet part of the country. There was a regular cockpit about twenty years ago, built in the open air, on purpose for the sport and for dog-fighting. It was suppressed by the magistrates. I was one of forty taken into custody by the police for attending it. We were all tied together with ropes round the body or arms, two by two, and were marched in procession through the principal streets of the town as an example, and then brought before the magistrates. The ringleaders, who actually got up the cock-fight, were fined, and the rest of us, who were spectators only, were discharged. The workmen are still to some extent fond of cock-fights. The fights are got up in public-house parlours, fitted up conveniently for the purpose. On Shrove Tuesday especially there are great numbers of cock-fights in tap-rooms and parlours, to which the admission is by ticket, at threepence and sixpence each. I think, however, there has been less of the amusement during the last five or six years than there used to be."

Within the last few years Birmingham has attained considerable reputation for its encouragement of music; and its triennial musical festivals are well known and appreciated. Of these, however, it is not consistent with the object of these letters to speak. The popular love of music, which has been much extended in every part of England and which forms, indeed, one of the most interesting characteristics of the present age, has seized all classes of the people in this town, and the purveyors of amusement have not failed to administer to it. No singing and dancing license is requisite in Birmingham, and the keepers of gin-shops and public-houses vie with each other in providing dramatic and musical entertainments for their customers. In the gin-shops—where no accommodation beyond a bench or two, or a seat before a barrel which serves as a table to put the liquor upon, is provided for the guests, and where in consequence the larger portion of the company have to stand at the bar and partake of their drams—it is not uncommon for the proprietor to hire a few fiddlers and banjo players, who sit in a kind of orchestra, overlooking the crowd, and make music from seven or eight in the evening until midnight. In one establishment of this kind, I was amused at seeing four men with blackened faces in a raised orchestra, smoking long clay pipes and playing the fiddle. In another, a fat boy was exhibiting his obesity taking advantage of the intervals in the musical performances to go his rounds, accompanied by his "keeper". But the tavern entertainments are of a higher class than is provided in the gin-shops. In many of these musical houses there is a regular stage on which farces and ballets are performed. At Christmas time they get up pantomimes, and incur considerable expense in their production. One of these roms is fitted up to contain upwards of 1,000 people, and is very handsomely decorated. Here the working classes resort with their wives and children, and have the enjoyment of a dramatic performance quite as good as would be provided for them at some of the minor theatres of the metropolis, together with those coarser enjoyments of smoking and drinking which are prohibited in the regular theatre. The price of admission is threepence and sixpence, according to the seat occupied, and the amount is returned in ale, beer, spirits, and tobacco. The number of young lads and boys in their teens—workmen on their own account earning their own wages, and responsible to nobody—who attend these places, is perhaps unparalleled out of Birmingham. The precocity in vice of these boys is one of the most melancholy results of the manufacturing system in this town. Factory girls of an age quite as tender, accompany them to such places, and sit for hours—especially on the Saturday, Sunday, and Monday evenings—drinking with their companions, and imbibing the odour of tobacco smoke, demoralising to every woman who is accustomed to it. On Sunday, when no dramatic entertainment is allowed, psalm tunes and other sacred pieces are played upon the organ. Some of these instruments are not only large and handsome in appearance, but powerful and rich in tone. In one public-house the proprietor stated that he had expended upwards of £800 upon his organ for Sunday evening performance, and there is no reason to doubt the truth of the assertion. The company is almost as numerous on Sundays as on the other nights of the week, and is composed of the same classes who frequent it at other times. The smoke and drinking form, it must be confessed, a strange accompaniment to the psalm and hymn tunes; and the conversation of the guests, if truly reported, would doubtless form an accompaniment, if possible, still more strange, incongruous, and improper.

. . . One other point in connection with the amusements of the working classes in Birmingham remains to be stated. Formerly, when the town was not half so large as it is at present, and before the railways cut up the neighbourhood, and took possession of the vacant land in the immediate vicinity on which to erect their stations and approaches, the better class of working men used to be fond of renting small plots of garden ground. These plots were let out by large landed proprietors, and produced a high rental. They were called "guinea gardens"— a guinea being the sum usually paid for a plot of an eighth, and sometimes for a sixteenth, of an acre. Here working men built themselves little summer houses of wood and brick, where, on the fine summer evenings, and on Sundays, they retired to smoke their pipes, and where they often took their wives and children to tea. They were fond of growing their own vegetables as well as flowers, and these little bits of ground were so much in request that, although the holding was precarious, and the tenant liable to a six months' notice to quit, the good-will of one of them has often been sold for as much as £20 or £30. The expansion of the town on all sides has almost swept the whole of them away, and the goods station of the London and North-Western Railway occupies the site of many scores of them. Only a few now remain, in the neighbourhood of the two Vauxhalls; and it is likely that these will be speedily swept away by the rapid extension of streets, factories, and railway stations. The working men of Birmingham cannot obtain land for any such purpose at the present time, and, more unfortunate than the dwellers in other large towns, they do not possess the privilege of a public park of any kind. But the railways, which have been instrumental in depriving them of their little plots of garden ground, have to some extent made them amends. Cheap excursion trains run on all, or nearly all, their holidays during the fine season, and convey them at almost a nominal rate to every popular place of resort in the beautiful county of Warwick, and sometimes into Shropshire or Wales, or as far as Liverpool to inhale the sea-breezes of the Mersey, and to visit the novel spectacle, to an inland population of the splendid line of docks in the great seaport of the west. Gipsy parties, as will have appeared from some previous allusions in this and other letters of the series, have also become exceedingly popular among the working classes, of late years. In almost every large factory, and in the small ones besides, the men and women, the boys and the girls employed, club up their money for an annual "gipsy party".

Clubs of Working Men and their Families

Letter XXI

There is perhaps no town in England in which the principle of association for mutual benefit, real or supposed, is carried to so great an extent as in Birmingham. Persons of both sexes and of all ages belong to sick and benefit clubs—to clothing clubs, and to associations of other kinds for almost every purpose for which a club can be devised. Even infants of two or three years of age are taught to club their half-pence, for medical attendance, or for the purchase of Sunday finery. Any one who walks along the streets, and looks at the placards on the walls, or the bills in public-houses, coffee-houses, and other shop-windows, may see at a glance from these announcements how deep a hold the club system has taken upon the affections of the people. In Birmingham the associative principle, if not worked out upon any great or comprehensive plan, is carried into a multiplicity of minor channels. The father of the family clubs for his Trade Society, or for the Odd Fellows, or for a Sick and Burial Society, or perhaps for the Freehold Land Society, or for a Money Club, or for a Watch and Seals Club, or for an Excursion Club. The mother joins a Medical Attendance Club, or a Coal and Coke Club, or a Flour Club, or a Shawl Club, or a Silk Dress Club, or, at Christmas time, a Pudding Club, or a Goose and Gin Club; while the children, if at school, bring their fortnightly halfpence to a Sick Club, or a Clothing Club; or if at work in a factory, contribute at a specified rate to the club of the establishment, to which it is a rule for every person, young or old, male or female, to belong. . . .

. . . If there were 40,000 club members in 1835, there are in all probability 60,000 or 70,000 in 1851. . . .

. . . The Building Societies are chiefly supported by respectable mechanics, and their meetings are mostly held at temperance hotels and coffee-houses. Their object is to enable each member to erect or purchase a house or houses, or some other freehold or leasehold property, from a common fund raised by the voluntary contributions of the members. The contributions vary in different clubs. In some it is five shillings for every share per fortnight, until the sum of £120 is realised for each share, and an equal proportion for half and quarter shares. In others the contributions are ten shillings per share per fortnight until the sum of £240 be raised. Whatever the contribution and amount of share may be, as often as the required sum is raised it is put up for sale. Every member who has not received his share of shares, or part of a share, is entitled to bid; and the share is awarded to the member who offers the highest premium for it, by ticket. If two or more members offer the same premium the bidding is repeated, and the one offering the greatest advance is declared the purchaser. No member can receive money until the land, building, or other premises offered as a security is approved of by the committee, in conformity with the recommendation of the surveyor.

At the termination of the society—that is, when each member has received £120 or £240 as the case may be, on every share he holds in the society—the securities are given up, and a receipt endorsed thereon, which by statutory enactment, has the effect of revesting the property in the mortgagor, without putting him to the expense of a re-conveyance.

"By way of illustration," says the prospectus of one of these clubs, which has now been in operation seven years, "it may be stated that a person, on purchasing one share of £120 for which he pays five shillings per fortnight—

Will pay, per annum, in contributions	£ 6	10	0
Interest at 5s. per share, per fortnight	£ 6	10	0
Premium, say £20, divided into ten years	£ 2	0	0
Total payments, per annum, for one share of £120	£15	0	0
The £120 invested in a house or houses, will yield			
say 10 per cent. per annum, or	£12	0	0
Which deducted from the £15, will leave every year a			
balance of	£ 3	0	0

only for the member to provide for, over and above the rents; which sum being continued for the term of ten years (the utmost period the society may be expected to last), he will have contributed to the funds of the society the sum of £30 only, and will then have his deeds delivered up to him, with a receipt of the whole £120 borrowed, and will thus become possessed of a dwelling-house or houses, worth £120, for the trifling sum of £3 per annum, paid during the period of ten years. But should a more advantageous purchase be made—say to pay 12 per cent.—the party would actually become possessed of property, unencumbered, and worth £120, for nothing at all on the dissolution of the society. And this is no imaginary case; for many instances of this kind are known in the societies now in operation."

These clubs, of which the number in the town is estimated at above a hundred, are continually dying out in the natural course, and are as continually being revived under new names. The rules of the whole of them are very similar, and differ only in minor details, as in the amount of shares, the fortnightly payments, and the fines for non-payment of interest or contributions. There is considerable rivalry among them in the inducements which they hold out to persons desirous of becoming members. Some of them adopt what they call an equitable adjustment of the rate of interest, in other words;—if a member has been subscribing five years for one share, of £120 at five shillings per fortnight, so that he has paid into the funds of the society nearly £33, and then gets his share advanced, value £120, although in fact he withdraws his own £33 and borrows only £87, he pays interest on the whole £120, and continues to do so although he reduces the principal by every subsequent periodical subscription. This is considered an injustice, and some of the newly established building clubs make a yearly reduction in the amount of interest, in proportion as the principal is redeemed. It seems to be admitted on all hands that these clubs are highly useful in promoting economy among working men, and in tending to their elevation from the ranks of the mere day labourer, into those of the capitalist. One result, not quite so agreeable, which has not been so much noticed, is that they tend to cover the town and its outskirts with small and mean houses and cottages, built without any pretension to beauty, and very often of the flimsiest materials or without proper regard being paid to the requirements of health or decency. . . . But the most numerous class of clubs in Birmingham are the "money clubs"—associations which are no doubt occasionally productive of good, but which, it is much to be feared, are still more frequently productive of evil. Out of the 1,200 taverns, public-houses, gin-shops, and beer-shops which are reckoned to exist in Birmingham, there is scarcely one—the taverns and gin-shops, which do not amount to above a tenth of the number expected—which does not hold a money-club at stated times. These clubs are for the most part got up by the landlords, with motives and objects which are clear to the meanest capacity; but others, got up by working men for mutual convenience, and as an investment of money, are held at temperance hotels and coffee-houses. There are £3 clubs, £10 clubs, £12 10s. clubs, £20 clubs, £25 clubs, £50 clubs, and £120 clubs. They are conducted upon similar principles to the building-clubs; and the money or share subscribed for is put up for sale by auction among the members in the same way— the only difference being, that the purchaser of the money is not obliged to spend it on a house, but may make whatever use of it he pleases. The purchaser must have two bondsmen to join in a promissory note for the repayment of the amount by the usual weekly, fortnightly, or monthly instalments. Birmingham, as is well known, abounds in ingenious mechanics. Many a man working at the bench or the lathe as a journeyman has an idea of an improvement in the mechanism with which he labours—or invents some new article which he imagines will make his fortune, if he can carry out his scheme—or discovers some new process likely to be advantageous to himself and to his trade. All he requires is money. In these circumstances, if he has not been a provident man, beforehand with the world, the money club is the only available resource; and such men have frequently been known to give these clubs £18 or £20 for £50;

in other words, to receive £30, and incur a debt of £50, repayable by weekly instalments. Those who know the working classes, and the private history of some of the cleverest among them for mechanical contrivance, report that many a useful invention has been brought to maturity by this means, although, in some instances, unfortunately not rare, the improvident man of genius has afterwards been compelled to part with his invention for a trifle, to an employer more ignorant and less ingenious than himself—and every often for no other reason than to be released from his liability to the money club. These clubs are also the resource of improvident working men, when their wives are confined, or when the quarter's rent becomes due, and they have not the means of paying it; and very often, also, the young workman, on contracting matrimony, has no other means of procuring furniture than the purchase of a share at the "Money Club". "This system," said the keeper of a temperance hotel, "has increased greatly within the last seven years. Indeed, all kinds of clubs are on the increase in Birmingham. The money clubs that meet in public-houses, used to be called 'Spigot clubs'. Money clubs are held not only in temperance hotels, but in private houses. A man may subscribe for a share, a half share, or a quarter share. The secretaries receive sixpence a quarter from each member for keeping the books, looking after defaulters, and attending to the general business of the club. Many young working men who are expert at figures, or who can write a good hand, make more money as secretaries to clubs than they can make at their trades. I know some who are secretaries of four, five, six, and even eight clubs, and who make it their regular business, and attend to nothing else. Some of them make as much as £100 per annum, or even more, in this way. There are good as well as bad points in the money-clubs, and although it would be better for working men to save their money than to buy loans at a high rate, I know many respectable tradesmen who have been enabled to set themselves up by these means in businesses that do not require much capital. One reason why these clubs are so numerous is that the banks do not afford accommodation to working men. They will have nothing to do with small accounts and small people. The banks with whom the money of these clubs is lodged charge commission for receiving it, and some of them will not receive such deposits at all, on the ground that it gives them too much trouble. At the end of the club, the money in hand is divided among all the members. The £10 clubs last eighty nights, and the £30 clubs on an average three years; but the duration depends to a great extent upon the amount realised by sales of money. The utmost I have ever known to be given were £24 for £30, and £60 for £120. In the panic of 1847 and 1848 very large sums were offered for loans, and there were a great many defaulters. Prices are now much lower.

One of the newest clubs of working-men in Birmingham has been constituted under the patronage of several of the most eminent manufacturers in the town, for the purpose of enabling the members to visit the Great Exhibition of the present year.

APPENDIX

In order to indicate to the reader the full range of the topics covered by the survey, we have included here a complete list of the letters published by the *Morning Chronicle*. The titles are those which were used by the correspondents.

LABOUR AND THE POOR

Morning Chronicle letters

INDEX

MANUFACTURING DISTRICTS

Date	District	Title	Letter
South Wales			
Mar. 4 1850	—	Mining in Merthyr Tydfil	I
Mar. 18 1850	—	Mining in Merthyr Tydfil	II
Mar. 21 1850	—	Mining in Merthyr Tydfil	III
Mar. 27 1850	—	Mines and Collieries—A Welsh Coal-Pit	IV
Apr. 1 1850	—	Aberdare Coal Strike	V
Apr. 8 1850	—	Merthyr and Dowlais	VI
Apr. 15 1850	—	Public Health: Religion in the Iron Works The Irish	VII
Apr. 22 1850	—	Merthyr & Dowlais: Public Charities— Education—Pauperism	VIII
Apr. 29 1850	—	Education of Pauper Children Pauperism—Crime	IX
May 6 1850	—	Truck In The Iron Works And Collieries	X
May 13 1850	—	Abercarn and Gwythen Collieries	XI
May 21 1850	—	Swansea and the Copper Works	XII
June 8 1850	—	Swansea and the Copper Works	XIII
June 14 1850	—	Swansea and the Copper Works	XIV
Aug. 14 1850	—	Swansea Copper Works and Potteries	XV
Apr. 22 1850	—	Welsh Lead Mines	XVI
Apr. 25 1851	—	Welsh Lead Mines and Works	XVII
Liverpool			
May 20 1850	—	Irish Pauperism	I
May 27 1850	—	The Docks, Their Management and Mismanagement	II
June 3 1850	—	The Prohibition of Fire and Light in the Docks	III
June 10 1850	—	The Porterage System	IV
June 17 1850	—	Dock Labourers and Their Families	V
June 24 1850	—	Shirt Makers and Needlewomen The Slop Trade and Sweating System	VI
July 1 1850	—	Tailors and the Slop Trade—the Sweating System	VII
July 8 1850	—	Dwellings of the Poor	VIII
July 15 1850	—	Emigrants and Man Catchers	IX
July 22 1850	—	The Departure of Stowaway Vessels	X
July 29 1850	—	The Mormons—Mormon Emigration	XI
Aug. 5 1850	—	The Mormons—Their Rise and Progress — Emigration from Liverpool	XII

Date	District	Title	Letter
Aug. 12 1850	—	Death of a Prophet—English Emigration	XIII
Aug. 19 1850	—	Education	XIV
Aug. 26 1850	—	Sailor's Homes	XIV
Sept. 2 1850	—	Literature and Amusements	XVI
Sept. 9 1850	—	Shipbuilding and Repairing	XVII
Sept. 16 1850	—	Ship Joiners and House Joiners	XVIII
Sept. 23 1850	—	Birkenhead and its Docks	XIX
Sept. 30 1850	—	The Present State and Prospects of Birkenhead	XX

Birmingham

Oct. 7 1850	—	Parochial and Moral Statistics	I
Oct. 14 1850	—	Sanitary Conditions	II
Oct. 21 1850	—	Metal, Florentine and Horn Button Manufacture	III
Nov. 4 1850	—	The Pearl and Fancy Button and Stud Manufacture	IV
Nov. 11 1850	—	Fire Arms	V
Nov. 18 1850	—	Fire Arms	VI
Nov. 25 1850	—	The Condition of Factory Women and Their Families	VII
Dec. 2 1850	—	Employment and Education of Children	VIII
Dec. 16 1850	—	Manufacture of Steel-Pens	IX
Dec. 23 1850	—	Glass Makers and Glass Workers	X
Dec. 30 1850	—	Makers of Swords, Matchetts and Bayonets	XI
Jan. 6 1851	—	Workers in Brass	XII
Jan. 13 1851	—	Workers in Brass	XIII
Jan. 20 1851	—	Heavy Steel Toys	XIV
Jan. 27 1851	—	Lightsteel Toys	XV
Feb. 3 1851	—	Tin Plate, Japan and Britannia Metal Workers	XVI
Feb. 10 1851	—	Die-Sinkers, Medallists and Coiners, etc	XVII
Feb. 17 1851	—	Gilders, Platers and Electro-Platers	XVIII
Feb. 24 1851	—	Industrial and Ragged Schools	XIX
Mar. 3 1851	—	Amusements of the People	XX
Mar. 10 1851	—	Clubs of Working Men and Their Families	XXI

Rural Districts

Oct. 20 1849		Introduction	I
Oct. 24 1849	Berks, Bucks, Wilts and Oxford	The Labourer's Home	II
Oct. 27 1849	Berks, Bucks, Wilts and Oxford	Wages and Diet of the Agricultural Labourer	III
Oct. 31 1849	Berks, Bucks, Wilts and Oxford	—	IV

Date		District	Title	Letter
Nov. 3	1849	Somerset, Cornwall and Devon	Condition of the Labourer	V
Nov. 7	1849	Devon, Somerset, Cornwall and Dorset	Physical Condition of the Labourer	VI
Nov. 10	1849	Devon, Somerset and Cornwall	Wages and Diet	VII
Nov. 14	1849	Cornwall	Physical Condition of the Labourer	VIII
Nov. 17	1849	Cornwall	Condition and Prospects of the Labourer	IX
Nov. 21	1849	Cornwall	Cornish Fisheries and Fishers	X
Nov. 24	1849	Cornwall	Mines and Miners	XI
Nov. 28	1849	Dorset	Condition of the Labourer	XII
Dec. 1	1849	Somerset, Cornwall Devon, Dorset	Intellectual and Moral Conditions	XIII
Dec. 5	1849	Norfolk, Suffolk and Essex	—	XIV
Dec. 8	1849	Norfolk, Suffolk and Essex	—	XV
Dec. 12	1849	Norfolk, Suffolk and Essex	—	XVI
Dec. 15	1849	Norfolk, Suffolk and Essex	— —	XVII
Dec. 19	1849	Norfolk, Suffolk and Essex	Herring Fisheries and Fishermen of Yarmouth	XVIII
Dec. 22	1849	Norfolk, Suffolk and Essex	—	XIX
Dec. 26	1849	Norfolk, Suffolk and Essex	—	XX
Dec. 29	1849	Norfolk, Suffolk and Essex	—	XXI
Jan. 2	1850	Norfolk, Suffolk and Essex	—	XXII
Jan. 5	1850	Durham, Northumberland, Cumberland and Westmorland	—	XXIII
Jan. 9	1850	Durham	—	XIV
Jan. 12	1850	Durham and Northumberland	—	XXV
Jan. 16	1850	Northumberland	—	XXVI
Jan. 19	1850	Cumberland and Westmorland	—	XXVII
Jan. 23	1850	Dorset	Swanage Stone Quarries	XVIII

* In *Morning Chronicle* printers error reads Dorset instead of Devon.

Rural Districts

Jan. 26	1850	Southern and Western Counties	Swanage Stone Quarries	XXIX
Jan. 30	1850	Southern and Western Counties	—	XXX

Date		District	Title	Letter
Feb. 13	1850	Southern and Western Counties	—	XXXI
Mar. 6	1850	Southern and Western Counties	—	XXXII
Mar. 30	1850	Southern and Western Counties	—	XXXIII
Apr. 5	1850	Herts, Beds, Hunts and Cambs.	Straw-plait and lacemaking districts	XXXIV

Letter 35 Missing from Morning Chronicle

Date		District	Title	Letter
May 8	1850	Herts, Beds, Hunts and Cambs	—	XXXVI
Sept. 27	1850	Herts, Beds, Hunts and Cambs	—	XXXVII
Oct. 18	1850	Herts, Beds, Hunts and Cambs	—	XXXVIII
Oct. 28	1850	Herts, Beds, Hunts and Cambs	—	XXXIX
Dec. 19	1850	Herts, Beds, Hunts and Cambs	Cottages of the Duke of Bedford	XL
Dec. 26	1850	Herts, Beds, Hunts and Cambs	—	XLI
Jan. 2	1851	Herts, Beds, Hunts and Cambs	The Spinning House	XLII
Jan. 9	1851	Northants, Leics Rutland, Notts, Derby	—	XLIII
Jan. 16	1851	Northants, Leics, Rutland, Notts, Derby	—	XLIV
Jan. 23	1851	Northants, Leics, Rutland, Notts, Derby	Boot and Shoe Makers of Northampton	XLV
Jan. 30	1851	Northants, Leics, Rutland, Notts, Derby	—	XLVI
Feb. 25	1851	Northants, Leics, Rutland, Notts, Derby	—	XLVII
Mar. 6	1851	Northants, Leics, Rutland, Notts Derby	—	XLVIII
Apr. 19	1851	Northants, Leics, Rutland, Notts, Derby	The Agricultural Labour of Northants	XLIX
Apr. 26	1851	Northants, Leics, Rutland, Notts, Derby	—	L

Metropolitan Districts

Date		District	Title	Letter
Oct. 19	1849	—		I

Date		Subject	Letter
Date		*Subject*	*Letter*
Oct. 23	1849	—	II
Oct. 26	1849	—	III
Oct. 30	1849	—	IV
Nov. 2	1849	—	V
Nov. 6	1849	—	VI
Nov. 9	1849	—	VII
Nov. 13	1849	—	VIII
Nov. 16	1849	—	IX
Nov. 20	1849	—	X
Nov. 23	1849	—	XI
Nov. 27	1849	—	XII
Nov. 30	1849	—	XIII
Dec. 4	1849	—	XIV
Dec. 7	1849	—	XV
Dec. 11	1849	The Operative Tailors	XVI
Dec. 14	1849	—	XVII
Dec. 18	1849	—	XVIII
Dec. 21	1849	—	IX
Dec. 25	1849	—	XX
Dec. 28	1849	—	XXI
Jan. 1	1850	—	XXII
Jan. 4	1850	—	XXIII
Jan. 8	1850	—	XXIV
Jan. 11	1850	—	XXV
Jan. 15	1850	—	XXVI
Jan. 18	1850	—	XXVII
Jan. 22	1850	—	XXVIII
Jan. 25	1850	—	XXIX
Jan. 29	1850	—	XXX
Jan. 31	1850	—	XXXI
Feb. 4	1850	—	XXXII
Feb. 7	1850	—	XXXIII
Feb. 11	1850	—	XXXIV
Feb. 14	1850	—	XXV
Feb. 18	1850	—	XXXVI
Feb. 21	1850	—	XXXVII
Feb. 25	1850	—	XXXVIII
Feb. 28	1850	—	XXXIX
Mar. 7	1850	—	XL
Mar. 11	1850	—	XLI
Mar. 14	1850	—	XLII
Mar. 19	1850	The Ragged Schools	XLIII
Mar. 25	1850	—	XLIV
Mar. 29	1850	—	XLV
Apr. 3	1850	The Coasting Trade	XLVI
Apr. 11	1850	—	XLVII
Apr. 19	1850	Sailor's Homes and Boarding Houses	XLVIII
Apr. 25	1850	Reply to the Secretary of the Ragged School Union	XLIX
May 2	1850	—	L
May 9	1850	—	LI
May 16	1850	—	LII

Date	District	Title	Letter
May 25 1850	—		LIII
May 30 1850	—		LIV
June 6 1850	—		LV
June 13 1950	—		LVI
June 20 1850	Workers in Wood and the Supply of the Material		LVII
June 27 1850	The Labourers at the Timber Docks		LVIII
July 4 1850	—		LIX
July 11 1850	Carpenters and Joiners		LX
July 18 1850	—		LXI
July 25 1850	Moulding, Planning and Veneering Mills		LXII
Aug. 1 1850	Furniture Workers		LXIII
Aug. 8 1850	Fancy Cabinet Makers		LXIV
Aug. 15 1850	Slop Cabinet Trade		LXV
Aug. 22 1850	"Garret Masters" of the Cabinet Trade		LXVI
[1]Aug. 29 1850	The Turners		LXVII
[2]Sept. 5 1850	Ship and Boat Builders		LXVIII
Sept. 12 1850	The Coopers		LXIX
Sept. 19 1850	On Transit of Great Britain and the Metropolis		LXX
Sept. 26 1850	Omnibus Drivers and Conductors		LXXI
Oct. 3 1850	Hackney Coach and Cabmen		LXXII
Oct. 10 1850	Carmen and Porters		LXXIII
Oct. 17 1850	Watermen, Lightermen, Steamboatmen		LXXIV
Oct. 24 1850	Dressmakers and Milliners		LXXV
Oct. 31 1850	Dressmakers and Milliners		LXXVI
Nov. 7 1850	The Journeymen Hatters		LXXVII
Nov. 15 1850	Tanners, Curriers etc.		LXXVIII
Nov. 21 1850	The "Live" Markets		LXXIX
Nov. 28 1850	The Meat Markets		LXXX
Dec. 5 1850	The "Green" Markets		LXXXI
Dec. 12 1850	The Fish Markets		LXXXII

[1] In some copies of *Morning Chronicle* this letter appears marked as LXII
[2] In some copies of *Morning Chronicle* this letter appears marked as LXVI

The dates given above are those of the original publication of the letters. Letter 1–19 for the Metropolitan, Rural and Manufacturing areas were, however, collected together and reprinted in Supplements to the Morning Chronicle. In order to make reference to these letters easier, the following table has been compiled.

Date of Supplement	Metropolitan Districts Letter	Manufacturing Districts Letter	Rural Districts Letter
Dec. 21 1849	I and II	I and II	I and II
Dec. 24 1849	III and IV	III and IV	III
Dec. 28 1849	V and VI	V and VI	IV and V*
Jan. 1 1850	VI (cont.) and VII	VII and VIII	VI and VII
Jan. 4 1850	VIII and IX	VIII (cont.) and IX	VIII
Jan. 8 1850	IX (cont.) and X	X	IX and X
Jan. 11 1850	XI	XI and XII	X (cont.) and XI
Jan. 15 1850	XII and XIII	XII (cont. and XIII	XII
Jan. 18 1850	XIII (cont.) and XIV	XIV	XIII and XIV

* Erroneously headed "Manufactured Districts" in Supplement.

Date		District	Title	Letter
Jan. 22	1850	XV	XV and XVI	XIV (cont.) and XV
Jan. 25	1850	XVI and XVII	XVI (cont.) and XVII	XVI
Jan. 29	1850	XVII (cont.) and XVIII	XVIII	XVII and XVIII
Feb. 1	1850	XIX	XIX	XVIII (cont.) and XIX

Index